T0345578

Karolinum Press

Matěj Spurný
Making the Most of Tomorrow
A Laboratory of Socialist Modernity in Czechoslovakia

VÁCLAV HAVEL SERIES

Matěj Spurný

Making the Most
of Tomorrow

A Laboratory of Socialist
Modernity in Czechoslovakia

KAROLINUM PRESS

KAROLINUM PRESS is a publishing department of Charles University
Ovocný trh 560/5, 116 36 Prague 1, Czech Republic
www.karolinum.cz

Reviewed by Michal Kopeček (Institute of Contemporary History, Academy
of Sciences, Prague), Eagle Glassheim (Department of History, University
of British Columbia, Vancouver), and Jakub Bachtík (Institute of Art History,
Charles University, Prague)

The Czech edition is the result of a postdoc project, 'A Great Experiment
in Socialist Modernity', which, as project no. P410-12-P596, was supported
by the Grant Agency of the Czech Republic. The making of the English version
of the book was supported by the European Regional Development Fund project
'Creativity and Adaptability as Conditions of the Success of Europe in an
Interrelated World' (No. CZ.02.1.01/0.0/0.0/16_019/0000734).

Originally published in Czech as *Most do budoucnosti. Laboratoř socialistické
modernity na severu Čech*, Prague: Karolinum Press, 2016.

Cover and graphic design by /3.dílna/
Typeset and printed by Karolinum Press
First English edition

Cataloguing-in-Publication Data available from the National Library of the Czech
Republic

ISBN 978-80-246- 4017-4
ISBN 978-80-246- 4018-1 (pdf)
ISBN 978-80-246- 4071-6 (epub)
ISBN 978-80-246- 4070-9 (mobi)

CONTENTS

ACKNOWLEDGEMENTS

The Czech original of this book, *Most do budoucnosti*, was years in the making and could never have been written without the support of family, friends, teachers, and colleagues. The idea of writing a book about the strange fate of the town of Most was born during long evenings spent in a cell of the Cistercian abbey in the north Bohemian town of Osek (Osegg), where, in 2006, I was working for an NGO called Antikomplex, recording conversations with people from villages that had been demolished to enable the mining of brown coal. I succeeded in making this idea a reality only several years later, thanks to the support of the Institute of Contemporary History in Prague and the Grant Agency of the Czech Republic. The writings of the historians Michal Pullmann and Michal Kopeček helped shape its conception, and both of them, as well as Ondřej Matějka, later also provided useful comments on various parts of the book as they were being written. In the passages concerning the environmental contexts of the Most story, Eagle Glassheim provided essential stimulus, and regarding technocratic thinking, I profited greatly from consultations with Jakub Rákosník and Vítězslav Sommer. For help with the context of the preservation of historic monuments, I am indebted to Jakub Bachtík for valuable advice. For making it easy to access records, I owe a debt of gratitude to the staff of the State District Archives in Most, especially Martin Myšička. I am also grateful to have had the opportunity to discuss the topic with a number of eyewitnesses, particularly the architect Václav Krejčí, the historian František Šmahel, and the archaeologist Jan Klápště. In the last stage of writing the book, I was helped by an informal group of friends, including crucial editing, in particular by Adam Šůra. For their meticulous translation, which entailed the addition of a good deal of new information, up-dating, and generally making the work more accessible especially to the non-Czech reader, I thank Derek and Marzia Paton.

PREFACE: COAL UNDER THE PAVEMENT

From a distance, the city, cobbled together from prefab concrete panel buildings, looks a bit as if someone had built it out of matchboxes. It is shot through with a regular grid of wide streets along which cars drive with ease. A church, separated from the town by a four-lane motorway, quietly looks on from a distance as people live the future they dreamt of. Instead of a church, an eighteen-storey tower now dominates this once regional metropolis, today a city of 60,000 people. It is the headquarters of a mining company. Everyone who visits the city quickly understands that something extraordinary has taken place here and may perhaps still take place. But what, actually? And why?

It is good to begin the account just outside the prefab concrete city, on the north slope of Hněvín Hill (399 metres above sea level). It was here that the royal borough of Most was founded in the Middle Ages. Today, below the hill there is only a lake. Its shimmering waters mercifully conceal an extraordinarily dramatic story of Czech history after the Second World War.

A human settlement was wiped off the face of the earth here. Another town of the same name was built on greenfield land a few kilometres away. One of the most valuable historic towns of north Bohemia vanished. Gothic and Renaissance monuments, the houses of burghers, convents and monasteries, churches, three town squares, stately buildings and boulevards – all gone. All of them were demolished and carted away as part of the worthless overburden. In compensation, a rationally organized city was built, the kind that not only Czech modernist architects and urban planners dreamt of. It was a city that was meant to open the way for people to a life with dignity.

The reasons seem obvious. The main reason was the 'black gold under the town'. Coal, thanks to which Most had become rich and grown, now, after the Second World War, in the years of single-mindedly building a 'fuel energy base', became fatal for the old town. Mining was moved from deep shafts to the surface, from the outskirts of the town right into the streets at its centre.

But to be satisfied with an answer like that would mean accepting the logic of the engineers of the state-owned company called Severo-české hnědouhelné doly (SHD – North Bohemian Lignite Mines). From their point of view, the existence of a coal seam under the city did not raise the question of what to do. Rather, it was in itself the answer: mine it. As a historian, not as a mining engineer, I start from the premiss that coal under the pavement of a historic town can be dealt with in various ways, and therefore that the story of the old Most could have developed in a number of ways. I am convinced that inquiring into the roots and circumstances of the decisions that determined the story of this town after the Second World War has not lost any of its urgency today. What at that time actually justified swapping a whole historic town for coal? Was it the context of the former Sudetenland, the local sense of uprootedness and lack of a real home? Was it the Utopia of progress and a life with dignity for everyone? Or was it rather a special form of the technical thinking of engineers, which reduced the world to economic indicators? What was particularly Communist and what was universal about the modernist discourse of the 1960s and 1970s? Can one find similar stories in the East and the West? During those three decades, when the destruction of one city and the building of another were under consideration and were then eventually carried out, was there a substantial change in the predominant way people thought about their environment, and about the meaning of the signs of being civilized and everything that belongs to a life with dignity? What aspects of the *Sinnwelt* (mental world or symbolic universe) of that time were reflected in the officially approved narratives about the fate of the city of Most and what was reflected in critical journalism and art?

We won't find the answer either below the surface of the lake, where the old houses once stood, or amongst the concrete walls of the new city. We have to travel back a few decades into the past and try, by following traces in the sources, to understand the *Sinnwelt* of the time, which was created by stories like the one of Most. And that is the aim of this book. It does not seek merely to tell the story of one north Bohemian town in the times of state socialism. It is about more than events that are several decades remote in time and about more than a single town. It is about understanding the world we live in and help to shape.

The Story

Where is Daedalus, so that he could search, cry out, and lament? Daedalus is not here; for decades now he has been standing at the steam hammer in the Louny workshops, making insulators in a porcelain factory, and has already somehow forgotten a bit about his wings. His son has set out alone, without him; he didn't need him; he listened only to his own voice, which invented wings for him, so that he reached the centre of his will and mastery, of seclusion and joy, his own heart. And maybe it was Daedalus who followed him with a sigh; maybe with a bit of envy, maybe with a knowing smile or sadness, which you will scarcely drive out even with a gulp of fire in your throat, gasping at a recollection. Daedalus was not here; he couldn't see that broken trunk, those wings broken apart, those bare bones, stripped of flesh [...] And after that blow the mountain did not even shudder.

(Emil Juliš, 1969[1])

1   From Emil Juliš, 'Ikarova proměna', in idem, *Pod kroky dýmů*, Most: Dialog, 1969, pp. 11–13.

It is reasonable to see the history of old Most as evidence of the self-destructive power of modern humankind. But it is also fair to see it as an example of the willingness to take a laboriously made, but already worn out, human creation and to sacrifice it to the newly built, better, and more rational world that is supposed to emerge on its ruins. It is fair to tell it as a story about pride coming before a fall, or as a modern variation on the theme of rising from the ashes. Though the history certainly contains a hint of both myths, of Icarus and the phoenix, it is wise to free oneself of these preconceived notions and to seek to become acquainted with the circumstances and environments in which the drama of the city took place. In other words, it is more useful to search for the answer to the questions of what kind of town old Most was, what the relationships were amongst coal mining, society, and politics in north Bohemia, what ideas guided the actors who played the key roles in taking decisions about the fate of the town in the 1950s and 1960s, and how its story was projected into the lives of the people who were at home there. The aim is not to confirm one's initial admiration or disgust, nor to make sure the story makes a simple point, but to seek to reconstruct what was probably the most dramatic period in the history of Most in its broader contexts, both with its contradictions and with its ambiguities.

OLD MOST

I do not wish to describe in detail, nor can I, the history of old Most (Brüx in German, Pons in Latin), from its foundation in the first half of the thirteenth century to the demolition of the last house just before the spring of 1987. Yet to grasp the context of the destruction of the town, one must get an overall idea of the historic traces that the old town represented, and of the state of the town in the late 1950s and early 1960s, when its fate was decided.

The history of the town of Most was, from its royal founding in the early thirteenth century, carried along by a principle that endured in different versions until the twentieth century. That principle was the interest of the powers that be in the existence of the town and its exact form. Most was founded as a royal borough at the impetus of King Wenceslas I (*reg.* 1230–53) of Bohemia, who, considering the strategic position and economic potential of the settlement, decided to build a new power base at the foot of Hněvín Hill in north-west Bohemia. Old Most was built on an urban plan with predominantly rectilinear divisions, though, owing to the shape of the terrain and the rapid growth of the town in the thirteenth century, this concept was not entirely adhered to. The interest of the powers that be in the existence of the town played an absolutely fundamental role also in one of the most difficult moments of its existence, the period after the fire of 1515, which in the course of two hours had destroyed almost all of Most. The rebuilding of the town was supported by King Vladislav II (Vladislav Jagiellon, *reg.* 1471–1516), and even the pope, Leo X (*reg.* 1513–21), contributed to it. It was at this time of unique restoration that most of the historically valuable buildings of Most were erected – the Renaissance houses of burghers and mainly the Deanery Church of the Assumption, an exceptional work of Gothic architecture and one of the largest churches in Bohemia – and these remained until the last third of the twentieth century.[2]

Apart from the monarch's, and then the State's, interest in the town, its development was determined from the beginning also by the mining of minerals in the Ore Mountains (Krušné hory) in the last two centuries, mainly brown coal (lignite), which existed even under the town of Most. The desire to mine intensified considerably in the second half of the nineteenth century, at a time of revolutionary changes in technology and the operation of capitalism. New actors entered into the planning of the town and its immediate environs. Their plans, needs, and opportunities opened up completely new and in some respects contradictory prospects, ranging from dynamic expansion to the complete elimination of the town. As we shall see in some detail, the life of the town and its people began largely to be subject to the needs of the market for coal. The existence and appearance of Most was thus again fundamentally influenced by a growing power, this time economic (which can reasonably be talked about in a special sense also in the period of state socialism).

The city did not of course comprise only a power structure beyond individual people, even though such structures have played an extraordinarily more important role in the history of Most than in other towns in the Bohemian Lands (Bohemia, Moravia, and Austrian Silesia). Here too, the people who have lived in the town have determined the particular form of its life and architecture. It is in this connection that we encounter the second distinctive factor that helped to determine the life of old Most – namely, heterogeneity. This consisted in a social diversity that had been present from the beginning, and helped to shape the town, both in the linguistic sense (of ethnicity) and – at least in the key period of the boom and

---

2   Karel Kuča, *Města a městečka v Čechách, na Moravě a ve Slezsku*, 4, Prague: Libri, 2000, pp. 161–201.

renewal of the city in the fifteenth and the sixteenth century – in the religious sense.

Most was from its beginning not only a royal borough but also a place with an intensive religious life. The Ves Svatého Václava (Villa s. Wenceslai, Wenzelsdorf), one of the core settlements of the future town, had not only the first church on the territory of the future Most, but also had a commandry of the Knights of the Holy Sepulchre and then the Knights of the Cross with the Red Star. Gradually churches and convents of the Order of St Mary Magdalene and the Minorites were built in the town, and, in the eighteenth century, a Piarist *collegium* was established. During the Hussite Wars (*c.*1419–34), Most was a bastion of Catholicism. It defended itself against a Hussite siege and, apart from the commandry of the Knights of the Cross with the Red Star, it was not destroyed. In the late sixteenth and the early seventeenth century, however, thanks also to the influence of the neighbouring land of Saxony, Lutherans dominated here for a while.[3] The struggle between the Lutherans and the Catholics left its mark on the long drawn-out construction of the central ecclesiastical building in Most, later known as the Church of the Assumption (kostel Nanebevzetí Panny Marie) or the Deanery Church. In the late Gothic style, it has an extraordinary design, with a remarkable interior that was, for its time, aesthetically modern.[4]

It is exceptionally difficult to determine the ethnic composition of the Most population before 1848. Indeed, in a certain sense it is impossible, even though Czech and German historians have for decades been happy to do so in the interest of justifying one claim or another. Until the mid-nineteenth century, ethnicity (*národnost* in Czech, *Nationalität* in German) was not important for individual or collective identity. Consequently, we now have little evidence

---

3   Kuča states that 'Lutheranism [...] completely prevailed in about 1590'. Kuča, *Města a městečka*, p. 174.
4   For more on this, see the 'Reconciliation' section.

1. The town of Most in the troubled times of social protests as a still mainly German town. Sterngasse in the 1930s.

of it, unlike religious affiliation. The history of Most was, however, clearly shaped both by people whose mother tongue was Czech and by people whose mother tongue was German. As a royal borough, Most was not founded in connection with the German settlement of the borderlands of Bohemia. But, beginning in the fifteenth century at the latest, the German language was making itself felt both in official records and amongst the population thanks to the influence of Saxony and, eventually, also the Lutheran Reformation. In the eighteenth century and the first half of the nineteenth, Most was linguistically a German town. Czech influence began to increase only in connection with the development of coal mining, when workers were recruited from more distant regions. This trend initially tended to change the ethnic structure of the countryside; the town itself remained mainly German (even in the 1880 census, ninety per cent of the people of Most declared German as their ethnicity, and in 1910 the proportion was eighty-five per cent).[5] Though this situation changed quite fast between the two world wars (in the 1921 census, already 9,261 people out of a population of 27,230, that is roughly one third of Most, stated their ethnicity as Czech, and in the 1930 census, 9,740 people out of a population of 28,212 did so),[6] by the Second World War, the vast majority of the Most bourgeoisie (that is, the stratum of owners of land and of houses) was German. Social divisions and conflicts thus to a certain extent overlapped with ethnic composition (though besides Czech miners and German 'coal barons', there were of course German miners and, less numerously, members of the Czech middle and upper-middle classes).

The situation changed radically shortly after the end of the Second World War in May 1945. Only a few hundred Germans remained in the town, most of them badly needed miners and specialists, together with their families. The pre-war structure of Most society had thus changed definitively. Unlike regions with continuous settlement, a sudden secularization took place here: religious life and, with it, the perceived reason for the existence of historic Church architecture almost completely vanished after 1945. In addition to the returning Czech inhabitants who had left with the German occupation, and newcomer Czechs from the interior, settlers also came here from afar, and would have a hard time becoming accustomed to life in an industrial and urban environment. Thousands of them would also leave in the coming years. Most and the Most district would never become their true home.[7]

But this history comprises more than just discontinuities. Even after the end of the Second World War we can trace continuities,

---

5   In 1880, Most had a population of 10,136, of which 1,026 were Czechs. In 1910, out of population of 25,577, only 3,965 were Czechs, and 21,267 were German. Kuča, *Města a městečka*, p. 164.
6   Ibid.
7   For more on this, see the 'Alienation' section.

particularly in the key influence that political and economic power had on Most. Although May 1945 marks a milestone in Czech history, we can still see the successful and uninterrupted development of the system on which Most had, in the fifty years before the war, become entirely dependent – namely, the mining and distribution of brown coal and the coal-fired generation of electricity. Whereas in a number of villages in the north Bohemian border regions the first weeks after the Liberation were marked by Czechs' unbridled murder and expulsion of their German fellow-citizens, in the Most district it was, in particular, long-time Czech inhabitants who concentrated on continuing the extraction of coal from shafts and large pits, continuing the production of fuel in the chemical plant in Záluží (Maltheuren, 5.5 km north-west of old Most), and continuing the generation of electric power, in other words maintaining the basic functioning of industries essential for the existence of modern society. Some people disappeared and others arrived. Monasteries, convents, churches, and whole urban structures became anachronisms, but the system, the basic relationships between industry, politics, and society, which had been forming the town of Most and its environs for decades before the war, was kept intact. Its operation was interrupted neither by the war nor by the Liberation, the expulsions, the resettlement, the post-war confiscations, and the nationalizations of the 1950s.

The characteristic contrasts of the old Most of the 1950s and 1960s were the resultant force of all these influences. They are the contrasts with which the town entered the period when the regional and state-wide economic and political elites would decide about the existence and non-existence of Most. First, there is the contrast between the great historic and architectural value of the old town and the neglect of its monuments, houses, and public space. The images of a dirty, dingy city, as old Most is still recalled today by many a visitor and former inhabitant, are not only the result of later efforts to justify what happened there. Testimony about the disastrous state of the city is provided by historical writings, photographs, and many period surveys and inquiries documenting what shape the city was in.[8]

On the basis of these materials, no matter how much some of the descriptions in them may be intentionally exaggerated, one can get a good idea of how old Most looked in the last two decades of its existence and what life was like there. About 15,000 people, more than 5,000 families, lived in Most at that time. More than one tenth of those inhabitants did not live alone: two or more families were squeezed into one flat; 60 per cent of the population lived in one-room flats, the vast majority of which were without bathrooms. Larger flats too were usually without bathrooms. Three hundred of the 1,300 houses were in serious disrepair, and required immediate repairs to their roofs and structures to make them habitable, including reconstruction of the plumbing and sewage. In the spring of 1963, several houses on Mírové náměstí (Peace Square) collapsed, which not only confirmed the relevance of the inquiries and reports, but also, indeed mainly, intensified the atmosphere of anxiety and discontent.[9] That was also the result of water and power cuts (the town water supply had been without real repairs for between forty

8   This was mainly a question of the detailed plan for the demolition of Most, of 4 February 1963, drawn up, tellingly, more than a year before the government decision to eradicate the town (Národní archiv, henceforth NA, fond 960, Ministerstvo paliv III, 1963–1965), inv. č. 430, sv. 419 and 420, Likvidační záměr města Mostu, 4. 2. 1963), Zpráva o efektivnosti likvidace starého Mostu from 1965 (NA, fond 1261/0/4, Předsednictvo ÚV KSČ, aj. 110, sv. 107), Důvodová zpráva byra KV KSČ v Ústí nad Labem ke zrušení staré části města Mostu a uvolnění uhelné substance v mosteckém uhelném pilíři a dalších náhradních investic (NA, fond 1261/0/43, Kancelář 1. tajemníka ÚV KSČ A. Novotného /1951–1967/, inv. č. 193, kart. 146). For documentation of the current state of historic monuments and various accidents (like the collapse of houses on Mírové náměstí [Peace Square]), see the record group of the State Institute for the Preservation of Historic Monuments and Environmental Protection (NA, Státní ústav památkové péče a ochrany přírody – nezpracovaný fond). Despite the impression that is made by some of these documents, there is no reason to assume that the numbers they are based on are irrelevant. Evidence of the state of the buildings is also provided by period photographs. The problem of the total lack of investment in the town is also mentioned earlier, before the decision to eradicate the town, indeed, even before the war.
9   See the chapter 'Everyday Life'.

and eighty years). The state of the historic monuments basically corresponded to the state of the other buildings, though several hundred thousand Czechoslovak crowns (Kčs) had been allocated for their repair in the course of the 1950s.[10]

The cause of this poor state of affairs was by no means only the cessation of all investment here in connection with the decision to demolish the town (most of the reports preceded the decision). Nor was it the public thematicization of reflections about this step, which began roughly in the second half of the 1950s. The state of the city was not the result of five, ten, or even fifteen years of intentional neglect. Rather, it was the consequence of half a century of uncertainty about its future. In the period between the two world wars at the latest, politicians, experts, and even members of the general public suspected that the future of the old Most was an open question, whose answer would reflect not necessarily the will of the population of Most, but rather the dynamics of economic development, which in turn stemmed from the needs of the population of the whole country or possibly the aims of those who would profit most from mining the coal.

This economic development, practically continuous from the late nineteenth century onwards, despite all the different economic systems, from liberal capitalism to the centrally controlled state capitalism of the Nazi years to the command-control economy of state socialism, is linked to the second contrast – namely, the contrast between the considerable strategic importance of the town and the interests of industry. This conflict is essentially paradoxical, because Most was of strategic importance to the development of industry. One of the largest towns in the North Bohemian Basin, Most continued to be an important place of settlement of miners and other members of the work force. The coal, from which the strategic

---

10 See the newspaper articles 'Statisíce korun na obnovu starého Mostu', *Svobodné slovo*, 2 March 1957, and 'Most dohání zmeškané', *Práce,* 27 October 1957.

importance of the town was ultimately derived, was, nevertheless, also under the town. In an environment where mining and industrial identity gained the upper hand over everything, this simple fact became the decisive argument determining the future of the town.

The transformation of the mining industry and the concomitant power of those whose thinking about the land was determined by the thickness of the coal seam could, up to a certain point in time, lead to an argument for the preservation of Most. The situation changed when it began to seem realistic to quickly build a substitute for old Most. The replacement town would not only provide housing for many more workers than hitherto, but would also have all the functions of an independent city. Particularly in this respect, the situation at the end of the 1950s differed from what it had been before and just after the Second World War, and even somewhat in the Stalinist years. The new reality was not, however, a direct result of the Communist takeover, nor even of the restoration of the Czechoslovak State or the resettlement of what used to be called the Sudetenland. It stems rather from the long growing influence of industrial interests, which in the twentieth century began to be decisive in the formation of the relationship between human beings and the land.

DEMOLITION

The Idea

If we searched the history of the old Most for the critical moment when the mineral wealth to which the town owed both its restoration after the 1515 fire and also its later boom turned against it, we would not get very far. Like most grandiose plans and projects, the idea of extracting the coal from under the town was not long in taking shape. It definitely was not born in 1964, which is often considered the turning point, nor with the start of the socialist dictatorship in 1948 and the concomitant emphasis on heavy industry and raw-material self-sufficiency.

2. Coal, especially in the second half of the nineteenth century, contributed to the development of the town of Most. The wealth generated by mining enabled the building of boulevards and impressive houses. Soukenická ulice (Tuchrahme) in 1905.

Though it is hard to demonstrate this precisely, the awareness of coal under the town very likely had an influence on the architecture and urban development of Most already in the late nineteenth century, and particularly on the inhabitants' growing reluctance to invest in the town. The rich bourgeoisie were therefore building their homes on the slopes of Hněvín, outside the original town boundaries, in places that were safe from possible plans to mine coal. Thus was born the district of Zahražany (Saras, in German). After 1910, it was the only large-scale investment of any real importance in the town. Still in the 1950s, as a whole it constituted about 90 per cent of the houses built here during the Austro-Hungarian Empire.[11] At the latest by the outbreak of the Great War, little was being invested in new construction or in the repair and modernization of flats or in public amenities and public utilities. With the development of surface mining, uncertainty grew and the memory of houses falling into mine shafts faded in the face of the ever more likely possibility of 'mining out' (*vyuhlení*) the town as a whole.

That possibility appears immediately in political discussions and particularly in internal plans of the mining companies which after the war were gradually merged into the SHD. Czech society and its politicians were distinctly of two minds about Most at that time. It had been mainly a German town, but from the late nineteenth century onwards was experiencing an influx of Czechs, particularly from the lower social strata. The town, the site of the largest strike in the history of interwar Czechoslovakia, was also a symbol of working-class struggles against oppression and social insecurity.[12]

The press of the period is full of the determination to make Most a living city again and a centre of the mining region. 'Come and see

---

11 Václav Krejčí, *Most: Zánik historického města, výstavba nového města*, [Ústí nad Labem]: AA 2000, 2000, p. 38.
12 For more on this, see the 'Alienation' section.

Most today!' runs a headline in the Communist regional weekly *Sever* (North) in early 1947. After the author of the article describes the atmosphere of destruction right after the war, he or she continues with a picture of a town that has already definitely recovered: 'The bustle of streets full of pedestrians, cyclists, motor vehicles, at all times of the day and night, illuminated signs above shops, restaurants, and cafés, the merry jingle of the bells of full trams, the ceaseless buzzing of places of the arts, entertainment, and sport – this is the mining town of Most today, after its resurrection [...].'[13] The eulogizing tone and the theme of resurrection reveal no doubts about the future existence of the town. Yet in government materials from as early as November 1945, comments appear to the effect that 'a great part of the town of Most, and also the surrounding villages, are certainly destined for mining within the next five to twenty years,' and that the town of Most must, with regard to housing for north Bohemian miners, be therefore considered a stopgap.[14]

More specific proposals and mainly the persistent pressure on 'fully extracting the coal pillar under Most', which in ordinary language meant the demolition of the whole town or at least the greater part of it, first originated at the SHD in the second half of the 1940s and particularly in the 1950s. It was the engineers in the service of the mining company who, regardless of the political takeovers, soon after the war counted on the demolition of not only villages but also the whole town of Most, which would have to yield to their interests.

---

13 'Kousek nedávné historie', *Sever*, 14 January 1947, p. 3.
14 NA, Archiv Ústředního výboru Komunistické strany Československa (AÚV KSČ), f. 23 (Osidlovací komise), arch. j. 193, stručné poznámky vládního zmocněnce pro účastníky schůze svolané úřadem předsednictva vlády ohledně osídlovací akce na Mostecku a Falknovsku, 22. 11. 1945.

Negotiation

Not until the mid-1950s did the SHD plans for the elimination of old Most, or most of it, run into criticism from the Most Municipal National Committee. Thus, not only in the period of the 'Third Republic' (from early May 1945 to late February 1948), but also, indeed mainly, in the period of 'building socialism' during the dictatorship of the Czechoslovak Communist Party, the local authorities were faced with the interests of industry, and tried to reach a compromise by eliminating only a smaller, peripheral part of old Most. This attempt at compromise offers remarkable insight into the negotiations amongst key players in the politics and economy of the country in the period of 'Czechoslovak Stalinism'.

By 1949 at the latest, representatives of the SHD at meetings of the Most Municipal National Committee openly declared their interest in mining on the territory of the old town centre. The representatives of the Most Municipal National Committee reacted quite angrily. The dispute came to head in 1951, when the representatives turned to the district and regional committees, demanding a decision on whether 'coal will be mined under Most and thus also whether the whole town will be moved southwards and south-eastwards', or 'whether coal will be mined only in part of the town, to be determined by the "Baseline Plan for the City of Most" [Směrný plán města Most], that is, to Stalinova třída [Stalin Avenue]'. The municipal national committee and the district national committee were unequivocally against the SHD plan, which at that time consisted in, first of all, the beginning of surface mining, which would separate the Podžatecká housing estate (then under construction) from old Most, followed by the demolition of the old city core. In addition to the 'incalculable consequences', which, according to a letter from the Municipal National Committee to the North Bohemian National Committee, would be manifested in the health and hygiene of the population, the chairman of the Municipal National Committee,

Václav Bubák (a brother of one of the miners shot dead during the general strike in 1920, who was from a mining family that had settled in Kopisty [Kopitz, in German], in the Most district, before the First World War), described the whole plan as unacceptable also in view of the high demand for housing for the work force, which, after all, the mining company needed. The SHD plan was thus described, in the event that it were implemented, as an 'absolutely disastrous intervention in the development of the town today and in the future', adding that 'from the standpoint of the Most Municipal National Committee and of urban planning, one cannot accept this act'. Even the historic value of the town was brought in as an additional argument: 'this regional centre has historically valuable buildings from various style periods, which are today irreplaceable and in themselves constitute a characteristic whole of medieval origin'.[15] According to research from that period, moreover, it seems that most of the population of old Most at that time tended to be critical of the possible destruction of the town or were at least highly sceptical about it, yet not because of the historic value of the town but because there were still no examples of an existing housing estate that could provide the thousands of people of old Most with a decent place to live. This attitude to the grandiose, complex plan would not begin to change until the second half of the 1950s.[16]

Though it discussed the matter, the North Bohemian National Committee, the available records suggest, came to no definite decision. At the meeting, representatives of the North Bohemian National Committee and the Most District National Committee gave presentations with neutral conclusions, for instance, that it was

15 Státní okresní archiv (SOkA) Most, f. ONV II, inv. č. 858, ev. j. 317, Budoucí vývoj města Mostu vzhledem k plánovanému těžení uhlí SHD v prostoru Most. Dopis MěNV adresovaný plánovacímu referátu KNV Ústí nad Labem, 22. dubna 1951.
16 Státní oblastní archiv (SOA) Litoměřice, f. 668 (SKNV), kart. 598, inv. č. 123, Důvodová zpráva o uvolnění uhelné substance v ochranném pilíři města Mostu, o výstavbě nového Mostu a dalších náhradních investic, pp. 13–14.

necessary to mine coal as part of raising the standard of living, and to decide on the concrete approach, but with the community as the main planner. The local government of the town and also the inhabitants thus had to wait in uncertainty. The local political authorities nevertheless had so far, in what is generally called the Stalinist period, to resist much more powerful actors, including the SHD. This was especially true because old Most so far had at its disposal substantial, if poor-quality, housing for thousands of miners and other workers. It had a functional city centre with a transport infrastructure, the necessary services, and cultural institutions.

It began to be clear to the managers of the SHD, and indeed to the whole economics and technology lobby, that if their efforts were to succeed (that is, if they were to get to those millions of tonnes of brown coal under old Most), it would be necessary to come up with a more sophisticated strategy. Among the necessary steps, they would offer (in collaboration with urban planners and architects) a complex solution to the problem and seek gradually to persuade the central Party institutions in particular of the inevitability of the whole operation and its benefits. That meant winning the support of a considerably wide range of influential actors, from experts in various fields to representatives of political power. The development of the Czechoslovak economy, the technological capabilities, and the *Sinnwelt* of that period nevertheless played into the hands of the engineers and officials of this mining enterprise. By the late 1950s and early 1960s, no obstacle stood in the way of their ambitions.

In the mid-1950s, with de-Stalinization and generational change, new people were hired in a number of enterprises or were elected to national committees and other political bodies. Revolution ceased to be the key concept of the times and a number of politicians and experts began instead to put emphasis on economic performance and efficiency. Consequently, there was of course greater pressure on extracting more raw materials and making the process more efficient. This, in turn was projected in thinking about the future of old

Most. Already in March 1954, the district planning committee divided the town in two, and each part was to have a completely different future. The committee was at that time already anticipating that the 'old town of Most, lying on a coal seam [...] should be completely or mostly mined out (*vydolováno*)'.[17] Although the Regional Planning Guidance of 1955 noted that it was 'necessary to weigh up the economic and technical possibilities of preserving the historic core [...], mainly because of its heritage and cultural values,' it still counted on the 'gradual demolition of the greater part of the old town in the interest of the indispensable mining of coal'.[18]

Only a couple of months later, towards the end of 1956, a general regional plan for the larger area (called a *generel*) of the North Bohemian Basin foresaw the 'extraction of the protective barrier pillar of coal under the town of Most' and the use of the resulting 'mined-out area' for spoil tips of the advancing pit.[19] The general plan, however, was influenced considerably by the management and engineering elite of the SHD mining company, which at that time no longer accepted any alternative to the complete elimination, that is, the mining out (*vyrubání* or *vyuhlení*) of the old town.

The fate of old Most was jointly decided by a wide variety of actors, ranging from the Municipal National Committee and the District National Committee to the SHD to the central bodies of the Communist Party and the Government. Indeed, it was the Government, the central institution, which was still trying, even in the second half of the 1950s, to prevent the destruction of the town, particularly its historic core. On the basis of the Government's efforts, at least to

17 SOkA Most, f. ONV II, inv. č. 858, ev. j. 317, Charakteristika města Mostu (OPK), 3. března 1954.
18 SOkA Most, f. ONV II, inv. č. 736, ev. j. 286, Technickohospodářské směrnice pro zpracování územních projektů města Mostu – podrobné rozvedení hlavních zásad (30. červen 1955), p. 21.
19 SOkA Most, f. ONV II, inv. č. 352, ev. j. 112, Generel SHR na léta 1957–1970, 1956/1957, p. 6.

stall the whole process,[20] the Most Municipal National Committee, for example in 1957, decided on a number of repairs to historic buildings and the re-landscaping of public areas of old Most. This entailed investment of about one million crowns to restore an area that, on the basis not only of the ideas of SHD engineers but also of expertly elaborated and binding plans, was in a few years to yield to mining.[21]

The political representatives of the town and of the district nevertheless acceded to the SHD plans because, among other things, the continuing provisional status (that is, of the town that was about to be literally undermined) put them in an extremely difficult position. The disproportion amongst the various ideas about the future of the town was reflected in the diverging plans of the architects, the municipal, district, and regional national committees, and the mining company. In such a situation it was practically impossible to govern the old town rationally. At the same time, however, it was difficult to determine the desirable size and form of the new town. The declared aim of building a town for between 90,000 and 100,000 people would no longer make sense if old Most were not destined for destruction. At a time of a rapidly rising demand for energy and, consequently, for coal, it was unlikely that the decision to rescue the whole town of old Most would be the desired solution. The situation thus irreversibly developed towards a decision, the germ of which had been present from the beginning of coal mining in the Most district – namely, to extract the coal under the town and, in order to achieve that, to demolish it first.

A decision of this scale and consequence naturally required official agreement and concrete steps to be taken by the Czechoslovak

---

20   On the basis of Government Decision No. 142, of 6 February 1957, the territory of old Most was to be partly mined, but in two stages, with the demolition of part of the historic town to be done only in about 1975.

21   For more on this topic, see 'Statisíce korun na obnovu starého Mostu', *Svobodné slovo*, 2 March 1957, and 'Nová tepna severočeské hnědouhelné pánve', *Lidová demokracie*, 4 April 1957.

Government. But the Government, even at the start of the 1960s, was reluctant to take such a step, probably because it feared the foreign-policy consequences.[22] The preparations for the elimination of the historic town, which had a population at that time of 15,000, were thus made with no legal basis that would have allowed the operation to be carried out. But amongst the main power holders in the region at that time there was already a consensus on the elimination of the town, in particular between the SHD mining company, the local and regional Party bodies, the municipal and district national committees, and ultimately even the Government (which, though it had not yet attended to it legislatively, had taken a number of steps that enabled the project to get under way).

This shift and the consensus did not, however, mean an end to disputes. The main division was now between, in particular, the representatives of the Most Municipal National Committee, trying for the smoothest possible course for the whole gigantic undertaking and the most architecturally imposing new town possible, and, on the other side, the leading officials of the SHD mining company, primarily concerned to achieve the quickest possible extraction of tonnes of 'high-quality' coal from under the old town. The Municipal National Committee repeatedly criticized the continuously changing plans of the SHD and the fact that the SHD was repeatedly presenting the town and the district with a fait accompli. The regional plan of 1961, which did not correspond to the current aims and hypotheses of mining, also turned out to be confusing. The members of the Municipal National Committee, furthermore, criticized the necessity of building new Most on the basis of the regional plan as a city for 100,000 people for whom the delimited area was not sufficiently large.[23] Even at the end of 1961 there were still fears at the mining company that

---

22 For example, the position of the country in UNESCO, of which Czechoslovakia was a founding member in 1945. For more on this, see Krejčí, *Most*, p. 83.
23 SOkA Most, f. ONV II, inv. č. 781, ev. j. 03, Zpráva o současné situaci ve výstavbě nového Mostu vzhledem k širším souvislostem podle předběžných návrhů rajonu SHP, 21. listopadu 1961.

the whole project would be stopped, as in 1957 when the Government came out against the hasty, overall demolition of old Most.

This time, however, the fears were not justified. The disputes were no longer about the existence or non-existence of historic Most, but only about the timing and way it would be demolished. The idea to eliminate old Most in the interest of mining would thus, on the threshold of the most liberal period of Czechoslovak state socialism, the 1960s, go from being a foggy alternative to be carried out at some future date, or an engineering vision, to being a real agenda of political and economic planning. From that point onwards, we can trace how the major actors of regional and state-wide politics related to the idea of demolition and how, considering the broad consensus, attention was shifted from whether it made sense at all to the technicalities linked with carrying it out as efficiently as possible.

This new chapter of the story is introduced by a few events that preceded the government decision on the elimination of old Most and the construction of the new town. They were to include the mining of the coal from under the town into the long-term plan of the fuel sector for the years 1960 to 1980, the elaboration of the plan to demolish old Most, the central Party bodies' discussion and approval of the gigantic project to 'move' the town, and the concurrent creation of the Government Commission for the Coordination and Oversight of the Demolition of Old Most and the Construction of New Most (Vládní komise pro koordinaci a kontrolu postupu při likvidaci starého Mostu a výstavbě nového Mostu).[24] To reverse these steps, which had been prepared by experts and were of considerable political consequence, was hardly possible. None the less, events of the following years provide extremely interesting testimony about the dynamics of the *Sinnwelt* of state socialism and, to some extent, also of Europe in general in the 1960s and 1970s.

---

24 Established by Government Resolution No. 1115 of 28 November 1962.

Organization

The moment that the decision about the demolition of Most went from being a question of the existence or non-existence of the old town to being merely a technical task is generally considered to be when the Government took the relevant decision in March 1964. Nevertheless, the fate of the town had actually already been decided between 1960 and 1962. This is not merely a matter of chronology. An apparent detail, it illustrates the opaque, chaotic manner of taking decisions on fundamental questions in socialist Czechoslovakia with its two decision-making hierarchies, that of the Party and that of the State.

The demolition of old Most was not ordered by the people of Czechoslovakia, the political headquarters of the Czechoslovak Communist Party, or the Czechoslovak Government. The Party and State bodies had no general knowledge of the logic of surface mining and they of course had to rely on information and proposals from the SHD mining company. The SHD in 1959–60, in the documentary materials for the general plan for the development of the fuel sector up to 1980, which was drawn up by the Ministry of Fuel and Power, presented the mining of the coal pillar under old Most as an indispensable part of the subsequent process. The planned SHD approach was incorporated into the overall conception of the next step for the mining,[25] and thus once and for all became the planned, binding reality. But because it entailed the demolition of the historic town, the moving of thousands of people, and a whole series of extraordinary investments, this step obviously required a political decision.

During 1961, regional planners discussed, concurrently and to some extent independently of each other, documents related to three broad

---

25 NA, f. 955 (Ministerstvo paliv a energetiky III, 1960–1963), kart. 189, inv. č. 249, Výpis základních ukazatelů generální perspektivy rozvoje do r. 1980; Návrh rozvoje SHR – Most, 28. 10. 1960.

areas: the North Bohemian Basin, the new Most, and the demolition plan for old Most. All three documents start from the same long-term perspective of mining all the coal under old Most, even though this prospect did not yet have the political backing of the Central Committee of the Czechoslovak Communist Party or the Government. The key role in debating the district plan was played by the North Bohemian National Committee, based in the town of Ústí nad Labem. The actual form of the plan in the Most district was strongly shaped by the district national committee and other district institutions.[26] The plans for the construction of the new Most, which started from the fact that the old town would be gradually demolished, were mostly a matter for the municipal and the district national committees, and in part also for the district and the municipal committees of the Czechoslovak Communist Party, as well as a number of other institutions at the city and district levels.

It is reasonable to see 13 May 1961 as the fateful date. On that day, with the consent of the North Bohemian National Committee and other bodies, the deputy director of the SHD, Josef Hojdar (1919–2000), sent a letter to the head of the Ležáky Mine, Karel Šamberger:

Dear Comrade,
Considering the intentions of the long-term hypothesis about the development of the North Bohemian Mining District (Severočeský hnědouhelný revír – SHR) and in connection with it and the mining plans for the pillar under the town of Most I enjoin you to ensure at your state enterprise the elaboration of the demolition plan for the old Most by the end of 1961. Because this is a problem without precedent in our country or even abroad, consent was given, at the proposal of the Regional National Committee, to the State Planning Committee

---

26 SOkA Most, f. 207 (ONV Most II 1960–1975), inv. č. 781, ev. j. 294, Schůze Rady Severočeského KNV a materiály Odboru výstavby SKNV.

for the State Institute of Regional Planning (Státní ústav rajónového plánování) also to participate in the elaboration of the demolition plan, especially concerning the replacement construction [of the new Most] and the political and economic conclusions. I enjoin you at the same time therefore, in the spirit of the effective agreement between the Regional National Committee and the State Planning Committee, to get in touch with the State Institute of Regional Planning and order the work. I ask you to inform me by the end of June about the measures you have taken to guarantee [the carrying out of] the task.

With comradely greetings,

Hojdar [27]

In the spring of 1961, the mining engineers and economists of the SHD then set to work on the now specific steps for the 'mining out' of the area of the old town and thus for its demolition in the interest of economic development. In the first phase, in May and June 1961, they elaborated a long report laying out the reasons for the elimination of Most.[28] This became the basis for the key plan for the demolition of the town.[29] And, following a decision of the SHD management, members of several SHD committees began to work on the plan before a political decision was taken. The Regional National Committee and the SHD therefore also prepared background materials both for the Politburo of the Central Committee of the Czechoslovak Communist Party (the supreme Party body) and for the Government for a government resolution.

---

27 SOkA Most, f. 207 (ONV Most II 1960–1975), inv. č. 781, ev. j. 294, Korespondence odboru výstavby KNV a Sdružení SHR.

28 SOA Litoměřice (pracoviště Most), f. SHD – generální ředitelství, spis 440 (Investice: likvidace starého a dostavba nového Mostu, přesun kostela), kart. 1, Důvodová zpráva k záměru na rubání zásob v ochranném pilíři města Mostu a přidružené materiály, červen 1961.

29 For the arguments for the elimination of old Most used in the accompanying report and in the demolition plan, see the chapter 'The Destruction of the City as an Investment Plan' in the 'Numbers' section.

At the June meeting of the development department of the SHD a timetable of the individual steps was drawn up, containing not only the elaboration of the demolition plan and other background materials for superior bodies, but also a suitable date, from the point of view of the mining company, for the anticipated approval of the plan – that is, by 30 June 1962.[30]

Not until 1962 did important political actors at government ministries responsible for mining and construction, together with officials of the Central Committee of the Czechoslovak Communist Party, begin to deal more systematically with the plan. In keeping with the general plan of the fuel sector and with their own continuous urgings that coal mining had to be increased and made more efficient, and also under the pressure of circumstances and the decisions already taken at the regional, district and enterprise levels, decisions were made in an attempt to put an end to the longstanding uncertainty about the demolition of the old town of Most and the form of the new town once and for all in favour of mining. It took a few more months before the Government and the Party took their final decision. In 1962 (within the period originally set by the SHD as suitable for the final approval of mining) the North Bohemian National Committee requested the Politburo of the Central Committee of the Party to take a binding position on the matter.[31] Though it was not a rule, the members of the Politburo who had been assigned the matter sought to ensure the prior agreement of other Party bodies and the state authorities. A consensus was thus prepared to ensure that none of the powerful political players would attack the resulting decision and again threaten the principal aim of the operation, that is, the extraction of all the coal from under Most.

30 SOkA Most, f. 207 (ONV Most II 1960–1975), inv. č. 781, ev. j. 294, Záznam z porady konané dne 6. 6. 1961 v odboru vývoje SHD.
31 SOA Litoměřice, f. 668 (SKNV Ústí nad Labem), inv. č. 2, k. 9.

The final decision (or rather the approval of the operation that was already under way) was thus taken by representatives of a few departments of the Central Committee of the Party (including planning, construction, finance, energy, and transportation), experts from the State Planning Committee, and representatives of the individual ministries and the Presidium of the Government. The final decision of the Politburo of the Central Committee of the Party, Resolution No. 215, of 2 October 1962, thus essentially substituted for the still non-existent government decision – it expressed consent with the beginning of the preparatory work for the demolition of the old parts of Most and bound individual members of the Government (Prime Minister Viliam Široký, and the ministers Alois Indra, Lux, and Oldřich Černík) to specific steps, in particular, to appoint a coordinating committee, to prepare the government measures, and to ensure the elaboration of the demolition plan.[32]

After long debates amongst the representatives of the ministries in Prague, of the Regional National Committee, and of the mining company, which took place concurrently with the internal-Party approval of the plan to demolish Most, the Czechoslovak Government, on 28 November 1962, appointed the Government Commission for the Coordination and Oversight of the Demolition of Old Most and the Construction of New Most'. In the Commission statutes, the Government expressly refers to the Party Central Committee resolution of 2 October 1962, thus, at least formally, conceding the primacy of the Party in an area that should in normal circumstances be legislatively attended to (that is, decided on by the legislative or executive body of government).[33] The Commission was meant to coordinate the creation of the plan for the demolition of old Most

32 NA, f. 1261/0/11 (Politické byro ÚV KSČ), arch. j. 458, sv. 365, Usnesení 213. schůze politického byra ÚV KSČ ze dne 2. října 1962.
33 NA, fond Úřad předsednictva vlády (dále ÚPV) – běžná spisovna (nezprac.), kart. 165, sign. 356/1/12, Statut vládní komise pro koordinaci a kontrolu postupu při likvidaci starého Mostu a výstavbě nového Mostu.

and assess it. It was also supposed to oversee the timely building of replacement housing for the population of the old town and the smooth moving of the inhabitants and also of the industrial plants, 'without disrupting production and in harmony with the needs of the workers'. The statutes also expressly mention that the Commission would oversee the thorough 'discussion of the demolition plans with the inhabitants'. It also points out that the Commission was not taking the place of the central bodies or national committees, which were fully responsible for carrying out their tasks in connection with the demolition of the old town and the construction of the new one.[34]

Though the first chairman of the Commission, which was supposed to coordinate, for perhaps the next two decades, the moving of several thousand people, the demolition of their former homes, and, mainly, the creation of a respectable new environment for their future lives, was the minister of construction, Josef Korčák (1921–2008), a few months later Josef Odvárka (1920–?), the minister of fuel and power took over as head of the Commission and would lead it for a long time to come. This 'detail' about who would be in charge of the Commission was hardly the result of random events – internal debates[35] were held about who would occupy this post endowed with considerable power and the result speaks volumes about the power relations amongst the individual departments and ministries and their briefs. The ten to fifteen members of the Commission usually included several ministers, deputy ministers, high-ranking members of the North Bohemian National Committee, the district, the City of Most, and the SHD mining company. Among them was Oldřich Černík, a future prime minister (1968–69). One of the members of the Commission who was also appointed at this time was the then little-known head of the Central Office

34 Ibid.
35 Ibid.

for National Committee Affairs, Miloš Jakeš (b.1922, who would, in 1987, become the last general secretary of the Communist Party while it was in power). He was, however, dismissed during the winter of 1963, when the office he represented on the Commission was abolished.[36]

The plan for the demolition of old Most lay down two fundamental principles for the process of moving and demolition. The first stemmed from the necessity to build a new infrastructure and an arterial road linking Most with other large towns in the Ore Mountains. For that reason the SHD was first meant to mine the coal from under the part of old Most adjacent to Hněvín Hill, so that the utility corridor could be built there. The inhabitants of this part of town were supposed to move to new housing by 1967, when demolition was to begin. The second principle was the necessity to leave the centre of the old town standing as long as possible. But this was not a matter of hesitating about whether actually to save the historic monuments; rather, it had to do with the fact that in this part of town institutions and services were still operating and were used by the inhabitants of both the old and the new Most. Consequently, demolition did not begin here until the second phase, in the early 1970s.[37]

Though the demolition plan did not deal with certain details (like the exact timing of the demolition of individual buildings), it did present a number of specific problems that required solving, ranging from the buying up of real estate that was still privately owned to finding replacements for the individual places of business, services, and shops to, for example, 'moving' the cemetery. The authors of the plan dealt with the cemetery as a technical task of the same magnitude as dealing with the rubble from the demolitions or the diversion of the River Bílina.

---

36 NA, fond ÚPV – běžná spisovna (nezprac.), kart. 165, sign. 356/1/12, Dopis předsedy vlády V. Širokého ministru paliv a energetiky J. Odvárkovi, 15. ledna 1963.
37 NA, f. 960 (Ministerstvo paliv III), inv. č. 430, sv. 419, Most – likvidační záměr, červen 1963.

3. Intentionally neglected and dilapidated, the town of Most in the 1960s. The photo is dominated by the Piarist church (originally the Church of the Order of St Mary Magdalene) on the third square (Šmeralovo náměstí).

The awaited government resolution was finally issued almost a year and a half after the Politburo decision. It was so far the only official document about the decision to demolish old Most in order to mine coal, at least at the state-wide level. In other words, it was at a time when dozens of experts and politicians at ministries in Prague, bureaucrats of the regional, district, and municipal national-al committees, and several departments of the SHD had already been systematically working on the elimination of the old town for more than a year. Government Resolution No. 180, of 25 March 1964, on the completion of the construction of new Most and the demolition of the old town, is thus essentially the expression of the Government's consent to a project that was already under way. The government resolution remarks that 'the housing in the old part of Most is superannuated and dilapidated', which, without costly repairs, would anyway soon make the town uninhabitable, that the 'freeing-up of the Most pillar for mining' would make it possible to obtain a hundred million tonnes of high-quality coal, and that the 'use of the freed-up space for a spoil tip' would markedly improve the spoil management of the open-pit mine called Ležáky.

Work on the new Most as a single planned city was to continue, and 'life would be transferred' there, the document states, from the old town. For the inhabitants of old Most, the government resolution – besides the statement that the Government, too, considered desirable what had been prepared for several years now – casts light on the years that were to follow. The moving of the inhabitants from the old town to the new was, like the systematic demolition, thus meant to begin in 1965. At least some people would, consequently, have to leave their homes in less than a year. Mining was meant to begin two years later.[38]

The idea to build a complex modern city a stone's throw from old Most emerged shortly after the Czechoslovak Government had, in 1957, indefinitely postponed the plan for the complete demolition of old Most. In other words, this was not only long before the formal government resolution, but even before the decisive Politburo resolution and the elaboration of the crucial demolition plan of the SHD. Who, then, was behind that plan? Who pushed it through and in what form?

No matter what the future of old Most was meant to be, one thing was certain already by the 1950s: the overpopulated and dilapidated old town would in future definitely not hold more people than had hitherto lived there. Yet mining and other related industries would

---

38 SOA Litoměřice, f. 668 (SKNV Ústí nad Labem), kart. 9, inv. č. 2.

need more and more workers and it was Most that, for various reasons, was meant to be the main centre of the North Bohemian Basin, the place where these newcomers, mostly miners and industrial workers, were to find a home and have their needs met. Still in the first half of the 1950s, Most was growing quite unsystematically, and now, in the late 1950s, that was meant to be stopped. The hitherto adding of housing estates to the historic town certainly did not correspond to the socialist State's demands for an emphasis on rational planning. People at all levels of government were aware of that. In the summer of 1958, a conference of the Most municipal, district, and regional national committees, together with planners and other experts, resulted in a straightforward conception:[39] the new Most would be a modern, rationally organized city with a suitable centre offering services for 100,000 people.

And, even in the conditions of state socialism, the relevant bodies admitted that 'this complicated, demanding task for urban planners can be solved only with a study obtained in a competition'. Its general terms and conditions on the course and requirements for the future centre of modern Most were, however, set by the North Bohemian National Committee, which had at its disposal the relevant experts in spatial planning. According to the official rules, specific teams or individuals (ultimately eight architectural practices from Ústí nad Labem, Prague, and Bratislava, the capital of Slovakia) were to be invited to the competition, which was to be held in two rounds.[40] On the commission to select the winning proposal sat well-established architects from throughout Czechoslovakia and representatives of the national committees of the town, district, and region.

In early January 1959, the architect Václav Krejčí (b.1928) received a telephone call from Jiří Porš, a member of the department

---

39   The conference is mentioned in the Usnesení schůze ONV Most z 22. 8. 1958, in SOkA Most, f. 207 (ONV Most II, 1960–1975), inv. č. 244, ev. j. 48.
40   SOkA Most, f. ONV I (1945–1960), inv. č. 56, sign. 127.3, kart. 4, Program výstavby na zpracování podrobného územního plánu Středu nového Mostu, odůvodnění, 7. 6. 1960.

of spatial planning at the North Bohemian National Committee in Ústí nad Labem. To his surprise, Krejčí, who was just then working on the spatial plan of Litvínov, the second largest town of the Most district, was told by Porš that if he were interested, he should choose people to work with and within three days enter the competition for the design of the centre of a brand new town. Krejčí accepted the offer without hesitation and approached his colleague Jaromír Vejl.[41] Though he was not a Party member and was clearly not as established as some of his fellow competitors, Krejčí won the competition. Thereby began, five years before the official decision to demolish the historic town, the history of the new Most – no longer only as a makeshift housing settlement, but as compact city built on the basis of complex considerations and a comprehensive urban plan. We shall return to this story later[42] – but it was important to mention here the architectural competition for the new Most as a whole, mainly because it opened the door not only to the construction of the new town, but also to the complete demolition of the old town. In a situation where replacement buildings were still in short supply and, except in the old centre, there was no infrastructure, the demolition of the old town would have been unthinkable if it had only meant worsening the social circumstances of the town's inhabitants, that is, the workers, most of whom were miners.

The large-scale plans for the gradual demolition of the old town, in which the town is divided into zones to be wiped off the face of the earth, look more like battle maps. They show the front lines (the coalface), the direction of their advance, the dates of the planned evacuation of the population and of the 'capture' of the territory.[43]

41 Krejčí, *Most*, pp. 20–21.
42 See the chapter 'City of Roses' in the 'Utopia' section.
43 See SOkA Most, f. 207 (ONV Most II, 1960–1975), inv. č. 777, ev. j. 291, Postup skrývky lomu Most (mapa, 1972); SOkA Most, f. 207 (ONV Most II, 1960–1975) – odbor výstavby, arch. j. 92, Studie dokončení likvidace Starého Mostu (plán, 1971); SOkA Most, f. 130 (MěNV Most), inv. č. 864, Vyklizování objektů ve starém Mostě pro postup Lomu Most (1976–1984).

The advance of the demolition depended on three factors: the needs of the mining company (that is, uninterrupted extraction), the tempo of building the 'replacement' housing (particularly the ability of the new Most to receive the displaced inhabitants of old Most, which depended on the number of completed flats for the new tenants) and the efficient organization of the legal and other steps (the purchase of real estate, the moving of the people and institutions). It was a task of dimensions no European state or industrial enterprise had ever been faced with in peace time. The old town, which was still inhabited by more than 15,000 people, could boast five churches and a number of other late Gothic and Renaissance buildings, and it had one of the best known theatres in north Bohemia, an important district hospital, another fifty buildings used by the health and welfare services, a spa, twenty office buildings occupied by important municipal and district institutions, twelve schools, fifteen restaurants, four hotels, 240 shops, 630 offices, seven industrial plants, a railway station, and more than 6,500 flats.[44]

The moving and demolition commenced according to plan at the beginning of 1965. The first task was mining out the space where the utility corridor was to be located. This included all the infrastructure and motor and rail transport that was meant to link the new Most with the rest of the Ore Mountains, in particular the town of Chomutov about 23 kilometres to the west and Bílina about 15 kilometres to the north-east, and Teplice another 14.4 kilometres north of there. In the direction of Chomutov, the corridor was meant to run along the foot of Hněvín Hill, that is, through a still built-up area of the old town, which was therefore, in the sequence of the individual steps of the project, the first that needed to be demolished. And, in 1965, it was here that demolition began, from the foot of Hněvín to

---

44 SOA Litoměřice, f. 668 (SKNV), kart. 598, inv. č. 123, Důvodová zpráva o uvolnění uhelné substance v ochranném pilíři města Mostu, o výstavbě nového Mostu a dalších náhradních investic, pp. 5–6.

the streets Palackého, Tylova and Žižkova. This was a strictly residential area on the edge of the old town, with 186 buildings containing 729 flats of 767 families. The moving of about 500 of those families to the new part of Most, and the rest mostly to Chomutov, Jirkov (Görkau, about 18 km due west of Most), and Litvínov took place gradually, street by street or block by block, which were then disconnected from the public utilities, and 'stripped down'. Most of the houses were then demolished by explosives and, after the useable material was carted off to the grounds of the former Capuchin monastery, heavy equipment spread the rubble.[45]

The second phase of the demolition took place from 1968 to 1970. Unlike the first phase, it included the historic parts of the old town of Most. But it mainly dealt with the area that had been built in the late nineteenth and early twentieth centuries, that is, the north and the north-east of old Most, which had been the most densely inhabited parts of the town. This was a compromise between the interests of the mining company and the need to preserve the centre of town at least for a few more years, because in the new part of Most it was not yet possible to set up a number of the institutions essential for the operation of the city.[46] That is why the demolition of the centre of old Most ultimately took much longer than had originally been foreseen: instead of being done by 1975,[47] it dragged on until the first half of the 1980s.

45 SOkA Most, f. 207 (ONV Most II, 1960–1975), inv. č. 785, ev. j. 295, Souhrnné stanovisko Okresní plánovací komise k předložené I. fázi likvidace staré části města Mostu, 8. května 1965.
46 SOkA Most, f. 207 (ONV Most II, 1960–1975), inv. č. 785, ev. j. 295, Studie o postupu likvidace starého Mostu v letech 1968–1970, území II. fáze likvidace, březen 1967 (SHD, oborové ředitelství Most).
47 SOkA Most, f. 130 (MěNV Most), inv. č. 863, Studie o dokončení likvidace starého Mostu III. fáze (1971–75), technická zpráva, červen 1970.

Everyday Life

It was the spring of 1968. In comparison with the previous twenty years, the Czechoslovak public was experiencing an unprecedented degree of freedom. The streets of the large towns were pulsing with continuous gatherings and in the various state enterprises one resolution after another was feverishly being drawn up. It was a time of hope and also, at least at first sight, of profound peace. But in Most a war was raging. On náměstí Ludvíka Svobody (Ludvík Svoboda Square) barricades sprang up and Chomutovská ulice (Chomutov Street) was captured by US Army tanks, until eventually only the ruins of houses remained, covered in red dust.

In Most, Americans were making *The Bridge at Remagen* (1969), a film that depicts in a largely fictionalized way events on the Rhine several weeks before the end of the Second World War. As the chronicler Antonín Mazanec wrote, 'our old town, condemned to extinction, has provided the most suitable backdrop' for a war film.[48] True, had they built film sets and spent more time and money, they could have filmed in some other town. But here in Most the ruins of the buildings were real, having been demolished by being blown up or were awaiting that fate, and they created the atmosphere of one of the final stages of the Second World War. The tanks in Chomutovská ulice could fire right at the houses because they were earmarked for demolition and would soon be blown up anyway. Indeed, shortly after the American tanks drove off, Soviet tanks appeared in the streets of the town on the night of 20 August and in the early hours of 21 August, but not to make a film.

That the Americans filmed *The Bridge at Remagen* in Most is remarkable in at least two respects. The first is that the Czechoslovak State decided that, in addition to the anticipated profit from the coal under the town, it would cash in on the spoliation of the town in

---

48 SOkA Most, f. 130 (MěNV Most), inv. č. 368, Kronika města Mostu 1968, p. 551.

another way as well[49] – namely, as the dismal backdrop of a war film popularizing a famous military campaign of an 'imperialist power'. To make money from the intentional destruction of irreplaceable values was clearly not considered to be in conflict with the moral imperatives of building a socialist society. The second respect is mainly what making the film here says about the state of old Most in the late 1960s. The town already at that time clearly provided a picture so similar to one from the end of the Second World War in Europe that it could without much effort be used as the setting for a war film. For scenes before fighting began, it was only necessary to repair a few buildings that were too dilapidated to have looked like that in wartime Germany and to put some German signs on them.

But the town had already experienced other situations similar to those during the making of the war film. For more than fifteen years, from 1965 onwards, its houses and streets were gradually demolished.[50] The atmosphere of the town, whose individual parts were being progressively emptied of people and anything that could still be moved, so that they could be blown up, is hard to imagine. We can, however, get some idea from period records and newspaper reports from Most, for example, the following, from 30 September 1968:

Rafters stripped bare, windows with nothing behind them, roads closed off. A dead street […] A primary charge is heard. Exactly 120 seconds later, Mr Šmída presses the button of the electrical detonator […] A few seconds later, half of Tylova ulice [Tyl Street], which had for decades formed an integral part of the historic core of Most, disappears […] Large blocks of flats sway and then vanish in an impenetrable haze of red dust. And then an unreal, unprecedented sight is revealed to us: Tylova ulice seems never to have existed. Only

---

49 The reports mention hard currency earnings of about one million US dollars. SOkA Most, f. 207 (ONV Most II, 1960–1975), inv. č. 779, ev. j. 292, Informativní zpráva o stavu likvidace starého a výstavbě nového Mostu [1967].
50 For more on the timetable of demolitions, see the previous chapter.

ruins – one house cut precisely in half –, in the background a church spire, a lone chimney, the beams of blocks of flats hanging in space.[51]

A month later, on 25 October, under the direction of Mr Šmída, the early Baroque Church of the Assumption (not to be confused with the Deanery Church) together with the adjacent Capuchin monastery from the early seventeenth century was also turned into a haze of red dust.[52]

For the greater part of the period when old Most was regularly shaken by explosions, people still inhabited the town. Until the second half of the 1970s, they lived here in the buildings that were left standing, and they went shopping in the shops and markets that remained open, met in pubs and restaurants, and attended theatre performances and concerts. It was a unique symbiosis between the destruction of a human settlement and a life that was, at least on the surface, presented as absolutely normal. Children, though by no means all of them, went to school,[53] and adults went to work. Buses were running and people filled the three squares of the old town. But this was of course not a completely normal life. Nor had it been even for the many years before the first Most house was blown up.

✕✕✕

The best contemporary description of the atmosphere of old Most in the 1950s is perhaps the one provided by the poet Emil Juliš (1920–2006). His poems about 'black darkness full of the smoke and dust of the mine shafts' rarely penetrated by islets of light, about the 'church on the third square, with its windows smashed' and a 'saint's knocked-off arms woven round with dusty cobwebs',[54] published in

51 'Starému Mostu jde o život: Deset minut pro kronikáře', *Průboj*, 2 October 1968.
52 SOkA Most, f. 130 (MěNV Most), inv. č. 368, Kronika města Mostu 1968, p. 654.
53 The problem of truancy, especially amongst children from Roma families, is further discussed in the chapter 'Gypsies' in the section 'Sudetenland'.
54 From Emil Juliš, 'Vzpomínka na noční Most v roce 1953', in idem, *Pod kroky dýmů*, pp. 31–34.

the 1960s, provide, together with paintings by Bohdan Kopecký (1928–2010), unrivalled testimony about the raw reality of the Most district of those times and about the people who made that society. The colourful society of old Most, which in the 1950s and 1960s was still inhabited by some old German burghers who had not been expelled after the war, Czechs from traditional mining families that had come to the area in the nineteenth century, newly arrived mining engineers from the interior, reimmigrants, and Roma (Gypsies) from east Slovakia, are discussed mainly in the section 'Alienation'. The background of the town, whose destruction had not yet been decided once and for all, consisted at that time not only of an impenetrable haze, the suffocating dust of summer, the snows of winter which quickly turned black with soot and fly ash, but also, indeed mainly, the houses that had for decades been left to go to seed, the streets full of potholes,[55] and the collapsing power grid, whose repair would in normal circumstances have been considered urgent.

It was pure luck that no inhabitant of old Most had been trapped under a collapsing house or part of one. The first unplanned collapse of a building took place on Mírové náměstí (Peace Square) in 1960, though the media and Most inhabitants had been drawing attention to the serious disrepair of the house for two years.[56] More often, however, ornamentation or individual structural elements, chunks of plaster, or roof tiles were falling off houses.[57] But the ramshackle state of the old houses and the character of their flats, which had not been remodelled for decades, affected people in many other respects apart from being a direct threat to their health or lives, as when buildings collapsed of their own accord. The dust and fly ash,

---

55 See the caption to the photograph in *Průboj*, 5 September 1959.
56 'Zapomněli Mostečtí', *Průboj*, 26 June 1958.
57 The chronicle of the town of Most mentions, for example, the oriel window on a house in Koněvova ulice, near the U Lva (Lion) pharmacy, which was, however, torn down in the course of 1967, before, fortunately, it could collapse on its own. SOkA Most, f. 130 (MěNV Most), inv. č. 367, Kronika města Mostu 1967, p. 253.

4. Despite the poor-quality housing and neglected public space, Most was still a lively town in the 1960s, with shops, markets, and a good offering of arts events. The photo shows náměstí Ludvíka Svobody (Ludvík Svoboda Square), dominated by the Deanery Church.

together with the many years of neglect, contributed to the overall atmosphere of the town, which contemporaries have unanimously described as a black tangle of streets full of potholes and gloomy grey buildings with crumbling plaster façades.

The standard of housing of the middle and lower social strata in pre-war Czechoslovakia and the immediate post-war period had in general never been particularly good.[58] But the situation in old Most, as a result of the special social milieu there and the absence of investment, was considerably worse than most other places in the country. In the mid-1950s, almost 60 per cent of the flats in old Most

---

58 See the chapter 'Czechoslovak Variations' in the 'Utopia' section.

had only one or two rooms (which included a kitchen) and more than four fifths of those flats lacked bathrooms. Most of the larger flats, of which there was an absolute shortage, had no bathrooms either. The housing department of the Most Municipal National Committee admitted in a report that about a fifth of the flats were excessively damp or had other problems that threatened the health of their inhabitants, and about 200 flats were described as completely uninhabitable.[59]

Apart from the unsanitary state of their flats, which lacked toilets and were too small, the people of Most, at least until the beginning of the 1960s, also struggled with an acute shortage of housing. Not even the distribution of flats confiscated from the Germans who were expelled after 1945, nor the dividing up of 'oversized' flats after 1948 and the building of two large housing estates (which later became part of the new Most), was able to satisfy the growing demand for housing. This demand stemmed both from the growing need for employees in heavy industry, particularly in the coal industry (that is, with the growing population in the Most district), and from the increased standards of housing. Thus in old Most after 1948, for example, 'basement flats', that is, flats below street level, which lacked daylight and were in fact mostly like damp cells, were removed from the housing stock. Because the authorities were unable to repair dilapidated flats quickly, indeed often not for several years, and were unable to divide up confiscated 'oversized' flats and reassign them to

---

59 According to a report from 1956, of the 4,644 Most flats managed by the Municipal National Committee, 8 per cent had one room and 46 per cent had two rooms; but these numbers also included flats on the new housing estates called the Stalingradská čtvrť and Podžatecká. The proportion of small and other flats in the other approximately 4,000 cases (mostly managed by the North Bohemian Mining District and other large enterprises) is not made specific in this or any similar report from the previous years. The 1956 report also mentions 188 vacant flats. See SOkA Most, f. 131 (ONV Most II, 1960–1990), inv. č. 255, sign. 460, kart. 15, Bytová situace – hlášení [1956]. The Chronicle of the City of Most in 1957 mentions that 60 per cent of the flats in old Most had one room or a kitchen and one room. In SOkA Most, f. 130 (MěNV Most), inv. č. 364, Kronika města Most, díl I. (1945–1965), p. 60.

5. The White Lamb Inn in Švermova ulice with the original German sign (Gasthaus zum weißen Lamm) still visible in 1965, when the demolitions were beginning.

several tenants (allegedly because there were no funds to do so),[60] some flats in old Most, despite the housing shortage, remained empty throughout the 1950s. That meant that they were arbitrarily occupied by people looking for better, or simply any, housing with their families in the place where they worked. The authorities sought to return such people to their original homes, but in a number of cases there was no longer anywhere to return them and the chaos only intensified.[61]

60 SOkA Most, f. 131 (ONV Most I, 1945–1960), inv.č. 255, sign. 460, kart. 15, Bytová situace – hlášení (1952–1956).
61 Ibid.

The situation began to change radically in the mid-1960s. The hitherto neglected, overpopulated town with its unhealthy environment now became something of a war zone in the 'camp of peace'. But it was not only a matter of demolishing individual houses and streets (the first houses to go were in the streets Palackého and Vrchlického in late February and early March 1965).[62] Before this compact urban housing area was turned into piles of rubble, all the inhabitants were moved out, the flats emptied, and whole streets were turned into desolate, dead zones. The town was divided into 54 demolition zones[63] and gradually the 'coalface front' of the great mine began to gnaw away at them. In addition to the houses and streets, places where people used to meet – quiet corners, fountains, squares with trees and benches – also disappeared. At the beginning of the 1970s, the dusty old town was thus already stripped of most of its green and, after the closing down of the last outdoor restaurant here,[64] the only shade in summer was offered by the now bare walls of the houses, marked by age, smoke, and fly ash.

From this moment on, all the inhabitants knew once and for all that their home in the old town was only temporary and that in the foreseeable future they would have to move away. That move was meant to take place systematically, from the demolished parts of old Most mainly to the newly built flats in the new part of town. By

62 See the brief press reports 'Likvidace města Mostu', *Svobodné slovo*, 25 February 1965, 'První dva domy', *Rudé právo*, 26 February 1965, 'Die ersten 3 Häuser, *Aufbau und Frieden*, 27 February 1965, 'Začala likvidace starého Mostu', *Rudé Právo*, 30 January 1965, 'Likvidace starého Mostu začala', *Svobodné slovo*, 6 March 1965, and also others, for example, in *Rudé právo*, *Práce*, and *Czechoslovak Life*.
63 'První fáze likvidace: Demoliční oblast starého Mostu rozdělena na 54 obvodů', *Průboj*, 4 April 1965.
64 See the speech by a certain Mr Petrtyl, a teacher, at the 15th plenary session of the Most Municipal National Committee, on 28 June 1966: 'In one fell swoop we deprived thousands of families of the possibility of sitting in the shade of big trees, where thousands of children used to spend their Sundays, co-op members celebrated their harvest home, factory committees their evenings, concerts, and variety shows [...].' SOkA Most, f. 130 (MěNV Most), inv. č. 366, Kronika města Most 1966, p. 75.

1972, half of the roughly 15,000 original inhabitants of old Most (as counted in the mid-1960s) had already been moved.[65] The press, understandably, reported in some length about the first family that was moved at the beginning of 1965, and thus it is no exaggeration to say that people in towns ranging from Ústí nad Labem and Havířov all the way to Prešov, in east Slovakia, knew about the Špaula family of Palackého ulice and their 'new home in the new part of Most, where, unlike in their previous dwellings, they would have all the creature comforts'.[66]

Yet unlike what one would have expected from a carefully constructed picture of a technically and humanely managed big project, not everything went quite according to plan. For example, the offices for the headquarters of a number of enterprises and institutions were not built on time, and thus temporary space had to be provided in old buildings, which were torn down in a few months or even years later.[67] Many families, too, found themselves in a similar predicament. In the early years, that was sometimes because the tempo of construction in the new town could not keep up with the destruction of the old town. Gradually, however, this was no longer true; construction in the first years after the restoration of the hardline regime following the Soviet-led military intervention in August 1968 became more efficient and in the Most district, moreover, inhabitants slowly (unlike the earlier rapid inflow of workers) began

---

65 From 1965 to 1972, 3,632 flats out of a total of about 6,000 flats necessary for moving the population of old Most were for people moving into the new part of town. Apart from that, another 3,445 flats were built in new Most in this period, and were assigned to newcomers from other parts of the district or even the republic. SOkA Most, f. 208 (ONV Most II, 1960–1975), inv. č. 780, ev. j. 293, Průběh likvidace starého Mostu a výsledky výstavby nového Mostu v roce 1972 (Zpráva pro zasedání Vládní komise, únor 1973).

66 'Vysídlování Mostu začalo', *Práce – venkov*, 28 January 1965.

67 For example, the state police (Sbor národní bezpečnosti – SNB) had to move from Vančurova ulice, which was demolished, not into the planned areas of the new Most but into a bank building in the old Most. See SOkA Most, f. 208 (ONV Most II, 1960–1975), inv. č. 780, ev. j. 293, Průběh likvidace starého Mostu a výsledky výstavby nového Mostu v roce 1972 (Zpráva pro zasedání Vládní komise, únor 1973).

to move in. At a time when almost the only people left in the old town were Roma,[68] however, it turned out that neither the authorities nor the 'white majority' of the new town wanted the Roma. Until an alternative solution was found, that is, segregation,[69] the Roma had to move from the demolition zones to the still standing old homes and streets – before these too were turned into ruins.

It was not only the living who disappeared from old Most. In addition to the efforts to preserve small historic monuments, which could be moved into the district museum, public spaces of the new town, or various repositories and historic buildings in the region, the town cemetery was also moved. Thus, apart from stone monuments and living people, the dead were moved out of Most as well.

From the time of its founding in 1853 to the late 1960s, 24,000 people had been buried in 7,500 graves in the Most municipal cemetery. Apart from the 2,000 graves that the town or family members had decided to move, 5,500 graves were eliminated and carted off together with tonnes of worthless overburden. The coal under the deceased had to be mined too. Their remains, none the less, were gradually moved in 'transports of the dead' to a new cemetery, mostly to a common grave.[70] The socialist state did not fail to look after its living and its dead. The second half of the 1960s, especially for people who had lived in Most for years, was thus, among other things, a time of the emotionally difficult parting with their forebears' final resting places, witnessing the gradual destruction and, ultimately, total elimination of those places.

The newspapers and the Most chronicle from the second half of the 1960s and the beginning of the 1970s contain not only a number of remarkable stories about criminals and drunks, which took place

---

68 See the chapter 'Gypsies' in the 'Alienation' section.
69 See the chapter 'City without Roses' in the 'Utopia' section.
70 See SOkA Most, f. 130 (MěNV Most, 1945–1990), inv. č. 367, Kronika města Most 1967, p. 362. For more on the destruction of the cemetery, see the chapter 'The Velvet Demolition' in the 'Reconciliation' section.

in the old town, but also show, using statistics, that crime and alcoholism were markedly more rampant than in other medium-large cities of Czechoslovakia at that time. The police sought to prevent crime (though, in view of the long-term lack of improvement in the situation, clearly without much success) by eliminating 'idleness', combatting drunkards and 'people with an aversion to work'. Thus, for example, in the spring of 1967:

Members of the regular police force went to a number of restaurants, rooming houses, and flats of questionable repute, where they detained individuals suspected of social parasitism, theft, alcoholism, or loafing, or individuals who were currently sought by the district court. The hunt for these birds has been a success. Several of the detained were escorted to Litoměřice prison [50 km east of Most] or put into cells for pretrial detention in Most. Twenty-five individuals were fined, ten were reported to the appropriate institutions for the crime of social parasitism, and sixteen others were reported for not fulfilling their duty to find a job.[71]

From the 1960s onwards, the town, with half-empty houses and living out its last days and then emptied of all people, became a paradise for a wide variety of small-time thieves, gold-diggers, and other adventurers. The statistics regularly mention that the number of crimes in Most greatly exceeded the Czechoslovak average (for example, the approximately thirty cases of robbery a year set a record in the country at that time), and juvenile crime in particular was rampant.[72] Old Most thus gradually became something like the Wild West of north Bohemia.[73] The remarkable mixture of the old

---

71 SOkA Most, f. 130 (MěNV Most, 1945–1990), inv. č. 367, Kronika města Most 1967, p. 228.
72 SOkA Most, f. 130 (MěNV Most, 1945–1990), inv. č. 366, Kronika města Most 1966, p. 7.
73 This term appears in connection with Most also in period journalism and other sources, no matter how much the people of Most in some cases opposed it. See SOkA Most, f. 130 (MěNV Most, 1945–1990), inv. č. 368, Kronika města Most 1968, p. 709.

6. Despite everything, people led a normal everyday life here. Švermova ulice with the museum building, September 1965.

world of mining, with its grubby pubs, and, on the other hand, the dark side of industrial modernity contributed to a keen sense of extinction and concomitant nihilism. It should come as no surprise, then, that there was a lot of drinking in old Most, that people here (and not only members of the local Roma community, which numbered several thousand) often physically attacked others, resulting in a wide variety of frequently tragic incidents and injuries.

Recurring police raids in pubs and restaurants, threats of high fines for selling alcohol to minors, even the work of various social commissions did not change things much. Thefts and offences against public morality committed since 1966 by several youth gangs were also connected with the above-average divorce rate[74] – which was in turn connected with job-hopping amongst people in the mining industry. The temporary living arrangement instead of a real home surely did not contribute to stable relationships and a sense of life satisfaction.

Despite all these factors, which were turning the neglected mining town into something like a war zone, normal everyday life was really lived here. The inhabitants of Most, with the exception of the big Roma families, often with only one breadwinner, were, compared to those in the rest of the country, amongst the materially well off. In a number of indices, like the consumption of foodstuffs, the inhabitants of the Most district ranked high above the state average and the average of the North Bohemian Region.[75] Still in 1967, old Most had twelve elementary schools with nine grades, some of which were attended also by children from the new town. In the streets that were still inhabited, grocer's, shops with mixed goods, haberdasher's, ironmonger's, chemist's, and others opened their doors every morning to shoppers from both the old town and the adjacent housing estates of the new part of Most.

'Normality', however, was not limited only to the daily routine, school, work, or the satisfying of consumer needs. Old Most, or what remained of it, until this role was partly taken over by the new Most in the mid-1970s, was an important cultural centre not only of the district but, in a way, also of the whole of north Bohemia. The flagship of the arts scene in Most had, since the end of the Second World War, been the local theatre, renamed, after the Communist takeover in February 1948, the Theatre of the Workers (Divadlo pracujících). The building of the Most theatre had been designed before the Great War by the Vienna-based architect Alexander Graf. Until the end of

---

74 For group juvenile crime in Most and its causes, see SOkA Most, f. 130 (MěNV Most, 1945–1990), inv. č. 366, Kronika města Most 1966, p. 77.
75 SOkA Most, f. 130 (MěNV Most, 1945–1990), inv. č. 367, Kronika města Most 1967, p. 208.

the Second World War, performances were given mostly in German. After the war, the emphasis tended to be on the tradition of Czech amateur companies (like Vlastimil, Vojen, Máj), whose history reached back to Austria-Hungary. The Theatre of the Workers had, at the latest by 1950, become not only popular, but also, it seems, a venue for high-quality drama. For the next fifteen years, it put on 129 different productions, from classic works of European theatre (including plays by Goethe, Balzac, Ibsen, and Dürrenmatt) to classics of the Czech stage (including works by Josef Kajetán Tyl, Jaroslav Vrchlický, and Julius Zeyer) to Czechoslovak premieres of new Czech, Slovak, and foreign productions. By the end of the 1960s, it had produced works by Shakespeare and other classics as well as adaptations of Passion plays, Wild West parodies, contemporary Czech dramas, English comedies, and even operas with the Ústí nad Labem opera company. The art director of the Theatre of the Workers at that time was Lubomír Poživil (b.1927), who taught at the Academy of the Performing Arts in Prague, and sought to popularize Czechoslovak drama in west European countries, for example, by lecturing in London in 1967.[76] In Most, a wide variety of theatre companies from other towns in Czechoslovakia and abroad gave performances. At this time, according to sociological research, the theatre was attended by 64 per cent of the inhabitants of Most.[77] Actors from here, like Vladimír Brabec (1934–2017) and Josef Velda (1930–1994), went on to join top companies, including the National Theatre, and figures long linked with the theatre, like the actor Miloš Kopecký (1922–1996) and the actor-director and Communist official Zdeněk Buchvaldek (1928–1987), were among the legends of the Czech theatre world.

Cultural life in the old town of Most naturally comprised more than the Theatre of the Workers. The town also had a puppet theatre

---

76 SOkA Most, f. 130 (MěNV Most, 1945–1990), inv. č. 367, Kronika města Most 1967, p. 232.
77 SOkA Most, f. 130 (MěNV Most, 1945–1990), inv. č. 366, Kronika města Most 1966, p. 154.

and a number of cinemas, which regularly organized a festival called 'The Demanding for the Discerning' (Náročné pro náročné), which screened art films and other non-commercial works from around the world. The actors of the theatre and other well-known figures then performed in regular evenings of poetry readings and dramatic collages, held in the 'Yellow House' in Žižkova ulice. The district museum and library regularly held discussions and exhibited works like the north Bohemian landscapes by the painters Emil Filla (1882–1953) and Bohdan Kopecký (b.1928), and the photographer Josef Sudek (1896–1976). A number of figures of the 1960s who were linked with north Bohemia were involved in the Most arts scene, for example, the writer Josef Jedlička (1927–1990, the author of *Kde život náš je v půli se svou poutí*, recently published in English

7. Most as a ghost town. The remains of Koněvova ulice (Konev Street) at Smetanovo náměstí (Smetana Square), waiting for demolition in November 1978. This is where the Anglo-Czechoslovak Bank once stood, with a photographic studio and a number of little shops on the ground floor.

translation as *Midway on the Journey of Our Life*) and the poet Emil Juliš. 'Musical Mondays' were held in the Deanery Church, with performances of works by composers ranging from Bach to Dvořák. It seems was the particularly existential atmosphere of a town which was gradually being blown up by wrecking crews and gnawed away by bucket-wheel excavators had, at least until the end of the 1960s, an inspirational influence on local cultural life. There were many performances and they were good.

Interesting artists and intellectuals took part in public discussions and remarkable painters and photographers showed their works here. And, most important, there was extraordinary public interest in it all. That may have been helped also by the constant awareness of the temporariness of the increasingly irreal microcosm of the old town.

The old building of the Most theatre became something like the last symbol of the cultural life of the demolished town. The last performance was given here in 1979. Dressed in their best, people attended performances week after week during the theatre season, walking through the now otherwise lifeless streets, clambering over the ruins of houses, and gingerly crossing makeshift footbridges over craters and ditches. While people entered the theatre to enjoy Shakespeare, František Hrubín (1910–1971), and Goldoni, outside, in front of the theatre, heavy equipment rumbled on the overburden of the big Ležáky Mine.[78] The other arts institutions, like practically all Most life at that time, had long ago moved to the new part of town.[79] Only the lights of the homes of the last few Roma families and the theatre still sometimes shone into the darkness as a reminder of the life that once was. In the winter of 1979/80, the actors also had to move, at first temporarily to the Community Arts Centre (Kulturní dům) and

78 'Město Most a jeho divadlo', *Naše rodina,* 4 June 1980.
79 For the character and everyday life of the new Most in the 1960s and 1970s, see the chapter 'City of Roses' in the 'Utopia' section.

then, five years later, to the theatre building in the new Most, which at that time was one of the most modern in central Europe.[80]

The Czechoslovak crime film *Stíhán a podezřelý* (Hunted and Suspected, 1978),[81] with a stellar cast (including Ilja Prachař, Jan Přeučil, Vladimír Brabec, Jiří Lábus, and Jiří Kostka), tells the strange story of an engineer, Karel Trojan (in the film, an expert in charge of moving the Deanery Church), who is on the run because he thinks he is erroneously suspected of having killed his wife. The last twenty minutes of the film, which is less than an hour and a half long in all, takes places in the soon-to-be demolished houses of old Most. In this harsh, bewildering setting, which stands in stark contrast to the otherwise organized, controlled, and controllable socialist country, the poor wretch on the lam can hide for days, before the good-natured detective, after an exhausting search, eventually discovers him just before the whole street on which the house Trojan is hiding in is blown up. He can thus save Trojan's life and finally tell him that the authorities know he is innocent.

And it was in old Most, in April 1978, when *Stíhán a podezřelý* was being filmed, that a story unfolded that could have served as an inspiration for the scenes that anyone unfamiliar with Most would surely find quite implausible. Ida Nováková, who the month before had been granted a lease for a flat in the new Most, was supposed to move in during the next few weeks. Her unregistered subtenant, one Mr Hruška, of course received no letter from the authorities, and because Nováková did not want a subtenant in her new flat, she left the unsuspecting Hruška, with his bed and wardrobe, in the old house in Oblouková ulice. Like the film *Stíhán a podezřelý*, this story too has a happy ending – a surprised Hruška poked his head out the window shortly before the detonation and heard the calls of

80   See also the chapter 'The Welfare Dictatorship' in the 'Utopia' section.
81   The Czechoslovak crime film *Stíhán a podezřelý*, Barrandov Studios, 1978, 1:22. https://www.youtube.com/watch?v=VOK-olcfZQM Accessed 10 December 2018.

8. One story ends. The demolition of the once famous Repre arts and community centre (also known as the Oblastní klub horníků, that is, the Regional Miners Club).

some even more surprised explosive technicians who were putting explosive charges into the masonry: 'Hey, mate, are we supposed to blow you up too?'[82] Nováková paid a 50 Kčs fine and had to move Hruška into her new flat.

Apart from pointing out the real risk that some people could also be physically eliminated with the large-scale elimination of Most housing, the film *Stíhán a podezřelý* also highlights another related fact that changed Most from a devastated and almost completely abandoned town into a unique environment. That fact is the uncontrollable, chaotic nature of what remained of the town, whose individual parts were now being neglected and left unguarded. This was something truly unique in an otherwise orderly and calm country. It should therefore not surprise anyone that the vacated town truly did provide

82 Josef Pavlíček, 'Opuštěný podnájemník', *Mladá fronta*, 26 April 1978.

hiding places for criminals. In the basements or attics of the abandoned houses in the late 1970s and early 1980s, people on the run found shelter – and so did people who simply wanted to make some money from anything they could find in houses earmarked for demolition. What morning looks like amongst these empty houses is described in an article in the Prague edition of the *Volkszeitung*:

> From the houses emerge dark figures, who warily look in all directions.
> [...] They slept in the abandoned houses on straw and rags, and are now hurrying with tin or copper pipes to the scrap metal dealers, to earn a few crowns for breakfast [...] Young runaways, fathers who don't pay alimony, fugitives from justice, the homeless, and the unemployed.[83]

The infernal environment of the abandoned town, whose streets had changed one after another into heaps of rubble, attracted not only screenwriters and directors of state-funded feature films and documentaries, but also independent artists, like Jiří Sozanský (b.1946). In what remained of old Most in the first half of the 1980s, he installed a variety of objects to draw attention to the desolation, absence of life, and human beings' alienation from their environment.[84] At that time, however, old Most or at least what remained of it was already an enclosed uninhabited zone, which Sozanský and his collaborators could enter only with special passes. The agony of the town, which had become an island between the coalfaces, like a continuously shrinking Atlantis, a mere shadow of the life of this now dead landscape, lasted until 1987. In spring of that year, the last house was blown up and the former royal borough was changed once and for all into part of the Most open-pit mine.

---

83 'Gibt es in Most Goldgräber?', *Volkszeitung*, 1 May 1969.
84 Jiří Sozanský, *Zóna*, Prague: Kant, 2013. See also the chapter 'In Defence of the Old Town' in the 'Criticism' section.

THINKING THE STORY

This book is an attempt to understand the *Sinnwelt* of the people who helped to create the history of socialist Czechoslovakia in the period when industrial modernity was reaching its peak. I understand the elimination of the historic town of Most, which was determined by coal mining and justified by, among other things, the building of the new town of Most, as one of the extraordinary yet somehow characteristic stories that enable us to identify the essential features of the thinking and behaviour of that period.

Five Perspectives

In the preceding chapters I have sought to identify the milestones and key decisions leading to the destruction of old Most and to the way people continued to live in the town as it was gradually demolished. The course of events alone does not, however, provide the essence of the story. We still have to get there, and in the following chapters I shall try to achieve that by means of a kind of triangulation, in other words, from several different perspectives, which will put the whole topic into its various contexts.

The name of the first of the perspectives that I have chosen, 'Alienation', might be somewhat misleading. Here, it does not pertain to the more general phenomenon characterizing the relationship of human beings, work, and the products of that labour, but instead to the special relationship between people and the land they inhabit (and also partly amongst the people themselves), which is characteristic of an area in which most of the old population had been replaced by a new one. In connection with Most, this is of course the phenomenon of the former Sudetenland, the expulsion of the vast majority of the German-speaking inhabitants, and the situation in which most of the subsequent population of this region after 1946 comprised newcomers who had no family or other roots here.

The peculiarity of this situation consists not only in the changed attitude to the historic cultural landscape, but also in the marked heterogeneity of the newly forming society.[85] From this perspective, what was decisive in Most was the complicated attitude of the majority population to the Roma, most of whom had come from east Slovakia. We can then see the alienation factor at several levels: in the attitude to the 'German' past, in the attitude to the land and the traces of the past that are present in it, and attitudes between the people forming the new society. The identification of the old Most with the Roma population, which constituted a substantial part of its population, especially in the 1970s, then served as a means to stigmatize this part of society and also as an instrument to justify the demolition of the historic town.[86] If, when trying to explain why people were willing to sacrifice the old town to coal, one relies solely on the phenomenon of the 'Sudeten sense of uprootedness' (*sudetské bezdomoví*) – that is, the loss of identity of a land that was deprived of its original inhabitants and their traditions – and the subsequent difficulty in finding a new identity, one encounters a whole series of obstacles. These range from the fact that the Most district had ben ethnically the most mixed area in the borderlands (that is, it was not at all purely German) to the important role of mining traditions and the memory of the struggles for social rights in the Bohemian Lands, one of whose most important symbolic centres was doubtless the town of Most. These aspects make it even more necessary to put the post-Second World War history of Most into other, transregional, indeed even global contexts.

The first of these aspects is necessarily linked to the factor that most influenced the landscape and society in the Ore Mountains

85 See Matěj Spurný, *Nejsou jako my: Česká společnost a menšiny v pohraničí 1945–1960*, Prague: Antikomplex, 2011.
86 See also Eagle Glassheim, 'Most, the Town that Moved: Coal, Communists and the "Gypsy Question" in PostWar Czechoslovakia', *Environment and History* 13 (2007), pp. 447–76. For more on this in the present publication, see the chapter 'Gypsies' in the 'Alienation' section.

from the nineteenth century onwards – namely, coal and the special interests and ways of thinking that had long accompanied its mining (and more generally the industrial exploitation of the land). This second aspect I call 'numbers', which refers to an even more general connection, going beyond the topic of coal mining (presented in the first chapter of this section) and the concomitant power constellations and ways of thinking. The reduction of the world to measurable quantities need not, after all, take the form only of productivism (that is, a special form of economic thinking aimed at an increase in industrial production), most often connected with coal mining (and the socialist dictatorship). In the capitalist and socialist countries from the second half of the 1950s onwards, a visible change occurred in governing linked with the scientific and technological revolution and optimistic visions of comprehensive management and planning based on recasting empirical knowledge into a complex system.[87] This technocratic vision changed the nature of state socialism and one has to investigate the extent to which it had an influence also on decision-making in the question of the demolition of old Most, its acceptance by the power elites and ordinary people, and the actual course of the whole experiment.

An important perspective from which one can fruitfully try to understand the demolition of old Most concerns in the promise to build a new Most and its actual construction. That is again part of the extraordinarily influential context of urban utopias, which is also vital to this study, that is, the visions and efforts to make them a reality, particularly in the first three decades after the Second World War. The section called 'Utopia' thus puts the Most story onto a wider spectrum, at one end of which are located the well-known concepts of Thomas More (1478–1535) and Tommaso Campanella (1568–1639). But it turns out that more important for us in this story are the figures

---

87 See below in this chapter and, in greater detail, the chapter 'Technocracy' in the 'Numbers' section.

who directly shaped modern urban planning and architecture, first and foremost Le Corbusier (Charles-Édouard Jeanneret, 1887–1965), and particular projects for the building of new cities in countries ranging from the Soviet Union to Great Britain. A link between this most general context and Most itself is the Czechoslovak and especially the Czech architectural and urban-planning debate, that is, the changes in Czech thinking about the forms and functions of the modern city from the 1920s to the 1960s. Nor is the topic of urban utopias a mere glimpse into the history of ideas; rather, it is directly linked to the social history of the populations of European and American cities of the nineteenth century and the first half of the twentieth century, that is, the poverty of working class areas, slums on the outskirts, makeshift quarters for miners, and the disastrous consequences of the absence of sanitation and hygiene in the growing cities. These are the phenomena, strikingly present in Bohemian towns ranging from Prague to Most, which were giving persuasive power to ideas about the clean modern city with decent housing for all.

Under the pressure of economic necessity from the decision--making of the political elites, the years when the old Most was demolished and the new Most was built constituted an historic watershed. Whereas at the start of the 1960s most Europeans and Americans looked optimistically towards the modern organization of industry, which would guarantee more efficient production, and therefore towards an increase in their standard of living and towards the possibilities of rationally running society, and they believed in the long-term planning of future developments, this image of a thoroughly organized world of technological solutions to all problems developed serious cracks over the next ten to fifteen years, both to the west and to the east of the Iron Curtain.[88] The gradually changing

---

[88] For that reason, it is fair to talk about the 1960s and 1970s as a time of the crisis of modernity, as I discuss later.

'criticism', which drew both on environmentalist thinking and on the increasingly more relevant emphases on the protection and preservation of the material traces of the past, therefore constitutes the fourth of my chosen perspectives. In Czechoslovakia, though the critical discourse developed in parallel with that in western Europe and America, under the authoritarian system it of course faced its own particular limitations – and mainly the phases determined by the political changes, first and foremost those brought about by the Soviet-led Warsaw Pact intervention in late August 1968 and the subsequent suppression of reform socialism in the course of 1969.

Whereas the absolute majority of decisions about the fate of old Most and the form of the new Most were made in the 1960s, and the sources of their ideas and the social contexts have to be sought chiefly in the period before 1965, the actual carrying out of the Most experiment mainly fell into the period of 'normalization' (the hardline policy of the Communist Party for the restoration of order from 1969 onwards). In other words, the decisions were taken in the period that in many respects follows on from the previous development, from the 'technocratic'[89] and reform socialism of the second half of the 1950s and in the 1960s, which, however, also strengthened the authoritarian regulation of public discussion. The particular context of 'real socialism', which influenced thinking about the demolition of historic Most, and of the degree and actual form of the preservation of some of its monuments and mainly the ultimate form of the new Most, therefore constitutes the fifth, and last, vantage point from which I seek to understand the Most story. Despite the return to bureaucratic and authoritarian rule, the attempt to integrate even some of the main points emphasized in the 1960s criticism into its ideological structure is – and this is a key proposition of my book – characteristic of the normalization period. It is precisely for this reason that I somewhat exaggeratedly use the word

89 For the term 'technocratic socialism', see below.

'Reconciliation' to describe the way in which the normalization period changed the discourse about the demolition of old Most and the construction of the new city, even though at this very time the final destruction of the old town was taking place.

Like most historians I too put my narrative into a certain theoretical framework, start from certain assumptions, and use terms whose precise meanings are by necessity not agreed on by everyone. Before I illuminate the stories from the first of my five perspectives, I shall try to reflect upon at least those assumptions of which I am aware.

The Landscape and the Society

This book is a discussion of the dramatic transformation of a town and a landscape, about an environment that was both a source of raw materials and the home of thousands of people. The changes and mutual influences of civilization and the landscape have for several decades now been the object of interest of a discipline that American historians in the 1970s began to call 'environmental history'. It concerns a methodological perspective that focuses on the relationship between human beings and their environment, including changes that people have made to that environment.[90] The starting point of this discipline of history writing, as it has been formed by a number of historians[91] who research specific changes to the landscape or to the relationship between human beings and the land in connection with the extraction of raw materials[92] (on the rare occasion, sometimes

90 Donald J. Hughes, *An Environmental History of the World: Humankind's Changing Role in the Community of Life*, London: Routledge, 2001, pp. 1–11.
91 Donald Worster, Alfred B. Crosby, and, in Europe, for example, Frank Uekötter.
92 See Richard H. K. Vietor, *Environmental Politics and the Coal Coalition*, College Station and London: Texas A & M University Press, 1980; Chad Montrie, 'Expedient Environmentalism: Opposition to Coal Surface Mining in Appalachia and the United Mine Workers of America, 1945–1975', *Environmental History* 5 (1), January 2000, pp. 75–98; and Timothy J. LeCain, *Mass Destruction: The Men and Giant Mines That Wired America and Scarred the Planet*, New Brunswick, NJ: Rutgers University Press, [2009].

about Czechoslovakia too),[93] was an inspiration for the interpretation of events examined in this book. Among the areas that the founders of environmental history, led by Donald Worster, intended to research was the relationship between technologies and the natural environment, environmental planning, and the changing value systems in individual cultural areas, which have had an impact on people's attitudes to nature and the landscape of their home.[94] All these strata (technology and technocracy, utopian visions and urban planning, the transformation of the dominant discourse about the environment) are the subject of research in this book, which thus, in its choice of topics, includes environmental history. Yet this is not a classic study of changes in the relationship between human beings and their environment written from the perspective of environmental history.

This is so because, first of all, the leading proponents of environmental history have in the past few decades satisfactorily explained how areas that less than a hundred years ago were untouched by human beings were exploited, and have demonstrated the influence of industry and technology on the rural cultural landscape. Considerably later and to a still not entirely satisfactory extent, as they themselves admit,[95] they succeeded in linking their field with urban studies, and demonstrated how technological developments and production have changed the environments of towns and cities.[96] This

93 Particularly the works of Eagle Glassheim, see below.
94 Donald Worster, 'Appendix: Doing Environmental History', in idem (ed.), *The Ends of the Earth: Perspectives on Modern Environmental History*, Cambridge and New York: Cambridge University Press, 1988. For a similar definition of the subject of environmental history, see also Timo Myllyntaus, 'Environment in Explaining History: Restoring Humans as Part of Nature', in Timo Myllyntaus and Mikko Saikku (eds), *Encountering the Past in Nature: Essays in Environmental History*, 2nd rev. edn, (1999) Athens, OH: Ohio University Press, 2001.
95 Maureen A. Flanagan, 'Environmental Justice in the City: A Theme for Urban Environmental History', *Environmental History* 5 (2), April 2000, pp. 159–64, esp. 159.
96 The trend of combining environmental history and urban history is a recent development, probably with particularly good prospects for the former discipline. In addition to the Flanagan article in n. 95, see also the articles in Dieter Schott, Bill Luckin, and Geneviève Massard-Guilbaud

slight one-sidedness may be linked with a second, more fundamental problem – namely, the so far not particularly successful combination of environmental history and social history.

The dichotomy between humankind and its activities on the one hand and nature on the other, as environmental historians tend to assume or at least implicitly construe in their works, has a natural tendency to conceive of 'human beings' or 'civilization' as a collective actor. This tendency to abstraction and personification of what is in fact a markedly heterogeneous reality, as it presents society with all its power relations, negotiations, partial identities, and interests, has recently been identified by environmental historians as a key problem of their field. On the other hand it is reasonable to think critically about the insufficient attention that social historians have so far paid to environmental changes brought about by human beings. The topic of social inequalities and their impact on the everyday practice of people from various social strata and environments in the past, the central topic of social history, is, though, ever more clearly connected with environmental problems and their varying impact on individual parts of the world and on the lives of various groups of the population. For this reason, there have been increasing calls for environmental and social history to find common ground.[97] This book, I hope, will also be seen as part of that search.

(eds), *Resources of the City: Contributions to an Environmental History of Modern Europe*, Aldershot: Ashgate, 2005, and the many articles that focus on a specific city, like Chicago or Pittsburgh. Similarly, William Cronon, Joel A. Tarr, and Christine Meisner Rosen devote themselves to the environmental history of the city in Christine Meisner Rosen and Joel Arthur Tarr (eds), *The Environment and the City*, a special issue of the *Journal of Urban History* 20 (May 1994). For more on the intersections of environmental and urban history, see Jonathan Keyes, 'A Place of Its Own: Urban Environmental History', *Journal of Urban History*, March 2000, pp. 380–90.

97   See Stephen Mosley, 'Common Ground (Integrating the Social and Environmental in History)', *Journal of Social History* 39 (3), 2006. Special Issue on the Future of Social History, pp. 915–33. For a more complex treatment, see Geneviève Massard-Guilbaud and Stephen Mosley, *Common Ground: Integrating the Social and Environmental in History*, New Castle upon Tyne: Cambridge Scholars, 2011.

The events forming the basic axis of this work are essentially linked with the human impact on the environment in its most extreme imaginable form – namely, the total destruction of both the natural and the cultural environment, of which only a greyish brown wasteland of a strip mine remained. Yet I do not want to tell this story exclusively as a dystopia of modernity and the emancipated powers of 'technoscience', which is served by an essentially cohesive, passive mass of people enslaved by these powers. I shall try mainly to provide a vivid depiction of the individual power groups and social groups (managers, politicians, preservationists, or, for example, the Roma of Most) and in some cases also specific actors, for example, architects, essayists, and intellectuals in the humanities, who decided and acted on the basis of certain interests or intellectual starting points, and pursued often different aims. In that sense, the book expands and deepens the interpretational framework, which for researching the transformations of north Bohemia, particularly Most, is offered mainly by the writings of Eagle Glassheim, a professor of history at the University of British Columbia. For me, Glassheim's works are without doubt amongst the strongest source of inspiration and I partly follow on from their basic arguments.[98]

This book builds on the assumption that the elimination of the old Most and the construction of the new one attest to more general links, continuities, and transformations of the modern age, and were hardly a random cluster of events and circumstances. At the same time, however, I do not wish to interpret this story – whose specific twists and turns and outcomes are formed by specific actors, changes in power politics, and the dynamics of the ideological

---

[98] See the long article by Glassheim, 'Most, the Town that Moved'. For a more general interpretational framework of industrial modernism and the transformations of identity in the Czech border regions in the period of state socialism, see Eagle Glassheim, 'Ethnic Cleansing, Communism, and Environmental Devastation in Czechoslovakia's Borderlands, 1945–1989', *The Journal of Modern History* 78, March 2006, pp. 65–92

patterns and the *Sinnwelt* – as an illustration of the inevitable scenario of modern technological civilization.

An essential particularity of this topic, which also influences the choice of suitable methodological approaches for its interpretation, is of course state socialism, in other words, the authoritarian power-politics system, in which the State, under the control of the Communist Party, not only provided the legal framework and had a monopoly of the legitimate use of force, but also concentrated and controlled all ownership and was the monopoly employer and sole actor that could invest in large projects and consequently carry them out. Amongst those projects was of course the extraction of non-renewable resources and the consequent large-scale destruction and reconstruction of the landscape. This framework of the Most experiment also distinguishes the book from the vast majority of works on environmental history, since that field emerged in the United States as a critical discipline pointing particularly to changes in the natural environment in connection with the development of capitalism. That of course opens up another level of this book – namely, observing the differences and especially the surprising parallels amongst the discourses about the environment and politics practised in the two political and economic systems.

Sources of Legitimacy

In an effort to understand the thinking and behaviour of people living under the state-socialist regime, I start from the conviction that the building of the socialist dictatorship[99] in Czechoslovakia (and elsewhere) and its largely stable operation cannot be properly explained by pointing to state-organized violence and, based on it, the

99 On the conceptualization of modern dictatorships as discussed by Czech historians, see Radek Buben, Michal Pullmann, Matěj Spurný, and Jiří Růžička, 'Diktatura,' in Lucie Storchová et al., *Koncepty a dějiny: Proměny pojmů v současné historické vědě*, Prague: Scriptorium, 2014, pp. 267–307.

absolute power of the Communist Party. The perspective I take in no way relativizes either the deplorable violation of human dignity or the essential differences between the system of authoritarian rule and, on the other hand, liberal democracy and the rule of law. We cannot, however, properly understand Czechoslovakia in the years of state socialism if we are unable to see state socialism as a form of domination, that is, as a constant struggle of the rulers for their own legitimacy based on the consent or at least the conciliation of most of the ruled with the power hierarchy, that is to say, with the right of the rulers to exercise power. Nor can the period that this book covers, from the second half of the 1950s to the end of the 1970s, be properly explained if, in addition to the differences, we do not take seriously the similarities and convergences between the two dominant economic and social systems at that time, capitalism and state socialism.

Czechoslovakia after the 1948 takeover was a 'participatory dictatorship'.[100] In the period of the events covered in this book, the execution of power was tied to the established decision-making procedures and, within the Czechoslovak Communist Party, to the norms of Party discipline. From the mid-1950s onwards, at the state and regional levels, the influence of the single authoritarian decision-maker gradually declined,[101] and the principle of collective leadership became stronger. The Communist Party in this period had, with various fluctuations, a membership of about 1.5 million people, who, together with their families, constituted an important part of the total population of about 13 million. Even the people who were not

---

100 This term is often used for the German Democratic Republic and other socialist dictatorships, for example, in Martin Sabrow, 'Sozialismus als Sinnwelt: Diktatorische Herrschaft in kulturhistorischer Perspektive,' *Potsdamer Bulletin für Zeithistorische Studien* 40/41, 2007, pp. 9–23, published in Czech translation as 'Socialismus jako myšlenkový svět: Komunistická diktatura v kulturněhistorické perspektivě,' *Soudobé dějiny* 2 (2012), pp. 196–208.
101 Concerning this aspect in Czechoslovakia, see Václav Kaška, *Neukáznění a neangažovaní: Disciplinace členů Komunistické strany Československa v letech 1948–1952*, Prague: Conditio humana ÚSTR, 2014.

Party members, and therefore usually had fewer privileges or decision-making powers, cannot properly be imagined as the passively suffering masses or blindly obeying the orders of the power-holders. The Party expended considerable means to monitor the mood of the population, consumer satisfaction, specific demands and complaints, not so that it could punish the dissatisfied, but because it was struggling for its own legitimacy and seeking to accommodate the needs of the times and of society, which the Party, or at least its elite, assumed it could lead to a brighter future. In this situation, most of the inhabitants of the country naturally sought not only to gain the best existential conditions for themselves, but also to project into their own lives their own understanding of the ideals of the period. Between the extreme and rarely populated poles of categorical (or even armed) resistance and unconditional obedience to the intentions of the powerful, there was a space of negotiation, everyday strategies, and headstrong, though not necessarily intentionally 'anti-regime',[102] behaviour. It was a sphere of life which enables one to understand and explain the changes in people's everyday life and *Sinnwelt*, that is, generally, historical change.

This book is not, as might perhaps be deduced from the preceding words, primarily research into the everyday strategies of ordinary people – no matter how much they occasionally come into play in the attempt to answer the most important questions. It is rather largely an attempt to reconstruct the thinking of ordinary people at that time and the influence of that thinking on changes in the world in which they lived and created together. If the question is posed like this, however, then the participatory nature, the efforts of the ruling elites to achieve consensus, and the continuous confirmation of their legitimacy by negotiation are the basic assumptions required to give

---

102 Concerning the term 'Eigen-Sinn' (one's own sense, one's own meaning), see Thomas Lindenberger, 'Die Diktatur der Grenzen: Zur Einleitung', in idem (ed.), *Herrschaft und Eigen-Sinn in der Diktatur: Studien zur Gesellschaftsgeschichte der DDR*, Cologne: Böhlau, 1999, pp. 13–44.

meaning to the attempt to understand and explain the relationship between changes in thinking and changes in the physical world. For if the world of socialist Czechoslovakia was, with the exception of islets of criminalized resistance, a mere derivative of an unchanging ruling ideology, there would be no point in trying to comprehend such a past. From the start, we would then actually already know everything substantial and would only be researching in order endlessly to reconfirm a simple explanation for existence of the *ancien régime*. Not only the necessity to explain historical change but also the sources of almost any origin demonstrate that the ways in which people living under the state-socialist regime thought about the world were neither merely a derivative of the prevailing doctrine nor, on the contrary, the uninfluential denial of reality, constrained and forbidden by that doctrine. At that time, as today, thinking about the world took place in dialogue, though undoubtedly within different limits and with different restrictions.

The questions that I ask in the short preface would be pointless if we did not perceive state socialism, like any other long-lasting social and political system, as a legitimate form of government. Legitimacy, as it was first defined by one of the founders of sociology, the economist Max Weber (1864–1920),[103] is not, however, a category we could use today to assess a certain historical stage or historical form in the sense of a good or a bad government. Legitimacy is the general public acknowledgement of the right of an authority to exercise power in a certain territory. A legitimate government thus has at its disposal the exercise of power or a set of characteristics that determine the willingness of individuals to respect the rules of living in a certain system and to participate in its operation. In a modern secularized society, however, legitimacy is not the result of the union of the ruler and the celestial order of things. Its construction must

---

103 Max Weber, 'Die Typen der Herrschaft', in idem, *Wirtschaft und Gesellschaft* I, ed. Johannes Winckelmann, (1921 and 1922) Tübingen: Mohr, 1956, pp. 157ff.

therefore be more complicated. Weber differentiated between legal--rational, traditional, and charismatic authority,[104] though these ideal types usually exist in some combination with each other, possibly expanded to include other factors, ranging from belief in the promise of future abundance to the non-existence of alternatives.

More recent approaches emphasize not only the sources of legitimacy consisting in the actual form of governance, the decisive role of prepolitical expectations, intuitions, or rituals of the 'ruled' – that is, the fact that legitimacy, whether of the capitalist order in a parliamentary democracy[105] or of authoritarian regimes (including states of socialist domination) is formed in interaction, by means of negotiation. This interpretation may not be in conflict with Weber's original explanation, but it puts considerably greater emphasis on the interdependence of the 'ruler' and the 'ruled'.[106] The concept of *Sinnwelt* has turned out to be extremely fruitful in analysis of the experience and expectations of the wider social strata or, simply, the ruled.[107] Difficult to translate, the term *Sinnwelt* links the level of conscious reflection of the world with mentalities and unconscious intuitions. It refers to the need and ability to make sense of the world around oneself, that is, on the one hand, to incorporate one's own ideas about correct, ideal operations into everyday conduct and, on the other, the continuous interpretation and assessment of reality on the basis of unconscious desires, ideas, and

104 Ibid.
105 See Jürgen Habermas, *Legitimationsprobleme im Spätkapitalismus*, Frankfurt am Main: Suhrkamp, 1973. Published in English as *Legitimation Crisis*, trans. Thomas McCarthy, Boston: Beacon Press, 1975.
106 See Alf Lüdtke, *Herrschaft als soziale Praxis: Historische und sozial-anthropologische Studien*, Göttingen: Vandenhoeck & Ruprecht, 1991.
107 The term *Sinnwelt* follows on from the interpretational approaches of the historians Alf Lüdtke, Martin Sabrow, and especially Thomas Lindenberger. Amongst the Czechs, the social dictatorship as a *Sinnwelt* has been researched mainly by scholars, including the author of this book, in an international project of the Institute of Contemporary History at the Czech Academy of Sciences (ÚSD AV ČR), in Prague, and the Centre for Contemporary History (ZZF), in Potsdam. See *Soudobé dějiny* 2, 2012, a special issue devoted to this topic.

experiences. The *Sinnwelt* thus includes the prepolitical acceptance of the value systems, constructing the meaning of the existing social system, and ideas, both articulated and unarticulated, about the best possible future. The scholarly debate about the sources of the legitimacy of the socialist dictatorships has been carried on for decades without reaching definitive conclusions. Briefly, it is fair to say, concerning the main pillar of the legitimacy of state socialism, that proponents of the central role of Marxist-Leninist ideology and the utopia of Communism (that is, a kind of self-serving rationality)[108] stand against those who are trying to historicize the ways various dictatorships sought legitimacy in their various stages of development, and to point out more specific experiential, material, and mental causes that led elites and the wider strata to accept the individual socialist dictatorships in their various phases as legitimate forms of government.[109] We may reasonably identify two strong historical sources of the legitimacy of Communist Party domination in post-war Czechoslovakia – one, the promise of social justice (which found wide acceptance particularly in the context of the Great Depression, the two world wars, and the social differences of interwar Czechoslovakia), and, the other, the project of a nation-state cleansed of most of its ethnic minorities, of which the Communists were able to present themselves as the guarantor immediately after the war.[110] An essential question in this research concerns the sources of legitimacy of state socialism in Czechoslovakia both in the post-Stalinist period, beginning in about 1956, when the two original promises, the social and the national (ethnic), had largely been fulfilled and were, from the standpoint of legitimacy, ceasing

108 See Thomas Henry Rigby, 'Political Legitimacy, Weber and Communist Mono-organisational Systems', in T. H. Rigby and Ferenc Fehér (eds), *Political Legitimation in Communist States*, New York, London, and Basingstoke: St. Martin's Press and Palgrave Macmillan, 1982, pp. 1–26.
109 See Agnes Heller, 'Phases of Legitimation in Soviet-type Societies', in ibid., pp. 45–63, and Michal Kopeček, 'Ve službách dějin, ve jménu národa', *Soudobé dějiny* VIII (1), 2001, pp. 23–43.
110 See Spurný, *Nejsou jako my.*

to be enough for the further existence of the dictatorship), and in the years of normalization. The cultural achievements, connected with industrial modernity, appear to be of central importance in the transformation of the town of Most in the period we are looking at. The *Sinnwelt* of the Communists throughout the period of state socialism was generally imbued with at least two other characteristic features that have a direct relationship with modernity – namely, respect for knowledge and faith in progress. Neither of those aspects was limited to the theatrical formulas of ceremonial addresses or ideological introductions written for Party publications. The initial orientation point for a member of socialist society looking at the world consisted in differentiating between the progressive and the reactionary, the scientifically substantiated or rational and the superstitious or alleged.[111] But the individual stages of Communist domination, with regard to emphases and to the forms of the desired progress, are also fundamentally different.[112]

With regard to official statements and political practice, we may, at the latest from 1956 onwards in the Soviet Union and the socialist countries of central Europe, observe a repeated emphasis on modernity, accompanied this time (unlike in the Stalinist discourse) by reflections about the convergence of its socialist and its capitalist versions. This trend was strikingly intensified in Czechoslovakia in the 1960s and it is fair to see it as a key starting point of what is generally known as 'reform Communism'. We can then observe at the beginning of the normalization period an intense effort to cleanse socialism of the silt of reformist notions about humanity and democracy, while trying to maintain the modernist emphasis and the

---

111   See Sabrow, 'Socialismus jako myšlenkový svět', pp. 204–06, with an English abstract on p. 379.
112   See Michal Kopeček, *Hledání ztraceného smyslu revoluce: Zrod a počátky marxistického revisionismu ve střední Evropě 1953–1960*, Prague: Argo, 2009, and Pavel Kolář, 'Čtyři základní rozpory východoevropského komunismu', *Soudobé dějiny* 22 (1–2), 2015, pp. 130–65.

real achievements of the State in modernizing the individual sectors of the economy and everyday life. The extent to which 'organized modernity'[113] constituted the common source of the legitimacy both of the liberal capitalist system and of the state-socialist system from the 1950s to the 1970s is one of the most important questions asked in this book. Through the Most story we can observe the actual face of socialist modernity and verify the extent to which it could truly have served to legitimate Communist Party rule, and possibly also, the conditions under which it ceased to perform this role and when.

Though I prefer the historicization of the specific social, cultural, economic, and political contexts to a monocausal explanation of the sources of the legitimacy of the state-socialist system, one cannot avoid the question of the role of Marxist-Leninist ideology. It is in the answers to this question that the various approaches to the history of socialist dictatorships considerably diverge. In the analysis of the role of ideology, it is possible to observe development over time, from the conviction about its primacy in the totalitarian explanation to its being almost completely excluded when emphasizing everyday practice in the revisionists' interpretations,[114] to the return of ideology (in a conception approaching discourse rather than doctrine) in

---

113 A term coined by the German sociologist Peter Wagner. Concerning the changing concepts of modernity, see the last two chapters of this section.

114 A chief aim of historians and Sovietologists who since the 1960s have rejected the totalitarian interpretation has been to return society as an active participant to our understanding of modern dictatorships, including dictatorships of the Soviet or even the Stalinist type. New research topics stemming from this conception first took shape in discussions gradually published in periodicals, edited volumes, the newly founded 'revisionist' periodical *Studies in Comparative Communism*, and subsequently also in classic monographs like Robert C. Tucker, *Stalin in Power: The Revolution from Above, 1928–1941*, New York: W.W. Norton, 1990; Sheila Fitzpatrick, *Everyday Stalinism: Ordinary Life in Extraordinary Times: Soviet Russia in the 1930s*, New York: Oxford University Press, 1999; J. Arch Getty, *The Soviet Communist Party Reconsidered, 1933–1938*, New York and Cambridge: Cambridge University Press, 1985; and Stephen Cohen, *Bukharin and the Bolshevik Revolution: A Political Biography, 1888–1938*, New York: Alfred A. Knopf, 1973.

the interpretations of the 'post-revisionists'.[115] At the same time, the emphasis on the role of ideology as well its very conception depends on what disciplines the individual analyses are anchored in – from political science to the history of ideas to cultural and social history.

This book is not intended to provide what no theorist has been able to achieve, that is, a generally acceptable and useable definition of the term 'ideology'.[116] To grasp the rest of the discussion here, however, it is, necessary to define at least broadly what I mean when I occasionally use the term. Ideology as an unchanging doctrine shaping the thinking and actions of people does not stand at the centre of my interest in this book, which is written mostly from the perspective of social and cultural history, informed by a revisionist approach to the socialist dictatorship and criticism of it. Rather, ideology here is a way of thinking, rooted by means of written and oral statements, but acquiring, in political practice, diverse forms and shades of meaning. The sources of contemporary history do not confirm Marx's proposition about ideology as a false consciousness produced purely for the purpose of legitimating a certain political and economic system.[117] If we applied Marx's interpretation to the

115 For interpretational frameworks, see Michal Pullmann, 'K sociální dynamice teroru,' the afterword to Wendy Z. Goldmanová, *Vytváření nepřítele*, Prague: Karolinum, 2015, pp. 267–86, the Czech translation of Wendy Z. Goldman's *Inventing the Enemy: Denunciation and Terror in Stalin's Russia*, Cambridge and New York: Cambridge University Press, 2011.

116 Eagleton lists almost two dozen different conceptions of ideology which he considers currently influential in the scholarly debate. They range from Marx's false consciousness to Foucault's production of meanings and signs to the theories of post-war American sociologists about ideology as being a closed system. Terry Eagleton, *Ideology: An Introduction*, (1991) London and New York: Verso, 2007, pp. 1–2.

117 Karl Marx and Friedrich Engels, *Die deutsche Ideologie: Kritik der neuesten deutschen Philosophie in ihren Repräsentanten, Feuerbach, B. Bauer und Stirner, und des deutschen Sozialismus in seinen verschiedenen Propheten*, (1845–46) Berlin: Dietz, 1953. Marx's conception of ideology was further developed and partly revised by Karl Mannheim (1893–1947), who emphasized that an ideology was a product of the social context it was created in, and Antonio Gramsci (1891–1937), who turned attention to ideology as praxis in forming the world. In particular, Gramsci's theory of hegemony has been an inspiration to me for the present book, though it is not the main starting point.

function of Marxism-Leninism itself in the system of state social-ism, we would have to claim that this ideology was merely an exterior, a façade, for the oppression exercised by the authoritarian regime, a mask behind which a completely different game was being played (much the way bourgeois ideology masks the exploitative nature of capitalism). Any conception that assumes the existence of two separate worlds, a false world of ideology and a real world hidden behind a curtain of language, cannot be defended if one is aware of the formative influence that language has on thinking and the real form of the world. The combination of ideology, the genuine wishes and desires of people, and the nature of governance has in any case far more aspects than could reasonably be reduced to a true–false dichotomy.[118]

The points emphasized by Michael Freeden (b.1944), a British professor of politics who specializes in ideologies, are essential to ideology as employed here, especially his emphasis on the complex, open, and dynamic nature of ideologies, which are not identical with doctrines or political concepts like socialism, communism, and liberalism, no matter how much they are necessarily defined in relation to political concepts. Ideologies are rather sites of meanings, developing around core values. Values, like freedom and progress, can, however, come into conflict with each other. This opens up the field to various conceptions and therefore also to a plurality of, say, liberalisms or Marxisms, as part of the originally unified ideology. The emphasis on the reciprocal relationship between ideology as a concept and a system and, on the other hand, its reception and adoption are also essential for the social historian.[119]

---

118   See Michel Foucault, *Les mots et les choses: Une archéologie des sciences humaines*, Paris: Gallimard, 1966. Published in English as *The Order of Things: An Archaeology of the Human Sciences*, New York: Pantheon, 1970.
119   Michael Freeden, 'Ideology and Political Theory', *Journal of Political Ideologies* 11(1), February 2006, pp. 3–22.

Definitely, after the Communist takeover in early 1948, Marxism represented in Czechoslovakia the most accessible way to formulate an approach to the world, to propose comprehensive solutions or prognoses.[120] Not only Communists adopted the language of Marx's key writings and used it to formulate their owns demands and ask certain questions publicly. But this 'instrument' also shaped their thinking, even though rival ideologies in the milieux of the central European Communist dictatorships were continuously casting doubt on its universal validity. With the arrival of the scientific and technological revolution, earlier discourses about the scientific and expert management of society and about the fundamental role of technological progress for its future form were transformed into a complex approach to the world, which is reflected in a number of exemplary writings. In this context, it is fair to talk about an 'ideology of technocratism', though real technocracy, like real communism, in state socialism and capitalist liberal democracies remained a mere utopian dream. The 1960s in Czechoslovakia saw not only a number of alternative visions of socialism and communism, but also a return of discourses rooted in liberal ideology, which, though forced out of the public space after the violent suppression of the reform movement in 1968, continued to be an abstract aim for a number of intellectuals opposed to the Communist regime. This then created the basic prerequisites for the disintegration of state socialism and the transformation in the first years after the Velvet Revolution of late 1989.[121] Other ideological currents formulated or reformulated during the 1960s, mainly in western Europe and the United States – for example, environmentalism –, also penetrated

120 This element was particularly evident in the last decades of the Soviet model of socialist dictatorship. See Alexei Yurchak, 'Hegemony of Form: Stalin's Uncanny Paradigm Shift', in idem, *Everything Was Forever, Until It Was No More*, Princeton (NJ): Princeton University Press, 2006, pp. 36–76.
121 See Adéla Gjuričová, Michal Kopeček, Petr Roubal, Jiří Suk, and Tomáš Zahradníček, *Rozděleni minulostí: Vytváření politických identit v České republice po roce 1989*, Prague: Knihovna Václava Havla, 2011.

Czechoslovakia, where, though marginal, they nevertheless formed an important breeding ground for the formulation of criticism of the existing system and its individual manifestations.

One difficulty is that the term 'ideology', as we have seen, should not only denote the closed system of ideas which serves the power-holders who are trying to gain legitimacy, but should also express a certain centre of gravity of influential writings and statements, which first enable it to be grasped as an ideology. The boundaries are thus hard to discern, particularly in a situation where various more or less established ways of thinking are in competition with each other, and overlap, as was the case for most of the period of state socialism in Czechoslovakia. Particularly in connection with an articulated plurality of opinions, as was gradually asserted in Czechoslovakia (including the mass media and the public space in general[122]) especially in the 1960s, it therefore appears more accurate to talk about individual discourses (such as humanist or productivist), that is, sets of utterances or speech acts, by means of which people construct their own conception of reality and individual social groups are established in opposition to other groups, classes, cultures, or events.[123]

The emphasis on negotiation, plurality of discourses, or efforts to achieve consensus (not always imposed or artificial) may be perceived as exaggerated or even dubious in connection with the key role of the large propaganda apparatus in all the socialist dictatorships. Communist propaganda (a term that the Party, particularly in the 1950s, openly declared to be a legitimate part of the building of socialism) really does manifest a number of structural differences

---

122 For the question of the existence of the public space in the conditions of an authoritarian system of government, see below in this chapter.
123 The concept of 'discourse', in the 1970s and 1980s, mainly thanks to the works of Michel Foucault, became a fundamental tool of analysis in the social sciences, enabling one to de-essentialize traditional social and cultural categories and to identify language as the form of behaviour, that is, praxis, which constructs and forms reality.

from the means of promoting ideologically tinged interpretations or dominant state-forming narratives in liberally democratic states. Though the institution of the censor and the social regulation of the mass media and belles-lettres existed on both sides of the Iron Curtain, the liberal capitalist model manifested a striking decentralization of the mass media and the concomitant pluralism. This deprived the state-controlled or paid media 'informing' the population of the monopolistic position it had largely maintained (with certain deviations) in the state-socialist countries. Even there, however, propaganda (information censored or otherwise regulated by the State) and agitation are not synonymous. As Stephen Kotkin has aptly put it, 'To be effective, propaganda must offer a story that people are prepared at some level to accept; one that retains the capacity to capture their imagination, and one that they can learn to express in their own words.'[124] I therefore see propaganda, whose elements also appear considerably in articles and documents concerning changes to Most for the greater part of the period we are looking at, to be an interpretation of reality, which has been produced by the rulers and disseminated with their support, and has the potential to be accepted as credible by a substantial part of the population, and also confirms the legitimacy of the existing power structure. Propaganda, at least if it serves its purpose, thus stems not only from the intentions or perspectives of the powerful but also from the continuously verified credibility or acceptability of the initial values and hierarchies to which it refers. That is why discourse reproduced in propaganda can provide us with a good idea of the values and the aims or perspectives which a considerable part of society related to and how it did so.

---

124 Stephen Kotkin, *Magnetic Mountain: Stalinism as a Civilization*, Berkeley, CA, and London: University of California Press, 1995, p. 358.

The Public Space and the Limits of Criticism

It is tricky to talk about criticism or even public debate taking place under an authoritarian regime that punished its opponents. One is absolutely justified in wondering what we can possibly know about what 'ordinary people', journalists, or experts, actually thought in times of fear and censorship. Yet not only the methodological starting points and instruments for researching a society and its thinking in a socialist dictatorship, but also the close reading of what was published in the mass media and other period sources does indeed enable one to research state socialism by examining the phenomenon of social criticism and, albeit in a limited sense, the public space. At the same time, and this is also fundamental to researching the debates about the Most experiment and its impact, from this perspective this researched section of Czechoslovak history splits into two very different periods – one beginning in about 1956 and ending in mid-1969, the other being the normalization period, which followed it.

Research on the period newspapers and magazines reveals that, despite the ubiquitous traces of the centrally controlled flow of information and news throughout the forty years of the Czechoslovak socialist dictatorship, a great many discussions were indeed taking place, at least below the surface. The criticism did not concern just purely 'operational' matters, though it usually did not go beyond the most basic values of the state-socialist regime in the Soviet sphere of influence. Nevertheless, for the brief period of 1968–69, socialism developing into Communism, the leading role of the Communist Party, and alliance with the Soviet Union continued to be factored out. A number of other key questions, ranging from the form of the planned economy (or a healthy measure of the market principle) to environmental criticism of productivism to questions of artistic freedom or urban planning and architecture, became the subject of lively debate, particularly in the 1960s. That is partly true also of the preceding period, especially after Khrushchev's 'secret speech' at the

20th Congress of the Communist Party of the Soviet Union in 1956, though the language of critical journalists and others in the public debate about the character of the State, society, and the arts was of course more coded in these years. In the normalization period, regulation of the mass media, particularly the daily press, increased and intellectual periodicals that before 1969 had provided the most space to critics and to the articulation of alternative visions of social-ist society and the State were closed down. Criticism, including environmental, sociological, and economic, did not vanish entirely, but it was limited to expert circles and their periodicals, which had a lim-ited reach, or it was sometimes published in samizdat, which had an even shorter reach. From the perspective of society at that time, this was a considerable intervention and in practice most people were cut off from independent critical reflections on central social and economic questions. The specialist periodicals and some popu-lar-science periodicals, like the science monthly *Vesmír* (Universe), are still important to the historian as evidence of 1960s social criti-cism and its specific forms. The space for dialogue began to expand gradually in the mid-1980s and some aspects of social criticism thus also penetrated the mainstream media, like the weekly *Mladý svět* (Young world). But that is the beginning of another story.

The fate of old Most was decided in the early 1960s. The first phase of its demolition was from 1966 to 1969. Concerning the relevance and possibilities of voicing criticism, I am interested here therefore primarily in the 1960s. Throughout the period from 1960 to 1968/69, but actually also in the period beginning in 1956, the phenomenon called, for lack of a better name, the public space or public debate was gradually spreading. In other words, I am using a term that has traditionally been linked with the liberal democratic system,[125] and

125 The terms 'the public' and, linked to it, 'the public sphere', discussion, or debate are connected to the analysis of the development of bourgeois society and liberal democracy, which was determined by this development. They stem from the classic liberal division of life into the private sphere and the public sphere (though the roots of this dichotomy are in classical

whose use in the analysis of one particular period of state socialism is unconventional.

What I then call, with some poetic licence, the public sphere or the public space was in state-socialist Czechoslovakia established in a milieu, especially before 1966, which was still considerably regulated, with numerous interventions by the censor and ubiquitous fear or at least uncertainty about where the limits of criticism were. Considering the gradual breaking through of barriers and the pushing out of the boundaries, one can, however, already from 1956 onwards, observe a growing number (though with certain downswings and setbacks) of critical voices, alternative proposals, lively debates and fields, which the participants in these debates were interested in and publicly sparred over. In the second half of the 1960s public discussion about fundamental social topics was shifted to the mainstream mass media and to the streets and squares. The time of public protests and demonstrations not staged by those in power had come.

The hybrid phenomenon of the expanding space of public debate in an illiberal milieu has several remarkable aspects. Most of them are linked with the quick development from the highly regulated stage-managed public and the thoroughly controlled media environment of the Stalinist period to the pluralism of the second half of the 1960s. The breaking through of barriers, together with the great expectations accompanying that, opened up a special space of focused attention, matter-of-factness, and intellectual persistence. Paradoxically, the still existing regulation also contributed to concentration on content and to the possibility, by following the same

antiquity). See Hannah Arendt, *Vita activa oder vom tätigen Leben*, Stuttgart: Kohlhammer, 1960, first published in English as *The Human Condition*, [Chicago]: University of Chicago Press, 1958. The classic theory of the public sphere as the fruit of the establishment of bourgeois society in the eighteenth century comes from the German philosopher and sociologist Jürgen Habermas, in his *Strukturwandel der Öffentlichkeit: Untersuchungen zu einer Kategorie der bürgerlichen Gesellschaft*, Neuwied Berlin: Luchterhand, 1962.

debates, of living intellectually in a shared world, which was in fact experienced by thousands or, in a certain respect, even hundreds of thousands of people. The number of critical periodicals was limited and the range of their boldness and openness towards what had not yet been tried was clear. Intellectually demanding periodicals like the weekly *Literární noviny* (Literature news), which already in 1956 was providing space for alternative voices and regularly allowing previously uncrossable limits to be crossed, thus had thousands of readers in the 1960s.[126]

Another of these aspects is linked not with censorship or regulation in the still authoritarian system, but, by contrast, with the absence of a phenomenon that in a liberal capitalist society squeezes out public debate and threatens its rationality. As critical reflections of the public sphere in the bourgeois society of a capitalist liberal democracy have demonstrated, the space of rational discussion may be connected with this type of organization of society, but it is also continuously threatened and driven back by the development of capitalist relations.[127] Theodor W. Adorno and Max Horkheimer wrote in the 1940s about the capitalist culture industry, about the spirit fixed on 'cultural goods', which are 'distributed for consumer purposes' and, consequently, must perish, and about the 'clearance sale of culture'.[128] This factor was not present in Czechoslovakia in its

---

126 The weekly *Kultúrny život* (Cultural life), the monthly *Plamen* (Flame), and mainly the monthly *Literární noviny* (Literature news) were published by the Writers Union in print runs of 120,000 copies and, in the mid-1960s, were read by about half a million people (the size of the print run and the estimated number of readers was occasionally announced, for example, in *Literární noviny*).

127 In Habermas, the 'dialectics of the public sphere'. See the chapter 'Dialektik der Öffentlichkeit' in *Strukturwandel der Öffentlichkeit*.

128 Theodor W. Adorno and Max Horkheimer, *Dialektika osvícenství: Filosofické fragmenty*, trans. Michael Hauser and Milan Váňa, Prague: Oikoymenh, 2009, p. 14, from the German original, (1944) *Dialektik der Aufklärung: Philosophische Fragmente*, rev. edn, Amsterdam: Querido, 1947. Published in English as *Dialectic of Enlightenment*, ed. Gunzelin Schmid Noerr, trans. Edmund Jephcott, Stanford: Stanford University Press, 2002. Available online at https://archive.org/details/pdfy-TJ7HxrAly-MtUP4B Accessed 2 November 2018.

full destructive force in the 1960s, though here too we may observe a particular form of consumer society.[129]

All these aspects – ranging from the phenomenon of the still-existing limitations and risks, which motivated the recipient to read carefully between the lines and to interpret small changes in formulations which were different from previous practice, to freedom from commercial pressures – contributed to the special strength and power of the word, which, though generally characteristic of authoritarian systems that limit freedom of speech, were penetrating more and more areas of the public debate in the period when restrictions were being lifted and barriers were being broken down.

Faces of Modernity

The Communists, like the post-Communist historians writing so far (though with different assessments), always emphasized the essential difference between their project and that of liberal capitalism. As the time that separates us from the immediate experience of the Communist dictatorship grows, its particular features recede into the background and the features that are typical of the modernizing world increasingly stand out. This trend is bound to continue. To understand the world we live in, comprehending the layers and mechanisms that are shared by both systems and therefore shape our times too will therefore become increasingly important.

Almost all the essential features of the Most experiment, from the emphasis on production and economic growth to the increasing power of the mining and power companies to the symbiosis between

---

[129] On socialist consumption, see Mark Landsman, *Dictatorship and Demand: The Politics of Consumerism in East Germany*, Cambridge, Mass.: Harvard University Press, 2005.
For consumption and the consumer society in Czechoslovakia in the late 1950s and early 1960s, see Jiří Knapík et al., *Průvodce kulturním děním a životním stylem v českých zemích 1948–1967*, 2 vols, Prague: Academia, 2011, and, especially, Martin Franc and Jiří Knapík, *Volný čas v českých zemích 1957–1967*, Prague: Academia, 2013.

destruction and reclamation, occurred in the countries both to the west and to the east of the Iron Curtain. The overall consensus on values, giving priority to the standard of living and economic productivity that determines it, is what linked West and East from at least the second half of the 1950s onwards. The events considered in this book, together with my theoretical starting points, thus contribute to such a reading of the Czechoslovak reality of the late 1950s, the 1960s, and the 1970s, which illuminate that reality from the perspective of the global changes in the practice and self-understanding of the modern age. Despite some of the almost feudal practices of Soviet Stalinism, the socialist dictatorship was an attempt at modernity. It was, moreover, an attempt that was not doomed from the start and so, like any historical period, it cannot reasonably be seen only through the prism of its end.

One of the particular features of the socialist dictatorships was the long emphasis (again seen by the Communists completely differently from how it was seen by post-Communist historians and political scientists) on the state-socialist approach to the environment. On the one hand, the emphasis was on the comprehensive welfare provided by the strong socialist State, unlike the exploitation practised under capitalism by the private owners of big businesses seeking to maximize their profits and, on the other, by the disastrous impact of the Communist regimes' one-sided orientation to heavy industry and production or their inability to react to the worsening living conditions. Particularly on the threshold of the 1990s, with the central role played by environmental problems and environmental criticism in the delegitimation of the socialist dictatorships, the strong conviction prevailed, amongst non-specialists and specialists alike, that the capitalist system had demonstrated its superiority in part thanks to its having efficiently solved environmental problems. This interpretation then led some observers to assume that in the future the least regulated capitalism would lead to minimizing both energy waste and therefore environmental damage.[130] But the future did not prove these visions right. With the benefit of hindsight, it is clear that we can see more similarities than differences between these two political and economic systems when it comes to devastation of the landscape brought about by industrial modernity.

For example, when comparing East and West Germany (which is possible because of their similar initial conditions and degree of modernization), contemporary historians, in contrast to historians right after the 1989 Changes,[131] tend to point to phase shifts rather than to fundamental differences. The statistical data demonstrate that from 1950 to 1970 the natural environment of the Federal Republic of Germany (including sulphur oxides and nitrogen oxides in the air, water pollution, and incidence of lung cancer) was becoming strikingly worse than in the German Democratic Republic. In East Germany in the 1960s, the problem had not yet assumed the dimensions that it had in West Germany, which was developing quicker economically. But in the 1970s and 1980s, the East German political leadership was unable to implement programmes to combat the worsening air pollution or the environmental degradation caused by the extraction of raw materials, not even to the extent that such programmes had already been successfully implemented in West Germany at that time. The greatest problem of East Germany remained, as it did in the neighbouring socialist countries, Poland and Czechoslovakia, the opencast mining of lignite and, related

130 See 'East Germany: Cauldron of Poison', *World Press Review,* March 1990, pp. 66–67 (originally published as the cover story, 'Giftküche DDR: Das Land der Tausend Vulkane', *Der Spiegel,* 8 January 1990); available online at http://www.spiegel.de/spiegel/print/d-13497006. html; Stanley J. Kabala, 'The Environmental Morass in Eastern Europe', *Current History* 90 (1991), pp. 384–89; K. Mazurski, 'Communism and the Environment', *Geotimes,* April 1993, p. 5; Friedhelm Naujoks, *Ökologische Erneuerung der ehemaligen DDR: Begrenzungsfaktor oder Impulsgeber für eine gesamtdeutsche Entwicklung?,* Bonn: Dietz, 1991; Daniel Charles, 'East German Environment Comes into the Light', *Science,* 19 January 1990, pp. 274–76; Lois R. Ember, 'Pollution Chokes Eastbloc Nations', *Chemical and Engineering News,* 16 April 1990, pp. 7–16.
131 'East Germany: Cauldron of Poison'.

to it, the coal-generated production of electric power. Despite this lag, which manifested itself fully in the 1980s, East Germany was producing increasingly less nitrogen oxides per capita and in the mid-1980s the average life expectancy was exactly the same in East and in West Germany – 74.5 years.[132]

I will not spend time trying to answer the rhetorical question whether state socialism is a way of carrying out the modernity project. Also in connection with the example we have just seen about the attitude to the natural environment, one of course asks whether considerable time lags are visible in the individual turnarounds and phases of modern civilization, both in the dominant discourses and in political practice. Modernity is linked to a great number of apparent contradictions. Its forms include an emphasis on technology and on human beings, on liberation and on disciplinary practices, on the key role of expertise and on radical democracy. All utopias and actual forms of modernity somehow combine (always with varying emphases) these opposing aspects of the ability to reflect on some of its problems and pitfalls while being astonishingly blind to other risks. Here it is useful to consider critically not only all the similarities, but also the differences between the liberal capitalist version of modernity and the state socialist version.

The first half of the twentieth century, especially in Europe, was marked by the protracted crisis of modernity, which may reasonably be described as a European civil war. At that same time, however, important prerequisites were being prepared (including equal and universal suffrage, mass parties, and comprehensive social security), which after the Second World War enabled the establishment of what Peter Wagner has fittingly called 'organized modernity', that is, a social system in which the individual freedom of the actors, at

---

132 Raymond Dominick, 'Capitalism, Communism, and Environmental Protection: Lessons from the German Experience', *Environmental History* 3 (July 1998) 3, pp. 311–32. See also the chapter 'Silent Spring' in the 'Criticism' section.

least in the liberal democratic countries, was woven into the fabric of organized practices, imparting considerable stability to the system.[133] Immediately after the war, the countries to the east of the Iron Curtain set out on a different path. Despite the changing ideological framework, state-organized violence, the logic of purges, and the mobilization of the masses against external and internal enemies, which had all characterized the previous period of crisis, persisted here. Theorists who do not link modernity solely with the liberal project, but also take into consideration its alternative forms, point to many shared features of the 'common boom of European capitalism and socialism'[134] during the 1950s and 1960s. Many of the features that Wagner links to organized modernity – a period we may usefully see as the Industrial Age at its peak – did indeed appear and develop in the industrialized countries on both sides of the Iron Curtain (though perhaps with a lag of several years in the east). In addition to the precipitous economic growth (the gross domestic products of a number of European countries, ranging from the Federal Republic of Germany to Bulgaria, were in 1965 more than twice what they were in 1950), it was also a matter of establishing consumer societies (with a certain time lag in the socialist countries, not until the post-Stalinist period), of the transformation of governance (the arrival of the scientific and technological revolution), of modern urban planning, and of making higher education accessible to the masses.

The years in which influential economists and politicians decided on the demolition of old Most and the building of the new town fall precisely into the period of organized modernity. This period is characterized by faith in comprehensive systems of management, in economic and urban planning, and by giving preference to the interests

133 Peter Wagner, *A Sociology of Modernity: Liberty and Discipline*, London and New York: Routledge, 1994, pp. 73–120.
134 Göran Therborn, *European Modernity and Beyond: The Trajectories of European Societies and Beyond, 1945–2000*, London, Thousand Oaks, and New Delhi: Sage, 1995, pp. 133–39.

of the whole, especially economic interests, over particularist interests or 'soft factors'. The carrying out of the project, however, fell mostly into the stormy period of the second half of the 1960s and the oil crises of the 1970s, which were characterized, at least in western Europe and some liberal democratic countries elsewhere, by the crisis of organized modernity, the growing criticism of the original modernist consensus, and the gradual breakdown of that consensus. Non-economic factors, including the natural environment and preservation of cultural heritage, and the lack of consideration for the particularist interests of various social groups, including individual generations, sexual minorities, and people of different skin colour from that of the majority. In the 1980s, the distinguished German sociologist Ulrich Beck (1944–2015) proposed the term 'reflexive modernity' for a qualitatively different form of modernity, one which had undergone the criticism and crises of the 1960s and 1970s and had also been affected by the transformation of the labour market which led to a loss of certainty.[135]

Beck's analysis importantly contributes to charting the changes in politics, society, and thinking in the last third of the twentieth century. It is also a fundamental starting point for this book. The question of the extent to which the 'second crisis of modernity'[136] and its new, 'reflexive' character were manifested in the nature of late socialism and what influence this global transformation had on its ultimate legitimacy crisis, certainly merits greater attention than historians have so far paid it. It is worth noting at this point that the changes in the discourse about the destruction of the old Most and the building of the new one in the 1970s and 1980s underscore the usefulness of Beck's and Giddens's analyses also when applied to the

---

135 Ulrich Beck, *Risikogesellschaft: Auf dem Weg in eine andere Moderne*, Frankfurt am Main: Suhrkamp, 1986. The term 'reflexive modernity' or 'reflexive modernization' is also used by Giddens, in Ulrich Beck, Anthony Giddens, and Scott Lash, *Reflexive Modernization: Politics, Tradition and Aesthetics in the Modern Social Order*, Stanford, Calif.: Stanford University Press, 1994.
136 Wagner, *A Sociology of Modernity*, pp. 123–71.

socialist dictatorships. Perhaps better than from anywhere else we can see from Hněvín Hill how the elites and society of Czechoslovakia were wrestling with the crisis of organized modernity, whose starting points and forms had given state socialism a considerable portion of its legitimacy in the course of a few decades. The changes in the strategies by which the whole experiment was justified to the public, and also its criticism (openly permitted or illicitly in samizdat) can at least begin to explain the causes of the breakdown not only of the consensus in normalization Czechoslovakia but also of state-socialist domination in eastern Europe in general.

Two Stories about Technology, Power, and Freedom

To the extent which man leaves the products of his past labours to operate as natural forces, with a consequent withdrawal of human labour power from the immediate production process, there enters into production a far more powerful force of human society, *science as a productive force* in its own right [...] The more man gives up the jobs that he can leave to be done by his handiwork, the wider the prospects opening up before him – prospects that would have been inaccessible without the backing of his own achievement.

(Radovan Richta et al., 1966 [137])

We live in a society where people have in many respects become alienated from the human way of life (which applies also to ourselves) and where many structures and processes have alienated people, that is, have been

---

137 Radovan Richta et al., *Civilizace na rozcestí: Společenské a lidské souvislosti vědeckotechnické revoluce*, Prague: Svoboda, 1966, pp. 26–28. Published in English as *Civilization at the Crossroads: Social and Human Implications of the Scientific and Technological Revolution*, trans. Mariana Šlingová, Prague: International Arts and Science Press, 1967, p. 27. See also the work of Vítězslav Sommer, for example, 'Scientists of the World, Unite!: Radovan Richta's Theory of Scientific and Technological Revolution', in Elena Aronova and Simone Turchetti (eds), *Science Studies during the Cold War and Beyond*, Basingstoke: Palgrave Macmillan, 2016.

emancipated, have become dislocated from their original purpose, which was to serve, and have been repeatedly dragging people into situations that they cope with only with great difficulty and great sacrifice – or no longer cope with.

(Ladislav Hejdánek, 1978[138])

Let us fast-forward directly to the events we are concerned with: the surface mining of coal over a vast area for the generation of heat and electrical energy, to which a whole historic town fell victim, and a modern urban area that had to be built because of that mining; the systematic moving of all the inhabitants and the moving of selected historic monuments; machines eliminating old Most; machines taking away the overburden; machines extracting raw material; machines, in a few steps, transforming raw material into electrical energy; machines reclaiming the devastated landscape. What was it all for? It was so that the energy obtained could drive other machines in factories or in households. And perhaps also so that people could lead better lives.

The Most project is the convex mirror of a key aspect of modern civilization, that is, technology, which became an instrument of progress in the hands of human beings but also an independent power. The most general, and perhaps most essential, level of inquiry about the events that are the focus of this book thus concerns the interpretation of the influence that technology has had on individual human beings and society. It is a question no less important than whether the modern age, by means of science and technology, has contributed to the liberation or to the enslavement of humankind. I am under no illusion that this book, or any other, offers a definitive clear-cut answer. It is even likely that this particular story, despite

138 Ladislav Hejdánek, *Filosofie a politika: Patnáct let nepolitické politiky*, Prague, 1978. This is a samizdat collection of articles written from 1963 to 1978. Quoted in Václav Tollar, 'Emancipáty a problém lidských práv', in Martin Šimsa (ed.), *Nepředmětné výzvy české filosofie: K myšlení Ladislava Hejdánka*, Ústí nad Labem: Univerzita J. E. Purkyně, 2013, pp. 333–57, here, p. 348.

the attempt to put it into the wider context, will not provide a satisfactory answer to this comprehensive inquiry. But it has seemed important to me to write it with this question in mind – and perhaps it will be more meaningful if read like this too.

Amongst the people who in the twentieth century have thought deeply about science and technology, there is general agreement on only one point – namely, the technicization of the world, determined by scientific development (whereby technology takes over human jobs), has not only led to increased efficiency and production, but has also meant an epoch-making change in the very nature of civilization and society. Individual intellectual views diverge, however, about where this transformation is leading, how to assess it, and how to react to it. Debates about the importance of technology and its formative influence on the operation of states, societies, and everyday life, gradually, especially in the first three decades after the Second World War, made their way into debates in the newspapers, amongst politicians, and the general public. To us, those debates now appear less like consistent standpoints than internally contradictory attitudes. From the start, the Enlightenment transformation of the world drew strength from its faith in the liberating power of knowledge-based rationality. That rationality was supposed to help not only to remove the injustice of feudal privileges and obstacles, but also to suppress physical violence both in interpersonal relations and in the relations of the State towards its population and to develop the creative potential of humankind.[139] The events of the twentieth century, particularly the experience of the two world wars and the Great Depression, complicated the formerly unambiguous nature of the Enlightenment vision,[140] but the post-war faith in rationality, science, and now also technology as instruments for building a better world, enabling all people to lead lives with dignity, was

---

139 See Bedřich Loewenstein, *Projekt moderny*, Prague: Oikoymenh, 1995.
140 For more on this, see the previous chapter, 'Faces of Modernity'.

based precisely on those intellectual traditions. In the post-Stalinist period, the rapid economic growth both to the west and to the east of the Iron Curtain, the inner conciliation characteristic of the majority of societies in the most developed countries, and the gradual convergence of the two dominant ideological and economic systems seemed to be proving right the emancipatory interpretations of modernity. The time of the scientific and technological revolution had come.[141]

In reaction both to the destructive power of technology, which during the world wars had been turned against human beings and their achievements, and to the internal transformations of science, there were, however, together with hope, critical analyses of the direction of modern thought, science, and mainly technology, which was going from being an instrument in human hands to being an independent power. The thinkers formulating this criticism, beginning in the 1930s, were mostly based in the German philosophical tradition. What they accentuated depended on whether they were arguing in the tradition of Romantic philosophy, sceptical of the Enlightenment, or based on the Marxist interpretation of alienation, which enabled criticism of specific mechanisms of the economic and political system while maintaining confidence in the emancipatory power of the Enlightenment project of modernity.

Among the first to formulate the idea that the power over the world which the natural sciences were giving to individual human beings and to humankind as a whole, in addition to all the conveniences making life easier and enabling an increase in the standard of living, had launched a fundamental crisis of humankind was the

---

141   One of the first to present the idea of a transition from the industrial era to the era of the scientific management of society, which would contribute to economic prosperity, the development of human capabilities, and the maintenance of peace, and who is also considered to have coined the term 'scientific and technological revolution', is the pro-Communist British biologist and writer on the history of science John Desmond Bernal (1901–1971). Of key importance in this connection is his work *The Social Function of Science*, London: George Routledge & Sons, 1939. See also J. D. Bernal, *Science in History*, 4 vols, London: Watts, 1954.

Moravian-born German-educated philosopher Edmund Husserl (1859–1938) in the 1930s.[142] Husserl was inquiring into the development and changing aims of European science, whose increasingly instrumentalist form was not living up to its original claims to be universalist and was not enabling science to be what it should in fact be – namely, an attempt at 'mankind's self-clarification' and the 'self-realization of reason'. Already while Husserl was writing his key work, one of his pupils, Martin Heidegger (1889–1976), was concerned with the question of the nature of technology. Heidegger was thus following on also from another German thinker, Ernst Jünger (1895–1998), who in 1932 characterized the technology-determined mankind of his day as reified and reduced to mastery of the means.[143] Heidegger, in a number of preliminary lectures and especially in 'The Question Concerning Technology' (published in 1954),[144] explains the 'commandeering'[145] nature of technology

---

142 See the essay, first published in the Belgrade periodical *Philosophia* in 1936, Edmund Husserl, *Die Krisis der europäischen Wissenschaften und die transzendentale Phänomenologie: Eine Einleitung in die phänomenologische Philosophie*, vol. 6 of the collected works, ed. Walter Biemel, The Hague: Nijhoff, 1954. See esp. the chapters 'Die Krisis der Wissenschaften als Ausdruck der radikalen Lebenskrisis des europäischen Menschentums' and 'Die Krisis der europäischen Menschentums und die Philosophie'. The full text is available online at http://ophen .org/pub-108581 Accessed 2 November 2018. The work was published in English as *The Crisis of European Sciences and Transcendental Phenomenology: An Introduction to Phenomenological Philosophy*, trans. with an introduction by David Carr, Evanston, Ill.: Northwestern University Press, 1970.

143 Ernst Jünger, *Der Arbeiter: Herrschaft und Gestalt*, Hamburg: Hanseatische Verlagsanstalt, 1932. Published in English as *The Worker: Dominion and Form*, ed. Laurence Paul Hemming, trans. from the German by Bogdan Costea and Laurence Paul Hemming, Evanston, Il.: Northwestern University Press, 2017.

144 Martin Heidegger, 'Die Frage nach der Technik', in idem, *Vorträge und Aufsätze*, Pfullingen: Neske, 1954, pp. 13–44. Published in English as *The Question Concerning Technology and Other Essays*, trans. and with an introduction by William Lovitt, New York and London: Garland, 1977. Available online at https://monoskop.org/images/4/44/Heidegger_Martin_The_Question _Concerning_Technology_and_Other_Essays.pdf Accessed 2 November 2018. For an online translation of the essay 'The Question concerning Technology,' http://www.psyp.org /question_concerning_technology.pdf Accessed 2 November 2018.

145 Heidegger uses the difficult to translate term 'das Ge-stell' to designate, first, 'enframing' and, later, 'commandeering', characterizing the function of technology, for example, in the framework of 'commandeering', that is, the instrumental and manipulative seizing of nature

(*Technik*, also meaning technique and engineering) and emphasizes its predictability, speed, and mass nature, which ultimately lead to flattening, emptiness, superficiality, vulgarity, boredom, and, mainly, the destruction of the power of the word.[146] Heidegger, however, despite the destructive power of technology, considers any attempt to limit and neutralize technology to be naive – technology, he argues, must be endured, like a disease, through the greatest danger, until ultimately one reaches deliverance.

The German philosopher-sociologists Theodor W. Adorno (1903–1969) and Max Horkheimer (1895–1973) critically analysed technology from another perspective in the 1930s. Unlike Heidegger, they clearly recognized the destructive power of the Nazi movement and warned against rejecting the Enlightenment project as such. In exile in the United States, they linked their criticism of the technicization of the world with the experience of capitalism and consumer society. In their co-authored book published in 1944, they argue that technology, consumerism, and modern antisemitism are examples of the manipulative nature of the Enlightenment project resulting in the 'mysterious willingness of the technologically educated masses to fall under the spell of any despotism'. But Adorno and Horkheimer understood their work as an attempt to salvage the core of the Enlightenment project, which is the exceptional ability to critically examine oneself, before self-destruction and 'the fear of truth which petrifies enlightenment itself'.[147] In the second half of the twentieth century a number of distinguished European philosophers, from the German-born and German-educated American philosopher, sociologist, and political theorist Herbert Marcuse

---

(as opposed to experiencing its aesthetic or other qualities). For an explanation of *Ge-stell* and its translation into English, and of other terms related to this essay, see Michael Inwood, *A Heidegger Dictionary*, Oxford: Blackwell, 199, pp. 210–12.

146 For more on this, see Heidegger, Martin: *The Question Concerning Technology and Other Essays*, trans. and intro. William Lovitt, New York and London: Garland 1977.

147 Adorno and Horkheimer, *Dialectic of Enlightenment*, p. xvi.

(1898–1979) to the German-born and German-educated American philosopher Hans Jonas (1903–1993), followed on from these various ideas, finding agreement in their criticism of the influence of technology on life and thinking. By the 1960s, this way of thinking was already reflected also in a wider social movement and eventually in politics (particularly green politics), which thus combines conservative and left-wing criticism of a modernity that lacks humility towards the natural order and manipulates the world with little regard for the damage this causes to the world that human beings inhabit and should be able to inhabit in the future.

Among Czechs, one thinks of Jan Patočka (1907–1977), a pupil of Husserl's and Heidegger's, who wrote about technoscience (*vědotechnika*), linking its destructive potential mainly with modern war. This is echoed in the works of other Czechs, for example, Václav Havel's (1936–2011) 'automatism' (*samopohyb*). The philosopher Ladislav Hejdánek (b.1927) wrote a remarkable analysis of the risks of modernity precisely in the form of technology; already in his articles from the 1940s and then particularly in his doctoral thesis of 1952,[148] he developed the concept of 'emancipated elements' (*emancipáty*) – originally human creations, which, however, in consequence of the inertia of their operation, gradually begin to function independently of their creators.

Though they can manifest themselves in the world only through the actions of people, these emancipated elements change autonomously and become independent powers to which people are drawn and then are in thrall to. For Hejdánek, the technician or engineer is a typical example of such a person alienated from power and manipulated by it.[149] Hejdánek argues, unlike Heidegger, that none of us can afford to shirk the task of getting technology back under

---

148 Ladislav Hejdánek, 'Pojetí pravdy a některé jeho ontologické předpoklady', PhDr dissertation, Prague, 1952. Available online: https://www.hejdanek.eu/digiarchiv.php?id_detail=265 Accessed 25 October 2018.
149 See Tollar, 'Emancipáty a problém lidských práv', pp. 333–57.

control, first by looking at its consequences and then by changing the way of life, which will henceforth no longer be under the sway of its dictates. In Czechoslovakia, Hejdánek's thinking influenced intellectuals in the 1960s and then in debates amongst dissidents in the 1970s and 1980s, and probably also had some influence, mediated by Havel and others, on environmental criticism concerning, among other things, the Most experiment.

Theorists of the scientific and technological revolution who saw technological development primarily as an opportunity to liberate human beings from factors that had so far limited them (especially the necessity of mindless repetitive work that stifles creativity and the development of humankind in general), naturally knew some of these critiques and worked with them. Mainly, they took issue with them about the great poverty, lack of freedom, and inability to break free from one's fate, which had been characteristic of most people's lives in the past. Under the state-socialist regime, moreover, some of the proponents of the liberating power of modern technology interpreted its risks as part of the alienation produced by capitalist exploitation and the orientation to individual profit – in other words, risks that socialism could successfully confront.[150]

The fundamentally different explanations of the meaning and power of technology have identified important contexts of the modern age. When considering the events discussed in this book, it is essential to bear in mind that both approaches, with many variations, existed when the events were taking place in the 1960s and 1970s – and that the events around Most could also be, and indeed were, understood by contemporaries both ways. As a historian, I seek to use real examples to show the connection between these intellectual concepts and specific transformations of society and the world inhabited by people, which I do mostly in the sections 'Numbers'

---

150 Radovan Richta, *Člověk a technika v revoluci našich dnů*, Prague: Čs. společ. PVZ, 1963, p. 61.

and 'Utopia' (where I point to the forms of thinking that set the Most experiment into the narrative of progress and the emancipation of humankind) and, on the other hand, the section 'Criticism' (the growth of the discourse pointing out the destructive and enslaving potential of industrial modernity, including the combination of mining and the destruction of the landscape). Whereas in the first case, the placing of the Most story into the narrative of emancipation, it is not merely a matter of agitation or propaganda, in the second case, criticism of the economist's or technocrat's approach to the world, it is not a matter of marginal or only supplementary intellectual reflections. In both cases we encounter a substantial part of the *Sinnwelt* of the times, which fundamentally influences the possibility of making sense of the whole Most experiment and thereby of its justification.

The demolition of old Most and the building of new Most may reasonably be seen as two chapters of two contrary stories, though both are based on the same facts. The power and persuasiveness of these stories changed over time. These changes influenced not only the perceived degree of legitimacy of state socialism, but also the specific forms of domination that the whole experiment initiated and carried out – and ultimately also the legitimacy of the technocratic form of modernity, which in Czechoslovakia and other countries of the Soviet bloc came to an end in late 1989.

Alienation

And what about the ones down here, at the foot of Hněvín Hill, that smoke-stained eye-witness to miners' demonstrations, long ranks in front of the employment office, where they hand out luncheon vouchers for unemployed dads! You're getting reading for a funeral. You're going off to meet the times that suit your dirty face so well. Well, then, go. And never come back! You'll end up like Ervěnice. You can expect a fate like the one that the old quarter of Souš met, not far from you. Whole streets of houses, which the bulldozers turned into rubble. Signboards that say 'Sinkholes! No entry!' And there is silence where children from mining families once ran barefoot. It is said that one should not speak ill of the dead. But you, grey old town, dirty and blind to human pain and desire, you have always been here, from the Přemyslids to Forty-five, ever a foreigner, an intruder, and yet master. There's little left of the House of Hrabiš, but lots of the king [Přemysl the Ploughman] who was ashamed of the origin of his forebears from Stadice [37 km northeast of Most], there at the outer limit of the coalfield. That's why they won't be playing a funeral march for you.

(Jiří Brabenec, Krásy domova, January 1964)

The Communist approach to society, like the expulsion of most of the German population from the Bohemian Lands, was a manifestation of the intentional and violent breaking of continuity. Here in the borderlands, this double rejection of bygone forms of society came together in a particular, concentrated way after the establishment of the socialist dictatorship. But does this mutually strengthening alienation of the past from what was then the present satisfactorily explain the Most experiment? In what respects is such an interpretation truly satisfactory and in what respects can one reasonably have doubts about it?

SUDETENLAND

In the demolition of Zvíkovské Račice [a little village in the Vltava River valley, near Zvíkov Castle, south Bohemia], which had to give way to the Orlík Dam, its inhabitants resisted moving into new family homes that were far better than their previous dwellings. If Chrudim or another town in the interior had been earmarked for demolition, the inhabitants would have defended themselves tooth and nail, even in the knowledge that their actions were futile. Something like that has not even occurred to the inhabitants of old Most, who in fact await this fate in the coming decade. Indeed, each of them is now looking forward to having a flat with large windows and central heating. If they have any fear at all, then it is only the fear that the public services in the new Most might not increase in proportion to the population.

(František Šmahel, 1963[151])

As the then director of the museum in nearby Litvínov, the now highly respected historian František Šmahel (b.1934), was, already in the early 1960s, expressing surprise at why the plan for the demolition of old Most, which was being pushed for, first by the SHD mining company and then by the ministries of the Czechoslovak Government and the Central Committee of the Czechoslovak Communist Party, did not meet with any appreciable resistance from the local population. The main reason, according to him, was, in combination with related influences, that after the Second World War newcomers had completely taken the place of the original population:

In the great population shift after 1945, the age-old relationships that had been formed by human beings during their many years of living in one place were torn asunder [...] It is reasonable to assume that most

151 František Šmahel, 'Karty na stůl', *Kulturní kalendář Mostecka,* June 1963, pp. 4–6.

of the local population still has no relationship with their town, the bond formed from a sense of being part of the architectural landmarks is weak, and ultimately almost no one has any idea about the historic value of these landmarks or their value as monuments.[152]

Šmahel's article was one of the first critical analyses of the problem, drawing attention to the approaching fate of old Most and its historically valuable buildings condemned to annihilation. At the same time, it identifies an idea, developed in greater depth by some Czechoslovak dissidents, like Ján Mlynárik, Petr Příhoda, and Petr Pithart,[153] and mainly Czech and foreign scholars abroad during the last twenty-five years – namely, the breaking of the bonds between human beings and the land, which took place in about a third of the Bohemian Lands, when, after the Second World War, the original population was dramatically substituted for with completely new inhabitants. This idea was later called, among other things, the 'Sudeten sense of uprootedness' (*sudetské bezdomoví*).[154]

After the Second World War, the regions until then known as the Sudetenland became a laboratory on several levels at once. The revolutionary transformation of the social and economic structures and the forms of the environment, which the dominant current of Czechoslovak politics led by the Communist Party had been striving for after the war in regions adversely affected by the mass expulsion of almost all the original population and by the precipitous settlement of new inhabitants, could no longer be slowed down or tamed by traditional institutions like the Church, various clubs, or the Sokol physical-training organization, since they were now far weaker than before the war or had completely vanished. The bourgeois

152   Ibid.
153   See Bohumil Černý, Jan Křen, Václav Kural, and Milan Otáhal (eds), *Češi, Němci, odsun*, Prague: Academia, 1990.
154   See Jitka Ortová, 'Sudetské bezdomoví', in Matěj Spurný (ed.), *Proměny sudetské krajiny*, Prague: Antikomplex, 2006, pp. 188–97.

elites were gone and so to too were the peasant families that had worked the land for centuries. Missing as well were the relationships between the land and people and amongst the people themselves, which would have acted as catalysts in the transformation of the identity of society and softened its impact on the environment. That is why in coming years the borderlands were, from the point of view of the new regime, meant to be a real jewel in the building of the new republic, an area where a great project would most likely succeed and do so quickly.

The new appearance of the Bohemian borderlands was shaped by resistance to anything of the old German world that had survived here. The result could only be the alienation of the new inhabitants from each other and from the cultural landscape, essential parts of which were material traces of the past (such as churches and roadside chapels, boundary stones, and low drystone walls) and a willingness and ability to read these traces. From the Bohemian Forest in the south of the country to the Eastern Sudetes (Jeseníky) in the north-east, there are many conspicuous signs of this lack of a human relationship with the land and the works of the past – three thousand defunct towns or villages or their parts, hundreds of church buildings, large and small, the remains of which can now be discovered in abandoned fields only by biologists or historical geographers, the overall devastation of historic buildings and the absence of care for the cultural landscape as a whole.[155] The causes are many--layered – from the impossibility that this large area could be completely repopulated to the special conditions along the border (particularly the western border) during state socialism, to more subtle questions of the identity of the society that was quickly stitched together here in the 1940s and 1950s. The unwillingness to look after someone else's heritage, even where attempts were made at least to

155 See Petr Mikšíček et al., *Zmizelé Sudety*, Domažlice: Pro občanské sdružení Antikomplex vydalo Nakladatelství Českého lesa, 2006.

take into one's own hands some of the tangible traces of the past, mingled with the impossibility of truly understanding the symbolic language and thousands of pieces of that heritage left in the landscape by those who were forced to leave after the war.[156]

The city of Most, whose elites up until the end of the Second World War had by far been mostly German, was of course fundamentally damaged by the demographic reversals of the second half of the 1940s. Only a few hundred Germans were allowed to remain in the city or, rather, were forced to remain, since most of them were badly needed miners and specialists. Original Czech inhabitants made up barely a quarter of the population of the whole Most district in the second half of the 1950s, and in the town of Most itself the proportion was probably even smaller. The newcomers, from the Bohemian interior and from Slovakia were mostly people with only primary school education, and they came to do manual labour, often just for a while. In the first fifteen years after the war, the town of Most grew quickly, from 25,000 to 45,000 inhabitants, but actually at this time not 20,000, but almost 35,000 people had gradually come to Most; in other words, in the same short period, more than 15,000 people had left Most.[157] For many people, Most became a mere stopover, a place whose future need not really have concerned them.

The changed population and the end of the German identity of Most meant not only severing the relationship between people and their environment but also a marked weakening of religious life. Consequently, lively places of religious gathering became largely superfluous buildings, which could be seen at best as historic and architectural monuments. Though this development was further accelerated by the establishment of the Communist dictatorship after the

---

156   See Miloslav Lapka, 'Sudety 60 let po odsunu: Návrat do divočiny, která člověka nepotřebuje?', in Spurný (ed.), *Proměny sudetské krajiny*, pp. 138–43.
157   For more on the changes in the population structure from 1945 to 1980, see Zdena Fröhlichová, 'Socialistické Mostecko', 3 vols, typescript, 1975, pp. 248–51. Deposited in the Library of the Most District Museum.

takeover of early 1948, the contrast between Most and the comparably large towns of the continually settled areas of south Bohemia and south and east Moravia point to the deeper causes of the almost total secularization: in north Bohemia it was connected partly with rapid industrialization, but mostly with the expulsion of the Germans and with the social structure and cultural identity of the new settlers.

✕✕✕

The new relationship of people to their environment, despite all of that, particularly in the industrial areas of the borderlands, cannot properly be described as only indifference and alienation. Particularly in areas with a strong minority of Czech-speakers and a mining or working-class tradition, like, for example, the Most district, this relationship was strikingly characterized by something that can usefully be called an industrial vision.[158] Glassheim offers a cogent description of Communist rule in the Bohemian borderlands: 'Rejecting romantic/pastoral German conceptions of Heimat, post-war Czechs sought to create materialist regional identities in north Bohemia that emphasized labor, productivity, and industrial modernity.'[159] After the Communist takeover of 1948, that was of course the result of heavy industry together with the ethos of the socialist dictatorship, but a fundamental role was also played here immediately after the war by the successes and failures accompanying the resettlement of the area and the renewal of the functions of the individual borderland regions and sectors of the economy. The vision of the new Czech borderlands was, as is convincingly demonstrated, for instance, by the catalogue to a 1946 exhibition entitled *Budujeme osvobozené kraje* (We're building the liberated lands), connected

---

[158]   For example, Zdeněk Forman, Vojtěch Jasný, and Karel Kachyňa, *Budujeme pohraničí*, Prague: Orbis, 1950. This picture book is full of photographs of mines and factories, but the rural idyll, which had formerly been the embodiment of the borderlands, rarely appears here.

[159]   Glassheim, 'Ethnic Cleansing, Communism, and Environmental Devastation', p. 68.

mainly with the idea of honest work, chiefly manual or, to be precise, factory manufacturing:

The transfer [*odsun*] of the Germans did not happen here in a vacuum. In less than a year, the borderlands are now teeming with hundreds of thousands of busy Czech hands and brains. In this area and frontier, that's no Pompeii rising up over the horizon; rather, it is one chimney after another, glowing with Czech fire, and machines, set in motion by Czech hands and Czech skill, are rumbling.[160]

It was the industrial towns of the north, unlike in the more remote mountain areas, that resettlement took place completely according to plan. Apart from that, there was, after all, something to follow on from here. Most itself, for that matter, because of the great Most strike of the early 1930s, symbolized, more than any other town in Czechoslovakia, the history of capitalist exploitation and the dramatic struggle of the mining proletariat (including Czech speakers) to eliminate poverty and unemployment – and it was thus a typical centre of the German Sudetenland. Even before the Second World War, the proportion of the Czech population was high here and the social unrest at the beginning of the 1930s in particular made the town a symbolic centre of the linguistically Czech collective memory.[161]

The restoration and development of industry in the borderlands, particularly heavy industry, were soon a demonstrable success. The high mobility of labour, the influx of new workers from the countryside to the industrial centre, and the high amount of state investment in industry and housing before long created suitable living conditions for the hundreds of thousands of new inhabitants in the

160 Albert Pražák, 'Budujeme osvobozené kraje', quoted in Svatopluk Technik, *Výstava Budujeme osvobozené kraje v Liberci roku 1946*, Liberec: Česká beseda, 2001, p. 49.
161 See the chapter 'Misery and Defiance: Most as a Site of Memory' in the 'Alienation' section.

borderland towns. This was partly because engineers and workers from cities in the interior were not tied to their original homes to the same extent as, say, the independent farmers who were supposed to resettle the rural areas of the former Sudetenland. Moreover, tens of thousands of German workers remained in industries here, enabling continuity in production and preventing a complete loss of knowhow.

Acknowledging the new industrial identity, successful resettlement, and the continuity of economic life in the relationship with the north Bohemian borderlands leads one to rethink the idea of 'uprootedness', that is, the absence of any collective regional identity. But the emphasis solely on industry and production in these areas of the former Sudetenland (and possibly even more thoroughly than in the abandoned west Bohemian borderlands, which were left wild) sidelined the premodern links and indeed all spiritual connections between human beings and the land they inhabited. The land became a reservoir of raw materials, an opportunity for even more massive and efficient exploitation, a quantity measurable by precise economic calculations. To perceive the land as a system of important references to the history of the community that inhabits it was clearly more complicated here than in the continually settled areas of what was then Czechoslovakia.

GYPSIES

A cluster of workers returning from their shift
Walk down the middle of the street.
In their pockets they clench the handles of their knives.
The Gypsies have mugged someone again.
Their footsteps are gobbled up by the night.

(Emil Juliš, 1969[162])

The society of the resettled Sudetenland in the post-war decades was colourful. The declared aim of the expulsion of the Germans from the Bohemian Lands and the resettlement of the borderlands was to regain these territories for Slav inhabitants and therefore for an ethnically (and, with time, also socially) homogeneous society. But the reality was fundamentally different from these nationalist visions. In the whirlwind of the expulsions, the confiscation of property, the breakneck colonization of the emptied-out lands, the replenishment of labour, and the forced transfer of other Czechoslovaks, the Bohemian borderlands during the first five post-war years were settled by more than 200,000 Czech and Slovak reimmigrants from Volhynia, Romania, Poland, Yugoslavia, and western Europe (many of whom no longer spoke Czech or Slovak), tens of thousands of Hungarians, about 15,000 Greeks, between 150,000 and 190,000 Slovaks, and tens of thousands of east-Slovak Roma. If we add to this sum the roughly 200,000 remaining Germans, it is clear that the members of these ethnically and culturally different groups constituted about a third of the society of the former Sudetenland in that period, which, according to statistics from the main settlement offices, had a population of 2,496,836 at the end of March 1947.[163]

---

162 From Emil Juliš, 'Vzpomínka na noční Most v roce 1953', Juliš, *Pod kroky dýmů*.
163 František Čapka, Lubomír Slezák, and Jaroslav Vaculík, *Nové osídlení pohraničí českých zemí po druhé světové válce*, Brno: Akademické nakladatelství CERM, 2005, p. 188. For ethnic relations and the heterogeneity of the borderlands after the Second World War, see also Spurný, *Nejsou jako my.*

All these minority ethnic groups encountered the animosity of the majority population, for they were fundamentally in the way of ideas about an ethnically Czech borderland. Though the source of the Czechs' most oppressive fears and the target of their fiercest hatred was of course the Germans, it was clearly the Roma who bore the brunt of their greatest contempt. The fate of the Roma (known at that time only as 'Gypsies') in the Bohemian Lands and Slovakia and their trials and tribulations during the war and in the first post-war years also considerably influenced post-war society in the Most district and, last but not least, influenced the character of old Most and the attitude that Czech majority society had towards this town in the decades after the war. We must therefore, at least briefly, stop and consider how and why the Roma began to shape the fate of the borderlands in this period.

Of the roughly 6,000 Roma that had lived in the Bohemian Lands during the first Czechoslovak Republic, mostly as settled inhabitants of south-east Moravia, the vast majority were murdered in Nazi concentration camps and death camps. To a considerable extent, local Czechs from Bohemia and Moravia had helped to organize the Roma 'centres' (concentration camps) in the Bohemian Lands – in Lety near Písek, south Bohemia, and in Hodonín near Kunštát, south Moravia. Only 583 Bohemian and Moravian Roma returned home from Auschwitz.

In the whirlwind of post-war migration (in addition to the hard-to-estimate number of itinerant groups), initially hundreds and then, a few months later, thousands of traditionally settled Roma from east Slovakia and south Slovakia began gradually to move into the borderlands. By 1947 probably between 15,000 and 20,000 had arrived, mostly in large towns and the borderlands, in search of a living or better housing. During the war, as a consequence of measures taken by the Slovak authorities and security forces, many of them had lost family members, their homes, and all their property. Now they were desperately searching for work, a livelihood, and a place where they could begin new lives.

Whereas before the war only groups of itinerant Roma had moved in large numbers, and the State sought to get this movement under control, things had now changed. The migration of mostly settled Roma from Slovakia to the large cities and borderlands of Bohemia and Moravia in search of work became part of the migration of many millions of other people. They thus found themselves not only in the sights of the authorities, who were supposed to regulate these migrations, but also attracting more attention from the wider strata of society in the Bohemian Lands.

In the early post-war years, the Czech population, in the spirit of First Republic attitudes and radicalized during the German occupation, basically did not consider the Roma to be part of human society. On the basis of this conception, journalists, bureaucrats, and politicians formulated various radical proposals to solve the 'problem'. 'The abundance of thieves means not merely that there is something to steal but mainly that theft is easy', commented one regional paper on the presence of Roma in the borderlands, continuing

it is therefore necessary [...] to set about 'delousing'. If there are refugees from foreign countries amongst the Gypsies, they must be moved away just as the refugees from other strata of foreign countries were expelled from our country. The rest must be divided up so that the handful of truly civilized ones can live like other Czechoslovak citizens; the rest would have to be settled in as many places as are necessary for them to be under absolute supervision and so they could not shirk work and roam the neighbourhood. The children would then [...] have to be absolutely and forever taken out of their surroundings and brought up to be accustomed to those of truly civil people. The internment of adults would perhaps be best arranged in settlements attached to farms belonging either to Bohemia or to towns and villages, on which, under proper management, they would carry out all the required work [...] It would be a facility as humane as possible and also economically the most efficient, with of course the requisite thoroughness and strict discipline.[164]

Other newspapers ran articles in a similar spirit. Only the Social Democratic and the Communist press occasionally reminded their readers that Roma were 'also people like anyone else'.[165] The need to give this truth special emphasis attests in itself to a significant continuity with the Nazi discourse, which in fact had singled out the Romani and the Jewish populations from human society, and this discourse now needed to be challenged. Also at Government ministries in Prague before the Communist takeover in February 1948, the 'solution of the Gypsy question' was being planned in a purely repressive spirit, by means of internment camps and forced labour.[166]

The post-war borderlands were full of people who had come here in search of easy earnings, and then soon left, without having really ever joined in the 'building work' that was so emphasized. In those respects, therefore the Roma who sought to earn some quick money and return to where they had come from or to continue in their travelling were no exception. They probably were involved in some petty theft or exhibited the poor work ethic of the Roma, yet a number of them were employed in heavy industry, construction, or building roads and railways elsewhere, often doing work that was not much sought after by the rest of the population. Slovak Roma lived

164 'Cikánské hordy v pohraničí – důkaz konsolidace?', *Náš hraničář,* 17 January 1947, pp. 7–8.
165 'Cikáni – metla nebo užitek země?', *Sever,* 20 May 1947, p. 5.
166 See NA, f. 315/1 (ÚPV – běžná spisovna, 1945–1959), kart. 1163, sg. 1424/b/1, Zařazení cikánů do pracovních táborů, návrh vládního usnesení (1947). For some of the considered solutions to the 'Gypsy problem' in the first years after the Second World War, see also Nina Pavelčíková, *Romové v českých zemích v letech 1945–1989,* Prague: Úřad dokumentace a vyšetřování zločinů komunismu PČR, 2004, pp. 23–31. For the legislative context, see René Petráš, *Menšiny v komunistickém Československu: Právní a faktické postavení národnostních menšin v českých zemích v letech 1948–1970,* Prague: VIP Books, 2007, pp. 113–16.

particularly in towns in very makeshift conditions, in basements and in buildings badly damaged during the war. These facts could of course, just like the ubiquitous antipathy, often arouse remorse. In themselves, they do not establish a real reason why a generally perceived antithesis crystalized so quickly between the Roma and the honest frontiersmen (*hraničáři*) – that is, the people with white skin and whose mother tongue was Czech. The roots of the 'popular' attitudes and opinions therefore clearly go beyond authentic experience, which is true particularly of the various proposed solutions to this 'problem'. In addition to the traditional prejudices about Roma, for instance, that they were 'work-shy' and caused 'outrageous squalor', created 'nests of filth' and 'hotbeds of disease', a role was also played here by the fact that most of the Czech population (apart from south Moravians) had had little experience of Roma before the war and was now shocked or outraged by the otherness of these people. A role was also played by the racialist discourse, which Czech society had, partly unthinkingly, adopted during the war.

A radical solution that entailed a combination of expulsion, internment, and institutional re-education was never implemented, for two reasons. The first reason was simply that, in contrast to the stereotype about their being layabouts and freeloaders, many of the Roma coming to the Bohemian Lands actually did the heavy work in a number of important industrial enterprises when, especially in the borderlands, there was a disastrous shortage of labour. This fact was pointed out, for instance, by the authors of the more benevolent articles in the Social Democratic or Communist newspapers; Roma, according to them, were the 'only element that accepted the heavy work in quarries, gravelling roads, and wherever others did not want to work'.[167] Paradoxically, a list of 17,000 'travelling Gypsies and vagrants disinclined to work' in the Bohemian Lands, drawn up by the Ministry of the Interior in 1947, stated that of the adult males

---

[167] 'Cikáni – metla nebo užitek země?'.

recorded in the list almost 80 per cent were workers.[168] In some cases, then, even their employers, who did not want to lose important labour, objected to the efforts to send the Roma back to Slovakia or intern them.[169]

The definitive end to radical solutions like internment, forced labour, or any other form or ethnically determined segregation came with the advent of the socialist dictatorship. The elites of the Czechoslovak Communist Party approached the 'Gypsy question' with great ambitions, based on faith in the possibility of radically making people appreciate freedom and dignity, on the condition that each individual succeeded in freeing himself or herself from the shackles of the past and the previous exploitation of man by man. The Roma, in the eyes of the new rulers, were the essence of the degradation of humankind, which was, from their point of view, the result of the capitalist relations of production. The struggle against their backwardness, and also against their traditional identity, which was now considered anachronistic, was also the Romani struggle to overcome the previous social order. The ideologically determined inadmissibility of a racist attitude, discrimination, and segregation did not of course mean either a quick redress of the actual social situation of the Roma or the elimination of the prejudices, animosity, and disdain which majority society felt for them. These attitudes and views were only temporarily pushed out of the public space, only to bewitch it again a few years later in the form of metastasis wrapped up in the discourse of welfare and equality.[170]

168 Pavelčíková, *Romové*, pp. 29–31.

169 The most striking case of this kind took place in the Ústí nad Labem district, where the Roma, at the instigation of the District National Committee, were interned and used to clear the ruins after the war. As unpaid labour, they were meant to take the place of the German inhabitants. See Pavelčíková, *Romové*, p. 28. Another dispute amongst employers of Roma, the authorities, and the local inhabitants, was recorded in the Broumov region of north-east Bohemia. See Spurný, *Nejsou jako my*, p. 245.

170 For more on the attitude of the State and society in the borderlands towards the Roma from 1945 to 1960, see Spurný, *Nejsou jako my*, pp. 237–85.

Already in the first wave of Romani migration from Slovakia to the Bohemian Lands right after the Second World War, a few thousand Roma headed for the partly depopulated industrial towns of north Bohemia, chiefly Ústí nad Labem and Most. They came in search of work, both as part of labour recruitment programmes and on their own initiative. The authorities did not know how to house the Romani workers, because they had not counted on the fact that Romani families usually follow their breadwinners even to places where they are employed only temporarily. Small flats, miners' barracks, and even cellars of post-war Most were thus filled with large Romani families. Women cooking on open fires and naked children in the streets of the old town thus represented the most visible face of its quickly stitched together and colourful society. Though the housing shortage was partly solved already in the 1940s and particularly in the first half of the 1950s by the building of the Stalingradská čtvrť (Stalingrad Quarter) and Podžatecká housing estates, Romani workers and their families did not move into the comfortable flats. They remained in the old Most, helping to create the strange amalgam of the heterogeneous community of the decaying town with an uncertain future.

In the mid-1950s, about 1,200 Germans and more than 2,500 Slovaks, together with Romanians, Hungarians, and members of other ethnicities were part of the total Most population of about 30,000.[171] Romani (Gypsy) ethnicity is not mentioned in the statistics; some of the Roma probably declared their ethnicity as Slovak. The roughly 4,000 members of ethnicities other than Czech did not of course include the reimmigrants, though a number of them shared the same customs, lifestyle, and mother tongue of the countries in which they had been born and where their families had lived for many decades rather than those of Czechoslovakia. Though society here was

---

171   SOkA Most, f. MěNV Most (1945–1990), arch. j. 986, Přehled o osobách jiné než české národnosti (Rada MěNV v Mostě, Plánovací komise, 18. března 1955).

markedly heterogeneous, there were clear differences also amongst the Czechs, who ranged from long-settled inhabitants who had spent the war here to long-settled inhabitants who, having been expelled by the Germans after the Munich Agreement in late 1938, returned after the war, and also newcomers. Most of the members of other ethnicities lived in the old part of town, with a population of 15,000, where these people constituted about a third of the population. In the mid-1950s, roughly 2,000 Roma were estimated to have lived here and, in the 1960s, when the population of the town otherwise began to decrease, the number was even greater.

✗✗✗

> The women of the Klíš family demolished the stove and threw the pieces into the courtyard below the window and did not clean them up by 25 November 1956 as they had been called upon to do by Estate Management No. 5 and Street Committee No. 12. Throwing potato peels and jam jars into the toilet, the toilet could get blocked [...] They pour human excrement down the plughole [...].[172]

Of the hundreds of 'complaints by citizens against Gypsies' in the old town of Most from the 1950s, 1960s, and 1970s, only several dozen have been preserved today. Yet even this fraction provides evidence of the dismal situation. Apart from toilets and plugholes being blocked with potato peels and excrement, neighbours most often complained about noisy drinking and parties that often (especially on payday) went on until the early hours of the morning, and about arguments and brawls, threatening and swearing at the other tenants or the house management, and about setting fire to the interiors of the apartment buildings, including the individual flats:

172 SOkA Most, f. MěNV Most (1945–1990), arch. j. 976, sl. Sociální péče – stížnosti občanů (1953–1979), Stížnost občanů zaslaná trestní komisi MěNV (27. 2. 1956).

In both houses, the Žolták family continues its destructive activity, wilfully destroying interiors [...] In house no. 1117 in Lidická ulice, Most, one leaf of double swing doors on the ground floor was purloined by Gypsies and probably burnt, the door to the kitchen of a ground-floor flat was considerably damaged and had to be replaced, one complete window was burnt in the same kitchen, and one electric switch was also destroyed, a whole new sash of a window onto the corridor [...] was burnt, one complete lavatory window on the ground floor and a sink in the corridor with the plumbing were purloined, and so was a well-preserved kitchen cooker [...] In the house in back, no. 1855, in which the family of the Gypsy Žolták stayed, Gypsies have so far burnt three complete exterior windows, one complete window (inside and out), one window above a door, two attic windows, two skylights, four doors at the sheds and eight square metres of flooring in the attic of this house [...].[173]

The cases that the municipal national committee or the district public prosecutor's office had to deal with need not of course have been absolutely typical. The many complaints and repeating pattern of behaviour occurring amongst them, however, testifies to the fact that these were not isolated incidents. As they had moved to other big and medium-sized towns of the Bohemian Lands, so too the Roma moved to Most, mostly from Slovak settlements, from milieux completely lacking not only the amenities of modern industrial society but also the basic furnishings of the typical Bohemian cottage of the time. They did not know door handles, keys, bathrooms, flush toilets, or electric appliances, and were unable to use them. The only heating fuel they knew how to use was wood, which they were accustomed to fetching from the woods behind the settlement. Their difficulties were comparable with those faced by people during the rapid urbanization of the nineteenth century. At that time, however,

---

173 Hlášení domovní správy č. 4 v Mostě Okresní prokuratuře (27. 9. 1962), ibid.

the towns to which people moved from the countryside were just gradually becoming special environments with other rules; electricity and flush toilets did not exist and a river or suburban woods long served people in the suburbs as a basic source of raw materials or the only place to wash laundry or to see to their personal hygiene. In this sense the situation of the east Slovak Roma in the whirlwind of rapid migration and moving to already modern centres of industrial society in search of a living was considerably less merciful. Moreover, as people were transplanted into a milieu whose operation and rules they did not understand, they found themselves together with hundreds of thousands of other proletarianized rural people (as was the case in the nineteenth century), but alone. It was therefore unlikely that they would find understanding in the ranks of majority society.[174]

As elsewhere, so too in old Most the Roma met with strongly negative reactions and efforts to get rid of them. The inhabitants demanded the expulsion of specific families and their punishment, sometimes even the expulsion of all the Roma from the town and their dispersal into other villages, towns, districts, and regions. Many sought to prevent the Romani families from moving into their buildings, often pointing out that one or two such families already lived there and that was more than enough. The arguments against Roma moving in were often remarkable – including, for example, that they 'have several musical instruments'.[175] The long-time inhabitants of Most in these circumstances even dared to complain to the authorities that in the first Czechoslovak Republic things were better in Most (without the Roma):

Comrade Chairman! Nowhere are there so many Gypsies as in Most. It is dreadful what they do, directly on the square, nothing but Gypsies,

---

174 See Pavelčíková, *Romové*, pp. 36–45.
175 A letter from all the tenants of house no. 1251 in Honzlova ulice to the secretary of the Municipal National Committee, 27 November 1969, ibid.

9. In front of the famous Opera café, 1970s.

every Gypsy woman is nursing a child on her breast publicly – that is, after all, a bit much. How then is one supposed to like living in Most? In Slovakia, they got rid of them. There, no Gypsy is allowed into town. But here they dare to say the worst things to everyone. The police should be on the square from 5 am to 9 pm and drive them away, move them to the countryside. They surely do not belong in town. This is total degeneracy!

Yours sincerely,

Věra Pospíšilová, Most

I hope that this is how it will be. During the First Republic, Most was a completely different place.[176]

---

176   A letter to the chairman of the Most Municipal National Committee, undated; the original is full of grammar and spelling mistakes, ibid.

Nevertheless, events in the 1960s took a different course than what was desired by the former 'white' inhabitants. It was not Roma but their 'decent fellow-citizens', who eventually were the first to move out of old Most.

In dealing with the question of the Roma in old Most, already in the 1950s the authorities alternated between efforts to implement resolute administrative measures (including a ban on the further moving of Roma to the town and criminal sanctions for causing a public nuisance and demolishing state-owned property[177]) and, on the other hand, by emphasizing patient explanation, the re-education of adults, and the bringing up of children. Whereas repressive and administrative measures were being pushed particularly at the lower levels of government, led by the Municipal National Committee and various citizens' committees, the District National Committee, in the spirit of Enlightenment absolutism, put emphasis on the gradual disciplining and civilizing of citizens as an inevitable effect of modern state institutions.[178] In the second half of the 1960s, all levels of government temporarily united in their efforts to disperse the Roma of Most to other districts of the North Bohemian Region, but the result of this long-term focused effort was that only twelve families were moved out.[179]

The decrepit condition of the town and the decision to demolish it in a number of years (and therefore not to invest at all in old Most except for the most necessary repairs made for security reasons and the operation of the public utilities) and a 1964 ban on further building, however, accelerated the exodus of its non-Roma inhabitants. The only group in old Most which did not decrease in size almost

---

177 SOkA Most, f. MěNV Most (1945–1990), arch. j. 969, Sociální péče – cikánská problematika (korespondence MěNV a ONV, 1953–1954).
178 Ibid.
179 See SOkA Most, f. 208 (ONV II), ev. j. 448, inv. č. 1283, sl. Komise rady ONV pro řešení otázek obyvatel cikánského původu (1966–1972); SOkA Most, f. MěNV Most (1945–1990), arch. j. 971, Evidence cikánských rodin v Mostě a návrhy na jejich rozptýlení (proposals for the dispersal of the Roma appear in materials from 1965–69).

at all until the mid-1970s, and in some years even grew,[180] was thus the Roma. The majority of them, after all, found that the freer environment of a town condemned to demolition, with its out-of-the-way little places, old pubs, vacated buildings, and opportunities to find wood and other useful material, was better suited to them than were the new strictly organized and supervised housing estates. In addition, sufficiently large flats were gradually made available, and they suited Romani families better than the modern but somewhat cramped rooms of the flats in the prefab concrete blocks of the new city. And, probably the most important reason, the rents in the old town of Most were markedly lower than elsewhere. Besides, new flats were usually not allocated to people who would have liked to move. The authorities and mainly most of the other inhabitants did not want Roma in the new city. Old Most, or what remained of it at the end of the 1960s, thus became one big Romani settlement – the only town in the whole of Czechoslovakia which was inhabited solely by Roma. On the edge of the big pit arose a 'Gypsy metropolis', unique in Europe.

The dismal state of the old town was not caused by the Roma but by the decades of uncertainty about its fate and by the unwillingness of the local authorities to maintain the town and its buildings. The houses, their crumbling façades, collapsing roofs, derelict plumbing and sewage systems and the dug-up streets full of mud and puddles – all were the consequence of the approach the State and its bureaucrats had long taken towards a town whose demolition had been decided in 1964. The future of the town and the indifference of most people to its current appearance could have intensified the destructive approach to the surroundings and in its own way justified

---

180 A report from the Most Municipal National Committee about work in the Department of Gypsy Welfare, dated 1 November 1976, states that the number of Roma living in the remaining houses of old Most (which are earmarked for demolition) had increased by 1,045 people (232 families). SOkA Most, f. MěNV Most (1945–1990), arch. j. 969, sl. Informativní zprávy o činnosti na úseku sociální skupinové práce v péči o cikánské obyvatelstvo (1973–1976).

it. The State and the powerful actors of majority society in Most in any case showed greater disdain for private and public property than the poorest and most neglected people, whose lives on the margins of society also included their occasionally throwing a piece of a door or a window frame into a wood-burning stove.

The way in which some Roma approached home interiors and their surroundings thus only added to the overall picture of rack and ruin. Furthermore, according to sociological research from the beginning of the 1970s, most Roma of the town lived in the flats with the lowest official rating (*4. kategorie*) in run-down buildings (often unsafe), but almost 70 per cent of those buildings had flats that were maintained and clean. The stereotype of Roma unable to look after their own homes is not confirmed by this research. Nevertheless, basic differences from this standard housing were found – in

10. Now partly evacuated and gradually demolished by the State, the old town of Most provided plenty of opportunity to collect junk, ranging from wooden roof trusses to scrap metal.

particular, in every fourth flat more than nine people lived together, often five or more to a room.[181]

Although sociological research has shown that the Roma had the same attitude as majority society to housing and many other social patterns (for example, the divorce rate), the various problems of the Roma, together with the overall bleak atmosphere of the decaying condemned town they inhabited, naturally attracted attention. These problems included truancy amongst some Roma children (there are no statistics about how widespread this was), shirking work (though this entailed a negligible proportion of the Roma), and mainly the damaging or theft of property (which was destined for destruction anyway), alcoholism, quarrelling, and brawling. Also because of its Roma, who were the sole inhabitants from the late 1960s onwards, old Most was increasingly perceived as a foreign town, quite alien to Czechoslovak reality, an exotic outpost of another civilization, a town that was 'not ours', not Czech (*ne naše*). News reports from what was by then essentially a Romani ghetto implicitly operated, but sometimes even explicitly, with that alienating effect:

There is still light coming from a few windows. They are now the last windows of the dying town. There are never many of them together at once; it's more like someone poured a bit of light into that smoggy dawn [...] the houses of the last 220 families, and that's it. Little islands of the sole survivors of Most in the midst of desolate abandoned walls and lights and out-of-the-way corners. Everybody is swarthy and black-haired and black-eyed, and speaks a strange language. When in the evening the last shop windows of the last shops begin to light up and when they go out into the streets, it's as if something of the atmosphere of southern

---

181   SOkA Most, f. MěNV Most (1945–1990), arch. j. 972, Sociologický průzkum cikánů ve starém Mostě (1972), a short version of which was published in a small number of copies, solely for the people who commissioned the research, as Jan Friš et al., *Cikáni ve starém Mostě: Výsledky sociologického průzkumu*, Most: ONV v Mostě, 1975.

towns on the coasts of the Aegean Sea had fallen to earth here, but for that intrusive November cold, raw and permeated with fog. The Roma.[182]

Not only popularizers of events in the Most district, but also authors of official documents intended for the internal use of politicians or experts, made it clear that the low standard of housing in old Most was connected with its inhabitants, the Roma. The problem of old Most, a town sacrificed to coal and allegedly the interests of the socialist state, was thus paradoxically interpreted as part of the 'Gypsy question' – and the demolition of the town could thus, naively or on purpose, be confused with the 'solution of the Gypsy question'. Yes, this term was used, probably without the relevant officials realizing its sinister connotations.[183] Minutes of meetings and a wide variety of reports thus, on the one hand, describe the disastrous situation of the 'Gypsy' town – alcoholism, brawls, dirty and lice-infested children not going regularly to school, and adults with a bad work ethic, a high crime rate, and pubs full of recidivists – and, on the other, adding in the same breath, or at least suggesting, that the problems in this instance would be solved with the demolition of the old town.[184]

Old Most, already in the years just after the war, became the home of several hundred and, later, several thousand, Roma. They came in search of work and a better life, but often hardly became accustomed to the urban environment, the forms of housing and sanitation connected with it, and mainly with idea of law and order which was held by majority society. In the last decade of its existence, old

---

182 Zdeněk Kropáč, 'Epitaf městu', *Rudé právo*, 27 November 1976, p. 3.
183 See NA, f. 850/3 (AMVD), kart. 1283, K návrhu MV na řešení cikánské otázky v ČSR, původce: Ministerstvo informací a osvěty, 28. listopadu 1951. The term is also used regularly in the Chronicle of the town of Most – SOkA Most, f. 130 (MěNV Most 1945–1990), inv. č. 364–366, Kronika města Mostu 1945–1965, díl I a II, Kronika města Mostu 1966.
184 See SOkA Most, f. MěNV Most (1945–1990), arch. j. 969, Minutes from a joint meeting of organizations of the National Front and state bodies, concerning questions related to the Gypsy population in Most, held at the Municipal National Committee.

Most became an exclusively Romani town. The connection between the dying historic town and its Romani inhabitants became an important aspect in the justification of its demolition. As old Most represented the residue of the German, capitalist past, which had no place in modernizing Czechoslovak socialist society, so too the Roma remained, in the eyes of majority society, a foreign element unable to adapt sufficiently to a modern industrial society based on education, rational planning, and productivity. Thus, both elements, the town and the people of the past, complemented each other in the majority thinking of the time, and in a remarkable symbiosis justified the great experiment that Most became in the second half of the twentieth century.

MISERY AND DEFIANCE:
MOST AS A SITE OF MEMORY

> Here in the streets on the outskirts, far from the capital, where very
> many now forgotten great men felt called upon to do historic deeds,
> the real history that our present day is connected with was made.
> It was a hard history, permeated with disasters, misfortune, misery, and
> continuously recurring struggles. The region is scattered with monuments,
> large and small, and memorial plaques. The history of those whom they
> commemorate is told by every miner who passes by. For what is today
> called history was until recently life, whose stories continue to circulate,
> told in the evening wherever a few miners get together. The stories are
> modified and grow the further they get from the day of the actual event.
> And the number of eyewitnesses, instead of decreasing, often even
> increases. But that does not change anything about the facts that
> took place.
>
> (Ivan Klíma, 1959[185])

The phenomenon of homelessness in the land after the Germans had
been expelled, together with the alien nature of the 'Gypsy town',
weakened the relationship of people with old Most, and was thus
able to contribute to the justification of its being swapped for coal.
Unlike these two factors, a third, which I will discuss in this part of
the book, had an ambiguous influence, if not even the opposite influence on the future of Most. It thus complicates the narrative of the
downfall of the town and its causes, but is undoubtedly an essential
part of the story.

Hardly anything at that time cast as much doubt on the legitimacy
of interwar Czechoslovakia, its liberal democracy, and the capitalist

---

185 Ivan Klíma, 'Kraj pod deštníkem, kapitola první', *Literární noviny* 8 (13), 28 March 1959,
p. 7.

order as fundamentally as the miners' living conditions. The people who came to the mining district in the nineteenth century, mostly from ever-poorer rural areas, gradually became hostages of the increasingly powerful mining companies. The contrast between the concentration of capital (visible in the ways of life and properties of the industrialists and their managers) and the heavy work performed by the miners, with its risks and fears of being laid off, was probably most conspicuous in this region. The miners working underground were often victims of a variety of small accidents and large disasters. Because of the influence of mining on the landscape and moving to different seams they often lived in makeshift quarters and colonies and, as a result of fluctuations in fuel prices, the risk of being laid off kept growing. Because of the unhealthy work environment, miners often became seriously ill with lung disease at a young age. They died early and their families suffered not only from hunger but often from tuberculosis too.

That was of course also the case in the Most district, which in this region from the late nineteenth century onwards led to several important collective protests, the largest of which was the great Most strike in the spring of 1932 – the biggest social protest in the history of interwar Czechoslovakia. The miners' fight for their rights at that time resulted not only in wounded and dead in clashes with the Czechoslovak police, but also in broad-based support throughout the country, including solidarity offered by leading left-wing writers like Vladislav Vančura (1891–1942), Ivan Olbracht (born Kamil Zeman, 1882–1952), Julius Fučík (1903–1943), Karel Toman (born Antonín Bernášek, 1877–1946), and Vítězslav Nezval (1900–1958). The strike ended with the acceptance of compromise demands (including the temporary suspension of layoffs and the elimination of some practices forcing miners to work without pay, in fact, servitude). Mainly, however, it became a symbol, a site of memory, of the miners, the Communist movement and the struggle for social justice in general.

Beginning in the 1930s and particularly after 1948, the miners' misery and mainly their collective resistance became a frequently recalled historical theme, which pointed to the injustice of the capitalist order and a central problem of interwar Czechoslovakia. It was not by chance that Most became a symbol of both the misery and the struggle for its elimination, regardless of the future of the town and the need to justify its demolition. The place that Most thus achieved in the collective memory of Communist-governed Czechoslovakia, albeit at the time when its future was being decided and then during its physical elimination, could not be ignored or bypassed.

The associations that Most evoked, intentionally sustained by the Press after 1948, were first and foremost unemployment, hunger, and hopelessness. It was recalled how during the Great Depression in the early 1930s the Most cemetery was soon covered with half a hectare of new crosses, erected in memory of those who had died of poverty and hunger or illness, which amongst the miners and their families spread more quickly in times of need.[186] And one recalled the grey, sad town under a blanket of fog, above which glowed the great houses of the coal barons. And one also recalled the mining disasters, which cost hundreds of miners their lives and here and there swallowed up a piece of the old town. And one also remembered the coal barons, whose names, like Weidlich, Bobbe, and Petschek, and characterizations were a reminder that they were allegedly doubly or even triply (as Jews) foreign here – as Germans and as merciless exploiters. Well into the 1970s the newspapers regularly recalled, for example, that

the bourgeois republic endowed this region with insatiable coal barons, blithely living from the blood and callouses of the miners, unemployment, police to put down worker unrest, toil, colonies of destitute miners with undernourished and hungry children, tuberculosis – the constant

---

186   Jaroslav Prášek, 'Život havířů je nový', *Československý svět*, 7 January 1960.

companion of penury – and narrow, filthy, dusty little streets.
The treasures of the depths brought profit and joy to only a small
circle of people. And jails and death were for those who did not want
to reconcile themselves to that.[187]

But as the lines of this chapter's epigraph, by the novelist Ivan Klíma
(b.1931), emphasize, negative images also played a part in forming
the collective memory of the place and giving it a bit of identity. Not
just among the eyewitnesses but also in a number of newspaper articles and made-for-television documentary films, the mining past of
old Most was presented with a dose of romance and nostalgia for the
'old, black, crumbling Most with its narrow, winding little streets'.[188]
The misery of the town with ramshackle dwellings on its outskirts,
its dirty corners, and its flats without running water and flush toilets
were a theme etched deep into the collective memory. These images
to some extent thus counter the image of the borderlands, including the Most district, as places with neither memory nor identity,
an image emphasized by some contemporaries and many historians,
including myself.

At the same time, however, it is true that the memory of poverty
and hardship could have the same effect as the absence of a shared
memory in general – that is, it could provide a reason for rejecting
the past and seeing the present as the opposite of what had been,
rather than as its continuation. But the tradition of the struggles
for social justice, which was full of dramatic gestures and sacrifices,
made it impossible to cut the present off from the past. Most and
the Most district had intentionally and thoroughly been building its
identity upon this since the 1930s and with renewed energy after the
Communist takeover in 1948.

187 M. Tolar, 'Ozvěny z Hněvína', *Obrana lidu*, 26 June 1976.
188 Ilja Bart, 'Pýcha a bolest Mostu', *Kulturní kalendář Mostecka*, May 1962, pp. 7–9.

A Czech TV series from 1987, called *Docela obyčejné město* (A quite ordinary town), included an episode devoted to Most. But there, the producers added a question mark, suggesting that Most was not such an ordinary town after all. The main characters and presenters/guides of the series here were not the secretary of the Most District Committee of the Communist Party of Czechoslovakia, the chairman of the Most Municipal or District National Committee, or the director of the SHD, but Libuše Pokorná (1946–2014), the manager of the Most District Museum, and Jana Sýkorová, who also worked there, and a teacher of the name Kvapilová. Sýkorová, together with Comrade Kvapilová and schoolchildren set off to visit the places related to the great Most strike of 1932. They look at locations of the mining accident and the eight trapped miners, which led to the strike. They talk to one another about the appalling conditions in which the miners lived, and they learn more about revolutionary traditions. The excursion and film were accompanied by quotations of the words of the Communist poet and one-time Minister of Culture Vítězslav Nezval and the martyred Communist journalist Julius Fučík, and by information about the violence of the police and about the miners who lost their lives in the struggle. 'It is good to know how the generations before us lived,' says the closing commentary, accompanied by footage of the new Most, including trams and parks, and remarking: 'Your now quite ordinary town has its own history. Wouldn't you like to discover it?'[189]

Docela obyčejné město is by far not the only television series or documentary film to pay attention to the strike. It is remarkable only because the whole episode was about the strike, though it was meant to be about the town of Most. The great Most strike became a central symbolic site of the Communist narrative, not only of the history of Most, but also of interwar Czechoslovakia as such, indeed,

---

189   *Docela obyčejné město*, documentary film, Československá televize (1987), IDEC 28736042891.

in a way, of modern Czech and Czechoslovak history in general. In the first fifty years from the time it took place, that is by 1982, more than 240 long articles, recollections, extended essays by MA students, works of belles-lettres, and scholarly articles had been written about it.[190] It became the subject of dozens of documentary and feature films, theatre plays,[191] and countless political speeches. Poems, newspaper reports, recollections, and history essays had been written about the 'black avalanche' that had been set in motion in the Ore Mountains in the spring of 1932. To mark the big anniversaries – twenty, twenty-five, thirty, forty, or fifty years after the strike – the press and other mass media were regularly filled with recollections and commemorations of this event.

A key role in this culture of remembrance was played by the riveting reports of Julius Fučík, but the image was also formed by the observations, sketches, and recollections of many other leading Avant-garde writers of interwar Czechoslovakia, for example, Ivan Olbracht, Konstantin Biebl (1898–1951), and Vladislav Vančura, and contributors to the Communist newspapers *Rudé právo* and *Tvorba*, but also, liberal democratic periodicals like *Přítomnost* and *Lidové noviny*.[192]

In a typical series of articles, 'Český sever v ohni' (The Bohemian north under fire) published in *Literární noviny* in 1957, Karel Nový (born Karel Novák, 1890–1980) pointed to several key contexts of the Most strike which were meant clearly to delegitimize interwar Czechoslovakia. Primarily, it was a matter of the oft-repeated fact

---

190 A bibliography, from 1982, lists 241 such works, but does not mention that this is hardly all the writings about the strike. In addition to in-depth articles, the strike was also the subject of hundreds of newspaper articles and short reports. Zdeněk Vojtek, Jarmila Trägrová, et. al, *Mostecká stávka 1932: Výběrová bibliografie k 50. výročí stávky*, [Ústí nad Labem]: Státní vědecká knihovna M. Gorkého v Ústí nad Labem, 1982.
191 See the play by Vojtěch Cach, *Mostecká stávka*, Prague: Orbis, 1953, or its adaptation for a small, village theatre company, *Pevnost na severu*, Prague: Orbis, 1955.
192 Marie Čutková (ed.), *Mostecké drama: Svědectví novinářů, spisovatelů a pokrokové veřejnosti o velké mostecké stávce roku 1932*, Prague: Mladá fronta, 1972.

that the police had stood behind those who had probably been responsible for the mining accident that had led to the strike – namely, the
owners and managers of the mines. Apart from that, Nový reminded
his readers that the profits of the mining company had not been, at
least in the early years of the Depression, significantly less than before, and also about the young miners who had died in the accident,
whose families he had visited. Sketches, recollections, and reflections
of this sort came across as authentic and were convincing – and
definitely again and again re-established old Most and its inhabitants at that time as part of the dominant narrative of recent history.

In his book of journalistic reports *Šachty splněných nadějí* (Mine
shafts of fulfilled hopes), the north Bohemian journalist Radovan
Brychta (1928–2008) has an aim similar to Nový's. But he seeks to
do more than just to present recollections of a past full of struggles.
He seeks also to construct a bridge to the present and to justify why
the demolition of this site of memory is ultimately what tradition
urges us to do and be:

> The old revolutionary tradition cannot be maintained only by recollecting.
> Formerly, revolutionariness was judged according to the thousands
> of miners who defied the mining companies. Today, it is measured
> according to the thousands of tonnes of extracted coal exceeding
> the plan. The ever-increasing flow of output is today an avalanche that has
> now buried and smoothed over the scars of the old days and is erecting
> a completely new structure. It is just as unstoppable as the backlash that
> the strike was. But it now reaches much, much farther.[193]

'The sentence passed on the old town' was anyway, according to
Brychta, 'signed before people even knew how to write'[194] – the coal

---

193 Radovan Brychta, *Šachty splněných nadějí*, afterword by Zdenka Fröhlichová, 'Veliká stávka',
Liberec: Severočeské krajské nakladatelství, 1962, p. 25.
194 Ibid., p. 53

under its streets, in short, has determined its fate despite all the emotion and nostalgia. About ten or fifteen years later, the Most strike was still being written about like this. On the one hand, authors were emphasizing that 'every remote corner, every paving stone of this town, is a faithful witness', but in the next breath they were adding that the time had come to say goodbye. The memory of the town must be preserved, but not those remote corners and those paving stones under which the black treasure lies. The time had come to build bridges to the future.[195]

✕✕✕

The town of Most played an important role in the historical memory not solely of the miners and their patrons amongst the Communists, but of Czech society as a whole. The uprootedness and discontinuity typical of what was once the Sudetenland could thus certainly have played its role after the war. Society here, as elsewhere in the borderlands, was considerably varied and many people simply did not feel at home here. That to a certain extent can explain the passivity of the local people and the acceptance of the great experiment in which old Most played the main role at the local level. But the phenomenon of the Sudetenland cannot explain the generally accepted logic of swapping the town for coal at the level of the key Czechoslovak elites and in some respects, as we shall see, even European political, economic, and cultural elites. It is not by chance that the role of the image of the 'German town' was unimportant in the period discourse about Most. The town of Most was perceived mainly as a site of Czech struggles for justice – its past belonged to 'us' (Czechs), not to 'the others'. This history could thus, in certain circumstances, also lead to a quite different future. Why that did not happen cannot be explained only by the context of the distinctive microcosm of the Bohemian borderlands. One has to go further, beyond its borders.

195 Kropáč, 'Epitaf městu', p. 3.

Numbers

Even a cursory look at the official sources concerning the demolition of old Most suffices to show that purely economic calculations were a fundamental factor in the considerations about the future of the town, the region, and the people. Precise numbers, down to the hundredths position after the decimal point, of the quantities of the coal extracted, profits, and costs, and the solving of simple mathematical problems, together constitute a kind of thoroughly constructed pyramid of evidence for the necessity of acting in one way and not in another. They are numbers, plain and simple, which withstand any precise way of trying to disprove or fundamentally cast doubt on them. The numbers stake out a one-way street from which there seemed to be no escape except at the price of losses that society could not afford.

This line of reasoning and the power with which it changed and continues to change our world is not a peculiarity of coal mining in the Most district or even of Communist productivism. We lack sufficient space in this discussion for a complex account of the emancipation of economic thought, reducible to calculable quantities, in the age of industrial and post-industrial modernity. I shall, however, try to cast light on this fundamental layer of the Most story at least from three perspectives that are directly related to it. I shall first point out the close connection between the mining industry (specifically, coal mining) and this way of dealing with the world. I shall then discuss the global transformation, in the 1960s and 1970s, in thinking about the management of society, a transformation linked mainly to the scientific and technological revolution. And, third, I shall demonstrate how these factors and changes are reflected in the internal debates and key documents justifying the Most experiment.

COAL

For an industrial country, coal means life.
And we must sacrifice everything for life.
(From the 1961 documentary film *Třikrát o dnešku*)[196]

The extraction and processing of non-renewable resources represents such an important aspect of the history of human civilization that historians have even named individual historical eras after some of them. Without this extraction and processing, civilization and progress could hardly have existed in human history – indeed, there is even a certain connection between the speed of the changes in human ways of life and the extent of the extraction of non-renewable resources.

From the mid-eighteenth century to the end of the twentieth, the volume of non-renewable-resource extraction throughout the world every year increased at least 130 fold.[197] In the second half of this period a watershed took place, which future historians may well consider more significant than the fall of the Roman Empire or the discovery of America: nature ceased to keep up with the tempo of its being exploited, and *homo sapiens* thus eventually became a serious threat to the future existence of life on Earth, that is, to existence itself.

At the end of the nineteenth century, the cycle of technological progress, which consisted in the demand for non-renewable resources, their extraction, consumption, the expectation of further progress, innovation, and, again, increasing demand, began to run up against the limits of the natural renewal of the land inhabited by people. At the latest from the outbreak of the First World War, this dynamic

196   *Třikrát o dnešku*, Krátký film Praha, 1961, directed by Jiří Papoušek, 26 min. Pt II.
197   John E. Young, *Mining the Earth*, Worldwatch Paper 109 (Washington, DC: Worldwatch Institute, 1992), pp. 7–8.

was not only depleting the natural wealth but also destroying man-made works. Technology, with its ability to exploit the earth, was by that time no longer merely an abstract threat to human life in the distant future. It had become an absolutely concrete manifestation of the force that human beings had unleashed and over whose momentum it had already lost control, and was now turning against humankind. The cycle of satisfying rising demand by means of technology had in many places on Earth begun to influence people's everyday lives; it was giving them what they wanted, but certainly not for free. One of the most visible manifestations of this was the opencast mining of coal, gobbling up the land, villages, and ultimately towns. Civilization had begun to devour itself.

Coal, which is associated with the whole period from the beginning of the Industrial Revolution to the present day,[198] is, like crude oil, closely linked to technological progress. The Industrial Revolution, from the steam engine to electrification, is unthinkable without coal. This fact makes the development of coal mining and its impact on society and the landscape that it inhabits a typical test of the dynamics of modern development. We may usefully look at these dynamics essentially in two ways: as evidence of the tremendous development and potential of civilization or as the story of humankind made unfree by a system it had itself set in motion and whose constantly increasing power was shared by anyone using products whose manufacture depended on the mining and processing of coal.[199]

Coal mining after the Second World War increased exponentially. That was particularly true of the surface mining of lignite (brown coal). At the end of the 1950s, about 100 per cent more lignite was extracted than at the beginning of that decade. In the 1960s and

---

198 In 2013, OECD countries were still producing more than 60 per cent of their electric energy from coal. http://www.cez.cz/cs/promedia/cislaastatistiky/energetikavesvete.html Accessed 15 April 2015.
199 See the chapter 'Thinking the Story' in the 'The Story' section.

1970s lignite mining continued to increase, though more slowly.[200] From the standpoint of industry, and therefore of economic stability too, coal was such an important raw material that agreements about its extraction and distribution became one of the two pillars of the best known peace projects of the second half of the twentieth century – the European Coal and Steel Community (ECSC), established in 1951 as a forerunner of what is today the European Union. Coal at the time was not only a basic raw material for the production of heat in households but also in the generation of electrical energy. In states that had been among the world's leading coal producers, like Czechoslovakia, Poland, and Australia, almost five metric tonnes of coal per capita were mined in the years around 1970.[201] Already in the 1950s, the serious environmental impacts began to be fully manifested, not only of surface mining, leading to the destruction of land and communities, but also of the preparation of coal, leading to air pollution and thus to a higher incidence of respiratory disease, including cancer and the deaths of thousands of people, as in the Great Smog of London in December 1952[202]). But coal was also the main motor of the increasing industrial production and therefore also of economic growth and the rising standard of living that stemmed from it. The main question was not whether to mine coal and prepare it but how to increase its production without increasing the costs of its extraction. In the underground mines it was necessary to extract at greater depths and some of the seams were gradually exhausted; less accessible coal, then, even with increased labour productivity,

---

200 In 1950, 381 million tonnes (in Czechoslovakia 27.5 million tonnes, that is, 7.21 per cent of the world's mined coal), in 1960, 634 million tonnes (in Czechoslovakia at that time 58.4 million tonnes, 9.2 per cent of the world's mined coal), and in 1968, 738 million tonnes (in Czechoslovakia just under 75 million tonnes, an astonishing 10.2 per cent of the world's mined coal). Václav Průcha et al., *Hospodářské a sociální dějiny Československa 1918–1992*, vol. 2 (1945–1992), Brno: Doplněk, 2009, p. 451.
201 In Czechoslovakia, for example, in 1968, it was 4,934 kg of coal per capita. Ibid.
202 Peter Brimblecombe, *The Big Smoke: A History of Air Pollution in London Since Medieval Times*, London: Methuen, 1987.

naturally became more expensive. Salvation, from the standpoint of the operation of the economic system, was therefore imagined to lie in the big mines that made it possible to extract coal efficiently and quite cheaply, even after factoring in the forced moving of whole communities and the construction of replacements for them.

The worldwide increase in the extraction of coal (mainly by surface mining) and its use as the basic fuel for households, industry, and the generation of electrical energy came to a peak in the 1970s. From 1940 to 1970, the production of sulphur dioxide emitted by power stations in the United States doubled every decade. Developments in this field in Great Britain and in the two Germanies were similar. The consequences were unexpected – the dying of forests and fish in lakes, poisoned by acid rain – was often also manifested hundreds or even thousands of kilometres away from the sources of pollution, for example, in north-east parts of the United States as a result of burning coal in the Midwest, or in the south of Scandinavia in consequence of the production of sulphur oxides in the Federal Republic of Germany and Great Britain. Though the situation, critical by the end of the 1970s, led to the gradual introduction of programmes for the desulphurization of power stations and the transition to other sources of energy, in many countries these programmes were in fact implemented very slowly. During the presidency of Ronald Reagan (1981–89), for example, the Republican Party in the United States rejected as an undesirable instrument the regulation of the market and the long prepared Acid Rain Program, which, consequently, was not passed by the United States Congress until 1990, as an amendment to the Clean Air Act.[203] Thanks to the preference for other energy sources and thanks to energy conservation since the 1980s, the limitation of the production of sulphur oxides has been reflected in the most developed countries in a slight reduction in coal extraction, but that has definitely not meant the end of the devastation of

203 Barbara Freese, *Coal: A Human History,* Cambridge (Mass.): Perseus, 2003, pp. 168–70.

the landscape by surface mining. In some cases surface mining has moved to other areas that have brown coal with a lower sulphur content, in the United States, for example, moving from areas east of the Mississippi to Wyoming and other states of the American West. Despite the negative environmental impact, the importance of coal as a local natural resource ensuring the independence of the local energy industry and industrial production was emphasized in the 1970s, particularly with its oil crises. Outside Europe and North America, the extraction and burning of coal has continued to rise in recent decades; economic growth in countries like India, Brazil, and particularly China has been based on coal. The fundamental relationship between progress and the extraction and burning of this natural resource is hardly, then, a thing of the past.

✕✕✕

One can rarely observe the interaction between coal mining, society, and the environment in which people live in a form as concentrated as in the Most district. Coal mining began here in the late sixteenth and the early seventeenth century, officially, in 1613, when Emperor Matthias (*reg.* 1612–19) granted Hans Weidlich, a citizen of Most, the right to mine coal in Hrob (Klostergrab) and Havraň (Habern). Until 1740, mining had been sporadic, but afterwards growth was marked. In the second half of the eighteenth century, the people of Most were opening coalbeds on the very edge of the town – at the foot of Hněvín Hill. At first, mining these seams was illegal, but in 1790, with the aim of supporting economic development in Austria, the approach to coal mining was greatly liberalized.[204] During the nineteenth century, coal mining gradually became a lucrative business, and by the end of the 1850s, local businessmen were opening the first large mines. This development considerably accelerated an event that

---

204 Václav Valášek and Lubomír Chytka, *Velká 'kronika' o hnědém uhlí: Minulost, současnost a budoucnost těžby hnědého uhlí v severozápadních Čechách*, Pilsen: G2 studio, 2009, p. 52.

completely changed the existing economic relations, putting the development of the Most district on an absolutely new trajectory. That event was the completion of the railway line of the Ore Mountains, running from Ústí nad Labem first to Duchcov (Dux), near Teplice (Teplitz), and, eventually, in 1870, to Most and on to Chomutov. The demand for Most coal rose tremendously because it was now becoming easily accessible from anywhere in the Bohemian Lands and other areas of the western part of the Empire (known as Cisleithania).

A year after the first steam locomotive stopped in Most in 1871, the first coal company, the Brüxer Kohlenbergbau-Gesellschaft was established. Small seams belonging to individual rich burghers or institutions (including the Cistercian abbey in Osek/Osegg, which began to mine coal in the eighteenth century) were soon unable to meet the needs of industry, and therefore companies established with Austrian and foreign capital began to organize the mining of coal. Thus began the stage of large-scale mining. Still in that same year, in addition to the Brüxer Kohlenbergbau-Gesellschaft, the Nordwestböhmischer Kohlenbergbau was established, with the help of the Anglo-Austrian Bank, which bought up land near Horní Jiřetín (Obergeorgenthal), eight kilometres north of Most. The following year, the Živnostenská banka (Gewerbebank für Böhmen und Mähren in Prag) sought to establish another mining company. In 1874 several companies were established, including the Dux-Brüx-Komotauer Braunkohlengewerkschaft, followed by the Brucher Kohlengewerkschaft (in Lom, Bruch in German), and the Duxer Kohlengewerkschaft (in Duchcov). At the very end of the nineteenth century, in addition to deep underground mines, the first surface mines were opened in the area between Most and Duchcov, which continued to grow during the Great War, when Most became an important centre of the war economy.

Though in some years, particularly during the war, the demand for coal as the fundamental raw material of modern industry rose quicker than at other times, it basically increased continuously. How much coal the mining companies would be able to extract depended therefore on technological progress and a sufficient supply of labour. The surface mines during the first half of the twentieth century, after mining by hand was replaced, first, by horse-powered and then steam-powered excavators, began to prove more promising than the old methods – more efficient and less risky for the miners as well as the mining companies. As demand rose in subsequent years and as coal mining developed faster during the Second World War, the mines of the area round Komořany (Kommern in German) near Most were gradually changed into large-scale pits with the electrification of rail transport. In that period, just before the end of the Second World War, the amount of lignite extracted in the North Bohemian Basin (by that time already 20 million tonnes per year) by surface mining already exceeded the amount extracted by deep underground mining.

After the war, though the total amount of extracted coal declined for a while to 11 million tonnes per year and the privately owned coal mining companies were nationalized, the basic trend continued. In fact, after the mining enterprises were merged to create the giant Severočeské hnědouhelné doly (SHD) in Most, in March 1946,[205] the enterprises were gradually reorganized and their operations were made considerably more efficient. At the same time, as everywhere else in Europe in connection with the post-war renewal and development of heavy industry, the demand for coal began to rise rapidly. The emphasis on heavy industry and the concomitant high demand for energy (and therefore also the consumption of coal for the generation of electricity) are usually explained by scholars as a peculiarity of state socialism. Yet at least until the 1960s this trend was typical of all the industrialized countries; after all, the first step towards the integration of western Europe came in the 1950s in the form of the European Coal and Steel Community.

205 Fröhlichová, *Socialistické Mostecko*, p. 63.

The first post-war ideas about the future of lignite mining in the Ore Mountains envisaged increases to 25 million tonnes per year. But this goal was already surpassed by 1954, and thirty years later the quantity of coal extracted annually had increased threefold, to almost 75 million tonnes in 1984.[206] Afterwards, a little later and a little more slowly than in the countries of western Europe, mining here gradually began to decrease.[207]

The period of preparations for the demolition of Most and then its actually being carried out is therefore also the period of the quickest increase ever in the mining of brown coal.[208] From the second half of the 1950s, moreover, the underground mines were gradually closed and by the second half of the 1960s about 80 per cent of the extracted coal was from large-scale surface pits.[209] The possibility of further expansion, particularly of the largest and most efficient of these pits, thus became, at the latest by the second half of the 1950s, the priority of the Czechoslovak economy and a priority of Czechoslovak state policy.

✕✕✕

The presence of non-renewable resources and the efforts to use them have shaped society and the landscape of the Ore Mountains since the Middle Ages. But, with the Industrial Revolution and the Most

---

206 Valášek and Chytka, *Velká kronika*, p. 101. For more on this aspect, see the chapter 'The Destruction of the City as an Investment Plan'.

207 Surface mining of lignite led to similar growth in other regions of eastern and western Europe as well. Whereas the mining of black coal reached its peak in a number of regions at the end of the 1950s (for instance, in the German Federal Republic in 1956, when 134 million tonnes were extracted), the greatest development of surface mining of lignite took place in the 1960s, 1970s, and 1980s. In the Rhineland, for example, the peak was recorded, as in north Bohemia, in 1984, when as much as 120 million tonnes were being mined. See Jens Hohensee and Michael Salewski (eds), *Energie, Politik, Geschichte: Nationale und internationale Energiepolitik seit 1945*, Stuttgart: F. Steiner, 1993.

208 For a closer look at this, see the next chapter, 'The Destruction of the City as an Investment Plan'.

209 Valášek and Chytka, *Velká kronika*, pp. 100–01.

district being connected to the Austrian railway network, the nature of the relationship between economic development and the local society changed fundamentally in the 1870s. A new era had arrived. During the next hundred years, the structure of society and the appearance of the landscape of the Most district would be thoroughly transformed.

The Most district used to be a fertile agricultural region, comparable to the neighbouring areas around Louny (Laun) and Žatec (Saaz). They typically had villages with large and small farming estates, surrounded by fertile fields and orchards. Until the 1860s, the main source of livelihood for most of the population here was agriculture. In the course of the quick development of lignite mining in the following decades, however, thousands of new job opportunities appeared for miners. The local sources of labour were soon exhausted and so miners were hired from the ranks of local German-speaking farmers and their children (mining labour was better paid than farming), but also from other mining areas of Bohemia. Even boys of fourteen, the legal age limit, were often working underground. From the interior or from the Bohemian Forest in the south came not only miners but also new labour to work in agriculture, substituting for those who would rather work underground. Indeed, the number of people who migrated here to take their place was even higher because the demand for farm produce also increased with the overall development of the region. The social and ethnic composition of the population thus changed, not only in the towns and mining colonies, but also in the countryside. Schools were at first only German and the children of Czech day labourers and miners either did not go to them or did but learnt to read and write only with great difficulty.

In the late nineteenth and early twentieth centuries, with the growth in demand for coal and mining, this development accelerated. Especially with the decline of the mines in Příbram, a town in central Bohemia, families of miners travelled the roads from the interior with carts loaded with all their worldly goods. They ended up in makeshift colonies of shacks and little houses, which the mines had quickly erected for them and could demolish again at any time when the advance of the coalface required it. Unmarried men ended up in shared rented rooms or in basement flats, where they took turns sleeping in beds while their roommates were on their shifts. In Most itself, Czech newcomers ran up again social and ethnic barriers; the predominantly German Most bourgeoisie did not welcome the influx of Czechs.[210] The miners in the colonies on the outskirts of town or in the gradually dying agricultural countryside constituted a significant part of the population in the Most district in the interwar years, and formed the absolute majority amongst the Czech speakers. From the perspective of 1945, we would consider them old-time inhabitants, but they were all affected by a particular modern sense of uprootedness.

The mechanization of mining and, beginning in the early 1930s, the temporary decline in the market led to mass layoffs and, in consequence of the increased number of people looking for work in the mines, decreased wages. The poverty of the miners, both the unemployed and those still working, became worse. The situation eventually led to the great Most strike, which became a central site of memory of the Most district in the socialist years and was to a large extent also formative in the whole country.[211]

The instability and risk which the people of the Most district were faced with in conjunction with the economic dynamics of mining and eventually also of the energy industry were manifested physically too – in sinkholes and mining-related accidents. There were dozens of accidents and hundreds of miners died in them during the fifty years of the most intensive underground mining. The town

210 Ladislav Štěpánek, 'Horníci na Mostecku', in Jiří Elman (ed.), *Regionální studie VII: Krušnohorský historický sborník*, Most: Dialog, 1968, pp. 127–37.
211 See the 'Alienation' section.

of Most was most strikingly affected by the mining disaster of 19 July 1895, when right next to the Most railway the overlying strata of the seam suddenly collapsed. Almost 40 houses were swallowed up by the earth, and others were damaged beyond repair. Two dozen people died and 2,500 Most inhabitants lost the roofs over their heads. Regarding the number of victims, the worst period was from September to November 1900, when 75 miners lost their lives.[212]

The changes in the natural environment, however, took place more slowly and, at first, less urgently than the changes in society. Their great importance, however, does not consist only in their having had a tendency to increase and that their potential elimination or restratification took even longer than it did with social problems. It would be erroneous to separate these two dynamics – social changes and changes to the environment – from each other; the one influences the other and the impact that changes to the environment has upon the lives of people and society may eventually be more substantial than the consequences of political revolutions or changes in economic systems. Most and the Most district were among the laboratories that enable us to document this interaction best.[213]

From the 1870s to the 1980s, farmland in the Most district was continually vanishing. First, bit by bit, under mining buildings and slag heaps, and then at a dizzying rate with the spread of surface mining. Where sinkholes and slag heaps had not yet appeared, miners' colonies began to spring up. Planned and long-term working of the land was replaced with provisional farming at the miners' colonies, which served to ensure the survival of the poor, often numerous families of the miners.

The compact cultural landscape – fields separated by boundaries, tree-lined roads, wells, small Church structures, conciliation crosses

212 Valášek and Chytka, *Velká kronika*, p. 64.
213 For more on the link between social and environmental history, see the chapter 'Thinking the Story' in the 'The Story' section.

and other little monuments –, which had been created in the densely settled basin areas between the ridges of the Central Bohemian Uplands (České středohoří or Böhmisches Mittelgebirge) and the Ore Mountains, thus disappeared. It was gradually reduced to being but a reservoir of raw materials essential for the further development of civilization. Until the end of the Second World War, the underground mines and opencast mines had avoided most of the villages, but people here were accustomed to moving continuously and to the construction of new makeshift colonies and their demolition in the interests of mining. After 1900, small villages in the Most district were 'moved' to make way for opencast mining – Ledvice in the Duchcov district, then Liptice near Most, and, still before the Great War, Zabrušany, whose church was dismantled and then reassembled a kilometre away.[214] Other villages met a similar fate. When, after 1940, with the transition to large pits as a more efficient method of extracting lignite, the elimination of larger villages and even towns, like Ervěnice, in 1958, and eventually old Most, was only a change in degree, not a new trend.

The symbolic centre of all these changes, but also the scene of most of the main events linked with them, was, and still is, Most. Few towns in the world are so essentially bound up with mineral wealth provided by the earth near it or even directly below its streets and houses. The first mining exploration that confirmed the existence of coal seams not far below the streets and houses of Most was carried out during the rapid industrialization of the Most district in 1867. By the end of the nineteenth century, it was followed by another 376 boreholes and shafts on the less than four-square-kilometre area of the town.[215] Surface mining at that time had not yet achieved the results that would lead to the transformation of this royal borough into a large-scale mine pit. Nevertheless, extraction

214 Valášek and Chytka, *Velká kronika*, p. 170.
215 Krejčí, *Most*, pp. 125–26.

from deep mines under the town was still carried on for a while. (to be exact, it continued until the previously mentioned accident of 1895, when almost 40 houses near the railway line were destroyed. From that time onwards, the coal reserves under the town were left untouched for a while. Though temporarily hidden from sight, that coal did not vanish from the plans of companies, mining engineers, the regional authorities, or the minds of the locals.

✕✕✕

That change entailed not only the impact on the structure of society and the natural environment but also more general features that tell us much about society in the Industrial Age, which the social and political theorist Peter Wagner calls 'organized modernity'.[216] Though this period partly overlaps, at least in the Bohemian Lands, with the growth of civil rights and individual freedoms (until the 1930s), we can observe in the Most district how the society and environment in which people lived and helped to create with no opportunity to resist, increasingly subordinated itself to the interests of impersonal economic forces and the apparently incontrovertible requirements of progress. As part of the established direction of the development of modern society, these changes and the price they exacted from society and the landscape, appeared to be irreversible, as if there had been no alternative: progress is determined by increasing industrial production, which itself is determined by the energy that drives the machines – and energy depends on a sufficient supply of coal. For industrial production to increase as quickly as possible, coal must be mined efficiently, with the greatest productivity possible. That can only be achieved by surface mining and the best

---

216 According to Wagner, 'organized modernity' continued until about the end of the 1960s, before it found itself in crisis and gradually changed into the post-industrial era. See Peter Wagner, *A Sociology of Modernity: Liberty and Discipline*, London: Routledge, 1994. It is fair, using this classification, to see the end of the era in the state-socialist countries as being in the 1980s. For more on this, see the chapter 'Thinking the Story' in the 'The Story' section.

11. Once fertile farmland, the excavated landscape of the Most district with smoke rising from the power stations in Ervěnice and Komořany.

conditions for that in Czechoslovakia were in the Ore Mountains. The landscape here thus had to yield to mining. People had to move away. And, mainly, they had to get used to the exploitation around them. The region thus served the people of the whole country. This was a necessary sacrifice made in the interests of the whole.

The social contradictions produced in north Bohemia by the released forces of mining and industry could be balanced out and subdued by the State (until the Second World War rather poorly, but afterwards with increasing success). The mining companies and later even the State could partly heal the increasingly large scars on the face of the landscape, the demolished settlements could be substituted for by new buildings, and it could be demonstrated, ultimately even by means of the monstrous moving of a magnificent church along rails,[217] that the interests of industry were not contrary to the

217   See the chapter 'Most between the past and the future' in the 'Reconciliation' section.

preservation of the cultural heritage. Nevertheless, it was not possible, and to a large extent remains impossible, to cast doubt on, let alone eliminate, the causes of all these phenomena. The increasing extraction of coal appeared to be the essential link in the chain of relations that ultimately ensured the rising standard of living of the population – a cornerstone of the legitimacy of liberal capitalism and of state socialism. That is why the rising standard of living had to be emphasized as an undeniable fact. The pace at which mining developed had changed. And though various political and technical solutions were sought, no alternative to the road already set out on was ever considered.

TECHNOLOGY AND REVOLUTION

Understandably, the Most story is usually perceived through the distorting lens of the Communist emphasis on material aspects of life, which are symbolized mainly by the increasing production of heavy industry. In the previous chapter, however, I sought to demonstrate that this way of thinking was, at least in the industrial regions (particularly where there was mining, like the Most district), dominant as early as the nineteenth century. Apart from these continuities, which enable us to understand why the aims of the authoritarian regime met with the prepolitical expectations of the population, the abstract term 'Communist regime' requires critical analysis from the other side, that is, by means of the individual stages of state socialism. Concerning both the dominant discourses and practice, this period is not as homogeneous as might seem from looking solely at the external political attributes. Examining the demolition of the old Most and the building of the new city, which reflect the nature of the post-Stalinist period, reform socialism, and also normalization, is extremely useful in helping us to understand this better.

State socialism in the Czechoslovakia of the 1960s and 1970s shares with the Stalinist period an emphasis on production, the just distribution of wealth, and a strong State run in an authoritarian manner by the vanguard of the working class, that is, the Communist Party. In other emphases, however, the two approaches to managing society diverge fundamentally. This difference, however, does not consist only in the evident shift in the perception of physical violence, which was, from the point of view of the governing elites, less and less acceptable as a legitimate instrument for holding power or pushing through the interests of the collective at the expense of the individual. From the end of the 1950s onwards, the Stalinist ideal of simply increasing production was sharply in decline. This aim and the instruments for its achievement (mainly directive, charismatic rule), together with manual labour, were replaced, in keeping with the dominant discourse in western Europe and the United States, by emphasis on a rational system of running the economy and society, based on expertise and technological progress.

Already in the 1930s, theorists and historians of science, from various normative positions, were pointing to the fact that science is not simply a discipline aiming at an ever more precise description of reality, but is, rather, mainly a dynamic force reshaping society and the world. Since the mid-twentieth century, it was science, according to these theorists, that would fundamentally change the nature of industrial society.[218]

The model of factory production with its human-controlled machines would be replaced by technologies changing not only the speed and scale, but also the character, object, and function of production. By means of science and the technological know-how derived from it, human beings were meant once and for all to be removed from their 'directly manual, machine-minding, operational and, ultimately, regulatory functions in production proper'.[219] Yet in this process it could not be a matter only of the transformation of industrial or other production. According to theorists of the scientific and technological revolution, the universal transformation of all the productive forces changed the status of human beings and thus also society. The rational world – in which science contributed to the development of technologies that, by means of automation and optimization, were meant to ensure prosperity, a life with dignity, and time for the wide-ranging development of human potential – was supposed to support not only the linking up of the potentials of individuals but also the convergence of what were at that time still antagonistic political or ideological camps. The scientific and technological revolution and the systems of rational management that

---

218 See Bernal, *The Social Function of Science*, and *Science in History*.
219 Richta, *Civilization at the Crossroads*, p. 26.

were emerging as a result of that revolution were thus also supposed to be a guarantee of peace.[220]

The transformation of the nature of the production process, whether we accept the hopes invested in that nature or view it sceptically in keeping with the dystopic interpretation of modernity, typical, for instance, of the thinking of Heidegger and Marcuse,[221] transformed the nature of power regardless of the actual political and economic system. The decisive role of technology, which was supposed to ensure prosperity and determine the form of work and ways of life of humankind, increased the power of those who were inventing technology and controlling it and those who most profited from that development. It is reasonable to see technocracy, a caretaker government, which the scientific and technological revolution lends legitimacy to, more broadly also as government based on the conviction that the management of society is a matter whose individual steps could, with sufficiently complex thinking, be calculated and optimized. In other words, it is not a matter of dialogue, moderated by elections and political parties, or central values and ideas about society, or of a dictatorship of charismatic leaders who, with the help of devoted bureaucrats, lead the people to a glorious future, but of government based on expert leadership and its application, optimizing the individual steps by means of complex calculation of long-term profits and losses. A number of studies by British, American, and French pioneers of this view of the organization of the modern state and society were published in Czech translation in the first half of the 1960s.[222]

---

220 J. D. Bernal, *World without War,* London: Routledge & Kegan Paul, 1958.
221 For more on this subject, see the chapter 'Thinking the Story' in the 'The Story' section.
222 Of period writings, see Peter F. Drucker, *The New Society: The Anatomy of Industrial Order,* (1950) New York and Abingdon: Routledge, 2017; idem, *Landmarks of Tomorrow,* New York: Harper, 1959; Norbert Wiener, *The Human Use of Human Beings: Cybernetics and Society,* Boston, Mass.: Houghton Mifflin, 1950 (published in Czech as *Kybernetika a společnost,* Prague: Československá akademie věd, 1963); of the 'how-to books', see Jiří Řezníček (ed.), *Moderní metody řízení v soudobém kapitalismu,* Prague: Svoboda, 1966. For reflections on the influence

In the United States in reaction to the Great Depression[223] and in western Europe after the Second World War,[224] the discourse about the scientific and technological revolution contributed to criticism of liberalism and to increasing faith in the strong State, enabling long-term systematic planning of economic policy, the fairer distribution of wealth, and the carrying out of grandiose technological and social projects. In east-central Europe the scientific and technological revolution in the political sphere was linked mainly with criticism of Stalinism. In Czechoslovakia, technocratic thinking and emphasis on government based on expertise not only led to a return to humanist tradition and the principle of pluralism, but also formed a cornerstone of reform socialism, one that the normalization elites also adopted to a considerable extent. The emphasis on government based on expert management, optimization, and the possibility of rationally planning the future – which were linked to the scientific and technological revolution – thus formed in Czechoslovakia the breeding ground for the long and otherwise heterogeneous period that began in the mid-1950s and closed at the end of the 1980s.

of technological change on governance and society, see Daniel Bell, *The Coming of Post-industrial Society: A Venture in Social Forecasting*, New York: Basic Books, 1973; and Geoff Crocker, *A Managerial Philosophy of Technology: Technology and Humanity in Symbiosis*, Houndmills, Basingstoke and New York: Palgrave Macmillan, 2012.

223 Among the American government programmes, public work projects, bank reforms and regulations, known collectively as the New Deal (1933–36), one often hears, for example, about the Tennessee Valley Authority. This is a federally owned US corporation that, among other things, built dams providing water and protection against flooding to nine million inhabitants of several US states. The system of dams, connected with the management of large areas of land, began as a federal project. They were planned and built as part of the New Deal but continued into the 1960s. It was seen as a model of rational and productive modernization of a region, and of support for employment and the use of resources. Criticism of the resulting radical interventions in the landscape was expressed only later. See David Ekbladh, 'Mr. TVA: Grass-Roots Development, David Lilienthal, and the Rise and Fall of the Tennessee Valley Authority as a Symbol for U.S. Overseas Development, 1933–1973', *Diplomatic History* 26 (3), 2002, pp. 335–74.

224 For the planning and building of about twenty new towns in Great Britain in the 1960s, see he chapter 'Utopia in Practice' in the 'Utopia' section.

In the early 1950s and late 1960s, it seemed not only to the Communists but also to many of their opponents that in education and science the Communist-led countries were overtaking the capitalist countries. The indisputable victories of the Soviet Union in the space race and superiority in rocket technology seemed to confirm the impression that the socialist system responded better to the challenges of modern technological civilization, which required a strong State capable of investing in education and science independent of volatile markets.[225] But in the socialist countries at that time, technocratic governance based on expert knowledge was actually more a distant aim than a reality.

The 'technological challenge of the Communist revolution' continued in many respects to be ignored in the system of authoritarian government. As early as 1963, the Czech sociologist and philosopher Radovan Richta (1924–1983), inspired by the writings of the polymath J. D. Bernal (1901–1971), and also by the leading thinker on management education Peter Drucker (1909–2005), the mathematician, philosopher, and originator of cybernetics Norbert Wiener (1894–1964), and other American and west European theorists, criticized comrades who were pretending that 'Communism could prevail on a global scale purely by extreme political means, only by the fact that the masses were, by their onslaught, demolishing the old order, without creating new productive forces, without overtaking capitalism in technology and labour productivity'. And he warned that such an attitude 'was reviving the monster of vulgar [...] Communism' and was in fact nothing other than the abandonment of the Marxist perspective.[226]

According to Richta and other champions of the scientific and technological revolution, the time had come at the beginning of the

---

225 Probably the most pro-Soviet interpretation by a west European author in this respect appears in the work of J. D. Bernal.
226 Radovan Richta, 'Máme se polekat vlastního stínu? O technické výzvě komunistické revoluce', in idem, *Člověk a technika v revoluci našich dnů*, Prague: Čs. společ. PVZ, 1963, p. 28.

1960s to surmount 'technological conservativism'. It was now time 'to orient oneself to the most efficient ways of engaging the productive forces of society – automation, chemical engineering, the qualitative restructuring of technology, the utilization of cooperation and combination'.[227] It was time to abandon the fascination with questions of power and the holy cow of manual labour; it was a time of a qualitative shift, which would be ensured by new methods of management, technological innovation, and carefully planned investment in projects for the comprehensive reconstruction of the environment of human life and labour.[228]

In Czechoslovakia since the mid-1950s, however, faith in the liberating power of science and confidence in a technology that would enable a fundamental transformation in the operation of society and the quality of human life were typical not only of the closed offices of leading theorists of the scientific and technological revolution, like Radovan Richta, Jan Auerhan (b.1925), an economist, theorist of automation and important member of the Richta team, the philosopher-aesthetician Jindřich Filipec (1926–2013), and the philosopher and cyberneticist Miloslav Král (b.1930). Beginning in 1956, articles by dozens of specialists appeared in the Czechoslovak press, providing information on the most important aspects of the scientific and technological revolution. In the 1960s, interviews about the influence of technology on human beings and society or about management became popular. Such interviews were conducted not only with experts and politicians, but also with representatives of a wide variety of institutions and with managers of industrial enterprises.

---

227   Radovan Richta, 'Má komunista právo zaspávat technický pokrok?', ibid., pp. 35–47. This article takes issue directly with Stalin's conception of productive forces.
228   The culmination of the work of the interdisciplinary team concerned with the nature and consequences of the scientific and technological revolution in Czechoslovakia was Richta et al., *Civilizace na rozcestí* (1966), which was soon published in English, French, German, Hungarian, Italian, Romanian, Slovak, and Spanish.

'The growing strength of socialism,' wrote Jiří Zeman (b.1926), from the Philosophy Institute of the Czechoslovak Academy of Sciences, as early as 1957, in what was then the widely read *Literární noviny*, 'goes hand in hand with the new achievements of science and technology, chiefly atomic energy, reaction engines, automatic machines.' Zeman was mainly concerned, however, with the last-named factor of progress, cybernetics, and his article was not only one of the first east of the Iron Curtain to present Wiener's work, but also, indeed mainly, it was like a manifesto of confidence in a future formed by developing science and the technologies that science was producing. According to Zeman, humankind was, thanks to science, entering the age of the integration and coordination of all the elements of life in the interest of the whole:

Human knowledge and practice are a struggle with chaos and meaninglessness. The whole development of society is a complicated journey to a brighter and more orderly life. Scientific knowledge of the laws of reality is gradually substituting certainty for uncertainty, orderliness for disorderliness, and coherence for fragmentation [...], it is beyond doubt that cybernetics will help man to achieve social welfare. Developments are, after all, heading inexorably towards the fact that Communist man will master the unrestrained social laws, will learn to control his own thinking and practical activity, and will be the sovereign master of himself.[229]

In a note just below Zeman's long article, the editors of *Literární noviny* informed the readers that with this article they had begun to 'publish essays that seek to acquaint the Czechoslovak public with the new scientific and intellectual impetuses of our age'.[230] In the coming months and years, hundreds of thousands of people regularly

229   Jiří Zeman, 'Člověk a stroj', *Literární noviny*, 18 May 1957, p. 3.
230   Ibid.

read in this weekly about the indivisible link between modernity and Communism, about man prevailing over the forces of nature, about the relationship between technology and revolution, and about the world of 'the people to come'.[231] The period of the first flights into outer space, demonstrating, from the perspective of many people, the superiority of Communist-governed civilization and its greater ability to really make a qualitative leap thanks to the scientific and technological revolution, was a time of infinite optimism, and of course not only in the East.[232] The chorus of cyberneticists, physicists, and sociologists was gradually joined by philosophers and other writers, all of whom shaped the narrative of technological modernity as an instrument for the next phase of the liberation of humankind. In the Czechoslovak public space on the threshold of the 1960s, this narrative became the predominant way to comprehend contemporary society, its tasks, and goals for the future.

The intellectual debates, however, were gradually accompanied by attempts, more or less successful, to actually implement the ideas. In the late 1950s, in connection with the first economic reform and particularly in the 1960s with the second economic reform, the introduction of the 'new system of management' became an agenda, which, at the instigation of the Politburo of the Central Committee of the Czechoslovak Communist Party and the Government, took over essentially every branch. Directors of each important industrial enterprise or agricultural operation had to deal with it. The system of top-down decision-making, to be gradually replaced by a modern system for running the economy, which would support performance, high quality, and initiative, found itself under fire from critics. The authoritative ideas and practical steps of reform were subordinated mainly to the technocratic viewpoint emphasizing the need for expert management in the interest of the whole, 'because truth is not

---

231 František Běhounek, 'Svět příštích lidí', *Literární noviny*, 4 January 1958, p. 3.
232 See Ivan Klíma, 'Nedávno tam sídlil jen Bůh', *Literární noviny*, 15 April 1961, p. 3.

voted on; truth is verified in expert discussion'.[233] This viewpoint, dominating internal debates about the management of the State and society from the end of the 1950s onwards, eventually, in the second half of the 1960s, became the subject of criticism by proponents of the fundamental democratization of politics and economics,[234] as a result of the changed political situation after the Soviet-led Warsaw Pact intervention in August 1968 and the events of the spring and summer of 1969. But the 'technocratic' consensus remained the determining starting pointing of governance in Czechoslovakia well into the 1980s.

Apart from the expert teams, in particular Richta's large interdisciplinary team, which considered at the most general level the consequences of the scientific and technological revolution and the possibilities of its implementation, a whole range of new institutions were established to ensure the efficient management of the economy and society, which was to be based on the latest and most complex scientific knowledge. Among the important ones were the Institute of Management (Institut řízení, originally the Institut pro řízení při vládě ČSSR), the State Commission for Management and Organization (Státní komise pro řízení a organizaci), the Centre (later Institute) for the Development of Automation and Computer Technology (Ústředí [later, Ústav] pro rozvoj automatizace a výpočetní techniky), and, in 1959, the establishment of the Ministry of Technology and the State Committee for the Development of Technology (Státní výbor pro rozvoj techniky), which, from 1963 on, was called the State Commission for the Development and Coordination of Science and Technology (Státní komise pro rozvoj a koordinaci vědy a techniky). A few of these institutions, like the Scientific Research

---

233 Miloš Kaláb, 'Denivelizací k technokracii?', *Dialog: Měsíčník pro politiku, hospodářství a kulturu* 4 (April), 1967, pp. 10–12 and 47.
234 For the duel between the technocratic managerial current and the radically democratic current in reform socialism in the second half of the 1960s, see Karel Kovanda, *Zápas o podnikové rady pracujících 1968–69*, Prague: Ústav pro soudobé dějiny AV ČR, 2014.

Department of Economics and Management of Scientific and Technological Development (Vědeckovýzkumné pracoviště ekonomiky a řízení vědeckotechnického rozvoje), and the Institute for the Scientific System of Economics (Ústav pro vědeckou soustavu hospodaření), were explicitly linked with the newly emerging discourse of the scientific and technological revolution. In 1966, there were about sixty such institutions in Czechoslovakia.[235]

With considerable authority, the leading members of these institutions entered the debate about the national economy. They symbolized the struggle against the incompetent old functionaries and bureaucrats and against the dogmatism of the Party ideologues, and were thus major proponents of the 'managerial' or 'technocratic' pillar of Czechoslovak reform Communism.

The shift from the romanticizing images of people manually at work on the 'building of socialism' to the complex use of resources and strategic planning for the future was visible not only at the central level, but also at the regional level – in the regional and district committees of the Czechoslovak Communist Party, in the national committees and other institutions, and in the regional press. In mining areas, and therefore in the Most district, a distinct continuity is apparent in the orientation to the quantity of extracted tonnes and the rhetoric of production or self-sacrifice. At the same time, however, certain phenomena that had at least until the mid-1950s tended to play a secondary role now came to the fore. Particular political decisions began to be taken to a much greater extent with a view to the long-term plans and strategies developed by experts in the fields of regional and land-use planning and economic development, which were often run by key actors in economic life. The Most district was primarily subject to the 'General Plan for the Development of the Fuels Branch to the Year 1980', which was made, in 1959–60, by

---

235 For a list of these institutions with brief descriptions of them, see the monthly *Moderní řízení*, 1966, no. 1, pp. 89–92, no. 2, pp. 90–92, no. 3, pp. 91–92, and no. 6, pp. 90–92.

officials from the Ministry of Fuel and Power together with experts from the SHD.[236] The individual resolutions about mining followed on from this plan, but so too did the debates about the regional plan of the North Bohemian Basin. Though coal mining remained, as before, the primary aim, to which all other plans and decisions were subordinated, now, in the second half of the 1950s, the approach to the future was considerably more complex. Questions of public health and sanitation, mainly air and water quality, were an integral part of the plan, which the authorities began to consider in the broader context of the socialist natural environment. Measurements, which began to be taken regularly in the Most district from 1959 onwards, confirmed the disastrous state of the air; in the Most environs, industry produced between 450 and 500 tonnes of fly ash daily and the concentration of sulphur dioxide here was for eight months of the year three times above the not very strict limits of the time. Other measurements confirmed a rate of disease of the upper respiratory tract, conjunctivitis, migraines, and other ailments far above the Czechoslovak average.[237] These findings could, paradoxically, provide support for the plans to demolish old Most and to build the new city, which was going to be at a higher altitude and with markedly less pollution.

A typical feature of technocratic thinking, which emphasized the complex and efficient welfare of society and its environment, was reclamation of the landscape after its degradation by mining. Individual attempts, for example, reforesting slag heaps, had been made in previous decades, but the systematic renewal of the land, devastated especially by the surface mining of coal, began in Czechoslovakia, particularly in the North Bohemian Basin, at the end of the 1950s. The founder and, to this day, doyen of reclamation in north

---

236 NA, f. 955 (Ministerstvo paliv a energetiky III, 1960–1963), inv. č. 249, kart. 189, Generální plán rozvoje odvětví paliv do r. 1980. For more on this, see the next chapter.
237 Krejčí, *Most*, pp. 39–41.

Bohemia is Stanislav Štýs (b.1930). A graduate of forestry at Prague, he was hired by the SHD in 1956. In the following years, he and his colleagues carried out detailed geopedological research (to discover the geomorphology of the soils) in all parts of the brown-coal basin, which were to be mined by 1980. Its purpose was to find out the 'pedogenic properties' of the overburden 'as a future soil-forming substratum'. The soils, which 'occur in the overburden of the formation of the North Bohemian Basin', were assessed with a view to their suitability for future reclamation as soils of classes I to VI. On the basis of the research, specialists, led by the young engineer, elaborated the 'General Reclamation Plan' (1959) for the North Bohemian Basin. Regarding the future repair of damages and the exploitability of the land after mining, the plan adjusted both the mining procedure and, mainly, the specific steps to be taken after the individual 'tracts' had been mined.[238] The conclusion of this more than sixty-page study about the research and prospects of reclamation, which Štýs presented at a seminar of employees of the State Environmental Protection Agency (Státní ochrana přírody) in January 1960, reflects the authors' confidence in a world that, though controlled and exploited by human beings, was always improving:

The current results and experience of reclamation already justify our hopes that if we adhere to mainly preventive principles, yet carry out careful biological reclamation of the devastated areas, we can also see the future optimistically in our coalfields. While being economically effective our coalfields can again be beautiful and not harmful to health.[239]

238 Stanislav Štýs, *Problémy rekultivace devastovaných pozemků v severočeském hnědouhelném revíru: Z celostátního semináře pracovníků Státní ochrany přírody*, Teplice v Čechách, 18–20 January 1961, Ústí nad Labem: Vydáno péčí Krajského střediska státní památkové péče a ochrany přírody v Ústí nad Labem, 1961.
239 Ibid., p. 64.

In 1961, people going to Czechoslovak cinemas had their first opportunity, thanks to a documentary film, to learn of Štýs and the reclamation of land degraded by opencast mining. They thus discovered not only that if they wanted to be better off, it was necessary to mine more: 'Coal means life for an industrial country. And we must sacrifice everything for life.' But they were also told that the life of the Most district, sacrificed in the interest of the standard of living of all inhabitants of the state, was not lost. The film presented the 'General Reclamation Plan' for the next twenty years and assured the viewers that modern technology was able not only to wrench millions of tonnes of high-quality coal out of the ground, but also to move away top soil and, with it, thousands of hectares of fields, meadows, and forests and then replace them.[240] Štýs, saving a 'land that was near death,' and contemplating a 'time that even his grandchildren will not live to see,'[241] has appeared repeatedly with similar messages on cinema and TV screens from the 1960s to the present.[242]

The reclamation linked with the Ore Mountains is but one of a number of phenomena that reveal the ambiguity typical of a whole range of expert projects and solutions carried out in the spirit of the scientific and technological revolution. The aim of governance based on expert knowledge is to deal with the world as a whole and to take into account all the factors influencing the future of human beings and their habitat. Governance, relying on technocratic factors, thus has the potential to integrate into prognoses and political practice previously overlooked factors such as health and hygiene, education, educating oneself, the possibility of self-realization, the changing needs and wants of human beings in the modern world, and the protection

---

240 Třikrát o dnešku.
241 Ibid.
242 In addition to Třikrát o dnešku, see the films by Československá and, later, Česká televize, Rekultivace Most (1975), První den stvoření (1978), Zánik a znovuzrození města (1988), and Ekoprůkopníci (2008, particularly the part about land reclamation).

of their environment.[243] To a certain extent, criticism of the one-sided state-socialist orientation to production, including environmental criticism, could thus rely on the scientific and technological revolution. This way of thinking and governing injected the orientation to production and profit with consideration for people in the distant future. The efforts to achieve a more complex conception and to link together the individual problems or phenomena thus opened the way to long-term sustainable development.

The optimism connected with the vision of an optimizable world, however, as is convincingly demonstrated by the reclamation of the devastated landscape, could at the same time justify the systematic exploitation to a hitherto unseen extent. By assuring not only television and cinema audiences but also governing elites that the world could indeed be broken down into little pieces, efficiently taken advantage of, and recomposed, again with net profit, into its original form or even improved, respected engineers and popular actors[244] perhaps did more, from the standpoint of the defensibility of the Most experiment and the possibility of actually carrying it out for several decades, than the managers of the mining companies or the fuel and energy ministers.

Technocratic thinking, based on rationality, efficiency, and cost optimization, and to a greater extent the policies that were based on it, paradoxically are inclined not only to complexity but also to reductionism. That is true also of the Stalinist years. Whereas the revolutionary period of building socialism entailed the intensive use of patriotic themes (with the tangible experience of liberation from social oppression and, mainly, with revolutionary pathos), the world, as a result of economic rationalization and the emphasis on

243 For the connection between the technocratic conception of the world, technology, and ecology, see Crocker, *A Managerial Philosophy of Technology*, pp. 108–12.
244 For example, the actors Miloš Kopecký and Pavlína Filipovská in *Dostaveníčko v Mostě* (Rendezvous in Most), a musical TV programme produced by Krátký film Praha for Československá televize, 1977, broadcast 26 March 1977. Archiv ČT, IDEC 277 531 21604.

expertise, was now reduced to the measurable and the demonstrable. Faced with rigorous economic calculations and rational plans, what had been lived, felt, won by defiance, and underlaid with the experience of charismatic leaders or mining foremen, was now becoming irrelevant. Despite the intentions of the theorists of the scientific and technological revolution, who in their analyses and prognoses were emphasizing the need to involve the most complex network of factors, from economics to the possibility of humankind's self-realization or with regard to the cleanliness and quality of the environment, the emphasis on the measurable and the verifiable usually resulted in the diktat of the language of economic advantage, understandable to all, in other words, consisting of easily comparable figures of financial profit and loss. We can see what such a reduction meant by looking at the key documents and political decisions which opened the way to the demolition of the old town at the foot of Hněvín Hill.

THE DESTRUCTION OF THE CITY
AS AN INVESTMENT PLAN

The demolition of the old part of the town of Most and the freeing up of the mass of coal in its protective barrier pillar with the commencement of mining as planned in about 1967 is necessary, efficient, and economical.

(Bureau of the Regional Committee
of the Czechoslovak Communist Party,
Ústí nad Labem, 1962[245])

As in many other industrialized countries to the west and the east of the Iron Curtain in the second half of the 1950s, the development of the economy, particularly heavy industry, in Czechoslovakia began to run into difficulties presented by dwindling non-renewable resources. Already in the first half of the decade, the mining and consumption of a number of these resources, including coal, had rapidly increased. This trend was amplified during the second five-year plan, from 1956 to 1960, which meant, for the brief period of 1954–55 (orientated to the consumer goods industry), a return to the preference given to heavy industry and the development of a 'fuel and energy' base. Industrial production in those five years rose by more than 60 per cent but, unlike during the first five-year plan, the standard of living of the inhabitants also improved markedly – real incomes rose by 40 per cent from 1955 to 1960.[246] These successes raised unrealistic expectations, in consequence of which, and also under pressure from the top levels of the Communist Party,

245   NA, f. 1593 (Politické byro ÚV KSČ), sv. 365–66, arch. j. 458, bod 4, Některé problémy zrušení starého Mostu a výstavby nového Mostu, Důvodová zpráva byra KV KSČ v Ústí nad Labem ke zrušení staré části města Mostu a uvolnění uhelné substance v mosteckém ochranném pilíři, k výstavbě nového Mostu a dalších náhradních investic, [1962].
246   See Průcha et al, *Hospodářské a sociální dějiny Československa 1918–1992*, pp. 300–01.

the plans and goals of the third five-year plan, from 1961 to 1965, as well as the long-term prognoses, were overly ambitious. The pressure on the current increase in the growth rate, the reduction of the working week, and the rising standard of living eventually led to the economic crisis of 1961 to 1963. The system of management of 1959 fell apart and the economy was run instead by means of stop-gap administrative interventions, which eventually called for more radical reforms.[247] When they finally came, from 1966 to 1968, they contributed not only to economic recovery but also to opening up the space for a broader-based discussion about the political-economic system and society.

The growth in industrial production and the rise in the standard of living (and the growing expectations associated with this) in the second half of the 1950s led to a need to increase the extraction or importation of non-renewable resources. For a number of these raw materials, this was no longer possible because they were in limited supply or inaccessible in Czechoslovakia and because of the tight raw materials inventory in the countries of the Council for Mutual Economic Assistance (Comecon). Czechoslovakia had considerable supplies of its own black and, especially, brown coal, the basic raw material of industrial development, and thanks to technological developments it was easily accessible. Though its share in the overall structure of energy sources was declining worldwide, this trend was slower in Czechoslovakia than in most of the industrial countries. In absolute values, the mining of brown coal rose from 27.5 million tonnes in 1950 to almost 59 million tonnes in 1960 – thus more than doubling in a decade. Czechoslovakia in the late 1950s and early 1960s was the source of almost 10 per cent of the brown coal extracted worldwide and this share increased further, until the end of the 1970s, when 75 million tonnes were mined. In absolute numbers

247 Ibid., pp. 313–16.

of mined tonnes it held fourth place in the world and in tonnes per capita even second place.[248]

Conscious of the key role played by coal in the development of the Czechoslovak economy, the guidelines for the coal industry in the third five-year plan were drawn up in 1959–60. Though these tended to accentuate the need for the efficient processing of brown coal rather than for further increases in extraction (while the plan was being drawn up, a slight surplus of extracted coal over consumed coal was observed), the guidelines mentioned the long-term goal of achieving first place in the world in lignite mining per capita.[249] But what was probably more important for the fate of Most than this five-year plan was the surprising shortage of brown coal in 1960. This one-off drop in supply was a sensitive topic because a chief goal of the five-year plan with regard to lignite extraction was to gain a 'permanent lead' for mining ahead of consumption.[250] Coal was not only a basic raw material for industrial operations; it was also an essential fuel ensuring heat for millions of Czechoslovaks. Its shortage could thus cast serious doubt on the ability of the political and economic system to ensure basic needs. Consequently, the central Party institutions were pushing for a quick fix and also for ways to increase the mining and preparation of coal to ensure that the situation would not reoccur.[251]

In these circumstances in the late 1950s and early 1960s, the SHD management, together with the Most district and north Bohemian regional Party bodies and national committees, debated the intensity and actual course of further mining in the North Bohemian Basin. Mining in the Most district was, however, absolutely essential, for it was the source of more than half of all the lignite mined on Czechoslovak territory. The SHD management long sought to extract all the

248 Ibid., pp. 450–51.
249 NA, f. 1593 (Politické byro ÚV KSČ), sv. 247, arch. j. 328, bod 2.
250 Ibid.
251 NA, f. 1593 (Politické byro ÚV KSČ), sv. 297, arch. j. 381, bod 1.

coal from the 'Most pillar' and to this end pushed for the demolition of the old town, which stood in its way. Even though local political bodies, particularly the Municipal National Committee of Most, were against the plan in the first half of the 1950s,[252] the managers and engineers of the mining company did not abandon it. The SHD general plan of 1957 again included the total extraction of all the coal from under old Most, and the SHD management successfully pushed to have this plan included both in the North Bohemian regional plan of 1958[253] and in the background material for drawing up the general plan for the fuel sector for the period from then until 1980.[254]

Following on from these later conceptions and plans, technicians and engineers of the Ležáky Mine (Důl Ležáky), at the impetus of the SHD management in the first half of 1961, elaborated an almost forty-page report explaining why the demolition of the old town and the complete mining out of the coal deposits below it were necessary. The authors of the report used economic arguments and also expertly referred to the decisions of the key political actors (the Party and the Government), which the SHD plan was supposed to be in keeping with – mainly, that is, the third five-year plan, whose chief goals included improved housing. And it was housing that the SHD was now offering in connection with the elimination of the derelict old town and investment in a brand new city. The alleged necessity to mine all the coal from below old Most was probably a cogent argument, in view of the recent acute shortage of this raw material. But it was less a matter of quantity (for even at the government ministries in Prague it was known that mining was possible in places other than under old Most) than of the conformity of these

---

252 See in the 'Demolition' chapter in the 'The Story' section.
253 See NA, f. 960 (Ministerstvo paliv III, 1963–65), kart. 419, inv. č. 430, Most – Posudek k investičnímu úkolu Koridoru inženýrských zařízení pod Hněvínem v Mostě, 15. 9. 1964.
254 NA, f. 955 (Ministerstvo paliv a energetiky III, 1960–1963), kart. 189, inv. č. 249, Výpis základních ukazatelů generální perspektivy rozvoje do r. 1980; Návrh rozvoje SHR – Most, 28. 10. 1960.

mining plans with the central values of the years of Czechoslovak President Antonín Novotný (1904–1975, President from 1957 to 1968) – namely, economic efficiency and economies of scale. In several pages of the report, the SHD economists point to the advantages of mining the Most pillar, that is, underneath the still-standing historic town and, further, below the railway line and station of Czechoslovak Rail. On this land, according to the calculations of the mining engineers, there was a total of 86,369,904 tonnes of coal reserves. It was therefore necessary to remove and cart away only 54,503,320 tonnes of overburden. (It was unusual that there was less overburden than coal under it.) About twelve metres below the overburden, there was said to be a layer of high-quality coal almost 45 metres thick. The explanatory report states that in addition to the overburden it would also be necessary to remove the town, since it stood in the way of the plan, but, in view of the otherwise outstanding mining conditions, the removal of 6,300 flats and the investment in replacement construction in the new Most should pay off. Another argument was the poor state of housing in the old town, which would allegedly require great investment in other circumstances. By a complicated calculation, the authors of the report then arrive at what is, according to the logic of the report, the incontestable fact that production costs for a tonne of coal in the Ležáky Mine extracted from under Most in the 1970s would come to 60.47 Kčs, but if mining under the town were to begin in 1967, it would cost only 26.58 Kčs.[255] Apart from these key arguments, the report also contains other emphases and points which the power elites would in coming years gradually accept and incorporate into legislation. These mainly concerned moving the preparatory and planning work directly to the new Most, strengthening institutions

---

255 SOA Litoměřice (pracoviště Most), f. SHD – generální ředitelství, spis 440 (Investice: likvidace starého a dostavba nového Mostu, přesun kostela), kart. 1, Důvodová zpráva k záměru na rubání zásob v ochranném pilíři města Mostu a přidružené materiály, June 1961.

of state power by entrusting employees with the supervision of the Most project and by setting up a coordinating commission for the demolition of the old Most and the construction of the new city.[256]

At the impetus of the SHD deputy director, Hojdar, the argumentation of the 1961 report regarding the mining of the Most coal pillar recycled, during that same year, variations on the plan for the demolition of Most, which had been elaborated at the Ležáky Mine, as well as the reports of the resolutions of the Politburo of the Central Committee of the Czechoslovak Communist Party in 1962 and eventually also of a government resolution from the spring of 1964. These ultimately amount to an equation, whose individual factors are (1) evidence of the extraordinarily high quality of the coal under the town, its easy accessibility, and also the possibility of an advantageous spoil tip radically reducing mining costs, (2) evidence of the advantageousness of the demolition of the old Most and the construction of the new city as opposed to the difficult and costly renovation of the run-down historic town, and (3) the overall economic balance, that is, a calculation demonstrating, from the perspective of the national economy, a considerable net profit, which would contribute to the affluence of Czechoslovak society and each of its members. The first part of the equation, as it appears in the demolition plan, reads as follows:

The compact nature of the coalbed of 100,000,000 tonnes of coal reserves is an exception in the North Bohemian Basin; a compact coalbed with similar uniquely advantageous mining conditions (geological stripping ratio/overburden/coal reserves/0.70, average thickness of the seam 23.34 m, average thickness of the overburden 25.02 metres, and so forth) does not occur anywhere else in the coalfield. In addition, this is high-quality coal, in which the proportion of coal with a net calorific value of more than 3,600 kcal/kg is greater than 45 per cent, and coal

256 Ibid., p. 37.

with a net calorific value of between 2,800 and 3,600 kcal/kg is greater
than 38 per cent, whereas, for example, the average net calorific value
of coal from the mining area of Slatinice [a village, 4 km south-west
of the new Most, demolished in 1965–68], is only a bit more than
2,500 kcal/kg, and in the mining areas of Bylany [5 km south-west
of the new Most, demolished in 1978], Třískolupy [a village near Louny,
demolished in 1970], Polerady [a village 6 km south of Most], and Vrbka
[a village, today part of the town of Postoloprty, near Louny]
it is about 2,000 kcal/kg. The complete extraction of the Most coal pillar
will therefore, from the mining standpoint, provide the national economy
with 100,000,000 tonnes of high-quality coal, which can be obtained,
considering the advantageous mining conditions, at minimal operational
costs, using current, tried and true machinery, and, apart from that,
the spoil tip, not taking up farmland, if used fully, will result in savings
of about 500,000,000 Kčs in the costs of transporting overburden.[257]

The second step of the calculations deals with the costs of the whole
investment – first and foremost, the demolition of the town and the
moving of its inhabitants. In other words, these matters were unusual after all, and could not, even in the technological and economic argumentation, be included under the heading 'Removal of
Overburden':

The costs for the demolition of structures in old Most, the buying
up of privately owned real estate, the moving of the inhabitants,
the relocation of cemeteries, and so forth, are considered
in the calculation of the operational expenses of the Most mine at an
average sum of 0.50 Kčs per tonne of coal.[258]

257 NA, f. 960 (Ministerstvo paliv III, 1963–65), kart. 419, inv. č. 430, Most – likvidační záměr
(technická zpráva), červen 1963 (zprac. SHR, důl Ležáky, národní podnik Most – odbor vyvolaných
investic a likvidace města Mostu).
258 NA, f. 1261/0/4 (Předsednictvo ÚV KSČ 1962–1966), sl. 110, Zpráva o efektivnosti
likvidace starého Mostu, n. d. [1965].

The calculation of the costs also had to take into account the obviously very costly construction of a complex modern city – new Most. The authors of some of the documents did not include this huge investment in their overall calculations, arguing that the old town had 'become so decrepit that its restoration would cost more than completing the new construction.'[259] In other words, if Most were not demolished, one would have to invest in its renewal, and so the money for the construction of the new Most should not be calculated as costs that in other circumstances would be unnecessary. Where construction was included in the calculations, only some costs needed to be taken into account – that is, only the part allegedly corresponding to the construction of replacements for the demolished structures of the old town (such as flats, public amenities, the utility corridor).

The triumphant result of the equation deciding the fate of the town and its people was the calculation of the total profit, which was made on the basis of the preceding two steps. According to the 'Report on the Efficiency of the Operation for the Demolition of Old Most, including the Construction of the Most Pit', the more efficiently mined Most coal was expected to take the place of the costlier extraction in deep underground mines, assuming a sales price of 58.34 Kčs per tonne. At this price, the reserves in the Most coal pillar had a total value of 5,190,455,626 Kčs. The economists also added to the assets one million Kčs, which would, in comparison with alternative mining, allegedly be saved thanks to lower costs for the removal of overburden. The costs for the extraction of one tonne of coal were calculated at 15.55 Kčs, that is, a total of 1,383,466,390 Kčs, the costs for the demolition of the town and for moving its inhabitants at 21,000,000 Kčs, and the costs for the replacement construction were reckoned at 2,099,200,000 Kčs. The result was a favourable balance of 2,686,789,236 Kčs. And that was

259   NA, f. 960 (Ministerstvo paliv III), inv. č. 430, sv. 419, Most – demolition plan, June 1963.

the estimate of earnings from the Most pit.[260] No one of course could have calculated what the actual balance would be twenty-five years later, that is, after the demolition of the old town, the building of the new city, and the complete extraction of the coal, taking into account all the changes in price and technology, and the overall conditions.

In dozens of internal documents from the first half of the 1960s, the basic line of argument justifying the gigantic project for the demolition of the historic town, the moving of its inhabitants, the extraction of the coal, and the construction of the new city almost exclusively followed these three steps, which always (no matter how much the included factors and actual numbers differed) triumphantly resulted in a favourable balance. The conclusion that the calculations were heading for was thus unequivocal, utterly indisputable:

> Compared to the slum clearance of other towns, the necessary slum clearance of old Most as a whole has an absolutely special feature. Whereas in other places slum clearance involves only costs, the slum clearance of old Most will provide the Czechoslovak national economy with high-quality brown coal.[261]

This argumentation, which lent the Most experiment an aura of one of the grandest displays of the rational planning, economy, and efficiency of the socialist economic system, was soon recast in a more digestible form, suitable for newspaper articles and other means of informing the public about the reasons for the demolition of the old town. An article in a 1964 issue of the Communist daily *Rudé právo* was probably based on slightly more cautious calculations, when it informed its readers:

> Mining activity in the area where the town has so far stood will have a great economic effect. It is not only a matter of extracted coal.

260   NA, f. 1261/0/4 (Předsednictvo ÚV KSČ 1962–1966), sl. 110, Zpráva o efektivnosti likvidace starého Mostu, [1965].
261   Ibid.

The possibility of placing the overburden into the mined-out seams will save 800 hectares of agricultural land. And despite the great costs for the construction of the new city, mining will have a great economic effect to the sum of almost 1.9 billion crowns.[262]

The same message could of course be formulated more satisfyingly for the reader, for example, in the fortnightly *Zápisník* (Notebook):

We often hear the words 'the treasure under the town' and 'billions under the town'. And one is not surprised, because it is a fact, a pure and simple fact – nothing more. No fairy tale. No fantasy. The pillar of the town, as we say, contains 100 million tonnes of high-quality brown coal, whose value exceeds four billion crowns [...] Is it, then, worth demolishing old Most? It is. There is coal under it. Treasure. Billions.[263]

Not only the author of these lines, one Jaromír Novohradský, but other journalists were also able to recast the economic reduction of the world, a simple equation, into a narrative many people believed. Opening up the 'mining space under Most' was, from the point of view of the SHD engineers and economists, their colleagues at the Ministry of Fuel, political elites, writers of articles in those days, and indeed perhaps even all progressively and rationally thinking people in the first half of the 1960s, utterly necessary. Any other solution had to be exposed as an economic gamble. The irrefutable logic of numbers, investments, and profits left little room for Communist ideology. But it did involve a lot of the modern thinking based on utilitarian rationality and the primacy of technological progress linked with economic growth. The reconstruction of the landscape in the interest of progress, and its absolute subordination to economic interests, was no longer merely one of several possibilities; it was the sole rational way, promising profits to every member of society.

---

262 'Starý Most ustupuje uhlí: 100 milionů tun uhlí pod městem', *Rudé právo*, 8 July 1964.
263 Jaromír Novohradský, 'Miliardy pod městem, *Zápisník*, 26 November 1964, pp. 9–11.

Utopia

within the urban space, using the topography to advantage,
taking the climate into account, and having the best exposure
to sunshine with accessible verdant areas at their disposal.

(Le Corbusier, 'Charter of Athens', 1933[264])

Why not go to Most? Today, part of the new city is surrounded
by woods, woven through with orchards, gardens, and parks,
the likes of which the residents of a big city can only dream of!
When you count twenty TV antennas on the roof of each
of the three-story houses [...] We no longer look with sympathetic
sadness at houses on their last legs. Everyone and everything has
to go into retirement one day. And this old revolutionary town, forever
written into the history of the struggles, must too make way for new life,
progress, and green.

(*Květy*, a woman's weekly, 1958[265])

264 Le Corbusier, 'The Athens Charter', http://microrayon.wikispaces.com/The+Athens+Charter
See also Thilo Hilpert, *Le Corbusiers 'Charta von Athen': Texte und Dokumente*, Braunschweig:
Vieweg, 1984, p. 131.
265 'Ustup černé město městu zelenému', *Květy*, 30 October 1958, p. 8.

A number of the period descriptions of the beauties and advantages of the new Most may now, fifty or more years later, reasonably be seen as part of state propaganda. But even in authoritarian regimes, propaganda is usually not simply one-sided political agitation; in order for it to be effective, propaganda must offer a plausible story.[266] The holders of power were by no means the only source of the publicly accessible documents, some less, some more trustworthy, which report positively on the new Most, especially in the 1960s. Key parts of the events considered in this book took place in the 1960s, when increasingly diverse groups of people were entering the public space that was opening up.[267] It was a time of focused debates, critical commentaries, and attempts to push outwards the boundaries of what could be communicated publicly. Politicians, journalists, and ordinary people of course had to know the rules of the game, but that is no reason to assume that we are unable to discern their authentic positions and opinions through the sediment of censorship and fear.

In the following pages I shall try to convey the experience of reading sources related to the plans for the new Most, its construction, and its reality. Perhaps I will not give too much away when I say right from the start that I will share with you a possibly surprising discovery, that is, that the utopian vision and reality of the new Most, with its emphasis on rational design, improved sanitation, and the solution to the oppressive social circumstances of tens of thousands of people really did, in its day, raise utterly genuine hopes for a better life – and that these hopes contributed considerably to justifying the demolition of the old town – as absurd as it may seem now, fifty years later.

---

266 For more on this matter, see the chapter 'Thinking the Story' in the 'The Story' section.
267 Concerning the unorthodox use of the terms 'the public' and 'the public space' in this work, see ibid.

To comprehend those hopes it is, I believe, essential to demonstrate that argumentation of this kind and its acceptance were not unique to north Bohemia, indeed not even to the countries of state socialism. They were rooted in modern European thinking about society, housing, architecture, and urban planning, and were based both on ideas from western Europe and, with regard to our story, on the intellectual traditions and actual practices of interwar Czechoslovakia.

THE IDEAL CITY

If we look for the roots of the intellectual tradition of the ideal city, which developed most importantly in the nineteenth century, and was successfully transformed into actual programmes and projects in the twentieth century, one has to imagine life in a nineteenth-century European city. The city, particularly the industrial city, at that time, became a place representing all the worsening contemporary problems: extreme inequality, economic exploitation, homelessness, huge social gaps, the absence of basic sanitation, and environmental degradation.

Apart from the bourgeois stratum, that is, the traditional bourgeoisie (entrepreneurs, white-collar workers, intellectuals), most people lived in overcrowded flats occupied by several families, in a wide variety of basement rooms, without sufficient daylight and fresh air, or in makeshift colonies without any infrastructure. Well into the twentieth century, most city dwellers lacked bathrooms; the sewage system was usually an open gutter flowing into the nearest stream or river. The distribution of water and electricity was developed at various tempos and was definitely still unusual in the majority of poor quarters of European cities even in the interwar period. Into the tangle of streets and houses stuck together in the shadow of factory chimneys belching clouds of smoke right onto the city, the sun was often invincible for weeks. In the toxic air and with no access to clean water, people were highly subject to epidemics and chronic respiratory disease.[268]

This situation did not necessarily happen to the same extent in all towns and cities of the industrial regions of Europe. In many places, the situation was not much worse than it had been in the

---

[268] For the situation in nineteenth-century English industrial cities, see Dennis Hardy, *Utopian England: Community Experiments, 1900–1945*, London and New York: Routledge, 2000, pp. 56–60.

pre-industrial period and in a number of towns, moreover, in consequence of state or private social programmes beginning in the last third of the nineteenth century, things gradually did improve. The picture of the poverty of the lower social strata in the growing towns, as in English industrial towns described in the nineteenth century in the works of Alexis de Tocqueville,[269] Friedrich Engels,[270] Charles Dickens,[271] Andrew Mearns,[272] and Jack London,[273] remained, despite small changes, the reality of a number of poor quarters well into the twentieth century. It was these images that became the frame of reference for all critics and authors of utopian projects seeking radical change.

Not only utopian socialists reacted to this situation; so too did urban planners and architects right into the 1960s. Bruno Taut (1880–1938), in his collaborative utopian project for the 'Stadtkrone' (City Crown, 1919),[274] and Le Corbusier in his 'Contemporary City for Three Million Inhabitants' (1922) emphasize the main question of contemporary society – namely, the social standing of people in urban civilization, the main justification for a completely new way of planning and building towns. The specific programmes and projects of the interwar period for a utopia of the rational plan were always accompanied by a utopia of the justly organized society.

It is not by chance that the first notions of the ideal city, as well as realistic plans for a new urban arrangement (like the garden city), were born in England. For it was there that mass urbanization occurred well before other places. In England, about 50 per cent of the

269 Alexis de Tocqueville's description of Manchester in 1835 is quoted in ibid, p. 56.
270 Friedrich Engels, *Die Lage der arbeitenden Klasse in England: Nach eigner Anschauung und authentischen Quellen*, Leipzig: O. Wigand, 1848.
271 Charles Dickens, *Hard Times*, London: Bradbury & Evans, 1854.
272 Andrew Mearns, *The Bitter Cry of Outcast London: An Enquiry into the Condition of the Abject Poor*, London: James Clarke & Co., [1883].
273 Jack London, *The People of the Abyss*, London: Isbister, 1903.
274 Bruno Taut, *Die Stadtkrone*, with contributions by Paul Scheerbart, Erich Baron, and Adolf Behne, Jena: Eugen Diederichs, 1919.

population lived in towns by the mid-nineteenth century, whereas in Germany this number was not reached until the end of the nineteenth century and in France not until 1931.[275] The term 'slum', used today mostly for the poor quarters of South American or African cities, has its origin in Great Britain – in Edinburgh, Birmingham, Manchester, and other towns of the first industrialized county in the world.[276]

✕✕✕

The utopias of the ideal city, which were envisaged as providing an opportunity for a happy life for all its inhabitants, are of course far older than the crisis of the industrial city. They have accompanied European thought from at least the early modern age. Even the first, precapitalist utopias, the best known of which are the those conceived by Thomas More (published in 1516)[277] and Tommaso Campanella (published in 1602),[278] are a remarkable mixture of an emphasis on the emancipation of human beings and the subordination of the plurality of individual ideas about home to the rational whole. Already at the dawn of the modern age, when the development of modern science had still not accelerated technological progress in practice, these utopian visions were accompanied by the notion of technology as an instrument by which human beings could have unlimited control over the world they lived in. In the industrial age, this trend was strikingly intensified in ideas about urban utopias.

For the future development of utopias, Campanella's scientific and technological vision of the city of the sun is more important that More's romantic notions of an ideal island of social justice, which gave

---

275 Helen B. Meller, *Towns, Plans and Society in Modern Britain*, Cambridge: Cambridge University Press, 1997, p. 11.
276 Ibid., pp. 20–22.
277 Thomas More, *Utopia* (1516), Available online in English translation, http://www.gutenberg.org/ebooks/2130 Accessed 28 October 2018.
278 Tommaso Campanella, *La città del sole* (1602). Available online in English translation, *The City of the Sun*, http://www.gutenberg.org/ebooks/2816 Accessed 28 October 2018.

birth to the term utopia. Among the first architecturally elaborated utopias is the Ideal City of Chaux (*c.*1775) by Claude-Nicolas Ledoux (1736–1806),[279] whose plans include features that appear later in cities that were actually built in the twentieth century, ranging from Chandigarh to Most: the emphasis on reducing the density of the built-up areas, the integration of gardens and other green areas into the whole of the town, and the separation of the main transport routes from the zones designated for housing.[280]

In connection with the Industrial Revolution and the worsening social and environmental crises of the industrial city, however, the utopias of the ideal city began to be increasingly urgent and real. The Welsh textile manufacturer and social reformer Robert Owen (1771–1858), the French philosopher Charles Fourier (1772–1837), and the French philosopher Étienne Cabet (1788–1856), and Cabet's followers who designed Icaria, perhaps the most rational and most influential model of the ideal state and town, all started from critiques of the poverty that was worsening in consequence of modern industry and concomitant urbanization. Unlike More and Campanella, spatial arrangement now played a fundamental role for these utopian thinkers of the mid-nineteenth century. Although it was not yet a matter of actual architectural designs, it is not too much of a stretch to call this urban planning.[281]

Especially in the second half of the nineteenth century, when utopian visions of ideal states and cities were subjected to Marxist criticism, a new kind of ideally organized town was also being developed in connection with factory production and consisting of architecture that rejected bourgeois survivals and the sentimentality

279 Anthony Vidler, *Claude-Nicolas Ledoux: Architecture and Utopia in the Era of the French Revolution*, Basle: Birkhäuser Architecture, 2006. Originally published in French, *Ledoux*, Paris: Hazan, 1987.
280 Mechthild Schumpp, *Stadtbau-Utopien und Gesellschaft: Der Bedeutungswandel utopischer Stadtmodelle unter sozialem Aspekt*, Gütersloh: Bertelsmann, 1972, pp. 40–51.
281 Ibid., pp. 52–72.

of Revivalism. These visions of modern architecture and urban planning, which would later be used both in liberal capitalist regimes (like the Baťa-built town of Zlín, east Moravia) and in state socialist regimes (like Magnitogorsk in the Soviet Union and Nowa Huta in the People's Republic of Poland), were first radically formulated, for example, by the Italian visionary of industrial cities of the future, Antonio Sant'Elia (1888–1916):

The decorative must be abolished. The problem of Futurist architecture must be resolved [...] through flashes of genius and through scientific and technical expertise. Everything must be revolutionized. Roofs and underground spaces must be used; the importance of the façade must be diminished; issues of taste must be transplanted from the field of fussy moldings, finicky capitals and flimsy doorways to the broader concerns of bold groupings and masses, and large-scale disposition of planes. Let us make an end of monumental, funereal and commemorative architecture. Let us overturn monuments, pavements, arcades and flights of steps; let us sink the streets and squares; let us raise the level of the city.[282]

The work of Sant'Elia contains all the ideas that theorists and, later, practitioners of modern architecture would develop in the interwar period, and would, after the Second World War, be followed on from in various ways in both western and eastern Europe: the social mission of modern architecture and urban planning, the emphasis on rationality, the application of scientific methods and principles, and the dominant role of technology, and, as a new trend, the fierce rejection of earlier traditions as such. The ideal city was ceasing to be an alternative vision and a dream for the distant future. Instead,

282 From the 'Manifesto of Futurist Architecture' (1914). Emphasis in the original. For a complete online English translation, see https://www.unknown.nu/futurism/architecture .html Accessed 11 November 2018. For the Italian original, see https://it.wikipedia.org/wiki /Manifesto_dell%27architettura_futurista Accessed 11 November 2018.

it was becoming a real competitor to the existing ways of creating an urban space and was soon to be an appeal not merely to update the earlier urbanism, but, if possible, systematically to replace the old and unsuitable with the new, rational, and, thus, perfect.

In the interwar period, it was mainly German, Swiss, and French architects who continued this discourse. In the jointly authored 'La Sarraz Declaration' (1928),[283] whose proposals and conceptions were intensified, made more radical, and, mainly, successfully codified in the field of architecture, urban planning, and building by the Swiss-born architect Le Corbusier (Charles-Édouard Jeanneret, 1887–1965). It was the people in the group around him who were able to implement the vision of the just distribution of housing, a life with dignity, a healthy environment for everyone, and rationally organized space on a large scale in the form of realistic plans and conceptions.

The basic starting points of the architects who gathered together in 1928 at the first International Congress of Modern Architecture (Congrès International d'Architecture Moderne – CIAM) are summarized in the 'La Sarraz Declaration'. The creation of cities and all their elements (urban planning, architecture, and building) had to serve, according to them, the desirable functions of the city, not 'aestheticism' or efforts to impress. These architect-theorists considered housing, work, and recreation (sport and entertainment) to be the only true functions of the city. The instruments to achieve these

---

283 The La Sarraz Declaration of 28 June 1928 was signed by H. P. Berlage (The Hague), Victor Bourgeois (Brussels), Pierre Chareau (Paris), Josef Frank (Vienna), Gabriel Guévrékian (Paris), Max Ernst Haefeli (Zurich), Hugo Häring (Berlin), Arnold Höchel (Geneva), Huib Hoste (Sint-Michiels), Pierre Jeanneret (Paris), Le Corbusier (Paris), André Lurçat (Paris), Ernst May (Frankfurt), Fernando Garcia Mercadal (Madrid), Hannes Meyer (Dessau), Werner Max Moser (Zurich), Carlo Enrico Reva (Milan), Gerrit Rietveld (Utrecht), Alberto Sartoris (Turin), Hans Schmidt (Basle), Mart Stam (Rotterdam), Rudolf Steiger (Zurich), Szymon Syrkus (Warsaw), Henri-Robert von der Mühll (Lausanne), and Juan de Zavala (Madrid). Quoted in Hilpert (ed.), *Le Corbusiers 'Charta von Athen'*, pp. 93–111. Available in English translation online: https://modernistarchitecture.wordpress.com/2011/09/08/ciams-la-sarraz-declaration-1928 /Accessed 28 October 2018.

functions were land subdivision, regulation, transportation, and relevant building codes. Architecture should, they claimed, continue to be seen as part of the life of the State; its principles, essential for the positive development of modern life, should be taught in school, and should, through the mass media, have an influence on public opinion.[284]

Although Le Corbusier regarded himself as the principal author or at least the instigator of the declaration, considerable differences exist between his emphases and its tone. The historical records suggest that the main author of the declaration was actually Hannes Meyer (1889–1954), who came out of the intellectual traditions of German garden cities.[285] That is why the declaration of the first CIAM emphasizes the 'organization of the functions of collective life' rather than their strict separation (which Corbusier, in particular, makes in his writings and plans). The signatories of the declaration also come out against earlier building approaches, though more in theory, but do not explicitly seek to do away with them and thus to adapt the world fully to their own modern vision. Le Corbusier went further, seeking to achieve a fundamentally new conception of architecture:

Contractors' yards will no longer be sporadic dumps in which everything breathes confusion; financial and social organization, using concerted and forceful methods, will be able to solve the housing question, and the yards will be on a huge scale, run and exploited like government offices. [...] An inevitable social evolution will have transformed the relationship between tenant and landlord, will have modified the current conception of the dwelling-house, and our towns will be ordered instead of being chaotic. A house will no longer be this solidly built thing which sets out to defy time and decay, and which is an expensive luxury by which wealth

284 Hilpert (ed.), *Le Corbusiers 'Charta von Athen'*, pp. 102–08.
285 Ibid., pp. 99–100.

can be shown; it will be a tool as the motor-car is becoming a tool. The house will no longer be an archaic entity, heavily rooted in the soil by deep foundations, built 'firm and strong', the object of the devotion on which the cult of the family and the race has so long been concentrated. Eradicate from your mind any hard and fast conceptions in regard to the dwelling-house and look at the question from an objective and critical angle, and you will inevitably arrive at the 'House-Tool', the mass-production house, available for everyone, incomparably healthier than the old kind (and morally so too) and beautiful in the same sense that the working tools, familiar to us in our present existence, are beautiful.[286]

In addition to their fascination with the technological solution to the demand for housing, these reflections often also include the notion that the new architecture will, thanks to a more just distribution and generally accessible opportunities for decent housing, be healthier, not only physically, but also morally. The absence of sanitation, threatening the physical health of the population, acquires a further meaning here as one of the most serious and visible problems of modern cities, particularly industrial ones. For the conception and practice of modern architecture, it was that meaning which would become fundamental as a force (rather than only an environment) leading the town's inhabitants to the correct way of life in future decades.

Probably the most authoritative and most influential document determining the basic prerequisites and rules of modern architecture is the 'Athens Charter'. It was formulated mostly by Le Corbusier in 1933, who first published it ten years later. Its main point of departure

---

286 Le Corbusier–Saugnier [Amédée Ozenfant], *Za novou architekturu*, Prague, 2004, p. 193. Translated from the French original, *Vers une Architecture*, Paris: G. Crès, [1923]. Quoted here from the English, *Towards a New Architecture*, trans. Frederick Etchells, (1931) New York: Dover, 1986, pp. 235–37, 263. This English translation is available online: https://archive.org/details /Towards ANewArchitectureCorbusierLe/page/n1 Accessed 11 November 2018.

is in accord with the 1928 CIAM declaration. The creation of the city was meant to be guided by the idea of justice and equality for all, with a right to decent housing. That could be achieved, it argued, by abandoning aesthetics, showiness, and tradition, and, by contrast, taking advantage of the possibilities offered by modern technology and industry. The Athens Charter[287] is elaborated in detail and, in addition to greater emphasis on the industrialization of construction, it also reflects the fundamental importance its author attributed to order and regularity. Details must be subordinated to the whole, private interest to the needs of society, individual processes to an obligatory plan. The individual zones of the city should be separated; the individual functions (living, working, free time, transportation) should be designed individually (though in interaction). A central role is to be played by forecasting and regulation – when building the city or its parts, the anticipated number of inhabitants and prospects for development over the next fifty years should be the starting points. The ideal density of the population should be calculated on the basis of that, and the results then determine the size and density of the built-up area. In the Athens Charter, Le Corbusier opposes not only tradition, in the form of the historic town, but also, to a considerable extent, Anglo-American modernism, which emphasizes the 'garden city' and lacks strong ties to industrial and technological development and an emphasis on efficiency and forecasting.

What is of relevance to our discussion, however, is the Charter passages in which Le Corbusier and his fellow signatories consider the topic of the old built-up areas and architectural heritage. The part about housing contains not only general rules (such as the layout of the housing blocks in verdant and sunny locations, the setting of

287   'La Charte', in Hilpert, *Le Corbusiers*, pp. 117–66; for an online English translation of the whole Charter, see https://modernistarchitecture.wordpress.com/2010/11/03/ciam's-"the -athens-charter"-1933/ Accessed 11 November 2018. From Le Corbusier, *The Athens Charter*, trans. from the French by Anthony Eardley, New York: Grossman, 1973.

the minimum number of hours of sunlight for each flat, and the diverting of main traffic routes) and the authoritarian statement that 'Unsanitary blocks of houses must be demolished and replaced by green areas' (Pt 36).[288] A passage about sanitation notes that 'entire districts', because of their disastrous lack of sanitation, 'merit only the pick-axe' (Pt 24).[289] In several separate points exclusively about the 'historic heritage of cities', the Charter is in favour of preserving 'architectural assets' 'if they are the expression of a former culture and if they respond to a universal interest' (Pt 66). The fundamental starting point, however, should be present and future needs – and the awareness that the 'whole of the past is not, by definition, entitled to last forever' (ibid.). Only outstanding works, then, should be preserved and in those cases, where the preservation of larger, particularly valuable historic units come into conflict with the needs of the contemporary city, only individual examples of historic architecture should be preserved, as a memory, as evidence, for the future. Any imitation of past styles or the completion of old built-up areas in the original spirit cannot be tolerated. An old built-up area, except for outstanding historic structures, should be mercilessly demolished. The authors of the Charter, led by Le Corbusier, admit that such slum clearances often destroy areas that have developed for centuries: 'This is regrettable, but it is inevitable' (Pt 69).[290]

Tall buildings with large windows, allowing sufficient daylight into the flat, the rational planning of the town, linking all its parts to the necessary infrastructure (such as transportation, water, and electricity), mass-produced houses, enabling the efficient provision of decent housing for wide strata of the population – all the imperatives became an inseparable part of the construction of city districts

288   Ibid., p. 138.
289   Ibid., p. 132.
290   Ibid., pp. 151–53.

12. Le Corbusier's Chandigarh, a problematic but respected work of high modernism.

in the industrialized countries from the 1940s onwards. This trend can also be observed as it developed over time beyond Europe and North America, particularly in connection with the construction of the new regional centres and capital cities of modernizing states. Apart from probably the best-known example, Brasilia, the capital of Brazil (completed in 1960 on what was a desert), the project for the construction of Chandigarh, the newly built centre (largely completed in the early 1960s) of the neighbouring Indian states of Punjab and Haryana, merits attention with regard to the building of the new Most. The main architectural consultant in the creation of Chandigarh was Le Corbusier. In its architectural features and some of its urban-planning elements, the centre of the city is indeed reminiscent of Most.[291] Unlike Most, however, Chandigarh is considered, at least by some theorists, to be a work of high modernism. Yet even admirers of Le Corbusier admitted that in a number of respects the city has failed to meet the needs of the people for whom it was built.[292]

The rapid technological progress, the bad condition of the old cities, made worse in Europe by the ravages of war, also opened the way, after the Second War, leading from individual experiments in modern social housing to the partial demolition (or non-renewal) of old built-up areas and their replacement with vast urban wholes now entirely in the spirit of modern architecture and urbanism – entirely in the spirit of the Charter of Athens. This 'renascence' of European cities grew, on the one hand, out of the criticism of the consequences of capitalism and industrial society in general, but, at the same, it was the fruit of this capitalism and industrial society. Modern mass-produced housing, unlike earlier construction, not only became in essence an industrial sector but it also introduced the principles of efficiency and rationalization into intimate spheres of human life, such as the creation of home.

291 Madhu Sarin, *Urban Planning in the Third World: The Chandigarh Experience*, London: Mansell, 1982.
292 Robert Fishman, *Urban Utopias in the Twentieth Century: Ebenezer Howard, Frank Lloyd Wright, and Le Corbusier*, New York: Basic Books, 1977, pp. 253–57.

UTOPIA IN PRACTICE

The founding and building of towns and cities has been part of human civilization since roughly the third millennium before the Common Era. One would probably find utopian traces in the earliest civilizations as plans for cities in regular forms embodying order or unity. But it is only with industrial modernity that it has become possible to build or rebuild complex settlements for tens or even hundreds of thousands of inhabitants in the course of only a few years. At this point, it is useful to consider two particular lines of development in the construction of cities in the twentieth century as the context for carrying out the idea to demolish the old Most and to build the new city. The first line is the building of new cities closely tied to industrial plants. This was typical mainly of the Stalinist phase of the socialist dictatorships, for instance, the cities of Magnitogorsk in Russia, Nowa Huta in Poland, and Sztálinváros (today, Dunaújváros) in Hungary. The second line is the building of new cities or parts of them at the expense of old built-up areas, which happened in a number of countries (for example, apart from Czechoslovakia, in Great Britain, France, and Germany) in the first two or three decades after the Second World War.

New Cities for a New Age

Nowhere in the world were the economic and ideological conditions ever more suitable for the building of new cities for tens of thousands or even hundreds of thousands of inhabitants as they were in the Soviet Union in the Stalinist period from about 1927 to 1953. The project for rapid mass industrialization was linked with the ideological rejection of the old tsarist or bourgeois city structure, that is, with the need to found and build the socialist city as something utterly new in human history. Collective ownership of the land, an authoritarian and powerful state that was able to invest on a massive scale and move labour by force, together with rapid industrialization connected with the building of a transportation infrastructure, rich deposits of raw materials, and an abundance of space – all of that created highly favourable conditions for the founding and rapid growth of industrial cities.

From 1926 to 1939 alone, the number of inhabitants of Soviet towns increased from 26 million to 56 million.[293] Names like Berezniki, Dzerzhinsk, Karaganda, Kemerovo, Komsomolsk-on-Amur, Norilsk, Novokuznetsk, and, mainly, Magnitogorsk represent but a fraction of the dozens of the new Soviet cities built mostly in the Stalinist interwar years.[294]

The vast majority of these cities were closely linked with the extraction of non-renewable resources like coal, oil, iron and other metals, and with industrial production, that is, the implementation of the idea of a new civilization based on the direct linking of the factory and the city. The number of inhabitants of many medium-sized old towns located in the European part of the Soviet Union increased between five and tenfold at this time. The centres of other towns, including the largest, were radically rebuilt.

Soviet debates between *urbanisty* and *dezurbanisty* (opponents of the influx of people into cities) probably had an influence on limiting the growth of the largest cities, in particular, Moscow, Leningrad, and Odessa, but did not really affect the intensive building of industrial settlements of between 50,000 and 150,000 inhabitants. Gradually, something of a comprise between the two theories began to be reached, based on the concept of the linear city promoted by Nikolay Alexandrovich Milyutin (1889–1942), which attracted

---

293 Kotkin, *Magnetic Mountain*, p. 18.
294 Harris mentions eighteen new large cities with populations of more than 100,000 people, which were connected with the mining of raw materials and the generation of electric power. Near machine-tool, chemical, and other large plants, however, dozens of smaller settlements emerged, tied to industrial operations. Chauncy D. Harris, *Cities of the Soviet Union: Studies in Their Functions, Size, Density, and Growth*, Chicago: Rand McNally, 1970.

attention in the competition for the design of the now legendary Magnitogorsk. The concept of the city divided into six parallel zones (specially assigned, for instance, to transportation, industry, parks, and farmland) suited the intentions of the creators of new cities, because it ensured short distances between where people lived and where they worked (thanks to fields and gardens in the built-up areas), together with easing the transitions of the inhabitants of the new Soviet town (most of whom came from the countryside) from farming to industrial production. Despite these advantages and the strong influence that it had on ideas about urban planning in the 1930s and even later, the linear-city concept was never carried out in pure form, not even in Magnitogorsk, which was ultimately built mostly on plans by the German architect and urban planner Ernst May (1886–1970). The building of new industrial cities in the Soviet Union stimulated the imaginations of urban planners, who, as Miljutin himself admitted,[295] also drew considerable inspiration from leading west European proponents of the modern city, particularly Le Corbusier and Walter Gropius (1883–1969).

The appearance of new districts of Soviet cities built from the beginning of the 1920s onwards reflects the work of Soviet and west European avant-garde architects who were drawing on Functionalism and Constructivism while rejecting any continuity between the past and the present. It also corresponded with the type of building that demonstrated the new way of life and mainly the emphasis on the collective ethos. In addition to arts and leisure centres (*doma kultury*) and kindergartens, there thus appeared the first collective housing, whose revolutionary character consisted more in the

295 Nikolaj A. Miljutin, *Socgorod*, Prague: Knihovna Levé fronty, 1931, p. 8. This is a Czech translation of Nikolay Alexandrovich Milyutin, *Соцгород: Проблемы строительства социалистических городов* (Sotsgorod: Problems of building socialist cities), Moscow and Leningrad: GIZ, 1930.

transformation of ways of life and the relativization of the family as the basic unit of society than in architecture.[296]

At the beginning of the 1930s, however, the development of Soviet architecture (unlike progressive urban planning) turned to the past, to the bombastic range of forms of Neoclassicism and classical antiquity. This turn is already evident in the competition for the V. I. Lenin State Library of the USSR in Moscow and was later definitively confirmed when, in an international competition for the Palace of the Soviets in 1932 the Revival-style design by Boris M. Iofan (1891–1976) won. The years of the most intensive construction of new towns linked with raw-material extraction and industrial production – the 1930s and, to some extent, the 1940s – were thus associated in the Soviet Union mainly with partly monumental Revivalist architecture in the style called socialist realism.[297]

This Soviet tradition, that is, the linking together of modern urban planning and traditionalist architecture referring back to classical antiquity, also strongly influenced the founding of the new industrial cities in east-central Europe in the first half of the 1950s – including Sztálinváros in Hungary, the royal borough of Nowa Huta in Poland, and Havířov and Poruba, both in northern Moravia, Czechoslovakia. From the mid-1950s onwards, however, the influential traces that the Soviet building of 'factory towns' left in the history of the twentieth century were already far less visible. Although the demolition of old Most and the building of the new city took place against the background of the ideological rejection of the bourgeois past, the intensive development of mining and heavy industry, collective ownership of the land, and the authoritarian state, it seems, from the standpoint of urban planning, architecture, and the overall ideological atmosphere

---

296 For more on the boom in avant-garde architecture in the Soviet Union, see Petr Vorlík, *Dějiny architektury dvacátého století*, Prague: České vysoké učení technické, 2010, pp. 84–92.
297 See Selim O. Khan-Magomedov, *Pioneers of Soviet Architecture. The Search for New Solutions in the 1920s and 1930s*, trans. Alexander Lieven, London and New York, Thames&Hudson and Rizzoli 1987.

of the new Most, that the context of the reconstruction and building of towns in the German-speaking countries and in western Europe in the 1950s and 1960s was more important.

A War on Tradition?

The radical programme of the CIAM and the even more radical propositions of Le Corbusier are evidence not only of the development of a phase of European thinking about home and the layout of human settlements. Despite their radicalness, even before the Second World War and mainly in the two or three decades after it, these ideas not only eventually enjoyed considerable recognition but were even carried out and transformed into generally binding rules, regulations, and other norms for modern urban planning, architecture, and engineering. Using the examples of post-war Germany and Great Britain, one can document different ways these visions were made a reality – not only as guidelines for the construction of new urban complexes but also as justification for the partial demolition of historic towns in the interest of building a new, rational world.

In the history of Europe, the Second World War was a new phenomenon, among other things, because of the vast scale of the destruction of built-up urban spaces – first as a result of the prosecution of the war by Nazi Germany, particularly the Blitz, and later, to a far greater degree, in connection with the air offensive by the western Allies, that is, the bombing of most German towns. As a result of air and ground operations, a considerable number of cities in Belgium, the Netherlands, and Poland were also destroyed. 'Of the large cities with more than 100,000 inhabitants in 1939, about 50 per cent of their built-up areas were destroyed on average. In Würzburg the figure was 89 per cent, in Remscheid and Bochum 83 per cent, and in Hamburg and Wuppertal 75 per cent.'[298]

298 Jeffry M. Diefendorf, *In the Wake of War: The Reconstruction of German Cities after World War II*, New York and Oxford: Oxford University Press, 1993, p. 11.

Already in the middle of the war, in 1943, modernist architects associated with the CIAM were involved in complex planning for the post-war rebuilding of European towns. Walter Gropius and Martin Wagner (1885–1957) were emphasizing the necessity of 'large-scale renewal that will be planned for an area of many square kilometres'. Experience demonstrated, they argued, that there was no point in renewing 'individual houses or blocks of houses' separately.[299] A 1947 appeal by leading German architects who had not been compromised by collaboration with the Nazis is even more specific in presenting the attitude to be taken towards historic towns. They assumed responsibility for the 'creation of a new world of life and work' and demanded the 'division of large towns into viable, clear districts by means of new construction'. 'New life should be breathed into' the old town centres and the 'destroyed heritage must not be renewed in an historic style; it can emerge again only in a new form and in the interest of new tasks'.[300]

Although the conservative criticism regarding the post-war reconstruction in the two German states has sometimes discussed the 'second phase of the demolition of German cities',[301] the post-war renewal of Germany, both East and West, is rather an example of the interaction between modernism and efforts to preserve the model of the historic town. In West Germany, a wide range of different approaches were evident, according to type of restored built-up area, region, or period. To put it simply, in the west there was greater willingness, when it came to partly preserved built-up areas, to respect the original structure of a district from the nineteenth-century or first half of the twentieth, which at least partly corresponded to the

299 Conrads, *Programme*, p. 139.
300 Ibid., p. 141.
301 These critics mean the demolition of the remaining parts of old built-up areas and the advocacy of modern urban planning and architecture in the service of industry and motor-vehicle transportation. See Klaus von Beyme et al., *Neue Städte aus Ruinen: Deutscher Städtebau der Nachkriegszeit*, Munich: Prestel, 1992, pp. 29–30.

needs of the modern city, than a partly preserved built-up area in an earlier historic centre. Approaches also changed with time: whereas until the mid-1950s a conservative spirit tended to predominate amongst the population and as part of local politics, resulting in efforts to preserve as much as possible of the appearance of the traditional German towns, the late 1950s and the 1960s are the most typical years emphasizing modernization and turning away from efforts to restore or renew historic built-up areas.[302]

This spirit of modernism gradually waned in the first half of the 1970s, which, throughout Europe, saw an emphasis on the preservation and development of national heritage – and also criticism of a whole range of the concomitant phenomena of organized modernity.

With the interplay of several factors – the actual condition of the built-up areas after the war, the periods of renewal, regional differences, and particular influential politicians and architects –, the situation varied considerably from one German city to the next. Some, like Hanover, Hamburg, Mannheim, Dortmund, and the centres of the industrial Rhineland, acquired a radically new appearance. In other cities, like Nuremberg, Münster, and Freiburg, conservative reconstruction, preserving the original urban fabric and most of the buildings that had not been razed by war, became generally accepted. Restoration of this kind soon met with bitter criticism from architectural theorists and urban planners. Whereas amongst the inhabitants, at least until the second half of the 1950s, support for conservative renewal predominated, the tone of public discussion, led by critical intellectuals and journalists, rejecting the legacy of Nazism and earlier German traditions that had led to it, often criticized the emphasis on heritage preservation, including

---

302 For the advocacy of modernism as part of the renewal and development of German towns in the 1960s, see Klaus von Beyme, *Der Wideraubau: Architektur und Städtebaupolitik in beiden deutschen Staaten*, Munich: Piper, 1987, the chapter 'Modernismus, Postmodernismus und die linke Stadtkritik', pp. 91–94.

the reconstruction of historic towns. We thus come across sharp criticism in which the restoration of historic centres is described as 'window dressing and waxworks' and the 'ghost' of the rebuilding of historic built-up areas, which are 'the more mendacious and antiquarian, the more they approximate historic truth'.[303]

In the 1950s and 1960s, in most of the large German cities, including East and West Berlin, under a variety of often contradictory influences, a compromise of sorts was reached between the modernist and the traditionalist approaches. The most valuable historic structures were restored and the basic urban fabric was preserved. In less damaged areas, particularly in city districts from the nineteenth century, façades were partly restored and original street networks were respected. At the same time, parts of old built-up areas, including largely well-preserved and restored areas, were sacrificed to modern conceptions. Thus, even in the centres of large cities space was opened up in the 1960s for modern urban planning and architecture. Despite 25 per cent of the built-up areas (half of which were in cities of more than 100,000 inhabitants) having been destroyed by war, the renewal and construction of big German towns ultimately meant a search for consensus between the modern and the traditional.

To a considerable extent, Great Britain provides an example of the opposite approach. At the end of the Second World War, at most 6.5 per cent of its built-up areas had been destroyed. The interventions carried out from the 1950s to the 1970s in the urban fabric of British historic towns are largely testimony to the fundamental influence of the policies of rational planning and technocratic approaches to the urban space.

In the nineteenth century, the quickly growing British industrial cities became a synonym for social inequality, poverty, and

---

303 Quotations from articles in the *Rheinische Zeitung* and the *Aachener Nachrichten* in the second half of the 1940s, in Beyme et al., *Neue Städte*, p. 16.

exploitation.[304] By the last third of the nineteenth century, initiatives were taken and political efforts were made to prevent cities from killing their inhabitants. In addition to Prime Minister Benjamin Disraeli's (1804–1881) 'cleansing' of London, these included mainly projects for garden cities, which started a tradition that has survived to this day in Britain and elsewhere. This trend in the planning of modern spaces and housing in the last quarter of the nineteenth century was a reaction to the extreme population density of British industrial cities and to the new possibilities of mass transport. (Apart from the rapidly expanding settled areas, the greatest problem of the garden cities was the using up of vacant land and the great distances between home and work.)[305]

But it was not until the Second World War that a large part of the British public became persuaded of the beneficial effects, indeed necessity, of central planning – economic, military, political, and urbanistic. The inhabitants of Britain seemed to have temporarily come to believe that plans and planning would provide answers to all present and future problems.[306]

The architect and main drafter of the development plans for post-war London, Sir Patrick Abercrombie (1879–1957), who gave the impetus to the influential British 'New Towns' movement, shared with the father of the post-war British welfare state, William Beveridge (1879–1963), faith in the necessity of the collective protection of individuals against the uncontrolled development and risks of urbanized industrial society. Like Beveridge, Abercrombie completely rejected the Victorian belief that poverty and suffering were consequences of individual moral failures. Though neither Abercrombie

---

304   See the chapter 'The Ideal City'.
305   For the west European and American conceptions of urban space and housing during the 'long' nineteenth century, see Anthony Sutcliffe, *Towards the Planned City: Germany, Britain, the United States and France, 1780–1914*, Oxford: Basil Blackwell, 1981.
306   Tony Judt, *Postwar: A History of Europe Since 1945*, New York: The Penguin Press, 2005, the chapter 'The Rehabilitation of Europe', pp. 63–99; Meller, *Towns*, pp. 67–84.

nor other urban planners and architects of that period necessarily considered themselves proponents of the radical left seeking to usher in socialism, they did share the utopian socialists' faith in the importance of a healthy environment, which forms a good society and enables its individual members to lead happy lives.

Abercrombie's main aim in these plans, which for the most part were indeed carried out, was the elimination of unhealthy conditions in the over-populated centres of British industrial cities. This entailed a number of steps – ranging from the demolition of 'defective' quarters, to the moving of industrial plants and populations, to the building of entirely new towns and cities. One aim was to raise the housing standard of British workers to a level that had for one generation been the common standard in the United States. The programme was, however, also the implementation of the utopian dream of building something like islands of a new civilization. New towns, like Stevenage, Crawley, Hemel Hempstead, Harlow, and Hartfield, were built autocratically, without the inhabitants being involved in their planning, but in the firm belief that everyone would ultimately benefit from the results.[307] On the basis of this plan, the British Government, in 1946, intended to build twenty entirely new towns over the next five years. Eventually, by the mid-1950s, fourteen of them were begun, but not finished. By the beginning of the 1990s, when the programme was halted once and for all, 32 new towns had been built in the British Isles. Their average size was, according to the original plans from the 1940s, to reach about 100,000 inhabitants; only those towns whose urban fabric was meant to be built on the existing urban wholes (Northampton, Warrington, Telford) were intended to have more than 200,000 inhabitants. The result was somewhat more modest. Eventually, in most of the new towns, between 20,000 and 70,000 people found

307   See Meller, *Towns*, pp. 70–75.

a home.[308] The building of these modern settlements, inspired both by the ideals of a town divided into zones according to function (as in the Athens Charter) and by the British tradition of garden cities, was from the start accompanied by reservations, especially from the local populations in the affected areas. On the whole, however, at least during the 1950s and the first half of the 1960s, the new towns tended to be judged positively, mainly because they fulfilled the purpose that the whole project had declared from the start – that is, they contributed to the decentralization of the population (especially in and around London) and to regional development, and at the same time created environments that had almost no social tension.[309] More consistent criticism, taking into account the 'soft' factors of neighbourhood and the sense of home, did not appear until the 1970s and then mainly in the late 1980s and early 1990s.[310]

But the spirit of planning and modernization in Great Britain was not usually limited to the building of new housing estates. For example, the necessity of renewing Coventry, London, and several other cities that had been severely damaged by German bombing in the Blitz provided the impetus in 1947 for a vast plan of reconstruction.[311] The aim was to restore only the most valuable architectural monuments, like Coventry Cathedral, whereas the other destroyed old built-up areas were to be cleared, and on their ruins, like phoenixes rising from the ashes, entirely new city centres, clean, airy, functional, efficient, were to emerge, marking a parting of ways with the past. These plans eventually affected not only the bomb-damaged cities of Coventry, Bristol, and Plymouth, but also cities of Northern England – Birmingham, Newcastle upon Tyne, Manchester, and

---

308 Carol Corden, *Planned Cities: New Towns in Britain and America*, Beverly Hills and London: Sage, 1977, pp. 86 and 107.

309 Ibid., pp. 85–122.

310 See Colin Ward, *New Town, Home Town: The Lessons of Experience*, London: Calouste Gulbenkian Foundation, 1993.

311 That was part of the more general Town and Country Planning Act (1947). See Meller, *Towns*, p. 75.

13. The demolition of the historic built-up area of Manchester, England, in the 1960s.

Liverpool. Thus it happened that post-war urban planning changed the face of British towns far more dramatically than the German air offensive.

Whereas in badly damaged Coventry the architect Basil Spence (1907–1976) to some extent succeeded in joining the modern and the historic aesthetic,[312] other architects and urban planners, together with the ever more powerful departments of urban planning at British town halls, did not share this respect for national

---

312 Peter Duignan and L. H. Gann, *The Rebirth of the West: The Americanization of the Democratic World, 1945–1958*, Cambridge, Mass.: Blackwell, 1992, p. 554.

heritage. The vision of the modern town, which had been dominant in the 1950s and 1960s, required sufficient space for grand buildings, public spaces, and, mainly, transport infrastructure. Apart from the demolition of the old districts of the poor, which met with a highly positive response particularly in the industrial towns of the Midlands, the rebuilding projects, particularly in Birmingham and Newcastle, required the demolition of valuable and compact historic built-up areas, thus destroying the social ties amongst the former districts of craftsmen and small shops.[313] Under the influence of the post-war enthusiasm for the modern, clean city, well connected by transport, and thanks to the close collaboration between architects and powerful heads of urban-planning departments, like the civil engineer Herbert Manzoni (1899–1972) in Birmingham and the politician T. Dan Smith (1915–1993) in Newcastle, the vision of the future thus became the present reality. The historic appearance of the oldest industrial towns in the world, the lived-in environments of the past, were irrevocably destroyed even before the wave of resistance rose up in the late 1960s and early 1970s against this way of planning and rebuilding towns.[314] As Le Corbusier put it, this was regrettable but inevitable.

---

313 Meller, *Towns*, pp. 80–81.
314 This was first represented especially by the conservative milieu, in architecture and urban planning, for example, in the New Classicism movement. See Martin Horáček, *Za krásnější svět: Tradicionalismus v architektuře 20. a 21. století*, with an English abstract, Brno: Barrister & Principal and VUTIUM, 2013.

CZECHOSLOVAK VARIATIONS

The materialist view of history teaches us to distinguish between different phases of social history, each characterized by its own way of providing food, clothing, and housing. Such a momentous change is happening in our own time, characterized by the birth of socialist cities and radical reforms in housing designed to satisfy the specific needs of working men and women (best described by the elimination of the old family-type household and its transformation into dwelling beehives), and providing a grand setting for society's development toward socialism. The synthesis of city and housing exerts its mighty influence on other domains of life as well, including ethics and the creative genius of humanity at large. The elimination of the bourgeois ways of dwelling does away with the remnants of the bourgeois 'home' (= way of life) and has delivered a mortal blow to bourgeois psychology and its despotic individualistic mentality. Even a cursory glance at the plans of the new socialist cities and settlements reveals the outlines of the unfolding of a mighty epic; its power signals the incontrovertible passing away of the old world and the birth of a new one.
Energized by the enthusiasm of the workers, socialist settlements and planned production bring us a quantum leap closer to what is popularly called 'the music of the future' and what we call the 'real realm of freedom'.

(Karel Teige, 1932[315])

In the winter of 1924/25, the Architects Club (Klub architektů), in Prague, together with the editors of the short-lived monthly *Bytová kultura/Wohnungskultur*, organized a lecture series about modern architecture. One of the initiators of the project, the avant-garde

---

315   Karel Teige, *Nejmenší byt*, Prague: Václav Petr, 1932, p. 338. For an English translation of this work, see Karel Teige, *The Minimum Dwelling,* trans. Eric Dluhosch, Cambridge, Mass.: MIT Press, 2002. The quotation is taken from pp. 371–72.

theorist Karel Teige (1900–1951), gave a talk on Soviet Constructivism. The names of the other lecturers provide eloquent testimony of the role played by Prague and Czechoslovakia in the international modernist community. For instance, Le Corbusier, Walter Gropius, and the Brno-born Adolf Loos (1870–1933, who was a member of the advisory board of the Klub architektů and of the editorial board of *Bytová kultura/Wohnungskultur*) welcomed the opportunity to acquaint Prague students and professionals with their views. After the lectures, these European stars of modern architecture went to the Café Slavia or the nearby Kavárna Union (a meeting place of Devětsil, the avant-garde artists' and architects' group of which Teige was the leading theorist) to discuss the modern city and the future of housing with Teige, Karel Honzík (1900–1966), and other members of the Purist Four (*Puristické čtyřky*), a group that initially comprised only Honzík, Jaroslav Fragner (1889–1967), Evžen Linhart (1898–1949), and Vít Obrtel (1901–1988). The positions and projects of Le Corbusier and the others were not new to the Czechs – the essays from the volume *Vers une architecture*, which had made famous Corbusier's definition of a flat as a 'machine for living' or the articles from the monthly *L'Esprit Nouveau: Revue internationale d'estétique* published in Paris from 1920 to 1925, were translated into Czech soon after they appeared and the few members of the Czechoslovak intellectual elite who may not have spoken French could get to know them when published in the Devětsil anthology *Život II* (Life II, 1922).[316]

Le Corbusier visited Prague several times and other Czechoslovak cities, including Zlín, in the 1920s, and kept up with the extraordinarily intensive building activity here, particularly in the new Functionalist style, for example, the Trade Fair Palace (Veletržní palác).

---

316 For more on cultural transfer and the Prague Avant-garde, see Derek Sayer, *Prague, Capital of the Twentieth Century: A Surrealist History*, Princeton NJ and Oxford: Princeton University Press, 2013, pp. 144–56.

Prague became a metropolis of modern architecture, and Czech intellectuals and young architects drew on this in their writing and designs. Some Czech left-wing theorists, particularly, Teige, also soon began to distance themselves from the stars of European modern architecture, who were accepting commissions to design luxury homes for progressive businessmen.

Already by the end of the 1920s and beginning of the 1930s, it was clear that, unlike the proponents of a mere 'urbanist revolution', the leading Czech proponents of modernism did not intend to abandon the close connection between the new architecture and social utopia, that is, between the new architecture and the revolutionary transformation of society as a whole, including restrictions on, or abolition of, private property. Modern architecture, argued Teige, 'was never supposed to become merely a new formal aesthetic formula, but was from the beginning conceived as a vehicle for changing the socioeconomic environment of humanity'.[317] Le Corbusier's designs, both built and unbuilt, were in this connection criticized as manifestations of how 'his radical technical ideas are tamely adapted within the context of today's social and economic conditions'.[318] Some members of Teige's circle considered Le Corbusier's assumption that it was possible to avoid social revolution by means of rigorously rational urban planning and construction to be an expression of servility towards the existing power hierarchy. Amongst Czech architects and theorists, even though this was an extreme, minority position, it could not be ignored.

Both for proponents of a purely technological approach, compatible with capitalism, and for the heralds of social revolution, the fundamental challenge remained how to ensure decent (that is, comfortable and healthy, yet affordable) housing for everyone. In other words, the challenge was how to solve the housing crisis as one of

317   Teige, *Nejmenší byt*, pp. 24; *Minimum Dwelling*, p. 13.
318   Ibid., p. 143; p. 145.

the most pernicious manifestations of poverty in which a large part of the population was forced to live.

If in this book I ask how it was possible to justify the demolition of a historic town or where the roots of the modernist utopia in post-war Czechoslovakia lay, the housing crisis of the 1930s is truly of central importance. This was a time in which the generation that would later give shape to the socialist Czechoslovakia of the 1950s and 1960s came of age. In consequence of the long-term trends, that is, the production of social inequality, characteristic of the capitalist system, or of urbanization, and also the acute economic crisis, most members of the proletariat lived in poor, even degrading conditions.

The considerable emphasis that Czech, especially Prague, theorists and modern architects put on the necessity to solve the social crisis may have been related also to the markedly more problematic situation in the large towns of Bohemia and Moravia-Silesia (in comparison with western Europe and especially with Germany). In Prague, at the beginning of the 1930s, one-room flats constituted almost 30 per cent of the housing stock and were occupied by one fifth of the population. The vast majority of the occupants were families, at least of two generations – for example, at that time more than half of Prague working-class families lived in one-room flats. In Berlin, such flats constituted less than 8 per cent of the housing stock and were occupied by about 2 per cent of the population.[319] Less than one tenth of Prague working-class flats were equipped with bathrooms and about a fifth had lavatories – the others mostly used a common toilet on the same floor or elsewhere in the house (but even that was unusual); workers and other socially needy people usually had no bathroom at their disposal.[320] If a whole family was able

319 Stanislav Holubec, *Lidé perferie: Sociální postavení a každodennost pražského dělnictva v meziválečné době*, Pilsen: Západočeská univerzita, 2009, pp. 121–23.
320 Ibid., p. 109.

to live in a one-room flat of their own with daylight and a common lavatory in the corridor, that was already quite an achievement. Tens of thousands of the inhabitants of large Bohemian and Moravian towns lived in far worse conditions.

What did this housing at the bottom of the ladder look like? First of all, there was a wide variety of makeshift workers' colonies. In Prague, where the situation was partly documented, about 10,000 people lived in such colonies in the late 1920s and early 1930s. Most of them were unemployed or were people who had come to the city looking for work in the previous ten or fifteen years.[321] These makeshift colonies lacked any infrastructure or sanitation; their inhabitants lived in a wide variety of abodes, ranging from wooden one-room huts to disused railway carriages.

Elsewhere too, in addition to the makeshift colonies and temporary abodes on the outskirts of town, that is, in the built-up parts of the cities, conditions could be appalling. Basements, attics, or individual rooms in larger flats were sometimes occupied by several generations. It was not unusual that a room intended for one or two people was rented out to between five and ten – its inhabitants slept in shifts, and the regime of the flat was thus adapted to the regime of factory production. In such flats, where people slept dressed in rags on plank beds and children slept in wooden washtubs, not only illness, but also growing frustration spread, and relations between the 'tenants' worsened. Housing was reduced to a place to get some shut-eye, and for these groups of people, especially the long-term unemployed, incomeless single mothers, and the disabled, privacy was a commodity that could hardly be associated with a room in such a flat.

It was these circumstances that led Czech social critics, theorists, and socially conscious modern architects to come up with radical designs, solutions, and visions. Many believed that it was impossible that

---

321 Ibid., pp. 131–37.

such conditions could be changed in the existing economic system; some of them, like Teige, believed that the old blocks of flats were so linked to the exploitation of tenants and their subtenants that in many cases it would be necessary to demolish them completely:

> Many of our cities are too old, with old districts decaying and ready to fall down; old houses are run down and are close to collapse, and indeed some have already collapsed [...] All over Europe, we still live in ancient, tumble-down houses [a] hundred years old and older, built so badly that they will not be able to last much longer. Any disturbances of their old walls during attempts to rehabilitate these old houses may cause their collapse. Other old houses are dirty and unhealthy, lacking light and air, and by modern standards are not fit for habitation. In certain old quarters tuberculosis has taken deep root. Here, it may not be sufficient to pull the houses down: doctors suspect that in order to disinfect these breeding places of germs, the only remedy now available is to burn them down to the ground; well, perhaps one day they will be decontaminated by shrapnel, gas, and bombs.[322]

The solution that was supposed to take the place of the 'old house' was, according to Teige, the principle of 'the smallest flat' (*nejmenší byt*, also translated as the 'minimal dwelling') – that is, an inexpensive space, as small as possible, which every family would have for itself (even a poor working-class family) or other intimate community. Such a space would consist of a living room with a bedroom – other functions (cooking, eating, relaxing, bathing, a place for children to play), as known from the large homes of the bourgeoisie or nobility, would be provided collectively for a large number of 'individual flats or units'. This was essentially the idea of collective or collective housing, which, though carried out in several cases in a somewhat altered

---

322 Teige, *Nejmenší byt*, p. 58; *Minimum Dwelling*, p. 54.

form in post-war Czechoslovakia, was never accepted on a large scale.[323]

An example of alternative modernist thinking about architecture, urban planning, and urban living in general is provided by the ideas of Karel Honzík. He was influential not only in the interwar years, but also in the public and specialist debates about architecture in the 1950s and at the beginning of the 1960s. As a member of the Purist Four and as the originator of many Functionalist projects he is usually mentioned as a typical example of an interwar Avant-garde architect. Whereas in his early writings he focuses chiefly on form and particularly the rejection of ornament (inspired by Loos), his articles from the 1930s and 1940s are remarkable criticisms of some modernist dogma, without, however, rejecting the progressive standpoint. Honzík thus, for example, distances himself from Teige's idea of the 'smallest flat',[324] emphasizes the 'inhabitability' (*obývatelnost*) of a town, and revives the function of the classic town square.[325] He also criticizes the cult of technology and particularly the destructive influence of the motor-car on city life. In his more

---

323 The best-known examples is the collective-housing project (*kolektivní dům*, popularly shortened to *koldům*) in Litvínov, north Bohemia, built from 1948 to 1958 on plans by Evžen Linhart, an erstwhile member of the Avant-garde art group between the two world wars, Devětsil, and Václav Hilský (1909–2001), a proponent of the architectural section of the Left Front (*Levá fronta*). It was preceded by the collective-housing project built from 1948 to 1950 in Zlín, Moravia. See Oldřich Ševčík and Ondřej Beneš, *Architektura 60. let: 'Zlatá šedesátá léta' v české architektuře 20. století*, Prague: Grada, 2009, pp. 91–94. For a look at everyday life in the Litvínov collective housing, see Josef Jedlička, *Kde život náš je v půli se svou poutí*, Prague: Československý spisovatel, 1966; recently published in English as *Midway Upon the Journey of Our Life*, trans. Alex Zucker, Prague: Karolinum Press, 2016. See also Lenka Kužvartová, 'Kolektivní bydlení v 2. polovině 20. století: K realizovaným kolektivním domům v Československu', M.A. extended essay, Charles University, Prague, 2012. The full essay and an English abstract are available online: https://is.cuni.cz/webapps/zzp/detail/123029/ Accessed 28 October 2018.

324 Today we see that the idea of the "minimal" flat will need some adjusting. The State or the municipality must guarantee its citizens "optimal" flats, not "minimal" ones if they are determined to solve the housing question.' From the essay 'Tvorba prostředí', written in the 1930s and published in Karel Honzík, *Tvorba životního slohu: Stati o architektuře a užitkové tvorbě vůbec*, Prague: Václav Petr, 1946, pp. 70–92, here p. 73.

325 See 'Obyvatelné město', *Přítomnost* 15, 1938, pp. 348–52.

general reflections, he even rejects the modernist 'faith in matter and reason', which had ceased to take into account the power of what lies 'beyond the horizon of objective reality' (*věcnost, Sachlichkeit*).[326] The Honzík of the 1930s and 1940s thus embodies an intellectual tradition full of contradictions, a tradition he and many of his followers continued in the 1950s and 1960s, often in contradictory ways, from praise for rational socialist planning to moderate criticism of Functionalism to emphasizing environmental aspects.

The rift between capitalist adaptations of modernist architecture and the emphasis on architecture as an instrument of socialist revolution, formulated most pointedly in Teige's writings, did not of course take place only along the boundary between Czech proponents of modernism and Le Corbusier. In Letná and other parts of Prague and also in Brno, progressive private investors built Functionalist blocks of flats and some social-housing projects, like the residential district Na Babě, in Prague, which eventually resulted in housing for rich clients, without helping to solve the living conditions of most of the inhabitants of the city. In reaction both to the rich bourgeois strata's increasingly greater acceptance of the Functionalist style and to the luxury Functionalist houses built in Czechoslovakia and elsewhere in Europe, part of the Czechoslovak avant-garde decided to make it clear as a group that these developments were not, in their eyes, carrying out the mission of modernist architecture. The Left Front was established, whose members included many architects, like Jiří Kroha (1893–1974), Karel Janů (1910–1995), and Jiří Štursa (1910–1995) – the last two of whom, together with Jiří Voženílek (1909–1986), established the Progressive Architectural Group – people who would later have a fundamental influence on urban planning and architecture in Bohemia and Moravia-Silesia in the 1950s and even, partly, the 1960s.

✕✕✕

326 Karel Honzík, 'Za obzorem věcnosti,' *Kvart* 1, 1930–31, pp. 29–32.

One of the focal points of the debates about the function of modernist architecture and the mission of the modernist town became the planning and construction of Zlín, east Moravia, built by the owner of the Baťa shoe factory, Tomáš Baťa (1876–1932). Zlín is a point of intersection of several phenomena, which would, decades later, influence the project of the new Most. In addition to the architectural conception of key buildings in the spirit of Functionalism, what is also important here is the close tie between industry and the modern city. In this sense, Zlín is a capitalist central European form of the Soviet city-factory, like Magnitogorsk. Unlike the project of new Most, which would be carried out twenty-five years later, Zlín urban planning was inspired not only by the French school but also, indeed mostly, by American and British garden cities.

In the mid-1920s, when its modernization began, the town of Zlín consisted of nothing more than the rapidly growing Baťa factory surrounded by temporary wooden structures. Ten years later, Zlín was a modern rationally organized town consisting mainly of multi-storey buildings in the centre and a large built-up area of small family houses. The emphasis on the single-family home (semi-detached, of two or four units) stemmed from the basic idea of the founder of the new town. It also stemmed from the rural nature of the area from which most of the employees came. That is also why the original designs included the possibility of the employees' farming their own land.

The decision to make Zlín a modern company town, which was eventually carried out in the late 1920s and early 1930s, had been taken even before the founding of the Czechoslovak Republic in late 1918. During the Great War, when, thanks to wartime contracts the number of Baťa employees grew from 400 to 4,000, it became clear that the small town of Zlín could not meet the needs of the factory. The employees lived partly in old poor-quality houses or in makeshift dormitories. Their accommodations did not even meet the low health standards of the time. Consequently, Baťa entrusted one of the most distinguished Czech architects of the first half of the twentieth century, Jan Kotěra (1871–1921), with elaborating a development plan for the future city. Kotěra's plans, inspired by the ideas of Ebenezer Howard (1850–1928) and his garden city, and Tony Garnier (1869–1948) and his *cité industriele* were taken up in the mid-1920s by Dušan Jurkovič (1868–1847) and František Gahura (1891–1958). The development plan elaborated by Gahura at the beginning of the 1930s anticipated that Zlín, which then had a population 30,000, would become a city of 100,000, composed into the green areas of the Podřevnicko Valley (Podřevnické údolí). The jury of the housing competition announced by the Baťa firm in 1935 included not only leading Czech architects, but also, for example, Le Corbusier, who visited Zlín a few times and was one of its admirers.[327]

Zlín was divided into individual zones for work, living, services, recreation, and education. The inhabitants – most of whom were Baťa employees and their families – were assigned accommodations on the basis of their position in the company hierarchy and their marital status. The employees with families, depending on their positions, thus lived in large and small single-family houses or semi-detached houses of two or four units. Single men and women (if they had not reached a high position in the hierarchy) lived in large dormitories of two kinds: halls of residence, called *internáty*, for young apprentices, and lodgings, called *svobodárny*, for more highly qualified young adults. The halls of residence were, apart from their low standards (one room shared by more than two people), closely supervised, with strict rules and a daily regime. The other kind of lodgings, the *svobodárny*, had at most two people per room, and many of these employees each had their own room. Even though 2,000 family houses were built in Zlín in the interwar period, their occupants

327 See Ladislava Horňáková, 'The Building of Interwar Zlín: Its Beginnings and Time of the Greatest Development,' in Ladislava Horňáková (ed.), *The Baťa Phenomenon: Zlín Architecture, 1910–1960*, Zlín: Regional Gallery of Fine Arts, 2009, pp. 57–93.

definitely did not constitute the majority of the town's population. To the idyllic picture of Baťa's town one must add the fact that production was largely based on both the unskilled and the skilled labour of young single men and women who were satisfied with the low-standard housing and highly supervised life in the dormitories or at least with the somewhat more decent accommodations in single or double rooms of the Zlín *svobodárny*.

Although the whole Zlín organism served mainly the gigantic business plan – that is, ensuring a steady source of skilled labour, increased profits for the Baťa business, and a return on investment in its buildings and land –, one can see in spheres other than architectural or urban-planning many parallels with later new towns of socialist Czechoslovakia. After the Second World War, the paternalism of company towns like Zlín was replaced by the paternalism of the socialist state, with similar benefits and risks. In Baťa's Zlín, as in other company towns, there was a clear interest in the workers' welfare and an effort to create the best possible living conditions for them. But the authoritarian approach also had its dark side.[328] Tomáš Baťa, who became the mayor of Zlín in 1923, bought up all the town land and had complete control over its subdivision. Until his death, in 1932, he was the sovereign ruler of the town and its development. He concentrated decision-making power over 'his' town in his own hands to an extent unparalleled even in the socialist dictatorship. Unlike in the north Moravian mining town of Havířov in the 1950s or in Most in the 1960s and 1970s, in Zlín no complicatedly negotiated compromise was required amongst the collective institutions of power, their individual parts (like the Central Committee, the Regional Committee, the Municipal Committee of the Communist Party), or between them and the state administration (the district and regional national committees) or between the political and

---

328 See Ondřej Ševeček, 'Socio-spatial Aspects of Zlín's Urbanization,' in ibid., pp. 37–55.

the economic spheres (like the Ostravsko-karvinské doly [Ostrava-Karviná Mines] or the SHD).

With regard to its architectural and social aspects, Zlín is unique in Czechoslovakia as an example of replacing an original small town with a modern rationally planned city, derived from the needs of industry. As a city that was establishing something like a new social order, Baťa's Zlín can reasonably be seen as a modern urbanist and social utopia in practice. Although this was a utopian project compatible with liberal capitalism, its inspiration for post-war projects in Czechoslovakia is indisputable, though never stated, whether in its complex planning, division into zones according to function, or the overall enlightened despotism of its political and economic elites.

✕✕✕

In connection with the political milestones of the years 1938 (the Munich Agreement and the Second Republic, 1939 (the beginning of the German occupation followed by the beginning of the Second World War), 1945 (the Liberation), and 1948 (the Communist takeover in February), there is a general tendency to perceive the thinking of the First Republic, from 1918 to 1938, including ideas about the public space, and the reality of the lives of the people living there (for example, the way Zlín operated) as something that existed within a closed period. Though Zlín was continually developing even during the war (under the supervision of the same architects) and afterwards, including after the Communist takeover (without the better-known architects, yet to a large extent based on their plans for many years after), this is even more true of the ideas of the interwar avant-garde. Teige, stigmatized by the new power-holders as too radical a modernist and an alleged 'Trotskyist', was silenced after the Communist takeover and died soon afterwards, yet figures like Honzík, Fragner, Voženílek, Janů, and Štursa shaped the debate about architecture and space, mainly urban space, in the 1950s and often well into the 1960s. It was largely the avant-garde architects of interwar Czechoslovakia who created the intellectual environment in which the vision of the new Most was born in the late 1950s and early 1960s.

Yet, after 1948, the post-war debate about architecture, urban planning, and the new towns developed in Czechoslovakia, paradoxically, with a number of detours and returns. The period of social revolution and the building of socialism, from the standpoint of a number of modernists, was seen as the gateway to making their dreams and visions come true. In its first phase, the period was marked mainly by a return to tradition.

Criticism of Functionalism and Constructivism, conforming to the Soviet environment, which during the 1930s returned to Revivalist architecture, could to some extent follow on from the interwar left-wing architects' departure from the formalism of modern Corbusierian architecture (which, according to them, had failed to solve the essence of the problem, that is, the lack of decent housing for the poor). 'Purism, Constructivism, and Functionalism,' wrote Honzík in the mid-1950s, 'were not based on a clear *Weltanschauung* [...], the connection with the *Weltanschauung* of Marxism-Leninism was tenuous, and if it at first seemed to exist, it became increasingly clear that the trends suited capitalism [...].'[329] Honzík would also follow on from his criticism of his own ideas in the interwar years, in which he distanced himself from the modernist dislike of ornament;[330] in the 1950s, he did not scruple to call the rejection of ornament 'purist dogma' from which architecture should now distance itself, just as it should now also distance itself from the anti-traditionalism promoted by the Functionalists and Constructivists.[331] The traditional, Revivalist use of elements on façades was, however,

---

329 Karel Honzík, *Architektura všem*, Prague: Státní nakladatelství krásné literatury, hudby a umění, 1956, p. 153.
330 See Karel Honzík, 'Toporná modernost', *Pásmo* 2 (1925–26), pp. 43–44.
331 Honzík, *Architektura*, p. 154.

defended by Honzík and other architects, mainly with regard to the ageing of buildings, though arguments were made about 'national folk art' as a fundamental source of inspiration.

The adoption of Revival styles, which in the Soviet Union were pushed through mainly after the conservative turnaround in the mid-1930s, thus led to a paradoxical development in Czechoslovakia. For architecture, the revolutionary period of state socialism – characterized in many spheres of life by the sundering of traditional social, economic, and cultural bonds and the creation of completely new structures – meant grandiose projects, for instance, the Ostrava district of Poruba and the town of Havířov. [332]Yet, with regard to style, it was the most conservative architectural wave since 1918. The Revivalist façades, colonnades, and the pathos mostly bring to mind Neoclassicism, a style without particularly marked national connotations for Czechs and Slovaks. This is another paradox in the story.

As has been demonstrated by the American historian Kimberly Zarecor, socialist realism never won widespread support amongst Czechoslovak architects. Few people had the courage or the need to reject this trend outright, the way Teige, for example, had done, comparing socialist-realist buildings to the architecture of Nazi Germany.[333] The term 'sorela', a portmanteau of the words 'socialistický', 'realismus' and 'lakomý' (Zdeněk Lakomý, 1914–1995, an architect loyal to socialist realism, who profited from side-lining former Functionalists like Voženílek and Janů) was originally meant ironically but came to be used privately by architects as shorthand.[334] This is further evidence of a growing distance from the style, particularly

---

332 For more on Havířov, see Ana Kladnik, 'The Formation and Development of the Socialist Town in Yugoslavia and Czechoslovakia, 1945–1965', PhD thesis, University of Ljubljana, 2013.
333 Karel Teige, *Vývojové proměny v umění*, Prague: Nakladatelství československých výtvarných umělců, 1966, p. 59.
334 Kimberly Elman Zarecor, *Manufacturing a Socialist Modernity: Housing in Czechoslovakia 1945–1960*, Pittsburgh: University of Pittsburgh Press, 2011. The whole book is available online: https://chisineu.files.wordpress.com/2014/02/manufacturing-a-socialist-modernity.pdf Accessed 28 October 2018.

by the older generation of modernists, amongst whom Kroha, a life-long proponent of Marxism-Leninism, was a rare exception. Kroha was not merely the main planner of the Slovak town of Nová Dub-nica;[335] he was above all the central figure in Stavoprojekt, a large state-owned planning office in Stalinist Czechoslovakia. In addition to Lakomý and Kroha, Vladimír Meduna (1909–1990) also personi-fied socialist realism in Czechoslovak architecture. Kroha's pupil, he was the chief planner of the continuous urban areas in the new, socialist towns around Ostrava, particularly Poruba (later incorpor-ated into Ostrava) and Havířov.[336]

The Stalinist and the traditionalist rejection of modernism did not last long in Czechoslovakia. Whereas in the late 1940s and early 1950s purely modernist buildings like the collective housing (*kol-ektivní domy*) in Zlín and Litvínov, were still being erected, only a few years later, with the first signs of turning away from socialist realism in the Soviet Union, discussion began – at first, cautiously and then, from 1956 onwards, intensively – about the rehabilitation of Functionalism. And there was also increased criticism of socialist realism in architecture. The close bond between the Revivalist archi-tectural intermezzo, Stalinism, and the Soviet Union, however, had created a special context in which the return to modernist architec-ture could become an expression of opening up to the West – and thus also, in a way, to the architectural and urban-planning forms of Marxist revisionism. In Czechoslovakia, in addition to the return of the sidelined older generation of left-wing modernist architects (like Janů and Voženílek), the way was now opened up for the youngest generation, who would soon shape architecture and urban planning, especially in the 1960s, but also often well into the 1970s.

---

335 The socialist town of Nová Dubnica, in central Slovakia, was built on plans by Kroha from 1951.
336 See Martin Strakoš, *Nová Ostrava a její satelity: Kapitoly z dějin architektury 30.–50. let 20. století*, Prague and Ostrava: NPÚ and ÚOP v Ostravě, 2010.

In September 1955, the Czechoslovak architects Josef Havlíček (1899–1961) and Karel Stráník (1899–1978) attended the official sessions of the CIAM in La Sarraz, Switzerland. Thus, seven years after all official contact had been broken between an organization that a number Czechoslovak architects had once drawn inspiration from but official Czechoslovak circles after 1948 had labelled merely a group of Western individualists, contacts were re-established. It took another four months, however, before *Československý architekt*, the fortnightly of the Czechoslovak Union of Architects, published any substantial report about the renewal of work with the CIAM.[337] Even before the end of 1955, however, readers of this periodical were encountering critical comments about several Soviet buildings, the individualism of architects, formalism, and things that were considered useless. The authors of these articles, who were architects and urban planners, emphasized mass-produced buildings, mass construction, and economic factors. Though readers would not yet see the terms Functionalism or Constructivism here, at least not in a positive context, the turn way from decorative Stalinist Revivalism was more than evident.

The repeated establishing of contacts with the world of Western architecture also meant a return to First Republic modernist traditions. The ending or suspending of the careers of the proponents of socialist realism in architecture, like those of Lakomý and Kroha, was only a less important side-effect of this change. What was far more important was the assertion of the discourse and practice which determined architecture and urban planning in Czechoslovakia at least until the end of the 1960s and, to a considerable extent, even into the 1980s.

For architecture itself, the departure from socialist realism was a watershed. In essence, the ideological criticism of Stalinism,

---

337 Karel Stráník, 'Navazujeme opět na spolupráci se CIAM', *Československý architekt* 2 (4), 24 February 1956, p. 4.

which gave strength to the return of modernism to architecture and urban planning, could also lead, and in fact often did lead, to the rejection of a whole range of arguments pointing out the risks of Constructivism in practice, such as too much sunlight and excessively hot rooms, resulting from the dogma about ribbon windows, the problem of ageing buildings with smooth, unarticulated façades, lack of diversity, and the debased aesthetics of urban built-up areas designed according to unified purist rules and constructed with mass-produced prefab units.

In 1956, in connection with the opening up to Western trends, the periodical *Architektura ČSR* published a detailed description of an assembled French-type prefab concrete panel building, originally designed by the civil engineer Raymond Camus (1911–1980) for a housing estate in Le Havre. This type would in later years be decisive for the development of Soviet towns, whereas in this respect the Czechoslovakia building industry was following on from local traditions – primarily the Baťa system, whose structural elements were, already in the late 1940s and early 1950s, further developed in Zlín, now called Gottwaldov (after Klement Gottwald [1896–1953], the first Communist President of Czechoslovakia), but also in Bratislava and in Prague. Czechoslovakia was thus, with France, part of the avant-garde in the construction of prefab concrete panel buildings, which were fully developed here already in the late 1950s and early 1960s. In that respect, the turning away from socialist realism meant a certain acceleration in their construction, but the close bond between industry and architecture was typical of the whole post-war period, both to the west and to the east of the Iron Curtain, despite of ideological trends.

Even with regard to thinking about the mission of architecture, the turn away from socialist realism did not of course mean a repudiation of all its starting points. Both of the ideological streams shared the emphasis on the future and on the moral mission of architecture; urban planning, in particular 'by creating an environment, was supposed to contribute to the education of Communist man and woman, to foresee the future forms of his or her material and cultural life, and to accelerate their becoming a reality'.[338] But apart from this utopian assessment, the architectural thinking of the second half of the 1950s was returning to Le Corbusier's idea of the house as a 'machine for living', although Czech and Slovak architects tended to distance themselves from such a radical reduction, and some even warned against an excessively technocratic conception.

'Science' and 'forecasting' were the terms that in future would gradually form the keystone between the technocratic and the utopian conception (and prevent slipping into either of the extremes). 'Questions of the urban-planning forms of a socialist settlement' were in future supposed to be solved 'on the basis of scientific forecasting of the development of life and its forms', 'in close connection with the development of the economy of socialist society'.[339] The close link between the future development of towns and the needs of contemporary and, mainly, future society shaped the attitude of specialists and the general public both to contemporary building and to the urban-planning and architectural legacy of the past.

As in the countries of western Europe, the general public was especially divided when it came to questions about the future of architecture, urban planning, and housing. Apart from radical proponents of modernism (and the demolition of dirty and cramped old towns), critics began to speak up in the late 1950s. Whether basing themselves on Revivalist socialist realism or on earlier traditions, these critics joined the debates on theory, but mostly spoke out in reaction to the newly built continuous urban areas, especially housing estates. The most common targets of criticism were the lack of services, the problematic layout of public space, the absence of foot

338 J. Klen, 'Bytová výstavba na Ostravsku', *Československý architekt* 5 (15–16), 30 August 1959, pp. 4–5.
339 Eduard Staša, 'O urbanismu a perspektivách rozvoje společnosti', *Československý architekt* 4 (12), 14 June 1958, pp. 3–5.

paths, or excessively small, cramped flats. In a public opinion poll published in the monthly *Literární noviny* in 1958, one reads, for example, the following messages to the 'planners':

> Please recall that a flat is not only for sleeping in or getting dressed in, that people spend their whole lives in it [...] For whom are things like fridges, washing machines, radio/record players produced, for whom are books written, if there is no room for them even in future flats? In modern flats, the walls are still taken up by windows and doors, and so there really isn't room for anything [...] It is obvious that in 29-square-metre flats, where a three- or four-member family is supposed to live, there isn't room even for a musical instrument, books, or toys. Do we want to disqualify a family from everything beautiful? [...] Did the planners consider that they would be demanding a greater area for garages rather than designing an environment for the inhabitants to live in?[340]

Apart from the usual complaints about the cramped nature of modern flats (and, by contrast, opinions in defence of their construction as the only possible quick way to provide at least some housing to hundreds of thousands of people who until the 1950s had been living in makeshift circumstances, or to young families living in flats with the parents of one of the partners) or about their lack of functionality (because, for instance, they had insufficient or no sound insulation) and various things going wrong (such as leaks), there was also more general criticism. Usually, however, it did not express basic scepticism about modern architecture. The criticism of some aspects of the revived Functionalist trend (unattractive façades and the general suppression of aesthetics) was usually mixed with astonishment that modern architecture and technologically rational solutions were implemented so slowly and inconsistently:

---

340 The section 'Kultura bydlení a architektura', *Literární noviny* 7 (2), 11 January 1958, p. 9.

New flats contain numerous archaisms. New houses are unsightly, depressing, they mar the landscape [...] The readers expected [...] at least to find out why a building from 1937, as opposed to its descendent from 1957, is a true pioneer of housing, why to this day kitchen sinks are still at knee-level, which means that a woman doing the washing up has to bend way down, why the façades are not plastered and painted suitably for the smoggy Prague air, what opinions are decisive for the rejection of progressive designs in favour of architectural monsters, why construction is so slow, why in the age of plastics bricks invented by Assyrians are still used, why a twentieth-century style which has become standard all over the world cannot make its way into our country, whereas in the twelfth and thirteenth centuries, when masons wandered from job to job, new Gothic elements were able to travel a distance of thousands of kilometres in five to ten years [...] Really, dear architects, [...] you have your union, your universities, it is therefore up to you to teach the institutions of public administration to adopt the correct standpoints, to discredit incompetent self-seekers, to instruct juries and to stand up everywhere for the interests of those who have to live in your houses and cities. The only thing the clients have is money. The responsibility for how it is spent is ultimately yours.[341]

Architects and urban planners used to answer criticism and attacks of this kind mostly by pointing out the complicated situation that the Czechoslovak building industry had been led to by the emphasis on the search for traditions and Revivalist façades in connection with socialist realism, which now, after 1956, was completely spurned. Even for them, the search for the right architectural expression was a markedly complicated manoeuvre between the Scylla of the Revivalist styles of the Stalinist period and the Charybdis of the alleged formalism of Western Functionalist architecture. For the uninitiated public, the situation was even less clear; considering that it took

---

341 Jiří Mucha, 'Hlas spisovatele', *Literární noviny*, 18 January 1958, p. 9.

several years from the designing of a building or urban area to its actual construction, the buildings and complexes with colonnades and ornamented façades, which had been banned by that time, were erected in the second half of the 1950s, from Ostrov nad Ohří to Poruba and Havířov to Nová Dubnica in Slovakia. Despite the criticism of small flats and a gradual turning away from radical plans for collective housing, it was also at this time that people were moving into similarly experimental buildings. Also with regard to the economic possibilities, planners and architects were forced to make a wide variety of compromises.

It was now, in the late 1950s and early 1960s, that an unprecedented opportunity to build an uncompromisingly modern city for 100,000 inhabitants, unspoilt by having to take into account any existing historic built-up area, presented itself to a group of young architects. It was an opportunity to distance oneself forever from the period of socialist realism and to take advantage of the inspirations both of interwar Czechoslovakia, personified by their teachers, and of contemporary western Europe. It was an opportunity to combine the advantages of Functionalism with the possibilities provided by the planned economy and egalitarian society, which emphasized equal – and decent – housing for all. An opportunity arose to build a modern city on greenfield land, to build the new Most.

CITY OF ROSES[342]

14. Most as a green city (a view from a temporary tram terminus) 1970s.

The new Most today has the reputation of being a big Communist concrete housing estate drowning in social problems. It has the reputation of a place no one wants to live in and where, consequently, only the poorest live, because they have no other choice. Through

342 This chapter is not intended to be a history of the urban planning and architecture of the new Most. The ideas from which the new city were born, its character and the picture that I will attempt to sketch out, however, together constitute one of the essential steps in the argument of this book. Concerning the creation of the new city, the most detailed source of information so far remains Krejčí, *Most*. For the architecture and urban planning of the new Most in the context of the architecture of other towns of the North Bohemian Basin, see Jana Zajoncová, 'Architektura a urbanismus Mostu, Litvínova a Teplic, 1945–1989', MA dissertation, Olomouc, 2011. A critical historical treatment of the new Most has yet to be written.

this lens, a depiction of the beauties of the future town, from the 1960s and 1970s, according to which only this city would provide the inhabitants of the old Most with a decent life, may seem like mere Communist propaganda, concealing the true state of affairs, or even as cynicism. But that is not the case.

Despite the weak environmental and historical consciousness of the population in the borderlands and despite the widespread consensus about the need to mine and produce more, the power elites of state-socialist Czechoslovakia realized that both radical intervention in everyday life and the discomfort that the demolition of old Most would entail would have to be compensated for with a vision of better days ahead, not only in abstract numbers of the economic use of the whole operation, but also in the concrete offer of a better life for those who in consequence of it would lose their home. The new Most unambiguously became this distant aim, a city of the future, a city of social justice, a city of roses, which was supposed to substitute (and indeed did substitute) for the historic Most that had been destroyed.

In their day, the utopian vision and, later, reality of the new Most seemed to be the opposite to what they seem today, fifty years after the fact. The emphasis on rational design, the improvement of sanitation, and the alleviation of the difficult social circumstances of thousands of people contributed substantially to justify the demolition of the old town and they raised hopes for a better life. But as should be clear from the preceding chapters, argumentation of this kind, like its reception, was not exclusive to north Bohemia, indeed even to state-socialist countries. It stemmed from a deep-rooted tradition of modern European thinking about society, housing, and architecture, drawing both on west European inspiration and on the intellectual ideas and practice of interwar Czechoslovakia.

Between Stalin and Le Corbusier

The teachers' hair turned grey from that, especially Professor Čermák's.
He was supposed to lead the project to socialist realism but he was
a Functionalist [...] And we were Functionalists. In our last years
of school we had to do sorela, but almost no one except for a few Party
members believed in it.

(Václav Krejčí, the chief architect
of the centre of new Most, 2012[343])

Initially, the new Most was not built as an independent city planned
in the spirit of modern urbanism and architecture. Rather, it was
built as two housing estates on the edge of the old mining town,
planned in the conservative style of Stalinist-period socialist realism.
In the history of Czechoslovakia, the first half of the 1950s saw the
most intensive development of industrial towns. A number of older
cities, like Ostrava, Sokolov, and Ostrov nad Ohří, rapidly expanded,
whereas others, like Havířov and Nová Dubnica, were established
on greenfield land.[344] The larger of the two Most housing estates,
Podžatecká, began to be built in 1951 (after the Stalingradská čtvrť,
built from 1947 to 1950).[345] It was thus only one of those grandiose
plans. Built of sturdy brick houses, into which about 10,000 people were gradually moved, the Podžatecká housing estate was not
paid as much attention as, say, Havířov or Nová Dubnica, partly
because, in view of its satellite character, it lacked the showy central space typical of Stalinist architecture. Aesthetically, however, it
greatly resembles the built-up areas of Havířov and other Czechoslovak towns or parts of towns which were established in this period.

---

343 From the author's interview with Václav Krejčí (2012), 45 minutes (in the author's archive).
344 See Zarecor, *Manufacturing a Socialist Modernity*, pp. 113–76, and Kladnik,
'The Formation', pp. 101–57.
345 SOkA Most, f. 207 (ONV Most II, 1960–1975), inv. č. 858, ev. j. 317, 'Budoucí vývoj města
Mostu (původce MěNV Most), 13. dubna 1951.

15. The Podžatecká housing estate still as a suburb of the old Most, 1950s.

Old Most, though somewhat hard to reach for the inhabitants of the new housing estate below the Žatecká street at the south foot of Hněvín Hill – many of the mining families had to go more than fifteen minutes to the nearest shop –, was still a centre of local government, shopping and so forth. By this time, it was already expected that a whole new town would be built, with a centre on the other side of the new housing estate from the still-standing old town. Nevertheless, Podžatecká is the largest housing estate built in the spirit of Stalinist realism in the North Bohemian Basin.[346] Both housing estates, the Stalingradská čtvrť and the Podžatecká,

---

346   Jaroslav Malý, 'Starosti, jež bychom nemuseli mít', *Práce*, 15 February 1957.

offered comfortable flats to almost the same number of people as had hitherto lived in the historic part of Most. These were mainly medium-sized flats, but there were also smaller units (so-called *svobodárny*) for single young miners or other workers. Some of the new inhabitants had moved here from old Most or from demolished nearby mining settlements, but there were also people who had come from all over the country. The SHD's pressure for the demolition of the villages and towns of the region and eventually also old Most, together with the large number of job opportunities in Most and its environs, underscored the necessity of solving, as soon and as well planned as possible, the construction of the new Most as a compact urban unit. According to the baseline plan of 1958, it was meant for a population of 100,000 people.[347]

These plans began to take shape during the second half of the 1950s and culminated in an architectural and urban-planning competition for the centre of 'New Most'.[348] In 1959, when the competition was announced by the North Bohemian Regional National Committee in Ústí nad Labem, the Czechoslovak debate about architecture had already fundamentally turned away from the principles promoted in the first half of the decade.[349] The Stalinist version of socialist realism in architecture was now seen as a blind alley and its proponents had either been sidelined or had to reorientate themselves once again to modernist purism. The heralds of modernist architecture from the older generation were coming back on the scene and, at the same time, the younger generation, who had never accepted sorela, were now, in the period of de-Stalinization, coming to the fore and were looking mainly to Western models.

347 For a detailed discussion of the development of individual baseline plans of the new Most from 1945 to 1958, see Karel Strejc, 'Urbanistické postřehy z Mostu', *Československý architekt* 4 (19), 14 September 1958, p. 4, and Petr Jančárek, 'Most město budoucnosti', *Lidé a země*, June 1957, pp. 241–43, here 243.
348 In the documents related to the architectural competition, that is, at the time when old Most was still standing), New (Nový) really is written with a capital N.
349 See the previous chapter, 'Czechoslovak Variations'.

The task of the competition for the centre of the new Most required architects and urban planners to create 'the basis for a definitive project for the construction of a new urban centre and main transport routes of the city, which will be economical and practicable'. The newly built centre was supposed to 'correspond to the importance and prospective size of 100,000 inhabitants of the city of Most, which is not only the main city of the district, but also, indeed first and foremost, an important political, economic, social, and cultural centre of the North Bohemian Basin.'[350] The assignment set the number of hectares and urban pattern of the new town, but not its architectural style, that is to say, the design of the individual houses and their aesthetics. Nevertheless, the socialist-realist blocks of the Podžatecká housing estate, built in the 1950s, which the projects of the centre of the new Most were supposed to follow on from, began to be seen critically. Architects and town planners were cautiously but increasingly making it known that the current style of construction was no longer desirable; the authors of articles in specialist periodicals wrote that the blocks of residential houses from the first half of the 1950s did 'not make a favourable impression', because construction had been dictated by 'short-term plans of the times' and also reflected 'various architectural views of the post-war period'.[351]

It was not by chance therefore that all the designs submitted in the competition, without exception, unambiguously drew on the tradition of interwar Czechoslovak modernism and current west European debates about Functionalism and Constructivism.[352] The jury, composed of leading Czechoslovak architects of all generations, assessed mainly the urban planning, the volumes of the individual

350   SOkA Most, f. 208 (ONV II, 1960–1975), inv. č. 873, ev. jedn. 332, Soutěž na řešení středu Mostu, Návrh na usnesení.
351   Miloš Mandík, 'Most: Výstavba nového a likvidace starého města', *Československý architekt* 10 (15–16), 18 August 1964, p. 4.
352   Krejčí, *Most*, pp. 28–31.

buildings (including a hotel, a theatre, and the building of the District National Committee) and their functionality with regard to their purpose.[353] In the two-round competition, the jury eventually selected the project submitted by the studio of young architects led by Václav Krejčí. He drew inspiration chiefly from his teachers in the Faculty of Architecture at the Czech Technical University (ČVUT), in Prague, a number of whom had been leading architects in the interwar avant-garde. He was attracted by a style that only a few years earlier had been stigmatized in Czechoslovakia as 'cosmopolitan'. Years later, Krejčí recalled how, with the help of acquaintances, he managed to get the bi-monthly *L'Architecture d'aujourd'hui* sent to him, and how reading it regularly influenced his attitudes and opinions.[354] The inspiration of west European modernism was not, however, found only in hard-to-access sources; at the latest beginning in 1956, specialist Czechoslovak periodicals, particularly, *Československý architekt* were reporting in detail on works by Western architects which had been erected in places ranging from Brazil to France to India.

The plans for the new Most were thus born during the general turning away from Stalinist architecture, as opportunities for collaboration with west European Constructivists and Functionalists were opening up and prefab housing began to be mass produced. The form of the project, the nature of the erected buildings, and the ideas that the architects and planners themselves used to discuss the new city of Most bear a striking resemblance to the ideas of Le Corbusier and some of his projects, for example, the one for Chandigarh, in North India, a brand-new administrative city of the united states of Haryana and Punjab, which he worked on from 1951 to 1965.[355]

353 SOkA Most, f. 208 (ONV II, 1960–1975), inv. č. 873, ev. jedn. 332, Soutěž na řešení středu Mostu.
354 Krejčí, *Most*, p. 19.
355 See Ravi Kalia, *Chandigarh: The Making of an Indian City*, New Delhi and New York: Oxford University Press, 1999, or Vikramaditya Prakash, *Chandigarh's Le Corbusier: The Struggle for*

The new Most was now being planned as a separate city without the historic town. Indeed, the fate of the old town was uncertain, to say the least, already when the new city was first being conceived in the late 1950s and early 1960s. The new city was therefore designed as a 'compact structure of a residential area and other zones each with a separate function'. The separation of living from other functions (especially the zone of industrial production in Velebudice and Sedlec, but also, for example, the hospital area and the recreational zones on the edge of town) was intended to ensure the highest quality of life for the inhabitants of the new Most. Through traffic, by motor car and rail, was integrated into the utility corridor running along the outer edge of the city. The north-south road, called třída Budovatelů (Builders [of Socialism] Avenue), and the east-west road running from the foot of Hněvín Hill to the railway station became the transport axes of the town. Though rather conservative for the 1960s, that solution was functional with regard to the future development of motor-car traffic.

Modernity in Postcolonial India, Seattle: University of Washington Press, 2002.

16. The centre of the new Most in the early 1980s. The třída Budovatelů (Builders [of Socialism] Avenue) and the partly erected Municipal National Committee building on the right.

Local government, the arts, social events, commerce, and offices were meant to be concentrated in the city centre. On the basis of the assignment of the competition, which was expanded, adding other requirements in 1960–61, a theatre, a hotel, a restaurant, a café, a post office, a department store, the buildings of the District National Committee and the Municipal National Committee, an arts and community centre, a cinema, banks, a delicatessen, a network of specialized shops, an office building, and the Mining Construction building were to be built where fruit trees had so far stood above an artificial lake. Until the second half of the 1960s, a bitter struggle was waged over the volumes of the individual buildings, between the construction companies and the architects, who were trying to anticipate the needs of the inhabitants and the local government of the still non-existent town by comparing similar housing estates in Czechoslovakia and abroad.[356]

In practice, the construction of the centre and other districts of the new town preserved the urban layout, but the precise siting of the individual buildings changed and so too did the volumes. The architects were thus unable, for example, to get a large shopping centre approved or to find contractors able to erect certain buildings using the originally intended technology. The most basic departure from the original ideas was that the city centre was meant to be finished and fully functional by about 1975, but was not in fact ready until roughly ten years later. The city, built in the spirit of late 1950s and early 1960s urban planning and architectural ideas, thus did not begin to be a truly functional unit until the first half of the 1980s.

Both for the experts and for the inhabitants, the absolutely key aspect of the modern city was sanitation. Today, fifty years later, the emphasis on the airiness of the new Most may well seem, in the context of polluted north Bohemia, like a bad joke or at least a paradox. But in those days, the architects, urban planners, and other experts

356 Krejčí, *Most*, pp. 184–85.

argued using meteorological measurements and other scientifically demonstrable facts. In the new Most the number of days without sunlight because of fog (and thus with higher concentrations of toxic fumes and dust) was markedly lower than in the area of old Most at the bottom of the North Bohemian Coal Basin.[357] The new town was supposed to have better air quality than old Most thanks to its being ten times bigger in area and with enough open spaces and wide straight roads through which not only cars but also air could circulate.

Cleaner air in new Most was also meant to be ensured by large parks and other green spaces. A key element of the urban conception was the sixty-hectare urban forest called Park Šibeník, running from the edge of the city right into the centre. A unique feature of north Bohemia was that the trees planted in Šibeník had to be chosen (in collaboration with land reclamation specialists) with regard to local air pollution – only sturdy species could grow and survive here.[358] But it was not just a matter of a central park; great emphasis was also placed on smaller green areas and in particular on flowerbeds. Most would become the 'City of Roses': in the course of the 1960s and 1970s tens of thousands of rosebushes were planted every year,[359] with the aim of an astonishing 200,000 planted by 1975.[360]

---

357 A 1962 report of the Bureau of the Ústí nad Labem Regional Committee of the Czechoslovak Communist Party mentions the dreadful climatic conditions and air pollution in old Most and notes that the number of days of sunlight here had declined to a mere 30 days a year, whereas the number of smoggy days had risen to 100. According to the report, the amount of sulphur oxides and dust in these circumstances was between five and ten times beyond what was then the rather high permissible maximum. NA, fond 1261/0/43 (Kancelář 1. tajemníka ÚV KSČ A. Novotného /1951–1967/), č. 193, kart. 146. According to studies of the Czech Hydrometeorological Institute from the first half of the 1960s, the climatic conditions in the new town of Most were considerably better (on average, fifty per cent better visibility, the smog here usually lifted after sunrise, and so on). According to the experts, this also had a fundamental influence on strikingly reducing the risk of air pollution. See Krejčí, *Most*, p. 41.
358 Krejčí, *Most*, p. 99.
359 15,000 roses were planted in 1966 alone. See 'Kronika města Most'. For excerpts, see http://www.mestomost.cz/kronikymestamostuzlet1966az1970/d4867 Accessed 10 December 2018.
360 'Město, které se stěhuje', *Zápisník* 21/1972, pp. 22–26.

Roses became a frequently used emblem of the new Most, appearing in a number of newspaper and magazine articles[361] as well as in popular documentary and feature films.[362] Green, whether in the form of urban forests or flowerbeds, became one of the most striking and frequently employed arguments justifying the replacement of the historic town with a new town. One of the first such narratives was by Jura Sosnar (1914–1989), published even a few years before the decision to demolish old Most. His 1958 article, in the weekly *Květy* (Flowers), of which he was deputy editor, was entitled 'Black Town Give Way to the Green Town!'[363]

From the point of view of the builders of the new town and the political authorities, sanitation played another role, the kind Michel Foucault (1926–1984) later described at a general level in his writings on the disciplinary nature of modern society as being like a jail without physical violence or on the construct of the categories of health and sickness.[364] The new, clean, rationally laid-out, well-lit, and safe city was meant to have an educative influence on its residents and their everyday lives. Its healthy and orderly environment would, the urban planners and local politicians believed, also change the residents' habits and eventually shape their spirits. The new Most was therefore depicted as the opposite of the old town, which had been

361   See 'Most, město uhlí a růží', *Svět v obrazech*, 25 September 1971; 'Most, město růží', *Květy*, 23 June 1973; 'Proměny naší současnosti: Od metropole měsíční krajiny k městu růží', *Naše rodina*, 22 February 1978.
362   .See *Dostaveníčko v Mostě*.
363   Jura Sosnar, 'Ustup černé město městu zelenému', *Květy*, 30 October 1958.
364   See Michel Foucault, *Surveiller et punir: Naissance de la prison*, Paris: Gallimard, 1975 (published in English as *Discipline and Punish: The Birth of the Prison*, London and New York: Alan Lane and Random House, 1977), and especially *Naissance de la clinique: Une archéologie du regard médical*, Paris: Presses Universitaires de France, 1963 (published in English as *The Birth of the Clinic: An Archaeology of Medical Perception*. London: Tavistock, 1973). The relationship between the urban space and its social consequences has been researched by urban historians with regard to the linguistic turn and the spatial turn, particularly in the 1980s. See Henri Lefebvre, *The Production of Space*, trans. by Donald Nicholson-Smith, Oxford and Cambridge, Mass.: Blackwell, 1991. From the French original, *La production de l'espace*, Paris: Éditions Anthropos [1974].

described as filthy paradise of criminals, disturbed individuals, and alcoholics.[365] It was meant to become the home of upstanding citizens who would look after their environment.

In this respect, the new Most was a typical example of a town built in the spirit of modern urban planning and architecture, a number of which were built in eastern and western Europe in the 1960s and 1970s. But unlike the new towns built in the same period, for example, in the South of England, Most has several special features.

The first special feature is the fact that the new town of Most had replaced the historic settlement whose name it had taken over, and explicitly saw itself as its continuation. The attitude to history and to the old town were, as we have seen, ambivalent. On the one hand, the old town was rejected and the sunny future was supposed to take the place of the filthy, poor past (as in Sosnar's article, 'Ustup černé město městu zelenému'). On the other, we see affection for the history of the mining town, an effort to save some of its historic monuments, and a wide variety of references to its 'glorious past'. Regarding the main topic of this chapter, however, we have to answer the question of the extent to which the existence of the historic predecessor of the new city was projected into its urban planning and was explicitly reflected in its streets. Although the plans for the new Most and its architecture were made somehow in opposition to the historic built-up areas (for example, the emphasis on air quality, public space formed with regard to motor-vehicle transport rather than pedestrians), old Most at the same time, surprisingly, played the role of an important model in part of the collective memory of its inhabitants, which was not meant to be erased.

The three town squares of the new Most were intended to echo the urban plan of old Most. Krejčí, the chief architect of the centre of the new town, years later emphasized that the 'main inspiration' for it was indeed old Most.[366] Not only the urban conception (whose

---

365 See J. Brabenec, 'Balada o Hněvově městě', *Krásy domova*, January 1963.
366 From the author's interview with Václav Krejčí (2012), 45 minutes (in the author's archive).

relationship with old Most is probably visible only in the plans and models, not in the terrain of the new town), but also a number of specific references, such as the statues, fountains, and other items that had been moved here, were supposed to bring to mind the town whose role had been taken over by the new Most. Some of the architectural plans supporting this historical consciousness, for example, the moving of historic pavement or a central monument symbolizing the demolition of the 700-year-old town, were never carried out. The reasons why these proposals were not accepted, however, appear to have been economic rather than ideological or political.[367] The surviving references to historic Most attest to the fact that neither its existence nor therefore its demolition was meant to be concealed or hushed up. Progress, which the new city was meant to embody, was supposed to be presented as the gateway to a better future, but that was meant to include humility and respect for the works of one's forebears, whose lives and labour should not be forgotten. Compared to the avant-garde proponents of modernist architecture, ranging from Teige to Le Corbusier, in whose works it would be futile to search for respect for tradition and emphasis on memory, the creators of Most, a town built to replace a totally demolished historic settlement, paradoxically placed greater emphasis on these conservative values.

A second peculiarity of the new Most, compared to most of its 'contemporaries', ranging from Brasília to Chandigarh, was its character as a mining town. Most has never been just any town of the North Bohemian Basin; it is a town that, by its very essence, has for centuries been closely connected with coal mining and was, in the twentieth century, clearly the centre of the north Bohemian mining region. The people who contributed to its design naturally thought about how to express this fact in the physical form of the town. The architects themselves eventually came up with a simple yet eloquent idea, without necessarily performing the political task one might

---

367 Krejčí, *Most*, p. 186.

expect.[368] The imposing 24-storey Head Office of the North Bohemian Mining Company (Oborové ředitelství SHD) became a symbol of the city. It was supposed to emphasize the nature of Most as an industrial city that owed its birth and further existence to brown coal.[369] Most thus acquired a landmark (eclipsing all other cultural and administrative buildings), which, compared to other towns, past and present, whose central and most visible buildings were churches and town halls, makes clear reference to the power of the state-owned mining company.

A central question, which had already been asked by contemporaries, was the extent to which the resulting appearance of the new Czechoslovak towns, including Most, reflected their socialist character – that is, the fact that they were the fruit of the 'building of socialism' and were meant to meet the needs of socialist society. Just as the contemporary narrative about the birth of the new Most was based mainly on the contrast between the past (of poverty and exploitation) and the modernist present (living with dignity), the alleged impossibility of carrying out a similar project in the capitalist West formed an important counterpart to a life of satisfaction in the new socialist city. The architecture and the general environment in socialist Czechoslovakia were supposed to contribute to the 'education of Communist man, to foresee the future forms of his material and cultural life, and to accelerate their becoming a reality'.[370]

Upon closer inspection, the urban plan and the architecture of the new Most certainly reveal many differences from the designs of Havířov, Most, Brasília, Chandigarh, and the new towns around London. Using only these criteria, it is harder to find the principal difference between the 'capitalist' and the 'socialist' variant of modernity. The Czechoslovak press of the period almost ritually

368 My interview with Václav Krejčí (2012).
369 Krejčí, *Most*, pp. 96–97.
370 'Bytová výstavba na Ostravsku', *Československý architekt* 5 (15–16), 30 August 1959, pp. 4–5.

emphasizes that the Most project would not have been possible in the capitalist West. They search for differences in the way the inhabitants would be moved, in concerns about their overall welfare, and who ultimately would profit financially from the whole operation. Even here, therefore, one finds few principal differences in the final form of the town, whose importance could then be verified.

The utopia of the rationally organized, airy city of the future thus seems to have been modernist rather than socialist. From the early 1960s onwards, the urban planning and architecture of the new Most were openly distanced from Stalinist Revivalist architecture and were inspired by, among other things, Western models. Its construction, including a wide variety of 'contractor-client' snags and the concomitant gap between plan and execution, and also the specific mission of the special-purpose buildings in the city centre illustrate the peculiarities of state socialism, but do not, at the level of architecture and urban planning, in principle differ in their final form from new towns that were built all over the world in the 1960s. One has to search elsewhere for fundamental differences – primarily with regard to the allocation of flats, the provision of care to the residents (from education to health), and the manner of meeting the consumer desires of the population.

The Welfare Dictatorship

The city has opened up to us all
Like our very own shopping mall.
The goods it has for everyone
Add beauty to the days to come.

The streets, like shop counters,
Offer many new encounters.
Where what you bought today
Is available every day.

I'm selling off bits of sunshine
For girls in their hair to twine,
And am giving it this song of mine
For bridges to future times.

These lyrics were sung in 1977 by the cabaret singer-actress Jitka Molavcová (b.1950), accompanied by the orchestra of Václav Hybš (b.1935), in *DostavQuestioníčko v Mostě*, one episode in a popular TV music show. They are about the superior range of products on offer at the then recently opened Most department store Prior. In the first part of the show, the main characters, played by the popular actors Pavlína Filipovská (b.1941) and Miloš Kopecký (1922–1996), wander through the bleak landscape, which they openly describe as 'lunar', where they encounter the singer-songwriter Pavel Novák (1944–2009) and the rock singer Alena Tichá (b.1944), who sing them the song 'Z těch kráterů mě jímá strach' (These craters give me the creeps), telling them 'very soon, everything will be in bloom' (za pár let bude to tady jeden květ). After the sweet sorrow of parting with the old town ('And so it is with you, Most: the old ends, the new grows [tak je to i s tebou, Moste, dávné končí, nové roste]), Kopecký, Filipovská, and Molavcová lead the TV audience to the new Most and astonish them with its modern buildings and infrastructure. The show reaches its peak in the Prior department store, where Kopecký enthusiastically rides the escalators up and down, while Molavcová sings, accompanied by dancers dressed as saleswomen. Later, Kopecký and Filipovská swim in a pool whose water is warm all year round. The music plays and the closing credits roll with the swimmers in the background. The picture of the idyll and abundance is complete.[371]

Throughout the 1960s and 1970s, the main ambition of all responsible institutions and individuals was not only to promote the vision

371 *Dostaveníčko v Mostě*, an episode of the *Dostaveníčko* TV series, produced by Krátký film Praha for Československá televize, 1977 (broadcast on 26 March 1977).

254

of the new Most as a complex city, but also to make it a reality and to breathe life into it. The creators of the town also intended that its inhabitants would enjoy all the conveniences of modern society and a decent life – from schooling and medical care to recreation, sport, and arts facilities. And, indeed, they were gradually able to achieve this. In the 1960s and especially in the 1970s, an important component of the vision of the new town, and partly also of its reality, was what was on offer to consumers – represented, for example, by the full shelves of the Prior department store.

These images of abundance, with which the new Most was often linked in the writing and films of the period, offer us useful insights into the peculiarly socialist version of consumer society, where the supply of goods was connected with the State providing infrastructure and social security. The fetish of choice, easy accessibility, and aesthetics of sale – typical of classic capitalist consumerism – were replaced here by material abundance as part of the all-embracing care of the socialist state, guaranteed equally to everyone. The care that was supposed to accompany every citizen of the state, even against his or her will, began at the maternity hospital and kindergarten, and then included high-quality schools, decent housing, and mass transportation, shops where ordinary people could buy anything they needed, and ended with security in old age and, ultimately, a modern cremation. Everything and everyone was looked after, literally from the cradle to the grave.

It is this feature, also evident in the way the Most project was justified, which points to what was likely the most fundamental peculiarity of the state-socialist version of modernity – namely, the comprehensive, strikingly authoritarian welfare provided to its citizens, from which there was no legal way to free oneself. The roots of this conception of the relationship between the State and the citizen or the State and society go back to the Enlightenment, and to a certain extent are politically applicable to Austria and Prussia in the second half of the nineteenth century.[372] But the socialist dictatorships, most effectively in the 1970s and 1980s, did not conceive of social care or welfare only as a 'safety net' or compensation for the legitimate differences and contradictions in capitalist society. This welfare served as an instrument to eliminate the existing social inequalities and hierarchies, in other words, to achieve social equality (which was manifested in the accessibility of all the key services that guaranteed a decent life to everyone) and economic certainties for every citizen at all the stages of his or her life. In this sense, the linking together of the apparently incongruous concepts of welfare and dictatorship is used aptly by the historian Konrad Jarausch when he describes the German Democratic Republic as a 'welfare dictatorship'.[373]

The central element of social welfare, which acquired even greater importance in the context of the forced moving of people from the town that was being demolished to the newly built city of Most, was housing. In the 1960s, housing in Most was not much different from what it had been in Czech towns before the Second World War.[374] Often, several generations of tenants were crammed into one small flat without a bathroom or flush toilet. The only real difference was that the houses of Most were in a worse state than before the war and it was surprising that only one of them collapsed (right on Mírové náměstí). Plumbing, sewage, and electrical wiring were in a disastrous state and a day did not go by without something going wrong. Heating was usually provided by little stoves – there was always lots of coal, but it had

372 Inge Zelinka, *Der autoritäre Sozialstaat: Machtgewinn durch Mitgefühl in der Genese staatlicher Fürsorge,* Vienna and Münster: LIT, 2005.
373 Konrad Jarausch, 'Realer Sozialismus als Fürsorgediktatur: Zur begrifflichen Einordnung der DDR' [1998], *Historische Sozialforschung* 24, 2012, pp. 249–75, available online https://www .ssoar.info/ssoar/bitstream/handle/document/37912/ssoar-hsrsupp-2012–24-jarausch-Realer _Sozialismus_als_Fursorgediktatur_zur.pdf?sequence=1 Accessed 28 October 2018; idem, 'Care and Coercion: The GDR as Welfare Dictatorship', in Konrad H. Jarausch (ed.), *Dictatorship as Experience: Towards a Socio-Cultural History of the GDR*, New York and Oxford: Berghahn, 1999, pp. 47–69.
374 See the chapter 'Czechoslovak Variations'.

to be carried upstairs from the cellar. Faced with that everyday reality, most residents saw that the new city, though initially only a housing estate of prefab panel blocks of flats, clearly had something to offer. Apart from the district of suburban houses called Zahražany, the whole of the new Most was built in the period of state socialism. Neither in the brick houses of the Stalingradská čtvrť and the Podžatecká housing estate nor in the districts of prefab concrete panel housing blocks, however, were the bold plans for housing reform carried out in the spirit of the left-wing avant-garde. In north Bohemia, the closest any of them got to Teige's ideal of the 'smallest flat', which assumed that residents would eat and spend their spare time in common rooms, was the collective-housing project (*kolektivní dům*) in Litvínov. Housing in Most was designed conservatively, in classic flats, ranging from a studio flat for a single or widowed person to a three- or four-room flat with a kitchen. These units took into account the need for privacy and assumed that the family was the basic component of society. Here, housing reproduced the lifestyle of the petty bourgeois, which, however, the architects and the political representatives of the emerging town were now offering mostly to the families of miners and other workers, who were accustomed to much worse conditions. Moreover, technological progress had made it possible to provide all flats with the luxury of central heating, flush toilets, and bathrooms with hot and cold running water. For most of the inhabitants of the old town, modern living in clean, prefab, concrete panel buildings with all the amenities was a convincing argument, reconciling them to the loss of their former homes. Moving from the old houses of the historic town, often damp, heated with coal-burning stoves, from flats in which people could only dream of having bathrooms, into 'comfortably furnished three-room flats with central heating',[375] could thus be effectively

---

375 K. Sedlecký, 'Začalo stěhování starého Mostu: První rodina v novém bytě', *Průboj*, 28 January 1965.

used in the mass media as the factor that justified the whole grandiose Most experiment and emphasized the advantages of the socialist system.

What made Most different from the majority of the new towns in the capitalist countries was of course the emphasis on equality and the just distribution of wealth, without housing as the priority. In this respect, the new town was unique even in socialist Czechoslovakia. Family houses here, in the mid-1970s, constituted a mere 5.7 per cent of the housing stock, whereas in other comparably large cities the number was about 40 per cent, sometimes even 50 per cent. The vast majority of flats were thus located in old-fashioned apartment houses and prefab concrete panel blocks, connected to public water, electricity, gas, and sewage. These flats were of various sizes but in other respects were similar in layout and had the latest amenities. This situation may have been seen as the utopian equality of all finally made into a reality. But by the 1970s at the latest, it was widely regarded as a serious problem, and not only by individuals with above-average or special demands on housing. The planners' internal reports, too, discussed the problem of the 'stereotypical categorization of flats and the generic composition of the houses'. It began to be seen as a defect that the city had practically no flats 'for people with special requirements (like doctors, artists, photographers, and so on)', and the reports therefore even called for the construction of family houses.[376] The problem of the same standard of housing for everyone did not, however, consist only in the impossibility of obtaining better or at least somehow different housing for the elites in the arts and the white-collar sector. The opposite pole consisted of those who, from the standpoint of majority society, did not deserve to live in new, perfectly clean, comfortable flats – in particular, the Roma of Most.[377]

376 SOkA Most, f. 207 (ONV II) – odbor výstavby, arch. č. 239, Územní prognóza Mostu (Krajský projektový ústav), duben 1974.
377 This is discussed in the next chapter.

Although the built-up areas of the emerging new city could already provide housing at the beginning of the 1950s, other areas of welfare expected from the socialist state, ranging from schools to shops and arts institutions to hospitals, long remained a mere promise for the future. Everything, apart from housing, was at that time provided by the historic part of the town, with its markets, little shops, offices of local government, cinemas, and theatre. In the 1960s, the new Most was thus still a synonym for a housing estate, not a city. That naturally became a subject of criticism in the public space and in the internal communications of the responsible individuals and institutions, who blamed each other for this state of affairs. Their criticizing the absence of public amenities (*občanské vybavenosti*) was not, however, meant to cast doubt on the whole Most project. It was only an urgent call for rectification of those shortcomings, made by proponents of the Most project who had some real experience of it. They were primarily people who lived in the new city and experienced the difficult everyday life of the local housing estates, which lacked schools, shops, and other services (in combination with continuous changes to the mass transport routes, including the closing down of the narrow-gauge tram lines and the rerouting of buses during the demolitions and the construction of the utility corridor).

One such critic was Radovan Brychta (1928–2008), a well-known journalist from the Most district, a writer who extolled the miners' struggle for social justice,[378] and a resident of an apartment block in Fibichova ulice (Fibich Street) in the new Most. In his book *Šachty splněných nadějí* (Shafts of fulfilled hopes, 1962), he complains that the 'everyday route march' people had to go on from the Most housing estates to buy even the most basic groceries, 'would not make anyone enthusiastic' about the new town. People in the new Most, he wrote, 'get comfortable flats, furnished in a truly modern way, but the streets to them come late, the construction of flats is far

---

[378] See the chapter 'Misery and Defiance', in the 'Alienation' section.

ahead of that of shops, nursery schools, kindergartens, and schools. Some things had to be overcome, but some difficulties were still in store.'[379] And other people in the early 1960s were of the same view. Gradually, the public and journalists were clearly losing patience. A year after the publication of this book, Brychta published the article 'Velkokapacitní bludiště' (A high-capacity maze) in which he describes the expanding new city as a sea of 'panels, concrete and steel', where 'someone who doesn't know his way around gets as lost as in a desert' and where 'only relations who live close to places of distribution are soon found, because there are so few shops in the newest city, that they serve as the ideal orientation points'.[380] It was not only shops and marketplaces that were missing. And the people of the new Most voiced their criticism not only in pubs and in conversations between neighbours, but also publicly, for instance, in the press, remarking that they had to travel three or more kilometres to old Most to get to a government office, the hospital or, say, the cinema. People also expressed more modest wishes that were difficult to fulfil in the new city: 'Young people on the housing estate have nowhere to go. You'd be hard pressed to find even a place in which to drive two posts for a volleyball net.'[381] At least until the early 1970s, the feeling that the new city was just a large-capacity dormitory, an unacceptable stopgap, was widespread. It was only at this time that the first shopping centres were opened; the centre of town, with local government offices and a department store, had only just begun to be built.

The promise of the future in the form of a complex modern city, offering its inhabitants an infrastructure with all the services and entertainment which were considered part of a life with dignity for the citizens of a socialist society, did not begin to become a reality,

379 Radovan Brychta, *Šachty splněných nadějí*, Liberec: Severočeské krajské nakladatelství, 1962, pp. 55–56.
380 Radovan Brychta, 'Velkokapacitní bludiště', *Průboj*, 21 April 1963.
381 'Bitva o domov', *Práce*, 16 October 1966.

however, until the second half of the 1970s. Most of the original plans were finally carried out at the very end of the decade. The book *Most 1932-1982*, published to mark the fiftieth anniversary of the Most strike, could thus already offer readers what was essentially a complete catalogue of the forms of welfare assured by the State and accessible to the inhabitants of the new Most.

Neither the limitations on publicly expressed criticism after 1969 nor the elimination of the greatest deficiencies of the new city put an end to the criticism. Criticism was limited to informal opposition groups or was voiced amongst teams of experts or in specialist and popular-science periodicals – and in reaction to the changing city it was aimed at more subtle factors of how it did or did not function. Amongst the probably not very influential, yet for the period remarkable, works by sociologists and urban planners are the now almost entirely forgotten critical essays 'Obraz Mostu' (A picture of Most) from 1977[382] and the 'These pro vypracování plánu sociálního rozvoje města Mostu' (Propositions for a social development plan for Most) from 1981.[383] Whereas the latter is concerned with, among other things, the loss of historical consciousness, demographic watersheds, and social dynamics, the authors of the 'Obraz Mostu' were mainly concerned with making a mental map of the new Most as seen by its inhabitants, in other words, how much the inhabitants truly identified with the new town, and which places were important to them, for instance, as points of orientation.

The most important topics of any welfare state, and not just an authoritarian one, were, and continue to be, accessible education

---

382 Jiří Ševčík, Ivana Bendová, and Jan Benda, *Obraz Mostu: Výzkum hmotné a prostorové struktury města*, Prague: Faculty of Architecture, Czech technical university, 1977 (published in very few copies). A short version for the general public was published as Jiří Ševčík, Ivana Bendová, and Jan Benda, 'Obraz města Mostu', *Architektura a Urbanismus* 12 (1978) 3, pp. 165–76. This article is available online at https://www.fa.stuba.sk/buxus/docs/udta /SevcikObraz.pdf Accessed 15 November 2018.
383 SOkA Most, f. 207 (ONV II – Odbor výstavby), arch. j. 239, příloha územní prognózy (These pro vypracování plánu sociálního rozvoje města Mostu).

and modern health care guaranteed to all. The ambitions of the new Most were thus to have a sufficient number of nurseries for babies and toddlers, kindergartens, and primary and secondary schools, which meant the possibility of free care of preschoolers and school-age children for every family. But something else became the main symbol of the achievements of civilization of the socialist State: the local hospital.

As a result of environmental damage, the Most district had the highest per capita rate of respiratory disease in the country. It also had in the long term a higher incidence of a number of cancer-related illnesses than the rest of the country. This was another reason why high-quality health care here was considered an absolutely fundamental service that the State should provide to its citizens. Unlike other buildings, such as arts and culture facilities, including the theatre, when it came to the hospital any lag between the demolition of the one in the old town and the opening of its replacement in the newly built city was unthinkable. And because of the necessity of quicker supplies of material and equipment in often unfavourable conditions, the construction costs of the large hospital complex, most of which was erected in 1975–76, were more than 50 million higher than expected, increasing to almost 700 million Kčs. Nonetheless, the main actors, including Czechoslovak cabinet ministers, realized that the existence of a high-standard hospital would have greater legitimating (or delegitimating) potential for the socialist State than any other comparable facility in the country.[384] The matter turned out well for the authorities, and one of the most modern hospitals in the socialist bloc could thus, before the bloc fell apart, serve as the setting for one of the most popular Czechoslovak TV series of all time, *Nemocnice na kraji města* (Hospital on the edge of town),

---

384 NA, f. ÚPV – běžná spisovna (nezprac.), kart. 183, sign. 356/1/12, Důvodová zpráva k návrhu usnesení předsednictva vlády ČSSR k návrhu na úpravu základních ukazatelů závazného úkolu investičního plánu stavby 'Nemocnice s poliklinikou v Mostě', únor 1976.

17. Final construction work on the grounds of the 'hospital on the edge of town' (*c.*1975).

which had a total of twenty sixty-minute episodes and ran from 1978 to 1981.[385] The legitimacy of the socialist State that guaranteed the most modern medical care to its citizens, and thus also indirectly the legitimacy of the Most project, was thus somehow confirmed for the millions of TV viewers by popular actors like Ladislav Chudík, Josef Abrhám, Eliška Balzerová, Ladislav Frej, Miloš Kopecký, Jana Štepánková, and Josef Vinklář.

When the inhabitants of Most, as in the 1960s, were dependent on the shops and marketplaces of the old town, it was of course the ambition of the Most Municipal National Committee to set things right as soon as possible. Another advantage of the modern town was supposed to be the concentration of formerly specialized shops, large and small, in large shopping centres where people could buy everything they needed in one place, from bread and cucumbers

---

385 Early episodes of the series were filmed in 1976 inside the new Most hospital. After the death of Karel Höger (1909–1977), who played the senior consultant, the series was, for various reasons, filmed mainly in TV studios. It even inspired the West German series *Die Schwarzwaldklinik*, which ran from 1985 to 1989.

to screws and TV sets. The shopping centres like Krym (Crimea), Sputnik, Obzor (Horizon), and Rozkvět (Flourishing) were built in the centre of town and also in the residential neighbourhoods. Their completion or opening was discussed a great deal in the press at the time, including the statewide newspapers and magazines. Later, in the second half of the 1970s, the Prior department store came to represent the fulfilment of the socialist citizens' consumerist desires. The theme of shopping, symbolized by shelves full of goods and by citizens with bulging shopping bags, formed a popular part of the newsreels and documentary films about the new Most.

The socialist system was meant to ensure not only the basic needs of modern society and its individual members, that is, housing, education, health care, and shops well stocked with food and other consumer goods. Another essential part of the promise was a suitable environment for rest and recreation, sports facilities accessible to all, and, last but not least, support for the arts and entertainment. All these things were supposed to be among the functions of the new city – tennis courts, playgrounds and playing fields, an ice hockey arena, an airfield for a flying club, a motorsport race course, and a recreational area on reclaimed land of the former Benedikt Mine. In these respects, actually, Most had it all.

One of the closely observed Most institutions, whose fate and form had long been uncertain, was the theatre. The original theatre in old Most, built at the beginning of the twentieth century, symbolized the emancipation of Czech-language culture in the borderlands (particularly in the interwar period) and its social dimension. In the postwar period, the theatre (called, since 1948, the Divadlo pracujících, the Theatre of the Workers) was also among the most important of north Bohemia and many actors who were well known throughout the country performed here.[386] Miloš Kopecký (1922–1996)

---

386 For more on the history and repertoire of the Most theatre in the 1950s and 1960s, see the chapter 'Everyday Life' in the 'The Story' section.

had performed in the Most theatre since 1952, and in the TV music programme *Dostaveníčko v Mostě* he expresses his regret over the demolition of a theatre with such a long tradition, a deed that the TV series' producers, however, interpret as necessary. In this 1977 programme, he expresses the hope that 'the new theatre building is erected as soon as possible so that the period during which the town is without a theatre is as short as possible and the theatre company can move to the new stage for its own pleasure and for the pleasure of all Most theatre-goers, which is our true mission.'[387]

The articulation of this wish in a popular TV programme may also have been motivated by current uncertainty. For a long time, there were discussions that the Most theatre company could always perform in the Máj arts and culture centre that was just being built, though not only for theatre, but for other purposes too.[388]

After the closing down of the old theatre, the company truly did move here in January 1980 and stayed for more than five years.[389] In the meantime, however, the idea to erect a separate building solely for the theatre was pushed through, supported not only by the architects of the new Most and the actors and creators of popular TV shows, but also to a great extent by the Most Municipal National Committee. Indeed, it was completed in 1985 and was in its day one of the most modern theatre buildings in Europe. The most modern theatre in Czechoslovakia, as we are reminded by one of the many TV documentary films about Most, *Zánik a znovuzrození města* (The death and rebirth of a town), from 1988, was not the only Most superlative: 'In connection with the cultural infrastructure, it is also important to remember that all the members of the theatre were

---

387 From the TV programme *Dostaveníčko v Mostě.*
388 See the comments by the chairman of the Most National Committee, Miroslav Fleišer, in 'Město uhlí a růží: Most od včerejška k dnešku', *Svět v obrazech*, 25 September 1971.
389 For the end of the last season in the Workers' Theatre in old Most, the atmosphere of the now deserted theatre building, and the prospects of the theatre company, see 'Město Most a jeho divadlo', *Naše rodina*, 4 June 1980.

18. The just-built theatre in the new Most (1985).

given flats here when they were hired – and that is an important superlative [*sic*]'.[390]

Comfortable flats, nursery schools and kindergartens with enough capacity, clean and functional school houses, modern hospitals with world-class medical care, a sixty-hectare municipal park, orchards, and ubiquitous beds of roses, playing fields, stadiums, an airfield for a flying club, and a track for car races, indoor and outdoor swimming pools, shopping centres and department stores, libraries, an arts and community centre, and a modern theatre continuing a great tradition. The new Most, about to begin the 1980s, constituted a state-socialist achievement of civilization and was somehow an argument against the scepticism and doubts of previous years about

390 *Zánik a znovuzrození města*, Československá televize, 1988, Archiv ČST, IDEC 288 430 51846.

whether the bold plans for the totally new city would ever come to fruition. The image of the new Most (and for a certain time also the reality) was a combination of utopian notions of the ideal town and the technocratic conception of a State that was, thanks to rational planning and technology, able to satisfy all the needs of every citizen. With regard to justifying the whole gigantic experiment and the legitimacy of the state-socialist regime, which wanted to use the experiment to demonstrate that it was governing a highly developed civilization, the form of the architecture and urban planning of the new Most (whether Stalinist conservative or cosmopolitan Constructivist modern) was not ultimately decisive. It was, however, of the utmost importance that it had helped to make the dreams of abundance and just distribution come true, ensuring the total welfare of each individual. The new town could fulfil these promises of the socialist system (and for many people it did indeed make them come true for a while) far more concretely and convincingly than solemn speeches and resolutions at Party congresses.

Obviously, despite the undoubted and quantifiable successes (at least in the short term), the State could turn some dreams into reality only very slowly. Many problems, ranging from the belated building of public amenities to the still disastrous state of the environment, became subjects of criticism.[391] In all these respects, however, the top-ranking political elites, together with the local officials and experts, could demonstrate that the situation was improving after all, or they could at least refer to the plans and measures that were supposed to guarantee gradual solutions in the coming years and decades. On one key point, however, the creators of the new town, fearing the unmasterable problems and conflicts, completely abandoned their own utopia.

---

391 See the following section, 'Criticism'.

A City without Roses

The central promise of state socialism was the creation of a world in which everyone could lead lives with dignity. That assumed the elimination of inequality amongst people, that is, the elimination of the poverty caused by feudal subjugation and above all the capitalist exploitation of one person by another. Socialist society was supposed to provide everyone – no matter what their social class, that is, the former social circumstances of their parents or grandparents – with the same conditions for life in the modern world. Although the task of building socialism in Czechoslovakia had been declared completed in 1960, it was clear that the residue of the 'former social orders' had survived here and there. Places like the new Most, however, were providing an opportunity to turn the utopia of a society of social equality into a reality. The Party secretaries and enterprise managers in Most were meant to live in the same kinds of flats as ordinary employees, unskilled labourers, miners, like those who once belonged to the poorest, lowest stratum. In a number of cases, that was really how it was, which of course the period propaganda did not hesitate to use.[392]

Since the early 1950s, the Communist elites realized that the 'citizens of Gypsy origin' were one of the groups whose integration into the socialist society of work and equality faced a number of obstacles. The Roma were mainly still living a miserable existence on the margins of society, spurned by the system and by majority society, and often living pretty much autonomously. If, however, the socialist project was to eliminate poverty and social inequality once and for all, then the Roma had to be among the main recipients of its care. How to go about 'making a Gypsy an equal, healthy, clean person

---

392 The third part of the film *Třikrát o dnešku* is about Jaroslav Maska, the manager of the Julius Fučík Mine in the Ostrava district, whose modest flat in a typical built-up area is contrasted with the great Empire-style house once belonging to the coal baron Salomon Mayer Rothschild (1774–1855).

consciously working for the good of the whole'[393] was the topic of complicated debates amongst politicians, bureaucrats, experts, and police officers. The original ideas about their gradual voluntary integration, which were raised in the late 1950s, eventually gave way to forced assimilation, connected with a ban on the Roma leading nomadic lives.[394] One thing, however, remained unchanged – that is, the systematic efforts, particularly by the central authorities, first and foremost the Central Committee of the Czechoslovak Communist Party, to limit their autonomous development, which, it was argued, would only intensify their differences and consequently their backwardness and poverty too. That is why their family ties were to be gradually severed and the Roma were to be settled and employed in small groups among the mostly non-Romani population. Though gathering the Roma together in one place was seen as risking a return to the earlier situation in which these people had been forced out of a society that did not want to have the Romani misery in plain sight, majority society thereby intensified that misery.

The fact that the Most district, particularly old Most, was an area with a high proportion of Roma who had come to this industrial region after the war, particularly from east Slovakia,[395] provided another reason to underscore the importance and historical mission of building the new, socialist Most. Modern architecture was attributed with great power to form the human spirit, to discipline, and to educate people to lead upright lives. The move from old Most and elsewhere, moreover, was fully under the control of the government

---

393 A frequently repeated formulation in the sources from the 1950s. Concerning the rhetoric and conceptions of this period, see Spurný, *Nejsou jako my*, pp. 237–85.
394 Zásadní směrnice o práci mezi cikánským obyvatelstvem ČSR, 8. dubna 1958', in Anna Jurová, *Rómska problematika 1945–1967: Dokumenty*. Pt 3, Prague: Ústav pro soudobé dějiny AVČR, 1996, pp. 459–64; and the subsequent Act on the Permanent Settlement of Itinerant Individuals 1958 (Zákon č. 74/1958 o trvalém usídlení kočujících osob ze 17. října 1958), NA, f. 05/3 (AÚV KSČ), ideologické oddělení, sv. 36.
395 For the situation of the Roma in old Most, see the 'Gypsies' chapter in the 'Alienation' section, or Glassheim, 'Most'.

authorities, particularly the Municipal National Committee, and the Party. All of this provided an opportunity, at least in the Most district, to make the old dream a reality and truly integrate the local Romani population thoroughly into socialist society. But the story had already taken a completely different turn back in the 1960s.

In the mid-1960s, the majority of old Most inhabitants longed to move away as quickly as possible from the dilapidated town with its crumbling houses and often non-functioning power grid, water pipes and other public utilities. At this time, therefore, unless otherwise destined by their occupation, education, or social contacts, people were not usually allocated flats in the new Most that was under construction. The vast majority of Roma fell into this category. At the beginning of the 1960s, about 3,000 Roma lived here, and because their population decreased considerably more slowly than the rest of the Most inhabitants,[396] their number as a proportion of the total population of the old town was increasing. And together with this, the disgruntlement of their non-Romani neighbours and the nervousness of the local authorities increased too. As part of the state-wide programme of dispersing people of Romani origin from places of their 'concentration'[397] to other districts of the North Bohemian Region, the authorities succeeded in moving only twelve families in the course of several years.[398] The operation thus clearly did not meet the aim of moving about 20 per cent of the Roma out of Most.[399] Yet it was the managers of industrial plants and

396 See the chapter 'Gypsies' in the 'Alienation' section.

397 The Most district, according to a 1966 report, had about 4,000 Roma (of whom 2,012 were registered in old Most). This was almost 4 per cent of the population, and was markedly above the Czechoslovak average. SOkA Most, f. 208 (ONV II), inv. j. 1283, ev. č. 448, Důvodová zpráva k Návrhu řešení rozptylu obyvatel cikánského původu v okrese Most vypracovaného Komisí rady ONV pro řešení otázek obyvatel cikánského původu dne 3. ledna 1966.

398 SOkA Most, f. MěNV Most (1945–1990), arch. j. 969, Rozbor současného stavu řešení otázek cikánského obyvatelstva ve městě Mostu (1. 6. 1971), p. 4.

399 SOkA Most, f. 208 (ONV II), inv. j. 1283, ev. č. 448, Důvodová zpráva k Návrhu řešení rozptylu obyvatel cikánského původu v okrese Most vypracovaného Komisí rady ONV pro řešení otázek obyvatel cikánského původu dne 3. ledna 1966.

heads of other enterprises, which often employed a high proportion of Roma, who prevented their dispersal. Sociological research conducted several years later confirmed that

> a whole range of enterprises, particularly municipal services, would be unable to carry out their tasks in the economy without these workers. But it must be emphasized that the majority of Gypsies, though they work mainly at unskilled jobs, have over the years in the work process acquired the relevant proficiency and it would be difficult to find equally proficient new workers to replace them.[400]

It was clear that the only thing to do was wait until the other districts of the new city were built. In the course of several years, however, the logical consequences of the 'Gypsy problem' in old Most began to get more complicated. The cause was not readily apparent, but the individual fragments of the story and mainly its outcome seriously spoiled the image of an integrating socialist society in which everyone could find his or her place.

The preserved complaints against Roma in Most from the 1950s to the 1970s[401] provide evidence that the tension between majority society and their Romani neighbours continued. Almost everything about the Roma bothered white majority society – their many children, their loudness, their destruction of their own flat interiors (though various investigations provided no evidence that this was a general phenomenon), that they played musical instruments, that Romani mothers nursed their babies in public.[402] The view of the Roma as 'anti-social elements' or at least as people unable or unwilling to adapt to modern 'civilized' society was also taken in a wide variety of internal reports, which associated a high proportion of the

---

400 Cikáni ve starém Mostě (výsledky sociologického průzkumu), ONV v Mostě, Útvar hlavního architekta, 1975, p. 56.
401 SOkA Most, f. MěNV Most (1945–1990), arch. j. 975. For more on this point, see the chapter 'Gypsies' in the 'Alienation' section.
402 Ibid. For a detailed discussion of this, see the chapter 'Gypsies' in the 'Alienation' section.

Romani population with crime, alcoholism, and other phenomena whose continuation in developed socialist society would otherwise be hard to explain from an ideological standpoint. Particularly the criticism of the 'destruction of values' by some Roma was typical of bureaucrats employed by a State that allowed a whole historic town to go to ruin and then be totally demolished.[403]

As in the late 1950s and early 1960s, so too in the early 1970s the Czechoslovak State sought by means of a thorough social policy to take a more systematic approach to the Roma. In addition to the emphasis on education and improved housing, this policy included various disciplinary measures and even outright repression. Apart from paying Roma women to be sterilized, which was practised in the early years of the normalization regime, the State returned to another traditional method – namely, the classification of Roma into three categories according to their alleged 'level of being civilized'. The authorities were then supposed to approach individual people according to the category they had been put in. People who fell into the first category could enjoy the same treatment as members of majority society. But people who had been placed into the third category were treated by the authorities as alcoholics or mentally ill, that is, as people who could not be left to live amongst the others without continuous supervision and permanent disciplining, or would possibly be temporarily isolated for re-education. In old Most, which in the meantime had become the largest Romani settlement in Czechoslovakia (with more than 1,500 inhabitants), the authorities, according to some research, placed as much as 83 per cent of the Roma into the third category.[404] In a period when law and order, were emphasized,

403   See SOkA Most, f. 208 (ONV II), inv. j. 1283, ev. č. 448, Důvodová zpráva k Návrhu řešení rozptylu obyvatel cikánského původu v okrese Most vypracovaného Komisí rady ONV pro řešení otázek obyvatel cikánského původu dne 3. ledna 1966, and especially SOkA Most, f. MěNV Most (1945–1990), arch. j. 969, Rozbor současného stavu řešení otázek cikánského obyvatelstva ve městě Mostu (1. 6. 1971)
404   An analysis by the Most Municipal National Committee of 1971 mentions that 1,290 of the 1,552 Roma in the old town of Most fell into the third category. SOkA Most, f. MěNV Most

and when the law-abiding citizen was placed on a pedestal, many people sensed an opportunity to express their reservations about living together with Roma. Whereas members of majority society had previously sometimes complained about specific disagreements, conflicts, and incidents with Roma (though these were often just stigmatizing normal manifestations of life such as playing a musical instrument or nursing a baby), now difficulties of coexistence were projected into the future. The non-Romani citizens of the new Most and the village of Obrnice (3.5 km to the east) thus rejected coexistence with their Romani fellow citizens and adamantly protested against Roma being moved to the finished or planned housing estates.[405]

After a few unsuccessful plans for mixed housing both for members of majority society and for the Roma on the edge of the new Most or on housing estates in the surrounding municipalities, a remarkable project thus began to take shape already in 1971. It entailed a solution that denied not only the basic attributes of the utopian vision of the newly emerging modern city, which was supposed to provide a home for everyone without exception and to bring them up to be law-abiding members of socialist society, but also the policy of assimilating the Roma as it had been applied since at least the second half of the 1950s. Thus, from 1971 onwards, the Municipal National Committee designated Roma from the third and even from the second category (that is, all the Roma still inhabiting the old town, with the exception of five families) as disrupters of socialist co-existence. As examples of the behaviour of this undefined 'delinquency' and juvenile crime 'at a much higher rate than amongst the other children', the Municipal National Committee explicitly mentioned 'little groups of youths, who, by their behaviour, provoke, harass, and pose a threat to citizens passing by' and 'mass theft and

(1945–1990), arch. j. 969, Rozbor současného stavu řešení otázek cikánského obyvatelstva ve městě Mostu (1. 6. 1971), p. 3.
405 Pavelčíková, *Romové*, p. 116.

the destruction of values' in the demolition zones after the flats had been vacated. For these reasons, then, the research concisely stated that 'moving second- or third-category Roma to the new part of town is out of the question'. The plan, which in the document is rather ominously called the 'final transfer of the Roma from the old part of town', was therefore to build a set of houses for second- and third-category Roma to the suburbs. The authors of the report swore that this 'was definitely not a so-called Gypsy settlement of the old type', because it would provide the Roma with high-quality housing and, furthermore, assumed that the hypothetical members of 'majority society, who probably have the same housing culture as the aforementioned Roma' would move there too. The abandoning of the doctrine of the reforming power of a civilized environment is also illustrated by a plan not to furnish the flats with, for example, kitchen counters and so forth, because they would only soon be destroyed anyway. In the conclusion, the authors admit that this was the only possible solution that met the 'needs and habits of the Roma', but also, probably primarily, it accommodated the 'demands of the other inhabitants of the town'.[406] The way to the soon-to-be legendary housing estate of Chanov was opened.

Officials of the Municipal and District National Committees and members of the relevant commissions for the welfare of the Romani population were aware that the plan, which accommodated the aversion that 'law-abiding citizens' had towards co-existence with the Roma, was largely incompatible with the ideological starting points of socialist society and also with the original ethos connected with the building of the new Most. Moving the Roma to an isolated housing estate (even though it was meant to be linked to the city by regular mass transportation) was not something that had to be defended to the general public, for they approved of this measure.

---

406 SOkA Most, f. MěNV Most (1945–1990), arch. j. 969, Rozbor současného stavu řešení otázek cikánského obyvatelstva ve městě Mostu (1. 6. 1971).

Rather, it had to be justified in the internal documents for the experts and the upper-level politicians. At any rate, in October 1971, the Czechoslovak Government Commission on the Gypsy Population did indeed express the fear that this could lead to a long-term problem. The chairman of the commission, the Minister of Work and Social Affairs, Emilian Hamerník (b.1922), did not even hesitate to call the concentrating of the Roma on an isolated housing state the 'relocating of hellholes' as used to be done in capitalist times.[407] It was probably for these reasons that in old Most, also in 1972, sociological research was carried out very quickly, probably with the aim of drawing attention to the particular way of life and needs of the local Romani population, and thus to justify their being moved outside the compact built-up area of the new city – that is, a solution that had been decided at the Municipal National Committee during the previous year. Though the research[408] did yield some interesting preliminary information about the composition of families and their financial circumstances, the employment of the adults, and mainly the housing conditions in the dying old town, its overall narrative reveals an absence of deeper knowledge of the topic and considerable expediency.[409]

Despite the many reservations about isolating what was at the time considered a problematic part of the Romani population in a separate housing estate outside the town, no one pushed sufficiently for an alternative solution. In 1973 therefore a plan for the

407 Pavelčíková, *Romové*, p. 116.
408 SOkA Most, f. MěNV Most (1945–1990), arch. j. 972, Sociologický průzkum cikánů ve starém Mostě (1972), zkrácená verze publikována (v omezeném nákladu, pro potřeby zadavatelů výzkumu) jako Jan Friš (a kol.), *Cikáni ve starém Mostě (výsledky sociologického průzkumu)*, ONV v Mostě, Útvar hlavního architekta, 1975.
409 Pavelčíková states: 'the organizers of the research either did not understand the researched problem at all or adapted their conclusions to the ideological intentions of state policy' Pavelčíková, *Romové*, p. 119. On the basis of accessible sources from the previous period, it nevertheless seems that the aim to support the proposition about the necessity of moving the Roma to a separate housing estate was typical mainly of local or district politicians, who, by contrast, needed to persuade superior Czechoslovak bodies of the benefits of this step.

housing estate was drawn up, and of the two proposed locations it was the slope between the River Bílina and the utility corridor near the village of Chanov which was chosen – in other words, an area absolutely cut off not only from the town but also from the surrounding area in general.[410] The local authorities, in connection with the decision and subsequent organization of the project, continuously sought to emphasize the advantages of this solution and also how much it differed from coldheartedly forcing out the Roma as had been done in capitalist times. In the documents of the Most Municipal National Committee, one thus reads, for example, that thanks to the project with 'housing units for inhabitants with a lower housing culture [...] it will be possible to have a better effect on the re-education of Gypsy citizens' and to 'observe the educational measures', whereas here 'Gypsy families of categories II and III will surely live more happily than in the new part of town'.[411] The original plan to move both Roma and non-Roma who manifested a problematic relationship to housing interiors and public spaces or manifested other social problems, to the Chanov housing estate, was somewhat revised even before construction began. Already in 1975, official documents mention that the 35 Romani families from the old Most, who were 'on a relatively high level regarding their willingness to work, housing culture, and their children's schooling', would be moved to Chanov, together with some Roma from the new Most.[412] A project that had been declared a special social measure had now once and for all become an instrument of local ethnic segregation.

The segregation of the poorest people – on the basis of ethnicity no less, which ran counter to the promise of socialist Most – did not, however, mean a retreat from all the attributes of a real-socialist

---

410 SOkA Most, f. ONV II – výstavba, arch. j. 425, PÚP Rudolice – Chanov – koncept (1973).
411 SOkA Most, f. MěNV Most (1945–1990), arch. j. 969, Informativní zprávy o činnosti na úseku sociální skupinové práce v péči o cikánské obyvatelstvo (1973–1976), zpráva z 11. 11. 1973.
412 Ibid., zpráva z 1. 12. 1975.

utopia in which people really lived. On the contrary, authoritarian welfare was supposed to be fundamentally linked to Chanov – to teach the local inhabitants to be better citizens, not just police supervision ('a redeployed police station with a sufficient number of qualified and experienced officers') was to be sent here, but also professionals with teaching experience. The 300 local flats were supposed to have not just a kindergarten for 170 children, a school with ten classrooms, after-school care, and a cafeteria, but also a community centre with a cinema, which could also be used for screening educational and training films, and, in addition, a restaurant and a medical centre. And of course there was also meant to be a village-type shop with a variety of general goods (probably taking into account the weaker purchasing power and lower expectations of the local population).[413]

The whole of Chanov was planned not only with regard to the lack of civilized habits amongst the Roma, but also with putative respect for the needs of their large families and the greater community. Children's playgrounds were built without equipment, because that could be easily damaged or dismantled. Nor were flats furnished in the usual way. The majority of them were big, with three or four rooms, which suited the Romani families. The buildings were always grouped into separate enclosed blocks, which created an inner courtyard-like area free of motor traffic, where people could meet. Bigger-than-usual common rooms, serving the same purpose, were also planned.[414]

From 1977 onwards, the Roma of old Most and, with time, from elsewhere as well, moved into the new concrete buildings between the colourful and poisonous River Bílina and the utility corridor with the north Bohemian dual carriageway. From the dwellings of historic Most, in which they lacked flush toilets and central heating, the Roma moved into flats of a much higher standard. From houses

---

413 SOkA Most, f. MěNV Most (1945–1990), arch. j. 974, Zajištění územní přípravy pro střediskovou osadu Romů (Útvar územního plánování a architektury ONV Most, 25. července 1971).
414 SOkA Most, f. ONV II – výstavba, arch. j. 425, PÚP Rudolice – Chanov – koncept (1973).

inhabited by extended families or by groups of neighbours that had befriended each other, they moved into prefab concrete panel housing blocks, whose inhabitants, in the best case, did not know each other and did not acknowledge each other or, in the worst case, were members of feuding groups. Everything had been planned for them as if they were one homogeneous group with clearly defined needs.

This artificially assembled mixture of people of a wide variety of lifestyles, cultural levels, and ideas about the good life, naturally did not comport with the ideas of the architects and planners. All of that soon left its mark clearly on the life and condition of the little concrete island between the river and the motorway. The problems here were intensified during the 1980s, but after the collapse of the socialist system with its constant but authoritarian care for the abandoned and uneducated they assumed utterly disastrous dimensions. The 'great experiment of socialist society'[415] became the first socially excluded locality of the capitalist system established after the collapse of the Communist regime in mid-November 1989. But that is a slightly different story.

Thus, beside the City of Roses a smaller city without roses was built in the 1970s. It was a city for the Roma, whom no one in the new Most wanted to live with. This was the result of the will of the regional and local politicians and bureaucrats, who were unable to find a solution for the co-existence of two different ethnic and social groups. And it was to the satisfaction of the 'law-abiding citizens', whose age-old dream of a tranquil world free of disturbers of the peace became, at least partly, a reality. With the segregation solution, the authorities, however, had refuted the integration theory that they had themselves come out in favour of, and implicitly cast doubt on the ability of the socially engineered utopia of the new city to educate and re-educate people. Chanov thus reveals the Communist elites' loss of faith in fundamental elements of their own ideology.

---

415 'Úkoly hornického města', *Průboj*, 17 February 1978.

Criticism

SILENT SPRING

The Global Rise of Criticism of the Ruthlessness of Industrial Modernity

No witchcraft, no enemy action had silenced the rebirth of new life in this stricken world. The people had done it themselves.

(Rachel Carson, 1962[416])

It is not often that an essentially specialist book on the effects of the products of the chemical industry becomes a national bestseller and leads to a lively debate in many spheres of society, including academics, the general public, members of the political elite, and CEOs and managers of large companies. But that is exactly what happened in 1962 with the publication of the marine biologist Rachel Carson's (1907–1964) *Silent Spring*, which documents the impact of pesticides and other chemicals on the ecosystem of the United States and on the lives of the American population. Like other experts and ordinary citizens, Carson noticed that in areas that had begun to use pesticides on a massive scale birds were dying in the thousands and that within two or three years some species had become extinct. These heralds of spring were not returning and new ones were not being born. A sinister silence set in which seemed to announce the future fate of those who with hubris intervene in the cycle of nature.

Silent Spring proved controversial and led not only to debates, but also to mass interest in environmental topics. And it contributed to intensifying the conviction that nature is not just a reservoir of resources enabling progress and prosperity, but is an endangered entity that needs to be actively protected against expanding modern civilization. Without this protection, not only nature but so too human beings themselves would ultimately pay for this lack of

---

416 Rachel Carson, *Silent Spring*, Boston: Houghton Mifflin, 1962, p. 3.

consideration. Carson thus importantly contributed to the fact that the protection of nature in the United States and eventually in Europe went from being a topic for experts to become a cause of whole societies.[417] A few years after the publication of the book, the legislatures of individual American states began to pass laws and regulations limiting or forbidding the use of pesticides. But, most important, people began on a mass scale to establish environmental movements and organizations, which in the course of ten years after the publication of *Silent Spring* came under the aegis of statewide institutions like the United States Environmental Protection Agency. This culminated in what is now international Earth Day, first marked on 22 April 1970.

The preparations for the first Earth Day exposed the conflict between, on the one hand, traditional efforts to protect nature and, on the other, environmentalism, a movement that was born mainly in the United States and western Europe during the 1960s. Whereas experts and small groups of original activists sought chiefly to protect the environments of their individual localities (stretches of river, meadows, woods, mountains, valleys) and to establish protected areas or new national parks, the new wave of the environmental movement sought to develop systematic criticism of the uncontrolled growth of industry. This criticism included limiting the development of some branches of industry, a determination to take a stand against economic growth if such growth depended on the devastation of nature, and the overall cultivation of the public's attitude to their natural environment.[418]

Though even in the earlier European tradition of environmental conservation one would find much inspiration and many practical steps for the protection of nature, until the 1960s most of the

417 Priscilla Coit Murphy, *What a Book Can Do: The Publication and Reception of Silent Spring*, Amherst and Boston: University of Massachusetts Press, 2005.
418 Robert Gottlieb, *Forcing the Spring: The Transformation of the American Environmental Movement*, rev. edn, (1993)Washington, DC, and London: Island Press, 2005.

reflections and activities were in the conservative tradition of preserving the old world and criticizing modernity and its Enlightenment starting points. An extreme version of this intellectual and political tradition is apparent in some emphases of the Nazi-promoted nineteenth-century ideology of *Blut und Boden* (blood and soil), particularly the concept of *Heimat* (homeland).[419] The 1960s were thus a watershed also in Europe, in two respects. The first is that interest in environmental questions led, as it had in North America, to the birth of numerous movements, and this time people with the potential to address wider social strata took the initiative, following on from experts. The second is that the Green movement was born, based on Enlightenment ideals and connected with the political left. Protection of nature and care for the natural environment were no longer meant to be in conflict with progress – on the contrary, they were discovered to be an essential part of the efforts to achieve a fairer distribution of wealth and a life with dignity for everyone in the present and the future. European environmentalism could find inspiration from the somewhat earlier politicization or protection of the natural environment in the United States, which was probably because of the more rapid and more destructive development of the chemical industry in America. The 7 April 1968, when the Club of Rome was founded, is widely considered to be a key date in European environmentalism. Among the reports and other Club of Rome publications on the state of the natural environment, Donella H. Meadows, Dennis L. Meadows, Jørgen Randers, and William W. Behrens III's *The Limits of Growth* (1972) stands out.

To what extent is the ecological crisis and mainly the awakening consciousness about this crisis characteristic also of the post-war history of the state-socialist countries? It might seem natural that

---

419 See Raymond H. Dominick III, *The Environmental Movement in Germany: Prophets and Pioneers, 1871–1971*, Bloomington and Indianapolis: Indiana University Press, 1992, especially the chapter 'The Völkisch Temptation'. For the connections between Heimat ideology and the natural environment in the Sudetenland, see Glassheim, 'Ethnic Cleansing'.

19. The intense and indiscriminate destruction of nature and the cultural landscape is a characteristic feature of industrial and post-industrial modernity. The photo shows coal mining in the Appalachian Mountains, in the United States.

a strong State, which controlled all the means of production and based its legitimacy largely on rational production and distribution determined by a long-term plan would have not only a fundamental interest in the protection of its natural wealth, but, even more so, sufficient capacity and powerful instruments to carry out such a plan in practice, and that this potential would also be obvious in comparison with capitalist states, the liberal democracies, which provided only a legal framework for merciless competition amongst rival businesses to make quick profits. The experience of state socialism, however, testifies to its long-term destructive approach to the natural environment. A key role in this was played by two factors in particular: the one-sided emphasis on industrial production and the suppression of criticism expressed by intellectual elites and ordinary citizens. In the liberal capitalist countries, however, it was such criticism that provided the decisive impetus not only to debates but also to political and legislative solutions.

Despite the inability or unwillingness of the socialist countries to search seriously for solutions to environmental problems (and it was perhaps the inhabitants of north Bohemia who felt this inability most), one should not go to the other extreme and believe that the capitalist system made this criticism possible and was eventually able to adopt it, thus quickly and effectively finding solutions to the problems, and thereby demonstrating its superiority. Nevertheless, such an interpretation was widespread, particularly in the early 1990s, when it was also assumed that the least-regulated capitalism would lead to minimizing both energy waste and, thus, environmental damage – and would consequently provide solutions to environmental problems.[420] These notions have since been proved wrong. Indeed, with some distance and without the prism of ideology, it turns out, even when looking at the past, that when it came to the devastating effects of industrial modernity, there were increasing similarities between the two systems.

The societies on each side of the Iron Curtain were, from the 1950s to the 1980s, going through years of the most ruthless and large-scale damage to the natural environment, though in the West, especially from the second half of the 1960s onwards, criticism could fully develop and lead to some measures more quickly and consistently then in the Soviet sphere of influence. Considering the different times when various societies entered the Industrial Age and reached its peak, before becoming post-industrial societies, it is hard to compare them. Yet one possible comparison does offer itself – namely, the two Germanies after the Second World War.

---

420 See 'East Germany: Cauldron of Poison'; Kabala, 'The Environmental Morass in Eastern Europe'; Mazurski, 'Communism and the Environment'; Naujoks, *Ökologische Erneurung der ehemaligen DDR*; Charles 'East German Environment Comes into the Light'; and Lois R. Ember, 'Pollution Chokes EastBloc Nations', *Chemical and Engineering News*, 16 April 1990, p. 7.

Was East Germany really that 'cauldron of poison' in contrast to the clean and considerate environment of West Germany, as was frequently emphasized in the 1990s by West German and American commentators?[421] As should be clear from the comparison I made in the chapter 'The Face of Modernity', the answer to this question cannot reasonably be yes.

This comparison, that is, a comparable or higher degree of pollution in the Western countries until the beginning of the 1970s, followed by a turnaround, is similar also in a wider framework than the comparison of only the two Germanies. If we compare, for example, the United States, France, and Britain with Poland and Romania, the results are partly a matter of time lags in the stages of modernity (the peak of the Industrial Age and the transition to the Post-industrial), whereas a comparison of the two Germanies points to another substantial factor – namely, the development and impact of environmental awareness amongst members of the population and its manifestations in the public space as environmentalist criticism.

In comparison with the explosion of criticism in the United States in the 1960s and then in western Europe, the situation in the authoritarian systems of state socialism was considerably less dynamic. With few exceptions,[422] environmental criticism here did not generally take the form of direct, massive confrontation with political or economic power – and where it did it was quickly pushed into the isolation of opposition groups and samizdat publications. The opposite pole consists of expert reports for official policy, which adopted a number of Western models and attempted to recast them for the conditions of state socialism. Writings that went beyond the usual constructive criticism only occasionally found their way

---

421 'East Germany: Cauldron of Poison'.
422 An exception may be the individual studies of the public speeches of environmentally minded intellectuals or the special period when public debate opened up more than usual in Czechoslovakia, especially in the second half of the 1960s, as we shall see in the next chapter.

in between the two poles (that is, those that were openly critical but were pushed to the margins and those that consisted of expert reports drawing attention to problems and proposing cautious, conflict-free solutions). An example of such a remarkable achievement is Valentin Rasputin's *Farewell to Matyora*, published in the Soviet Union in 1976. In this novel, Rasputin, basing himself on classic conservative values like patriotism, memory, and family, comes out sharply against the technological exploitation of nature in Russia and brutal interventions in local communities.[423]

In the 1970s and 1980s, the power elites of the socialist states supported or at least tolerated organizations concerned with the natural environment, for example, the Liga Ochrony Przyrody (League for the Protection of Nature) in Poland or the Český svaz ochránců přírody (Czech Union for Nature Conservation). At the same in the socialist states, many experts and expert groups were working at a semi-state level. They linked together the scientific, political and non-state spheres, including opposition groups. Yet people such as those around the biologist-environmentalist János Vargha (b.1949) in Hungary and the environmentalist Josef Vavroušek (1944–1995) in Czechoslovakia in the 1980s were walking on thin ice: official policy in the socialist states did not allow open confrontation and therefore avoided dialogue about large-scale environmental problems that had structural causes. In this way, however, as it turned out in the 1980s, official policy thus found itself in a cul-de-sac. Unlike the limitations on civil rights, the worsening environment, especially air pollution, had a tangible impact on the quality of life and human health. The attempts of the political elites to trivialize this state of affairs, their inability to quickly and clearly inform the public about the risks, and mainly their postponing effective solutions became, in

---

423 Valentin Rasputin, *Proshchaniye s Matyoroy,* first published in the miscellany *Наш современник,* No. 10, 1976. Published in Czech as *Loučení,* trans. Dagmar Šlampová, Prague: Lidové nakladatelství, 1980, and in English as *Farewell to Matyora,* trans. Antonina W. Bouis, New York: Macmillan, 1979. See also the chapter 'The Velvet Demolition' in the 'Reconciliation' section.

the second half of the 1980s, particularly in the most industrialized countries of the Soviet bloc (that is, East Germany, Poland, Hungary, and Czechoslovakia), a key factor in casting doubt on state-socialist domination as such. The younger generation of environmental activists in various organizations, like Wolność i Pokój (WiP – Freedom and Peace) or Wolę być (I prefer to be) in Poland, or opponents of the large technocratic projects like the hydroelectric power plant at Gabčíkovo-Nagymaros on the Czechoslovak-Hungarian border, combined environmental topics with human rights and the peace movement, and thus contributed to the considerable politicization of environmental topics. As had happened twenty years earlier in the West, now in the countries of the Soviet bloc a combination of moral appeals, scientific arguments, and the ability to make the phenomenon a key topic of political debate began to actively transform the political sphere. For the authoritarian regimes, however, such a transformation meant a fundamental threat to the legitimacy of their rule, resulting in radical changes in the nature of governance and the economic system.[424]

In the West and the East, the surface mining of coal played a fundamental role not only in the degradation of the natural environment but also as an impulse to protests and environmental criticism. In the Appalachian Mountains of the eastern United States such protests first emerged in the 1950s. Fishermen and nature lovers began to form various associations and to put pressure on the individual state legislatures to pass laws as soon as possible to limit or stop surface mining. In the 1960s, the protests of local farmers and other people who had long lived in those parts did not take place without violence, which came to a peak in 1967–68. At that time, local people caused damage to the facilities of coal-mining companies,

---

424 For more on the nature of environmental criticism and its impact in Czechoslovakia from the 1960s to the 1980s, see the next chapter. For the context of reflexive modernity and the delegitimation of state socialism, see the chapter 'Destruction as the Achievement of Victory' in the conclusory section 'Laboratory of Modernity'.

amounting to hundreds of thousands of US dollars. What is also remarkable is that, despite threats and reprisals from the mining companies, the protests were joined by some of their employees and some miners who had lost their jobs because surface mining requires considerably less labour than underground mining.[425] Much as in other parts of the United States and Europe, protests against the destruction of the land by surface mining had a greater impact in the 1970s; before that time, mining companies were able effectively to defend themselves against environmental activists, the local population, and part of the government, which was pushing for regulation.[426]

✕✕✕

The protection of the natural environmental and the preservation of the cultural heritage are discussed in the scholarly literature and in politics as two distinct agendas, stemming from different roots, as the concern of different social actors and focusing on different aspects of life. The demolition of old Most, however, raises the question whether the intellectual sources of both kinds of preservation and criticism are not, in fact, common to both. At the most general level, it is on the whole clear that the criticism of the ruthlessness, risks, and mistakes of industrial modernity can justifiably be supported by the experience of both spheres – awakened environmental consciousness and respect for the man-made works of the past. What, however, did this criticism of the reification of our world mean in practice for both movements and for the spread of environmental and historical consciousness amongst the broader social strata? Does not the fact that both perspectives gained in strength

---

425 Chad Montrie, 'Opposition to Coal Surface Mining in Appalachia and the United Mine Workers of America, 1945–1975', *Environmental History* 5 (1), January 2000, pp. 75–98.
426 Vietor, *Environmental Politics and the Coal Coalition.*

and persuasiveness in the world at basically the same time provide evidence of their actual connection?[427]

Though the first institutions for the preservation of cultural heritage had been established in European countries in the nineteenth century, the preservation of historical monuments experienced a watershed from the late 1950s to the mid-1970s. Though classic specialist historic preservation fighting to save individual buildings or architectural elements continued even after this period, a sense of dissatisfaction with this approach, which on the whole did not challenge the ruthlessness of modernity, was growing from the 1960s onwards.[428] Similarly to the preservation of the natural environment, the struggle for the preservation of the cultural heritage in this period became a society-wide phenomenon that reacted to the expansive character of modern civilization which was destroying everything that stood in its way or at least forcing it to adapt to itself. The search for a new language of historic-monument preservation was sometimes even inspired by the preservation of the natural environment.

Both these 'preservationist' trends are thus a manifestation of the same crisis and the fruit of what in many respects was related critical reflections. They were born of the feeling of irrecoverable loss and could be articulated on the common basis of both the growing criticism of the fetish of economic growth and of questioning the boundless faith in the ability of humankind to plan rationally.

The emphasis on preservation and care moved from individual phenomena, like wonders of nature or historic monuments, to efforts for the conservation of broader relations between society and the cultural or natural landscape, first in theoretical writings and

---

427 Here, I limit myself to a few global contexts of environmental criticism and heritage preservation. For more specific contexts of the search in Czechoslovakia in both languages, Czech and Slovak, see the next chapter.
428 See Miles Glendinning, *The Conservation Movement: A History of Architectural Preservation*, London and New York: Routledge, 2013, pp. 293–95.

demands of activists, but then also at the legislative level. Whereas the earlier approach was characterized by arguments based on notions like 'Washington slept here', organic ties between human beings and the land were now becoming the focus – that is, relations that were created as a result of historical development rather than particularities. This appears in the most dynamically developing economies, where modern quarters or the transport infrastructure most quickly gobbled up old towns, beginning in the late 1950s.[429] In the preservation of the cultural heritage, this change in thinking, is aptly recorded in one of the first official political documents, a 1965 report of the Special Commission for Historic Preservation under the Auspices of the United States Conference of Mayors:

If the preservation movement is to be successful, it must go beyond saving bricks and mortar. It must go beyond saving occasional historic houses and opening museums. [...] Second, the new preservation must look beyond the individual building and individual landmark and concern itself with the historic and architecturally valued areas and districts which contain a special meaning for the community. [...] In sum, if we wish to have a future with greater meaning, we must concern ourselves not only with the historic highlights, but we must be concerned with the total heritage of the nation and all that is worth preserving from our past as a living part of the present.[430]

The institutional ties between the preservation of the natural environment and the cultural heritage are the closest in the United States. The National Park Service, which oversees the efficient conservation

429 Laura A. Watt, Leigh Raymond, and Meryl L. Eschen, 'On Preserving Ecological and Cultural Landscapes', *Environmental History* 9 (October 2004) 4, 620–47.
430 *With Heritage So Rich: A Report of a Special Commission on Historic Preservation under the Auspices of the United States Conference of Mayors*, New York: Random House, 1966, pp. 207–08. The 1999 re-edition is available online: https://www.slideshare.net /PreservationNation/with-heritage-so-rich-compressed Accessed 18 November 2018.

of nature in national parks, has been fighting for the preservation of historic monuments since the 1930s. From the beginning of the 1950s, this agenda was taken over by separate organizations, committees, and specialized initiatives, but the gradual expansion of the scope, ranging from individual places or things to ties and an organic whole, continued to take place in the mutual communication and interaction of both preservationist currents.[431]

Besides the conservation of the natural environment, criticism of the modern planning and construction of cities constitutes the second pillar upon which the new historic preservation or, more generally, the struggles for the preservation of historical traces rests. Amongst Germans, Alexander Mitscherlich's (1908–1982) work about the 'inhospitableness' of West German towns was a breakthrough.

Originally a doctor and psychoanalyst by profession, Mitscherlich had a special ability to cut to the quick. The best known of his works in this respect is *Die Unfähigkeit zu trauern: Grundlagen kollektiven Verhaltens* (1967, translated into English as *The Inability to Mourn*, 1984), written with his wife Margarete. It became a key work reflecting upon the German silence about the Nazi past, and in the late 1960s it helped to change West German society. Already in the mid-1960s, however, Mitscherlich was one of the first Germans to warn about another development that for years could not be criticized amongst intellectuals – namely, the uncontrollable growth of modern cities and the reshaping of old towns in the modernist spirit. The expansion of German towns was, he argued, destroying the cultural landscape that until recently had surrounded them:

> If we had a reason to lament the destroyed cities and the ways they have
> been restored, we now have reason enough to regret the destruction
> of the land that surrounded the cities – and we have little hope that this
> damage can be repaired. When trees are felled, cranes rise up and former

---

431 See Watt, Raymond, and Eschen, 'On Preserving'.

gardens are covered with asphalt. We look at this with great indifference only because we have become accustomed to it and any sensitivity towards these things has been dulled.[432]

Mitscherlich also sharply condemned the mass production of blocks of flats and single-family houses which did not take into consideration the existing order of the urban built-up area. The city as an environment-home was, he argued, becoming a mere accumulation of buildings stripped of identity – and not only in Germany. Mitscherlich also looked in some detail at the creation of new towns in the South of England.[433] Their rationality, dictated by the egotism of planners and investors, according to him, would strip societies of their diversity, as it had already done in American cities. Cities produced as if they were motor cars (in contrast to the habitats of the old towns) are not perceived by Mitscherlich, unlike Le Corbusier, as the promise of a splendid future.

'The old towns had hearts,' claimed Mitscherlich, without, however, calling for a return to tradition. He merely pointed out the nonsense of some modernist dogma, like the separation of areas for living and for working (especially where most people were not employed in heavy industry). His criticism, born in a particular economic and political context, included the sharp condemnation of the 'fetish' of private ownership, particularly of building plots, which, he argued, made it impossible to carry out truly innovative and well-considered large-scale projects. Nevertheless, he admitted that the experiment of Soviet Communism was not a model to follow, but he also pointed out that a failed experiment does not delegitimize an admirable aim or the search for an alternative.[434] His criticism of 'supermarkets' as a general ideological prerequisite of the modern

---

432 Alexander Mitscherlich, *Die Unwirtlichkeit unserer Städte: Anstiftung zum Unfrieden,* (1965) Frankfurt am Main: Suhrkamp, 1969, p. 10.
433 See the chapter 'Utopia in Practice' in the 'Utopia' section.
434 Mitscherlich, *Unwirtlichkeit,* p. 20.

city led Mitscherlich to, among other things, rehabilitate the concepts of neighbourhood and helping one's neighbour. Though Mitscherlich did not directly criticize the destruction of old towns and monuments, his book anticipated a watershed between, on the one hand, a way of thinking about urban space, interwoven structures of historic built-up areas, and, on the other, the modernist utopia of rational towns of the future, divided up into zones according to function. Criticism of the modernist vision and practice was wrenched away from the purely expert circles or circles of lovers of what is old, and gradually became part of the shared beliefs of wider strata. In future, the criticism no longer necessarily had to be in conflict with a left-wing political identity; the new left would combine environmentalist emphases with faith in progress and modernity as a project of emancipation. That meant an important turning point in the post-war history of west European societies – which appears in various forms also in Great Britain, the United States, and other industrial countries in the mid-1960s.

In all these countries, social support for preservation of the built environment was harder to muster and took longer than support for preservation of the natural environment. The transformation from being a matter of experts into a society-wide struggle for the preservation of irreplaceable values was, nevertheless, common to both streams – the protection of the environment (especially the natural environment) and preservation of the cultural heritage – and activists of the two streams were aware of this connection since at least the early 1970s.[435]

As in the Federal Republic of Germany, so elsewhere, pioneers of the criticism of the inhospitableness of modern towns and the concomitant ruthless demolition of old urban units appeared elsewhere too, even before the mid-1960s, especially in the English-speaking

---

435 'Old buildings are irreplaceable, like oil,' said Peter Davey, an editor of *Architectural Review.* Quoted in Glendinning, *The Conservation Movement*, p. 322.

world. Among them these pioneers are the American-Canadian journalist and activist Jane Jacobs (1916–2006)[436] and the British architecture critic Ian Nairn (1930–1983). Nairn was already voicing his
criticism in the second half of the 1950s.[437] Jacob's *The Death and
Life of Great American Cities* (1961) may not have had the impact
of Carson's *Silent Spring* (1962), but with regard to the depth of its
criticism of a certain modernist stereotype (claiming that the technological and urbanist modernization of large cities meant a life
with dignity for its inhabitants), Jacob's feat is comparable to Carson's. 'But look what we have built with the first several billions,'
Jacobs writes in the introduction to her book, and continues with
a damning enumeration:

Low-income projects that become worse centers of delinquency,
vandalism and general social hopelessness than the slums they were
supposed to replace. Middle-income housing projects which are truly
marvels of dullness and regimentation, sealed against any buoyancy
or vitality of city life. Luxury housing projects that mitigate their inanity,
or try to, with a vapid vulgarity. Cultural centers that are unable to support
a good bookstore. Civic centers that are avoided by everyone but bums,
who have fewer choices of loitering place than others. Commercial centers
that are lackluster imitations of standardized suburban chain-store

436 Jacobs was an activist and pioneer critic of the alienation of the big modern city. She
became particularly influential with her book *The Death and Life of Great American Cities*,
New York: Random House, 1961. In connection with the argument in the following section
('Reconciliation') of my book, it is interesting to note that Jacobs was published in Czech in this
period: Jane Jacobsová, *Smrt a život amerických velkoměst*, afterword and editing by Jiří Hrůza,
trans. Jana Solperová, Prague: Odeon, 1975.
437 Already in the 1950s, Nairn began to consider the particular qualities of the British towns
and landscapes which surrounded him. Amongst the most important of his writings on the topic
are 'Outrage' in a special number of *Architectural Review* vol. 117, no. 702 (1955), later published
as a book, *Outrage: On the Disfigurement of Town and Countryside*, London: Architectural Press,
1959, *Counter Attack: Counter Attack Against Subtopia*, a special number of *The Architectural
Review*, vol. 120, no. 719, December 1956, and *Your England Revisited*, London: Hutchinson,
1964.

shopping. Promenades that go from no place to nowhere and have no promenaders. Expressways that eviscerate great cities. This is not the rebuilding of cities. This is the sacking of cities.[438]

Important works that not only contributed to the public's understanding of the seriousness of the situation but also showed ways to radically change attitudes towards the material monuments of the past, and particularly towards the interwoven historic built-up areas, including those of the nineteenth century, were not published in Britain and continental Europe until the 1970s.[439] In addition to more general critical writings about the destruction of historic built-up areas of British, German, and French settlements during the 1970s, brochures, studies, and other writings calling for action were published, focusing on particular historic towns under threat.[440] But the 1970s in western and eastern Europe were a time of increasing emphasis on heritage and its preservation, not only by the critical public but also, indeed mainly, by the mainstream media and the government. The modern State and European society were thus entering a fundamentally new phase of development, characterized by an effort not to lose the consumer fruits of industrial modernity, but also to cultivate its relationship with the environment and the cultural heritage – that is, a period when not only ideas about the just organization of people's lives in the future but also respect for and humility towards the past were a sign of being civilized. But reconciling the apparently unreconcilable is a topic discussed later in this book.[441]

438   Jacobs, *The Death and Life of Great American Cities*, p. 4.
439   For example, David Sturdy, *How to Pull a Town Down: A Handbook for Local Councils*, [London]: British Museum, 1980; Karl Ohlenmacher, *Sind die Dörfer zum Sterben verurteilt?*, Limburg: Self-published, 1975; and Colin Amery and Dan Cruickshank, *The Rape of Britain*, foreword by John Betjeman, London: Elek, 1975.
440   Probably the best known of these activist publications was Adam Fergusson, *The Sack of Bath*, Salisbury: Compton Russell, 1973.
441   See the 'Reconciliation' section.

CITY, FOREST, SMOKE

The Birth of Environmental Consciousness in Socialist Czechoslovakia

Let us not, however, flatter ourselves overmuch on account of our human victories over nature. For each such victory nature takes its revenge on us. Each victory, it is true, in the first place brings about the results we expected, but in the second and third places it has quite different, unforeseen effects which only too often cancel the first. The people who, in Mesopotamia, Greece, Asia Minor and elsewhere, destroyed the forests to obtain cultivable land, never dreamed that by removing along with the forests the collecting centres and reservoirs of moisture they were laying the basis for the present forlorn state of those countries. [...]
Thus at every step we are reminded that we by no means rule over nature like a conqueror over a foreign people, like someone standing outside nature – but that we, with flesh, blood and brain, belong to nature, and exist in its midst, and that all our mastery of it consists in the fact that we have the advantage over all other creatures of being able to learn its laws and apply them correctly.
[...] But the more this progresses the more will men not only feel but also know their oneness with nature, and the more impossible will become the senseless and unnatural idea of a contrast between mind and matter, man and nature, soul and body, such as arose after the decline of classical antiquity in Europe and obtained its highest elaboration in Christianity.

(Friedrich Engels, 1896[442])

---

442 Though written in May-June 1876, the essay, unfinished, was published twenty years later. Friedrich Engels, 'Der Anteil der Arbeit an der Menschwerdung des Affen', *Die Neue Zeit* 14 (2), 1896, pp. 545–54. The English translation from the German quoted here, 'The Part Played by Labour in the Transition from Ape to Man', is by Clemens Dutt and was published by Progress, Moscow, in 1934. It is available online: https://www.marxists.org/archive/marx/works/1876 /part-played-labour/ Accessed 3 November 2018.

Marxist thinking, as undoubtedly the most influential intellectual current of post-war Czechoslovakia, at least in its emphases, lacks an environmental dimension. From the time it emerged, it was a reaction to the problems of industrial towns and their inhabitants. Nature was, in this regard, mainly a source, a reservoir of raw materials or a state of affairs existing beyond human beings, against the backdrop of which important battles took place. The ones that Marx and his followers were most concerned with were the struggle for the just distribution of resources, for labour, and for the corresponding remuneration for that labour. It was a matter of preventing the exploitation of human beings but not of nature. Productivism therefore was not born only of Stalinism or state socialism, but has its roots already in Marxist thinking.

As can be seen in the epigraph, this thinking was never monolithic. Particularly in Engels's later works, but also, for example, in the early Marx, emphases appear which relativize simple dichotomies, like man versus nature, base versus superstructure, matter versus spirit/mind, and could at least provide another conception of the world. Marxist thinking, like the Enlightenment rationality in which it is rooted, thus offers opportunities for self-criticism and self-reflection. That is what played the essential role in Czechoslovakia in the 1960s and also in the criticism of the Most experiment.

In Czechoslovakia, as in other countries of eastern and western Europe and North America, the first ten years after the Second World War were characterized mainly by an emphasis on building up industry, increasing production, and raising the inhabitants' standard of living. But in this period too, intellectuals were occasionally heard drawing attention to the soft factors of landscape or of home as important aspects of a better future. With regard to the topics of urban planning, architecture, and housing, probably the most important Czech critic of the technological optimism of post-war industrial society was the painter, architect, theorist, and teacher Ladislav Žák (1900–1973), though he was never called a pioneer of environmental thinking. 'The protection of nature in Czechoslovakia and abroad is conceived with unnecessary modesty as the desperate preservation of the last, negligible islets threatened by the predatory stream of the economic and technological life-sustaining commotion which is considered the only real and correct manifestation of life and progress,' Žák wrote only six months after the Liberation, continuing in an almost prophetic spirit:

The scientist-conservationists and the most civilized technicians and landscape architects share the mistaken notion that the conservation of nature and the landscape can be applied to only small parts and areas like the preservation of historic monuments, which cannot be applied to the whole country. These experts, devoted to their own aims, are, however, too modest, and do not realize that a new conception of progress is possible, in which, on the contrary, preservation and a considerable unchanged continuation of values is the basis and requirement, which are just as vital and life-giving as the principles of construction and change [...] It is impossible to foretell what housing, production, mining, and transportation will look like in a hundred years. But it is possible to foresee quite precisely and confidently that in a hundred or a thousand years open space, clean air, a balmy breeze, sunshine, crystal-clear water of a mountain stream, worn-down cliffs, and lush forest trees will for the next generation be precisely the kind of valuable, or even more valuable, gift of life which these age-old natural values are to us [...] The natural values that we preserve and create will never become an outdated, bothersome burden for the future world, unlike what many of the bad and inappropriate works of technology have already become to us today.[443]

Žák largely remained, at least until the end of the 1950s, a prophet in the wilderness. Even in the years of de-Stalinization, the periodicals

443 Ladislav Žák, 'Technika a příroda', *Věda a život* 11 (November) 1945, pp. 536–43.

published by the Union of Czechoslovak Writers (like *Plamen*, *Literární listy*, and *Kulturný život*), which after 1956 were otherwise quite critical, were singing the praises of the great building works of socialism, from the dams on the River Vltava[444] to the newly erected industrial cities like Nová Dubnica in Slovakia.[445] The subjugation of nature was welcomed by writers as the demolition of old 'unsanitary' districts, which were replaced by modern blocks of houses or gradually also by prefab concrete housing estates. When, in 1959, the Prague district of old Holešovice was demolished, it was not an event that the mass media was expected to remain quiet about to avoid awakening unnecessary criticism. Indeed, journalists wrote about the end of poverty and the beginning of hope for modern housing for other Prague inhabitants and they praised the admirable speed and efficiency of the slum clearance. Prefab concrete panel houses could, according to an article in *Literární noviny*, be expected in the coming years also by inhabitants of other districts and the author added:

> I hope for their sake that they meet with this good fortune as soon as possible and I think that nothing would happen if even the rest of old Holešovice were soon demolished. The housing here is not good and we are not worried about the old image of this remarkable district. Filmmakers have filmed it for us and our grandchildren will thus not have lost anything.[446]

In parallel with the articles praising the great works of technology and the subjugation of nature, alternative voices, based on the

---

444 See Jiří Světozar Kupka, 'Stavba známá i neznámá', *Literární noviny* 5 (10), 10 March 1956, pp. 1–2; or Jan Smetana, 'Podrobíme si sílu vody', *Literární noviny* 5 (29), 7 July 1956, p. 2.
445 See Jarmila Urbánková, 'Po cestách povstání', *Literární noviny* 5 (36), 25 August 1956, p. 1.
446 Vašek Káňa, 'Sbohem, minulosti!', *Literární noviny* 8 (27), 4 July 1959, p. 2.

20. At the beginning of the 1960s, the predominant artistic interpretation of the transformation of the landscape gradually began to change. The great Czech photographer Josef Sudek (1896–1976), for example, no longer celebrating the land of work and machines, now perceived northern Bohemia as a 'sad landscape'. Here is his photograph *The Shores of Soot* (1960).

criticism of Stalin and Stalinism, began to penetrate the Czech and Czechoslovak public space, at the latest beginning in 1956. In addition to political debates or historical reflections on the forms of the Stalinist dictatorship, this wave of criticism included a philosophical layer, which sought the essence of the problem rather than individual phenomena. Marxist revisionism, as this intellectual current is most often called, may have been lacking environmental criticism well into the 1960s, but in some of its emphases it was opening the door to critical thinking about the attitude of socialism and socialist society towards the environment. Marxist revisionism made it possible to find a new language and to formulate largely still unexpressed doubts. 'A philosophy that refuses to investigate reality in its full breadth and totality and instead plucks "currently relevant tasks" from reality as simplemindedly as a small child picking flowers in a garden who is surprised when they visibly wilt in his or her hands [...] ceases to be any philosophy,' wrote the distinguished Marxist philosopher Karel Kosík (1926–2003) in *Literární noviny* in November 1956. He continued his criticism of thinking that 'naively assumed it was defending socialism and serving the Party when it observes development with regard to a particular moment and a particular need'.[447]

Concurrently with developments in the United States and western Europe in the late 1950s, in Czechoslovakia too, besides general criticism of productivism and the orientation to the needs of 'the moment', criticism or at least doubts were published about the dominant approach to the natural environment – even though in the conditions of the slow thaw in the authoritarian regime such criticism could at first be articulated only cautiously and usually in the local press or intellectual periodicals. In 1957, the term 'lunar landscape' was already familiar to readers of *Literární noviny* and one could read about the River Bílina, 'whose brown stream ploughs through the brown earth'; if little children are taught that they should clean up after themselves, why do we not behave like that in mining areas; and the harmful effects of smog.[448] Nevertheless, the demolition of Ervěnice, a north Bohemian town with a population of 3,000, was still being described by reporters in 1959 as a victory of the socialist system and socialist man, even if entailing difficulties and the dissatisfaction of the locals, and as the road to prosperity, though purchased with necessary sacrifices, ranging from the loss of the nice square to the bees that would no longer have anywhere to graze.

Two years later, as Carson was getting ready to publish *Silent Spring*, other emphases, this time related to surface mining, were already perceivable. 'Statistics already testify to the state of the environment in the Komořany area: this year, 619 tonnes of fly ash fell on one square kilometre,' writes Brychta in a front-page story of the November issue of *Kulturní kalendář Mostecka* in 1961. And he continues with a vivid description of a journey from Litvínov to Most, during which 'you force your way through what are literally zones of a variety of mixed stenches, ranging from ammonia to hydrogen

447 Karel Kosík, 'Hegel a naše doba', *Literární noviny* 5 (48), 17 November 1956, p. 3.
448 Jaromír Tomeček, 'Zemský ráj to na pohled', *Literární noviny* 6 (3), 1957, p. 2.

sulphide'. The culture of life, he argues, is also markedly influenced by how clean the air we breathe is – and in that respect, according to him, 'the Most district, perforated with lunar hills, suffused with smoke, dust, and fumes from the chemical plant', has to change.[449] Articles by other writers in subsequent issues of the monthly are in the same spirit – they point to the unenviable primacy of the Most district in the quantity of toxic agents per litre of air and they appeal to the relevant authorities to take vigorous action before it is too late. And more specific analyses were also written. For instance, 'Les a kouř' (Forest and smoke, 1962), in which the anonymous author writes that half the forests of the Most district have been seriously damaged by emissions from the burning of coal, and points out that sulphites are causing irreparable damage to the soil, with the danger that the forests will die on a large scale.[450] In this period, articles about the current devastation of the land, or the threat of it, began to be published in state-wide periodicals as well. The effects of lignite mining in north Bohemia,[451] however, was only one of the topics discussed in addition to criticism of the poor management of forests and meadows or the brutal interventions in the river regime. Thus the first criticism of the large hydroelectric dams, including ones that had hitherto been extolled, also appeared outside specialist circles and their periodicals. For example, in *Literární noviny* in 1963, the botanist and philosopher Jiří Úlehla (1924–2009) and his wife, the biologist-ecologist Blanka Úlehlová (1927–2018), wrote about the 'ravaging of the land' and pointed out that the 'final result of human activity should be the most natural possible landscape, not a landscape destroyed by countless technological interventions'.[452]

449 Radovan Brychta, 'Kolem nás', *Kulturní kalendář Mostecka*, November 1961, p. 1.

450 'Les a kouř', *Kulturní kalendář Mostecka*, April 1962, pp. 9–10.

451 See the warning about the necessity of further mining, which would be possible only at the cost of devastation of the north Bohemian landscape and the demolition of the town of Most, in Dušan Pokorný, 'K věci', *Literární noviny* 12 (11), November 1963, p. 3.

452 Jiří Úlehla and Blanka Úlehlová, 'Nehazardujme s krajinou', *Literární noviny* 12 (24), 1963, p. 6.

In consequence of the visible deterioration of the natural environment in the course of the 1960s and thanks to greater openness in the public space, in which heated debates could now be held, the language of criticism in Czechoslovakia continued to change – and it became more radical. By the mid-1960s at the latest, the environment acquired a new, more complex meaning than it had as the 'socialist environment', which had emphasized sanitation, health, and order.[453] Czechoslovak debates about the environment, however, were not taking place in isolation. On the contrary, the inspiration of the environmentalist emphases of west European and American activists was one of the important components that gave them dynamics and contributed to the formation of a new language of criticism. Reviews of Carson's *Silent Spring* appeared in Czech periodicals soon after its publication[454] and translated passages from it began to appear in the press[455] and on the radio[456] in 1966.

The change in discourse – determined by dramatic changes in society and individual lives, inspired by debates in the Western countries, and enabled by greater openness in the public space – ran through various milieux, from circles of experts, through popularizing literature and journalism, to legislation, institutions, and political strategies. In other words, it was hardly restricted to the pages of the traditionally critical *Literární noviny* or other specialized periodicals and publications linked with intellectuals in the humanities. In the popular-science monthly *Vesmír* (Universe), for example, one can observe how the section 'Vytváření krajiny, urbanismus'

---

453 For the natural environment in this earlier definition, see 'Výsledky podrobného průzkumu a návrh na zlepšení hygienických podmínek měst SHR (1953)', in SOkA Most, f. ONV I, inv. j. 274, sign. 480, kart. 16.
454 See the long review by M. Čapek, *Vesmír* 42, 1963, p. 140.
455 Rachel Carsonová, 'Mlčící jaro', *Vesmír* 45, 1966, pp. 143–46.
456 A radio series, *Mlčící jaro*, named after a Czech translation of the book, was broadcast on Československý rozhlas every Thursday evening from February to June 1966. See https://plus .rozhlas.cz/rachel-carsonova-poslala-lidstvu-varovani-a-zemrela-jeji-bible-6510783 Accessed 18 November 2018.

(Shaping the landscape, urban planning), which had originally reported on the draining of swamps, new cities, new dams, new valleys, new mountains, and successful socialist building projects in general, changed in the course of 1963–64 into a critical platform, with articles by leading Czechoslovak biologists, physicians, economists, geographers, and other experts warning against water and air pollution, soil contamination, dying forests, and generally about the looming or already existing devastation of nature and the landscape. The change in discourse was ultimately also reflected in 1966 by a change in the name of the section to 'Ochrana přírody a tvorba životního prostředí' (Protection of nature and environmental engineering).

Using the example of north Bohemia, numerous authors from various fields increasingly pointed to the dangerous situation of the natural environment and its consequences for people living there. And they warned that it would get worse. In an article entitled 'Krajina je stav duše' (The landscape is a state of mind), published in 1964, the psychiatrist Jiří Semotán (1908–1982) and his wife Milada Semotánová (1914–2001), an expert on mental hygiene, may not have yet written about specific municipalities or districts, but it was not hard to locate the landscape 'where sunshine hardly penetrates the clouds of smoke' and 'where impurities from the air fall on everything, even forcing their way into human dwellings'.[457] In a *Vesmír* article two years later, the scientist Václav Smil (b.1943) described the disastrous impact of the current extent and form of coal mining and electric-power generation on the Ore Mountain region, including its air, and he made concrete demands and suggestions. Mainly, he demanded that the population be thoroughly informed about the situation, that the land be reclaimed more quickly, that the capacity of the mines and power plants be limited, and that

457 Jiří Semotán and Milada Semotánová, 'Krajina je stav duše', *Vesmír* 43 (11), 1964, pp. 338–39.

municipalities in the worst affected parts of the coal-mining district should no longer exist.[458] In this article, specific criticism of air pollution and devastation of the natural environment is mixed with the hitherto pragmatic, technocratic approach to the cultural heritage and the phenomenon of home and the lifeworld of people. In the same issue of *Vesmír*, the geographer Otakar Tyl (1916–1976) describes the North Bohemian Basin as a 'lunar landscape',[459] and Ladislav Čepek (1899–1974), a former head of the Geology Institute of the Czechoslovak Academy of Sciences, points out that whereas in Czechoslovakia degradation was only discovered and enterprises gave reasons why nothing could be done against damaging the landscape and contaminating the air, in the most industrialized capitalist states they had already gone from merely talking about things to taking actual steps to protect the water, the soil, and the air.[460] Only gradually were aesthetic questions, in addition to factors influencing the health of people, coming to the fore – that is, the awareness that this had to do with more than just clean water and clean air, but also had to do with the beauty of the cultural landscape in which human beings restore their strength and cultivate their minds.[461]

The new language of criticism, already quite remote from the former commentary on the possibilities of improving the socialist environment, was not limited to communicating concrete and more complex information about the state of the environment, but gradually grew into substantial questioning of the modernist optimism that was so characteristic of the first fifteen or twenty years after the war. Among the articles published in the state-wide press about Most and the Most district, which were pointing in this direction is,

---

458   Václav Smil, 'Energie, krajina, lidé', *Vesmír* 45 (5), 1966, pp. 131–33. In 1969, he and his wife Eva, a physician, emigrated to Canada. Smil, the author of dozens of books, is Distinguished Professor Emeritus in the Faculty of Environment at the University of Winnipeg.
459   Otakar Tyl, 'Vracet zemi život', ibid., pp. 134–35.
460   Ladislav Čepek, 'Vážné škody, které způsobuje průmysl', ibid., p. 135.
461   See Alois Myslivec, 'Estetické vzdělání těm, kdo vytvářejí krajinu', *Vesmír* 48 (5), 1969, p. 136.

for example, an essay by the literary historian and critic Vladimír Karfík (b.1931) published in *Literární noviny* in 1966:

> For more than twenty years, a poisoned, dead river flows here. But during the war, trout still migrated through the town. When I first saw the black fetid river here shortly after the war, I could not understand the ghostly transformation. Today, I understand. The transformation of the river was at that time just too sudden – and it was the first.
> It was followed by the gradual transformation of the landscape, of beautiful vital nature, into a lifeless desert. The air, poisoned, does not flow above it, but hangs motionless [...] I have read quite a bit about devastated land, dying forests, vanishing waters, industrial emissions, and smog. I am afraid that that these things are generally read more out of curiosity about the pathology of civilization than to protect a living organism. And it seems not to upset people very much. They will calmly walk down the streets until they suffocate. I would like to know how human beings can live in a dying land. Live? [...] The idea that a single species – although admittedly the human species – could flourish in a dying natural organism defies logic.[462]

In parallel with journalism about the 'denaturation of man' and polluted air or specialist articles empirically charting the damaged natural environment, there also developed a more broadly conceived critical debate about the achievements and risks of the scientific and technological revolution and technicist civilization in general. The devastation of nature and the historic cultural landscape and the breakdown of natural bonds between human beings and their environment was, at the latest by 1964, the subject of a number of debates, conferences, and research projects involving a wide range of specialists. These topics were also considered here by the Richta team (which is rather surprising, considering the commonly perceived

462 Vladimír Karfík, 'Most – obležené město', *Literární noviny*, 25 June 1966.

opposition between technocrats and environmentalist critics).[463] In *Civilization at the Crossroads*,[464] which, like the Karfík article quoted here, was published in 1966, Richta urgently pointed out that 'the vast uncontrollable amassing of civilization's fruits brings man back to the elementary problem of the "habitability" of the artificial environment.' (Here Richta was referring to Honzík's 1940s writing on the problem of the habitability of towns). The analysis of the situation and the reaction that this state of affairs requires, according to Richta, was described in this book, which was influential in Czechoslovakia in the 1960s, in keeping with the emphases of west European and American environmental criticism:

However, such a power over nature must ultimately bring man (and society) back within his own limitations: in an industrial society it is, after all, merely an external, and in that sense quite limited, power based on the separation of man from nature; the outcome is, therefore, nature reduced to a mere means or mechanism – a machine for human life. The artificially constructed environment again manifests itself as a power confining man, reducing him to a 'denatured being' or machine. The natural ground having been lost, the certainties it afforded are also lacking and civilization inevitably appears as a harbinger of doom. [...] However, the present century has witnessed the acceleration and extension of man's intervention in the material, ecological, vegetational, biotic, and climatic factors of his environment, while hand in hand with this process grows concerns about 'the man-made world'. The *technical world* seems to have come for good. The artificial environment reaches out, encroaching step by step on all the refuges of nature. There is nowhere to run away. [...] At the present rate, a few decades will see the devastation of the landscape. The only salvation lies in a considered and consistent policy for conserving nature, [...] A society that proved

---

463 See the 'Numbers' section.
464 See the chapter 'Technocracy' in the 'Numbers' section.

incapable of mastering the production of a balanced artificial environment, of turning the global and often unbalanced onrush of technology to man's advantage, would undoubtedly be faced with the devastation of its natural conditions and a tragic disturbance of the biological and mental balance of its people.[465]

In Czechoslovakia, particularly amongst the Czechs, from the second half of 1966 to 1969, the environmental discourse quickly and basically without interruption continued to become more critical. In a certain part of the public space, that is, in intellectual, specialist, and popular-science periodicals, it became dominant and thus contributed, especially during the Prague Spring, to an unprecedented expansion of freedom of speech. An important role in this was played by north Bohemia. Both the state-wide and the local press at this time were regularly reporting on air pollution, threats to human health, and the lunar landscape of north Bohemia. In 1968–69, together with the condemnation of the Stalinist show trials that had been held in Czechoslovakia about fifteen years before and of coercion in general, public discussion began about the reprehensible mistakes, the lies about the true state of affairs, and the lack of consideration for future generations.[466]

At that time, long after reflections on other topics, like the natural environment, the problem of the attitude towards the cultural heritage began increasingly to be critically discussed even in Czechoslovakia. Specialists and journalists who were concerned with the modern town's attitude towards traces of the past were able to follow on from earlier local 'preservationist' traditions, for instance,

465 Richta et al., *Civilizace na rozcestí*, pp. 208–11. English, pp. 188–91.
466 See the articles 'Gordický uzel českého severu', *Svobodné slovo*, 23 January 1969; 'Proč se člověk dusí', *Rudé právo* 14 February 1969; the interview with the medical doctor and founder of Czechoslovak endocrinology Josef Charvát (1897–1984) 'Lidstvo je ohroženo, ale odvrátí katastrofu', *Práce,* 25 February 1969; 'Krajina k nepoznání', *Mladá fronta,* 3 April 1969, and also a number of articles in *Kulturní kalendář Mostecka* from 1966 to 1968 and the *Dialog* monthly run by Emil Juliš, Bohdan Kopecký, and other leading artists and intellectuals linked with north Bohemia.

21. Mining, which was gnawing away at the former cultural landscape of the North Bohemian Basin, had become a topic of increasingly radical criticism since the early 1960s.

the late nineteenth-century struggle against the slum clearance of the Prague district of Josefov (Josefstadt), the Klub za starou Prahu (Club for the Preservation of Old Prague), and the work of the State Institute for the Preservation of Historic Monuments and Environmental Protection (SÚPPOP – today's National Heritage Institute), and also from inspiration outside the country. In 1967, for example, the historian Bedřich Loewenstein (1929–2017), in a long essay about the 'cramped nature of civilization', discussed Mitscherlich's *Unwirtlichkeit unserer Städte*, pointing out that Mitscherlich's conclusions were also fundamentally relevant to Czechoslovak socialism: 'we were unable to plan with real foresight and aware of the contexts, or to shape the natural environment [...] Real human needs were of no interest to the planners.'[467]

---

467 Bedřich Loewenstein, 'Stísněnost z civilizace', *Literární noviny*, 22 September 1967.

In this connection, when at least the better informed part of the public began to reconsider the attitude to traces of the past and specifically to the historic town, the planned demolition of Most finally became a topic,[468] several years after reflections on the attitude to the natural environment.

✕✕✕

With regard to the public space, social dialogue, and criticism, the advent of normalization truly did mean a watershed. The mass media that had created a large forum for critical debate about the environmental risks of modern society and had also identified concrete manifestations of the crisis in north Bohemia and elsewhere were either closed down during 1969 or their editorial boards were at least seriously purged. The opportunities for intellectuals, that is, people not employed directly in the mass media, to communicate to the public were radically limited. In critical reflections on the natural environment and the treatment of the cultural heritage,[469] there appear not only breaks with the past but also striking continuities between the period before 1968 and the first decade of normalization.

As in the surrounding world, particularly in the West, the first half of the 1970s meant a fundamental expansion of environmental awareness in Czechoslovakia too. The organization TIS – Svaz pro ochranu přírody a krajiny (YEW – the Association for the Preservation of Nature and the Countryside), which, since its creation in 1958, at the National Museum, in Prague, operated more as a group of enthusiasts. Yet it did not die with the coming of normalization policy, despite what one might assume from the generally accepted narrative about this period. Indeed, on 15 November 1969, TIS became fully independent and was one of the few organizations completely

---

468 See the next chapter.
469 Since I discuss historic preservation during the normalization period, from 1969 to 1989, in some detail in the 'Reconciliation' section, in the next few pages I offer only an outline of the criticism of environmental pollution in the course of the 1970s and early 1980s.

outside the National Front (the coalition, established just before end of the Second World War, of all Czechoslovak political parties and most organizations) and the Socialist Youth Organization (Socialistický svaz mládeže – SSM). It gradually expanded its membership and range of interests during the 1970s. Neither, in 1971, when representatives of TIS read passages of *Silent Spring* on Czechoslovak Radio, to which they added information about the increased use of pesticides in Czechoslovakia, nor couple of years later, when they officially protested against the plan of building a dam in the Jeseník Mountains, did their activity lead to their being banned. On the contrary, it only helped to strengthen the organization. Eventually, by the end of the 1970s, TIS had 35 group members and 16,000 individual members. In 1978, just before it was de facto disbanded, TIS began to publish *Nika*, a critical environmentalist periodical. Beginning in 1979, its publication, in several thousands of copies, was continued by the state-run Czech Union for Nature Conservation (Český svaz ochránců přírody), though still outside the National Front.

When the State succeeded in not only disbanding TIS de facto, but also neutralizing anticipated resistance by establishing the Czechoslovak Union for the Protection Nature (Československý svaz ochránců přírody – ČSOP), another environmentalist group already existed in the Czech Republic – Brontosaurus. Its establishment, in 1974, was linked with the Socialist Youth Organization and *Mladý svět* (Youth world), the organization's weekly. The popularity and activities of Brontosaurus are, however, comparable with those of the independent TIS, and attest to a growing environmental consciousness, particularly amongst young people.[470]

Throughout the 1970s, the mass media did not remain silent about environmental preservation. The tone was of course more cautious than in the late 1960s, but that did not mean a return to the approach

---

470 See Miroslav Vaněk, *Nedalo se tady dýchat: Ekologie v českých zemích v letech 1968–1989*, Prague: Maxdorf, 1996, pp. 31–43.

taken in the years before the problem had been raised in the public space. In the *Vesmír* monthly, even during the profoundest 'silence' of the first half of the 1970s, at least regarding criticism and the formulation of alternative standpoints, general articles continued to be published about modern man's problematic attitude to the environment and on specific questions, ranging from pesticides to nitrates in the water to air pollution. Not only was the new name of the section of *Vesmír*, 'Ochrana přírody a tvorba životního prostředí' (The protection of nature and environmental engineering), left untouched, but the number of articles published in it markedly increased, from five to ten articles in the 1960s to almost fifty in the mid-1970s. Compared to the previous period, global topics now dominated. These topics testify to the lively contacts – surprisingly so in the early years of normalization – between natural scientists and other academics from Czechoslovakia and their colleagues in the West. One of the most important books that signalled the change in American and European attitudes to the natural environment, *The Limits of Growth* (1972),[471] became a subject of discussion amongst specialists and the general public of Czechoslovakia.[472] These general debates and criticisms of the ruthlessness of modern industrial civilization consuming itself, led to criticism of the Czechoslovak situation, which, in some cases, was even described as worse than that of the Western countries. The authors of these articles warned of the high industrial emissions in Czechoslovakia and criticized the obsolete and environmentally harmful conception of fuel

---

[471] Donella H. Meadows, Dennis L. Meadows, Jørgen Randers, and William W. Behrens III, *The Limits to Growth*, Washington, DC: Potomac Associates – Universe Books, 1972. For an online version of their *The Limits to Growth: The Thirty Year Update*, see http://www.peakoilindia.org/wp-content/uploads/2013/10/Limits-to-Growth-updated.pdf Accessed 25 October 2018.
[472] See Bedřich Moldan, 'Meze ekonomického růstu na planetě Zemi', *Vesmír* 52, 1973, pp. 40–42.

and energy policy.[473] Only a few of the articles, at least in the first half of the 1970s, were concerned with the continuing devastation of the land in specific areas, including north Bohemia. That did not change until after 1975.

Unlike what one might conclude from what has long been the dominant view of normalization,[474] the 1970s were not a period of decline for environmental criticism. It is true, however, that by tolerating 'small-scale' environmental activities, which at least temporarily contributed to the legitimation of the existing regime, the powers that be succeeded in this period to draw attention away from the most fundamental environmental problems that they had been unable to solve, without remaining completely silent about them – as for instance, in articles in *Vesmír* or at Ekofilm, an international film festival held every year in Ostrava since 1974. Until the 1980s, there was basically no direct relationship between research and criticism, on the one hand, and politics or the management of industry, on the other. The reasons for this disconnect and inability to push through solutions to fundamental environmental problems are, to be sure, also economic (as commentators have usually noted). The gaps that opened up between the liberal democratic countries and the state-socialist countries during the 1970s and mainly the 1980s, however, consisted to large extent, on the one hand, in the

---

473 See Květoslav Spurný, 'Co bude lidstvo dýchat v roce 2030?', *Vesmír* 50 (5), 1971, pp. 148–51.

474 The normalization period has been written about by historian-eyewitnesses and other historians in the first two decades following the Changes beginning in late 1989, and has been interpreted as a period of a general damping of any independent political initiatives, the renewal of oppression, and moral crisis. See Milan Šimečka, *Obnovení pořádku: Příspěvek k typologii reálného socialismu*, samizdat, Prague: Edice Petlice, 1978, published in English as *The Restoration of Order: The Normalization of Czechoslovakia*, with an introduction by Zdeněk Mlynář, trans. A. G. Brain [Alice and Gerald Turner], London: Verso [1984]; Vilém Prečan, *Die sieben Jahre von Prag, 1969–1976: Briefe und Dokumente aus der Zeit der 'Normalisierung'*, Frankfurt am Main: Fischer, 1978, and from the publications of the Institute of Contemporary History at the Academy of Sciences, Prague, in the 1990s. Of the more recent works, the interpretational framework of Petr Blažek (b.1973), for example, is heading in this direction.

incompatibility of the continuing technocratic and productivist conception of industrial modernity in the socialist countries and, on the other, in post-industrial environmentalism and taking into account unquantifiable factors of human existence on Earth.

Circles of experts, which had in the 1960s still sought to link these two currents of thought as if they were only apparent opposite poles of the scientific and technological revolution, diverged in Czechoslovakia during the 1970s, as they did in a number of other socialist countries, into, put somewhat simply, experts in the service of modernist optimism, on the one hand, and principled critics gradually drifting into the political opposition, on the other.

Richta is undoubtedly an example of someone from the first stream who, after 1969, remained in a leading position at the Czechoslovak Academy of Sciences and continued to develop some ideas of his *Civilizace na rozcestí*. What is central to understanding the essence of the normalization period and its attitude to what is called 'macroecology' is that an important figure of the reform movement of the 1960s could continue to work as an academic, travel abroad, formulate expert briefings for some political decisions, and also the emphasis on only certain aspects. Richta and Filipec's *Vědeckotechnická revoluce a socialismus* (The scientific and technological revolution and socialism, 1972) does not include the earlier work's sharp criticism of the treatment of the natural environment or warnings against the one-sided technicization of the world, which lacked a 'carefully thought-out and consistently pursued conception of environmental preservation' and would therefore lead to 'disrupting the mental balance of man'. Environmentalism thus again temporarily disappears from the repertoire of the big topics of the Communist conception of the scientific and technological revolution.

Nevertheless, continuity between the previous period and the 1970s did still exist amongst academics and other experts. This too makes it possible to understand the roots of environmental criticism in the 1980s, when it played a fundamental role in the gradual change and disintegration of state socialism in central Europe. As late as 1969, some biologists attempted to establish the Environmental Society (Ekologická společnost) at the Czechoslovak Academy of Sciences. Because of the political changes in the spring and summer of that year, however, this attempt led nowhere. Nevertheless, a group around the economist Jaroslav Stoklasa (1926–2007), the lawyer Václav Mezřický (1934–2018), and the geochemist Bedřich Moldan (b.1935) met regularly to discuss environmental problems in Czechoslovakia and the rest of the world and, beginning in 1976, they repeatedly tried to establish themselves officially. Three years later they eventually succeeded in founding the Environmental Section (Ekologická sekce) of the Biological Society as part of the Czechoslovak Academy of Sciences. In the 1980s the Environmental Section played an important role as a platform for expert criticism, the expansion of environmental consciousness, and, ultimately, political change.

The unofficial criticism, represented by Charter 77, did not begin to consider environmental questions until the beginning of the 1980s. Since the experts amongst the Chartists, led by Ivan Dejmal (1946–2008), were dissidents, they were of course unable to communicate their criticism to a wide audience. But in samizdat publications they could be open. One of the first Charter documents on environmental questions, from 1981, mentions not only air pollution and water pollution, which were topics in many newspaper articles and expert reports at that time too, but also the politicians' inability to truly solve these problems and their disastrous future consequences – namely, the further large-scale degradation of the land and contamination of the natural environment. The authors of the document then mainly propose what the regime would have considered radical solutions, mostly a completely new way of thinking about energy and energy policy, the possibility of closing down production that had a markedly negative influence on the natural environment, and the setting up of a committee for the protection of the natural environment as an independent civil initiative.[475] In addition to their being able to ignore the ruling consensus and the limits to 'constructive criticism', the Chartists also had instruments at their disposal to inform the world about the state of the Czechoslovak natural environment. This could, as well, influence institutionally based experts and politicians in Czechoslovakia.

The 1980s were not only a period when environmental problems in Czechoslovakia were coming to a peak and, consequently, state institutions and expert groups and dissidents were taking a greater interest in them. It was also a time of expert analysis of the natural environment, carried out in official scientific institutions. This was again drawing closer to the environmental criticism made by people in opposition. The first Charter 77 report on the natural environment, incidentally, drew on materials from the Environmental Section of the Biological Society. Indeed, the links between these two circles were even closer. By and large, the example of actors involved in environmental criticism can thus convincingly help to deconstruct the notion that the powers that be, the opposition, and society in normalization Czechoslovakia were totally separate spheres.

From its beginning, the Environmental Section held regular meetings and seminars lasting several days. They were participated in by Chartists – the first of whom was the historian-journalist Jiří Vančura (1929–2015) at a seminar at Klínovec, the highest peak in the Ore Mountains, in 1981 –, but also by senior bureaucrats, Party members, and representatives of the government. The seminar held in Jánské Lázně, in north-east Bohemia, in 1983, was actively participated in, for instance, by Václav Nešvera, who was an adviser to Lubomír Štrougal (b.1924), the Czechoslovak Prime Minister, and he reported some of the conclusions of the environmental analysis both to Štrougal and to Gustáv Husák (1913–1991), the President

---

475 Reprinted in Blanka Císařovská and Vilém Prečan (eds), *Charta 77: Dokumenty 1977–1989*, vol. 1, Prague: Ústav pro soudobé dějiny, 2007, pp. 381–90.

of Czechoslovakia. Štrougal then requested a more comprehensive analysis of the environment in Czechoslovakia. It was compiled by members of the Environmental Section of the Biological Society in the Hotel Hubertus, in the village of Jíloviště, just west of Prague. The analysis was then not only provided to the Czechoslovak Government but was also published by Charter 77, in December 1983, though against the Government's wishes of course and at considerable risk. From there, it was then quoted in West German and French mass media.[476]

These not entirely foreseeable contexts illustrate the extraordinary potential of environmental criticism. Thanks to it, the Environmental Section of the Biological Society became more than just an expert group, whose members elaborated a highly critical expert analysis. It was also was a mediator between the upper levels of politics, who had ordered the analysis, independent discussions in dissident circles, and the international public. This convergence of the individual social and political milieux, contrary to the dominant interpretation of the undignified role of the social sciences in the normalization period,[477] gradually started an overall transformation in the thinking of people and led to uncertainty within the decision-making system. But that is a topic that requires more time and space than is available here.

With regard to shaping the land, environmental thinking, and environmental criticism, the North Bohemian Basin, stretching from Sokolov to Ústí nad Labem, had been a special region since the beginning of the twentieth century. But whereas until the 1960s, the Ore Mountains were only one of many areas in western and eastern Europe where coal mining had led to the destruction of the land

---

476   See Vaněk, *Nedalo se tady dýchat*, pp. 68–69.

477   See Alena Míšková, 'Vývoj mimouniverzitní vědy v Československu a ČSAV po roce 1945', in Alena Míšková, Martin Franc, and Antonín Kostlán (eds), *Bohemia docta: K historickým kořenům vědy v českých zemích*, Prague: Academia, 2010, pp. 418–93 (particularly the part about the years from 1969 onwards).

and human settlements and to the deterioration of water and air quality, during the 1970s, the extent of devastation here surpassed the usual benchmarks. This was because of the large size of the mining district, geographic conditions (a valley surrounded by mountains, in the rain shadow, and with no way to disperse the pollutants), and the population density of the region, which, apart from the usual demolition of small villages and former mining colonies, led to extreme interventions not only in former farmland, but, as in the demolition of old Most, also in the historic built-up areas of the town.

On this land, comprising a structured cultural, largely agricultural, landscape until the twentieth century, 73 per cent of Czechoslovak brown coal was mined here in the 1970s and the electric power plants, without flue-gas desulphurization, produced almost 40 per cent of the country's electrical power. The high number of power stations on such a small surface area was also unique in the world. The combination of poor-quality coal and the inability of the Czechoslovak politicians to install technologies to remove sulphur dioxide from the flue gases (which was, it is true, extraordinarily costly until the 1980s) resulted in an annual production of about a million tonnes of sulphur dioxide (which was almost half the emissions of this gas in the whole country), the dying of the woods in the Ore Mountains (first noticed at the end of the 1960s and seen everywhere from the second half of the 1970s), and a marked deterioration in the health of the population. In addition to these phenomena, this was anyway a region whose appearance was unattractive, disfigured by surface mining, various stopgaps, and sluggish reclamation that often ignored aesthetic values. The members of the district and regional national committees were of course aware of these problems.[478] From 1970 to 1975, the Most District National Committee was systematically trying to draw attention to the 'extensive devastation

478   For a detailed account, see Vaněk, *Nedalo se tady dýchat*, p. 47.

of the countryside'[479] and its commission for the natural environment demanded putting a halt to some operations, improved information about air quality, and a reduction in emissions of dangerous gases.[480] The cautious efforts to slow down or stop the further construction of heavy-industry projects and power stations, and to enact stricter mining regulations ran up against the limited interest of upper-level politicians and the economic mechanism that demanded above all the smooth extraction of coal and its cheapest possible transformation into electrical energy.[481]

Though the economic and political authorities in Prague were able to neutralize the unwillingness of the District National Committee and regional officials, they could not limit the continuing breakdown of society-wide consensus in which industrial production had occupied a privileged position and north Bohemia was seen as a region that must be fully subordinated to progress. Despite the critical studies on the natural environment in Czechoslovakia which were published in the course of the 1970s in *Vesmír*, few articles from this period focused on the environmental problems of north Bohemia. Nevertheless, the image of this region in the public space was visibly shifting – instead of being seen as a showcase of progress and part of the building of socialism, it often came to be associated with pollution and a 'lunar landscape', a metaphor that was even used in made-for-television documentary films (in some respects propagandistic) like *Rekultivace Most* (The reclamation of Most)[482] or the Most episode of the *Dostaveníčko* (Rendezvous) series.[483] Articles mention fly ash and sulphur fallout on villages and people in

---

479 See SOkA Most, f. 207 (ONV Most II, 1960–1975), inv. č. 244, ev. j. 49, Návrh plánu a rozpočtu na období 1970–1975, 21. srpna 1970.
480 SOkA Most, f. 207 (ONV Most II, 1960–1975), inv. č. 497, ev. j. 166, Zápisy Komise životního prostředí ONV Most (1969–1971).
481 See the 'Numbers' section.
482 *Rekultivace Most*, a documentary film shown on Československá televize (1975), Czech television archive (Archiv ČT), IDEC 275 531 18350.
483 *Dostaveníčko v Mostě.*

the North Bohemia Basin and the forests of the Ore Mountains, and the fact that the people of north Bohemia now had only the Jizera Mountains (Jizerské hory) to vacation in, though that was where the fumes from the Turnov power station and East Germany were blowing. And they also mention the unbearableness of the situation and the unkept government promises to improve the natural environment of north Bohemia.[484]

In the late 1970s and early 1980s, biologists and environmentalists, whether in academia and research institutions or in opposition groups, began to consider the topic of north Bohemia more intensively than before. From the beginning of the 1980s, the devasted landscape of the Ore Mountains was of fundamental importance in the interaction between the Environmental Section and Charter 77. Both groups had been concerned with the region systematically from their first analyses and reports, including the Environmental Section's crucial 'Rozbor ekologické situace v Československu' (An analysis of the environmental situation in Czechoslovakia), written up in 1983. North Bohemia was thus, in the first half of the 1980s, even the sole subject of several analyses. One of the first such analyses, discussing the environmental, health, and social problems of the North Bohemian Region, was in the form of a letter by Charter 77 signatories addressed to the Presidium of the Government of the Czechoslovak Socialist Republic. In the letter, the authors return to the late 1960s rhetoric used in criticism of the way the natural environment was being treated ('north Bohemia has been cynically and consciously exploited as if to say "Après moi, le déluge"'), but their letter intentionally links the environmental topic with the mood in society ('In the suffocating atmosphere of Czechoslovakia, north Bohemia is amongst the regions with the most unbreathable air').[485]

484 See Terezie Habigerová, 'Hořká abeceda', *Tvorba*, 13 September 1972, pp. 10–11.
485 A letter to the Presidium of the Government of the Czechoslovak Socialist Republic, concerning environmental, health, and social problems in the region of north Bohemia, with

Apart from the occasional cautiously critical article in *Vesmír* or *Architektúra & urbanizmus*, or at small seminars held in private flats or elsewhere, however, the interests of industry and of state-wide policy faced a more serious obstacle – demographic movement. It was becoming increasingly difficult to maintain enough labour, particularly enough skilled labour, in the North Bohemian Basin. This was a clear demographic phenomenon, not merely an argument of the local governments of the district or region by means of which officials sought at least to gain advantages in supply and in wage policy for the region (since it had not succeeded in radically changing the form of its industry and consequently the environment). Thousands of people were leaving. They were chiefly members of the middle generation, families with children, and skilled workers, who were sufficiently informed of the consequences that toxic fumes and long-lasting inversions were having on their health. In the course of the 1970s about 50,000 people left and in the 1980s the exodus was even greater. But unskilled young people were coming in their place, often in search of decently paid temporary work, and so too were some of the absolutely poorest people, who had little other choice, mainly Roma from east Slovakia. Thus gradually evaporated the vision of the new Most as a city with a population of a hundred thousand, an industrial centre of a prospering region, a city of roses, which, like a magnet would draw the best engineers and top workers from the whole republic. The utopia, which in the 1960s was still attractive not only to urban planners and Communist elites, but also to the general public, was now, in the 1970s, becoming less convincing. Face to face with the suffocating inversions and dying forests, it was eventually ceasing to be credible even in the eyes of those who had long worked on making it a reality.

an attachment about police and judicial persecution of local non-conformists (19 July 1983), in Císařovská and Prečan (eds), *Charta 77*, vol. 1, pp. 531–36.

IN DEFENCE OF THE OLD TOWN

One has to stop [...] and chart a different course. To be specific, that means saving Most – there's still time – to decontaminate the whole region and elaborate a kind of plan for the extraction of raw materials for the whole of north Bohemia, one which will not destroy the country.

(Ivo Kořán, *Mladá fronta*, 1969)

22. Bezručova ulice, looking towards Mírové náměstí, before demolition (May 1978).

The engineer Josef Odvárka (1920–?) was an experienced bureaucrat and politician. As the minister of fuel and power from 1963 to 1965 and then first deputy minister of mines, he chaired a number of committees and commissions, including the Government Commission for the Coordination and Supervision of the Demolition of Old Most and the Building of New Most. An organizer and official, he was accustomed to solving things in his jurisdiction efficiently and without much discussion, by means of internal agreements amongst the relevant institutions, and subsequently supervised the carrying out of decisions of the Government or the Presidium of the Central Committee of the Czechoslovak Communist Party. In 1966, however, Odvárka was suddenly forced to discharge what had hitherto been an utterly inconceivable task. Tens of thousands, possibly even hundreds of thousands, of people had read several precisely argued and effectively formulated newspaper articles, whose authors not only attacked specific shortcomings in the work of Odvárka's commission, but had also fundamentally questioned the way the Czechoslovak State was treating the land and human settlement in the Most district. As a minister of the Czechoslovak Government, Odvárka had no choice but to enter the debate, though not as an indisputable authority authorized by the Party and the State, but merely as a representative of a particular institution that was defending his work.

The first of the articles of the whole debate was by the literary historian and critic Vladimír Karfík (b.1931), entitled 'Most – obležené město' (Most, a city besieged), published in *Literární noviny* on 25 June 1966.[486] Apart from a description of the overall disastrous environmental situation in the Most district, Karfík drew attention mainly to the pointlessness of building a new main town of the district at a contaminated location, where one power station after another was being erected. Thus, he argued, the wind would bring deadly

486 Vladimír Karfík, 'Most – obležené město', *Literární noviny* 15 (26), 1966, p. 6.

sulphur oxides into town from the power-station chimneys surrounding it, no matter which direction the wind was blowing.

Karfík's article was followed by a large debate, again published in *Literární noviny*. Mainly only developing his view, its authors included a Most district conservator, Břetislav Logaj (1921–1980), physicians, and academics from an agricultural college.[487] Some of them, in addition to voicing criticism of the polluted air and devastation of the land, also deepened and made more pointed the criticism of the new Most. For example, Logaj argued that the new city made a 'mockery of all architectural principles', and that it was a 'repulsive accumulation of tasteless and slipshod buildings' and a 'gigantic defective housing estate'.[488] Other authors, including readers of the periodical, took up the topic in letters to the editor, and put the Most problem into the context of the productivism and 'economic fetishism' of the times.[489]

Odvárka went to considerable pains when crafting his reply. He worked on it for about three months, requesting materials from the Ministry of Mines, the SHD mining company, the Most Municipal National Committee, the Most District National Committee, and the secretariat of the Government Commission, which he chaired. He asked his colleagues at the Office of the Presidium of the Government to comment on his article and to make any necessary additions. Ultimately, he omitted several sentences from his reply, in which he had pointed out to the reader that the authors of the articles 'had not provided the public with an overall, objective view of these problems'.[490]

---

487 *Literární noviny* 15 (30), 1966, pp. 6 and 7, and no. 51, p. 8.
488 Ibid., p. 7.
489 'Názor čtenáře Miroslava Mašíka', *Literární noviny* 15 (30), 1966, p. 6.
490 NA, f. ÚPV – běžná spisovna, kart. 167, sign. 356/1/12, složka 'Zrušení starého města Mostu a výstavba nového (1966)', Návrh odpovědi předsedy vládní komise pro koordinaci a kontrolu postupu při likvidaci starého a dostavbě nového Mostu na články v *Literárních novinách* (1966).

He was probably thus trying to make as accommodating an impression as he possibly could, sticking closely to matter-of-fact arguments. He admitted that the development of mining, energy, and other industry 'also has its unpleasant sides, which are being manifested in large-scale devastation, air pollution, the deterioration of the natural environment, and so on,' and that the SHD and the State authorities were still not able to mitigate these influences and reverse the developments in the natural environment. Otherwise, Odvárka's argument is made entirely in the spirit of productivist thinking and faith in a technological solution. Increasing energy consumption in this view is an incontestable fact, which not only is not seen as a problem, but is, indeed, considered a sign of economic prosperity, a high stage of social development, and therefore also the door to a life with dignity. Hence, the emphasis on increased mining. In Czechoslovakia, until a time when the development and construction of atomic-energy plants will have progressed, it was argued, brown coal had to be mined, and it made no sense to criticize this. Odvárka therefore focuses on promises of compensation for the devastation and on the possibility of reducing emissions. He vigorously dismisses criticism of the construction of the new Most, for he sees the problem purely with regard to 'construction capacity' and it is clear that the criticism of the alienated environment of a city consisting of prefab concrete panel housing had no effect at all on the chairman of the commission that helped bring that city into being. Though they were not part of the preceding discussion, in his article Odvárka seems to have felt a need to repeat arguments justifying the demolition of old Most (which originally appear in internal documents and commentary on the legislation) – namely, the one hundred million tonnes of coal under the town, the disastrous condition of the old Most utilities, roads, and buildings, and the character of the new city, which would, better than the old town, ensure a 'decent standard of living for its inhabitants'. The Planning Office of the Chief Architect of Most (Útvar hlavního architekta

Mostu) 'is watching closely the further construction in keeping with the principles of modern architecture'.[491]

The whole exchange of views, which was held 'live' in the public space amongst experts, intellectuals, and high-ranking politicians, constituted the first big debate on the point of extracting all the coal from the Most district or, more generally, the North Bohemian Basin, and therefore its destruction. Despite the openness and critical quality of the prevalent productivist thinking and, for example, the conception of the new Most and real life there,[492] none of these authors had so far questioned, at least not explicitly, the rationality of demolishing the old town.

For a surprisingly long time, the fate of the historic town in the middle of the brown-coal basin, soon to be wiped off the face of the earth, and the topic of cultural heritage in general continued to be ignored by critical journalists and other members of society who were becoming active. Here and there, one encounters attempts made by historians and preservationists,[493] but this criticism was making its way into the more widely shared discourse only very slowly. And the people who were most directly affected by the demolition of the old town, that is, its inhabitants, though they had been critically speaking out about the problems of the new construction from the moment it began to be carried out – the dearth of services and other infrastructure on the housing estates and the 'difficulties with the Gypsies', the principle of demolition, mining, and construction was not called into question even at this local level.

---

491 Josef Odvárka, 'Odpověď na články Most – obležené město a Z obležení musí být cesta ven', *Literární noviny* 15 (43), 1966, p. 7.

492 Though criticism was not a new phenomenon here, its openness, that is, how much was argued in the mass media, was new. For example, the internal critical debate amongst experts and politicians about environmental damage had been carried on longer. Similarly, in parallel with public criticism, there are internal analyses of the problems of new Most which go beyond criticism of mere initial shortcomings. See SOkA Most, f. 208 (ONV II), inv. č. 770–778, ev. j. 777, Hodnocení úrovně architektury nového Mostu (1967).

493 See František Šmahel, 'Filipika proti misomusům', *Kulturní kalendář Mostecka*, 12, 1961, pp. 7–8.

The thinking that considered the preservation of the cultural heritage a value at least comparable to current production and the needs of the national economy had not yet asserted itself in the public space. As is clear from the sharp tone of the debate in the summer of 1966 and from the seriousness of the topics (ranging from economic policy to responsibility for the destruction of the land and the health of the population), this was not because of censorship or fear. Whereas environmental criticism of damaging the landscape appears in somewhat independent periodicals beginning in at least 1958,[494] the language of criticism of the destruction of the cultural heritage seems not yet to have been discovered. That does not mean of course that Czechoslovakia was, until the late 1960s, a country in which no one would have stood up for heritage preservation, that is, the conservation of architectural monuments of the past. Indeed, this care, particularly in Bohemia and Moravia-Silesia, had a long tradition, going back to the nineteenth century. But from the creation of the K.K. Central-Commission zur Erforschung und Erhaltung der Baudenkmal (Imperial and Royal Central Committee for the Research and Conservation of Historic Buildings) in Vienna, in 1850 (which became the basis of the Státní památkový úřad after the Great War, renamed, in 1958, the Státní ústav památkové péče a ochrany přírody – SÚPPOP, the State Institute of Historic Preservation and Environmental Protection) to the late 1960s, this was mostly work performed by institutions created for the task and by the specialists working in them. Only a few cases, related to the earliest historic monuments, and mostly in Prague, such as the demolition of the district of Josefov (Josefstadt) in the 1890s, met with a wider public response that could endow them with some power if they came into conflict with the economic or political interests of the modern State. But in those cases, it was the critical reaction of a limited number of intellectuals, and was only partly able to prevent modernist projects.

494 See the previous chapter.

Since the mid-1950s at the latest, the socialist State also began to see the preservation of historic monuments (and by far not only those related to the history of the labour movement) as one of its tasks. The discourse emphasizing national traditions and following on from the glorious past – as it was promoted by important political figures like Zdeněk Nejedlý (1878–1962), minister of culture from 1945 to 1946 and minister of education from 1948 to 1953, and Václav Kopecký (1897–1961), minister of information from 1945 to 1953 and minister of culture from 1953 to 1954 – was influential throughout the 'revolutionary stage' of the building of socialism, that is, from 1948 to 1953. But the discourse was strikingly exclusive. In the post-Stalinist period, by contrast, it became one of the most important policies demonstrating the cultural achievements of the socialist State. It also accompanied legislative developments that came to a peak with the passing of the 1958 Cultural Monuments Act (Zákon o kulturních památkách č. 22/1958 Sb.), which established the State Institute for the Preservation of Historic Monuments and Environmental Protection (including a network of regional branches). Regarding historic monuments, it was run by the Central Committee of State Monument Preservation (Ústřední komise státní památkové péče) attached to the Ministry of Culture (originally the Ministry of Education and Culture).[495]

To be responsible for the protection and preservation of the cultural heritage in the former Sudetenland of north Bohemia in the second half of the twentieth century was definitely no enviable task. The surface mines swallowed up not only large areas of the former cultural landscape, but also historic buildings, at first little chapels standing in the open landscape, and then, gradually, also compact built-up areas of demolished villages and – what was most important with regard to monument preservation – their churches as well. In

---

495 Concerning the further development of institutionalized historic preservation, see the 'Reconciliation' section.

the Most district, for example, there were still 22 listed churches in the early 1970s. The list into which the preservationists had recorded the kind of care these buildings would receive in the coming years assumed that ten of them would be demolished by the year 2010[496] (and that is indeed what happened, with the exception of the church in Horní Jiřetín, which is today again threatened by coal mining). The work of the specialist in monument preservation thus often resembled, especially in the Ore Mountains, that of a pathologist. It was a matter of documenting a former life before it vanished from the face of the earth.

23. Josef Sudek, *The New Most* (1962).

Whereas this metaphor applies to the whole of the North Bohemian Basin with some exaggeration, it characterizes the preservation of historic monuments in Most nearly literally. But that 'nearly' is important, because the preservationists, in addition to their efforts to document the about-to-be demolished historic town in as much detail as possible, nevertheless sought to fight for the preservation of traces of the past on at least two fronts: smaller monuments, ranging from statues to doorways of historic houses or churches and ecclesiastical

496 SOkA Most, f. 207 (ONV II), inv. č. 1223–1233, ev. j. 444, Seznam památkově chráněných kostelů v okrese Most, 1. 9. 1973.

items) and especially the costly rescue of the Church of the Assumption. To that end, they took advantage of the increasing state emphasis on socialist legality requiring that in matters of supreme state or economic interest (like the mining of coal and the concomitant demolition of Most) all signed contracts and all legislative steps and bureaucratic measures stipulated by the constitution or acts of the National Assembly be respected. For that reason, the Regional Centre for the Preservation of Historic Monuments and Environmental Protection (Krajské středisko památkové péče a ochrany přírody) refused to delist individual monuments – even though the Municipal National Committee, with the support of the North Bohemian Regional National Committee in Ústí nad Labem, had demanded it, for example, regarding Minorite monastery and church.[497] At the same time, in 1963–64, the preservationists were still proposing that seven Most monuments be placed on the list of state-protected historic monuments, which was at that time being drawn up on the basis of the 1958 Cultural Monuments Act.[498] In addition, the State Institute for the Preservation of Historic Monuments and Environmental Protection was keeping another list of several dozen Most monuments of interest to preservationists.[499] The Regional Centre for the Preservation of Historic Monuments and Nature, in 1970, then made it possible to delist historic monuments[500] if all the conditions agreed

497   NA, f. SÚPPOP (uncatalogued), documents, including correspondence, on the question of delisting the Franciscan monastery (1959–62).
498   NA, f. SÚPPOP (nezprac.), Most: seznam památkových objektů, pp. 3. Apart from the Church of the Assumption, eventually moved to safety, and the Church of the Holy Spirit, the buildings on this list were churches, convents, and monasteries condemned as part of the complete demolition of the old town.
499   NA, f. SÚPPOP (nezprac.), Most: seznam památkových objektů, pp. 4–6.
500   NA, f. SÚPPOP (nezprac.), Žádost o upuštění od památkové ochrany nemovitých památek v Mostě, 10. srpna 1970. This request concerned the following architectural monuments: the bell tower of the Deanery Church, the Church of the Order of Friars Minor Conventual and its monastery, the Capuchin Church and its monastery, the former Piarist Church, the town walls, the Church of St Wenceslas, the fourteen stations (chapels) of the Way of the Cross in Žižkova ulice, the former hospital of the Knights of the Cross with the Red Star, the building of the theatre, the Komuna, the Na Střelnici pub, and twenty residential houses.

by the State and the SHD were met (especially the saving of small historic monuments and the completion of documentation).[501]

The fate of old Most, which was indisputably tragic concerning historic preservation, also includes some partial successes of the institutionalized preservation and protection of historic monuments, such as the decisions taken in the 1960s to save the late Gothic Church of the Assumption, the preservation of many small objects and architectural elements, and the meticulous archaeological research and documentation of the historic town as it was being demolished.[502] On the whole, however, the demolition of Most also exposes the toothlessness of state institutions of socialist Czechoslovakia when their agendas came into conflict with key power interests, especially if these institutions and their missions did not enjoy wider social support.

Like experts and institutions for the care of historic monuments, critical intellectuals, including those who worked in the region, did not seriously try, until the second half of the 1960s, to question the extraction of all the coal from under the historic town. Some, like the medievalist František Šmahel, joined the struggle to save the main church of the town and also smaller monuments that could be moved to safety.

In about 1966, the consensus regarding old buildings and unnecessary monuments yielding to industry and the modern town began gradually to breakdown, at least amongst the cultural elites. The general enthusiasm for technological progress sustained by mining and the destruction of the land was increasingly disrupted by voices drawing attention not only to dying nature and bad air but also to the loss of works of historic value. And yet thoughtfulness towards treasures of the past could have been promoted as a socialist value. Writers

---

501 For more on the approach to historic buildings, their preservation, or documentation by the authorities, see the 'Reconciliation' section. The work of the preservationists in 1968–69 is discussed later in this chapter.
502 See the 'Reconciliation' section.

associated with *Literární noviny* were thus following on not only from the existing institutional care for the material monuments of the past, but also from the revisionist philosophy of man, whose leading figure in Czechoslovakia from the late 1950s onwards was Kosík. Socialism was no longer to be understood as the way to material prosperity dependent on technological progress, economic growth, and just distribution. The one-sided orientation of state socialism after 1948 to economic factors was perceived as a cul-de-sac, at least amongst humanist intellectuals, who were becoming increasingly less marginal. The discourse, emphasizing non-material values, beauty, and humility towards the works of the past generations, gradually moved from the philosophers, writers, historians, and art historians into mainstream Czech and Slovak journalism and began to change the *Sinnwelt* of people strikingly. Their once marginal voices were heard and their points of view were adopted by others.

That of course also influenced thinking about the demolition of the historic core of Most. The so far generally accepted starting point of all reflections about the future of the region, including the most critical ones, was thus challenged, initially only in allusions but then increasingly in unequivocal judgements. The first conspicuous step in this direction was the shift in discourse, which dates from before 1966. In discussions about the fate of the town of Most at that time, in addition to individual, separate, and in the main precisely quantifiable agendas of mining, construction, public amenities, clean air, or preservation of specific monuments, the term 'domov' (home or *Heimat*) appeared considerably more often than it had before in the sense of the lived-in environment of people, created by long-term ties, which cannot be measured or produced like pre-fab concrete-panel housing or utilities. 'Home,' wrote the *Práce* (Labour) daily on 16 October 1966, in connection with the demolition of the old town and the construction of the new Most, 'is hardly born the moment one gets the keys to a comfortably furnished three-room flat in a pre-fab concrete block. Home is also an avenue lined

24. Václavské náměstíčko (Wenceslas Square) – a view of the Church of St Wenceslas. Until the end of the Second World War, the house on the righthand side of the photograph used be home to the Neue Welt pub.

with ash trees, along which one hurries on the way to work in the morning; it is a little playground, where one goes to play volleyball, a poster-covered kiosk, where one chooses films and theatre performances to attend; and it is also, say, a pleasant club or café where one meets with friends. Home can be all those things together and probably even more, but not greyness and uniformity.'[503] Apart from the debate mentioned at the beginning of this chapter, the article 'O jeden kostel' (About one church), by Václav Vilém Štech (1885–1974), an art historian and theorist, which was published in *Literární noviny* in 1966, was also an important step towards the limits of everything that hitherto had been said and challenged. Like Šmahel before him, Štech advocated saving the Deanery Church of Most. Unlike Šmahel's article (which, after all, had been written in the less free atmosphere of the early 1960s), Štech's is strikingly emotional and radical. According to him, this had to do not only with the past and its monuments; it was also a matter of the spiritual life and cultural level of the nation:

> Money is a fine thing. But equally important are values that are uncountable and to many officials incomprehensible: ideas, vivid ideas, works of art. Indeed, for the life of the nation they are usually the more important values. [The historian-politician František] Palacký [1798–1876] was here before Škoda Works and the Živnobanka, and [the author of the first Czech novel] Božena Němcová [1820–1862] is today an economic factor. The Most church, with its timeless wholeness and vitality, is also this kind of value for the whole [nation] [...] I would not like it if we were again impoverished and heard that a mistake had been made. For today we need first and foremost a cultural will – an awareness of values and the link between the past and the present, active efforts to apply them in life. After all, it is a matter not just of this church, but of the inner atmosphere of the times, of the spirit and direction of the collective life of the State.[504]

503 Václav Vondra, 'Bitva o domov', *Práce*, 16 October 1966. See also JJ, 'Co je domov', *Kulturní kalendář Mostecka*, September 1968, pp. 2–4, or the critical reflections about the new Most, 'Stroj na bydlení kontra člověk', *Výtvarná práce*, 29 June 1967.
504 V. V. Štech, 'O jeden kostel', *Literární noviny*, 4 June 1966, p. 2.

Regarding the Most project, the lively social debate of 1968 did not of course stop at saving the church. It made it possible to reformulate more general reflections about the loss of home and the priceless traces of the past in specific criticism of swapping the whole old town for tens of millions of tonnes of brown coal and chiefly to establish this criticism in the main currents of the mass media. The hot phase of the debate was launched by an article entitled 'Chystá se kulturní zločin' (A crime against culture is about to be committed), published in the popular daily *Mladá fronta*, on 8 May 1968.[505] The article was like a bolt out of the blue. What had so far been respected by everyone, including many critics, at least on the surface, as an indispensable concession to energy policy was suddenly being called a 'crime' in the mainstream media. Because of the overall atmosphere of the time, the article did not lead to police questioning or increased supervision over the content of the daily, but the *Mladá fronta* journalists were summoned to a 'meeting of involved institutions and bodies of the "people's administration"' in Most.[506] The negotiations with the representatives of the city, the district, and the SHD mining company, however, neither suppressed nor mitigated the debate. On the contrary, it became more heated. In late June of that year, the critical discourse about the demolition of Most temporarily dominated the state-wide press, particularly several editions of *Mladá fronta*. In an article entitled 'Odepsané město' (A town written off), the journalist Olga Hníková, together with the former head of the Most Museum, the historian and preservationist, Ludvík Losos (b.1929), reacted to the clash of discourses running along two oblique lines, at the May meeting in Most. On 21 June, therefore, readers of this popular daily were confronted for a second time, but now on a considerably larger scale, with the fundamental criticism of the Most project:

---

505 M. Brožovský, 'Chystá se kulturní zločin', *Mladá fronta*, 8 May 1968.
506 See NA, f. SÚPPOP (nezprac.), Záznam ze schůze (14. 5. 1968).

In the name of profitability – they say – and economic effect, in the name of values that in the course of ten or fifteen years ceased to be valid, we destroyed values that had been created over the centuries. When and where will it stop? Who will provide guarantees that towns will not fall again only on account, say, of investments for several years? [...] We razed a number of villages in the borderlands so that the Czechoslovak People's Army had somewhere to train. We turned great country houses into barracks, warehouses, granaries, and dormitories, and turned churches into sheds for farm machinery. What was human increasingly yielded to the economic, and eventually it was neither human nor economic. Nevertheless, everything was duly justified; everything was assigned an exact number. Let there be no doubt that the numbers about the Most coal have also been justified. As sure as eggs is eggs, the numbers seemed to us precise, consistent, and simple. When we looked at those eggs in Most, we saw that we didn't have the slightest chance against them. We didn't have calculations of our own. We weren't able to calculate the price of human life or how many litres of clean air and how many months of health have to be paid out for one tonne of cheap coal, and what social insecurity amounts to. We were unable to express in numbers the extent to which the officially blessed devastation of the countryside, old settlements, and churches plays a part in shaping the character of people and their increasingly destructive attitude to this country. We did not calculate what per cent the decrepit state of a community is projected into the decrepit state of the thinking of its inhabitants [...] We were unable to multiply the unit of beauty by the factor of centuries, and were unable to calculate the module of affability of the environment. We argued with emotions, attitudes, and the future of coming generations. This was met with laughter, smirks, and impatience. We lacked the figures, a set of tangible pieces of evidence; we lacked the eggs. And yet left with a feeling, a very strong feeling, that the truth is on our side, and that we have to fight for that dirty, dingy, old town.[507]

507   Olga Hníková and Ludvík Losos, 'Odepsané město', *Mladá fronta*, 21 June 1968. The article is a reflection of the debate between its two authors and representatives of the town of Most and

The article met with stormy reactions, despite the fact that sharp criticism of a wide variety of projects, small and large, of Czechoslovak socialism had for months been developing rapidly. What was new about the two articles published in May and June in *Mladá fronta* ('Chystá se kulturní zločin' and 'Odepsané město') was not their frank criticism but its target – namely, the generally accepted swap of old Most for coal and a modern new city. To the criticism of the devastation of the land and the character of the new town, Odvárka's successor as the head of the relevant coordinating committee, the engineer Otakar Novák (1905–1979), took a considerably sharper tone than his predecessor had in his reactions two years before. But since then, the dynamics of public debate had greatly accelerated and Novák, unlike Odvárka, could not spend three months elaborating his reply. *Mladá fronta* published it only two days after the article 'Odepsané město'. Novák accused the journalists of the daily of having failed to understand the complexity of the whole matter and of having reacted emotionally. He repeated the well-known reasons used to justify the demolition of old Most. Apart from the reply of the journalist Hníková, which was heated and ironic, the same issue of the newspaper included a remarkable essay by the architect, preservationist, and leading theorist in his field Otakar Nový (1918–1999) about the end of 'Gründerzeit' socialism. Comparing the last twenty years to the Gründerzeit capitalism of the mid-nineteenth century, Nový was probably the first, and for a long time the last, architect to come out against the demolition of historic Most and the whole project of the new Most, and not just how it was carried out in practice:

> The centre [of the new Most], which is just being built, will never totally take the place of the one that is vanishing with the old Most, that beautiful medieval town, wonderfully situated in the landscape, a town

the SHD mining company, which they had been invited to after publishing brief critical remarks on the demolition of old Most, which were published in an earlier issue of the *Mladá fronta* daily.

whose ground plan and system of three squares are a rarity in Europe. Of all of that, we will now be left only with a church, our awful alibi. I hope that this will be the full stop, a warning, to this Gründerzeit.[508]

In the essay, Nový then reflects on the latest developments in the global architecture debate, which, according to him, was reconsidering the ideas of modern urban planning and was returning to the historic core of the town as the fundamental symbolic centre from which a feeling of home develops. In the debates, he claims, it is becoming increasingly clear that, regarding the inhabitability of space, no one has so far succeeded in creating anything better than streets and squares. Nový thus in a nutshell combines criticism of state-socialist productivism with doubts about the fundamental modernist dogma of architecture in Czechoslovak and elsewhere during the past fifteen years. Hníková, the co-author of 'Odepsaného města', then closes the page-long discussion about Most with a forceful statement: 'The damages increase exponentially with time. But who cares about that? Now we need coal. Après nous, le déluge.'[509]

Few of the debates were as heated as this one in *Mladá fronta*. But other people, including some readers who explicitly joined 'those who were speaking out against the demolition of old Most', rallied to the defence of the old town.[510] The criticism naturally met with the strong disapproval not only of the political elites and regional officials, but also, indeed mainly, of managers, workers, and miners, first and foremost of the SHD mining company. On many fronts, those who disagreed with the criticism warned against abandoning the existing energy policy, which, they claimed, ensured Czechoslovak self-sufficiency, emphasizing that continuing coal mining, or even increasing it, was the absolute priority: if the town or nature were

508 Olga Hníková, 'Po nás potopa?', *Mladá fronta*, 23 June 1968, p. 4.
509 Ibid.
510 See the letter to the editor, by Pavel Koukal of Ružomberok, north Slovakia, published in the daily *Lidová demokracie*, 28 June 1968.

standing in its way, that might be unfortunate but life required sacrifices.[511] The most essential critical articles were published during the year after the Soviet-led intervention and occupation of Czechoslovakia. Now journalists and intellectuals, following the example of earlier critics of the devastation of the natural environment, were putting this criticism into the context of industrial modernity. The art historian Ivo Kořán (b.1934), again in *Mladá fronta*, emphasized that the struggle for Most, which the preservationists had recently given up, was not yet lost. He did not, however, see this only as a struggle against specific political and economic elites:

We entered the stream of the world-wide Industrial Revolution, in which we are can hardly swim, being carried further and further away. Increasing the standard of living, we are simultaneously destroying the foundations of our own existence. This is a world-wide problem and it is also a problem of the socialist countries [...] If our existence and work today are to have some point, we must again set the goal that had inconspicuously gone missing in the late 1950s and the early 1960s. That goal, we believe, is in the highest development of human capabilities and the maximum opportunity to employ them. The destruction of towns and nature and the plundering of our own wealth is clearly and irreconcilably counter to this aim.[512]

Kořán, like the other critics, in a remarkable way links criticism of productivism and classic industrial modernity with the discourse of the scientific and technological revolution such as we know, for example, from Richta's works. The following decade in particular provides evidence of how easily the universal aims and critical potential of thinking connected with the scientific and technological

511 See the opinion of the SHR mining company regarding the solution of the fuel-energy balance, in 'Potřebuje republika severočeské uhlí?', *Rudé právo*, 9 April 1968.
512 Ivo Kořán, 'Dokud stojí Most aneb o krizi země i památek', *Mladá fronta*, 12 April 1969, p. 3.

revolution results in highly contradictory conclusions, from reducing the world to economic indices to defending beauty and love.

At a time when critical debate about the rightness or wrongness of demolishing old Most was being carried on in full force, proponents of historic monument preservation were, after years of cautious struggles to save individual monuments or parts of them, beginning to speak up.[513] Now, when their views were beginning to be shared or considered by at least part of the public, the proponents of preservation were seeking to seize the opportunity to save at least part of the old town. The impulse was not only the meeting with the *Mladá fronta* journalists, at which representatives of the Regional Centre for Historic Monument Preservation (Krajského střediska památkové péče), in particular František Peťas (1912–1976), first formulated a proposal for the preservation of the historic core of Most,[514] together with the completion of the four-year preservationist research of the old town, in which specialists led by the architectural historian Václav Mencl (1905–1978) made surprising discoveries. It turned out that about twenty originally Gothic houses in the centre of Most were concealed by a variety of façades, and that in this respect the historic core of the town was, together with Prague, Kutná Hora, Kadaň, Kolín, and Jihlava, amongst the most valuable in Czechoslovakia. Under pressure from the SHD and the Most Municipal National Committee (which, unlike in the early 1950s, stood decidedly against the preservation of historic Most, for at this moment it would only further complicate things), the government commission, in the autumn of 1968, nevertheless unequivocally rejected the proposal for an overall revision of the plans to demolish the old town.[515] At the same time, the Municipal National

---

513 NA, f. Státní ústav památkové péče a ochrany přírody (nezprac.), Výzkum středověkého Mostu, červenec 1969.
514 NA, f. SÚPPOP (nezprac.), Záznam ze schůze (14. 5. 1968).
515 See SOkA Most, f. 207 (ONV II), inv. č. 1223–1233, ev. j. 444, Záznam z konference k otázkám záchrany měšťanských středověkých domů ve starém Mostě, 20. 3. 1969.

Committee awarded Mencl's group the Prize of the City of Most for outstanding research.[516]

A compromise version of the plan included efforts to save at least a set of the most valuable Gothic buildings, without aiming to preserve the spatial relations amongst them. This entailed taking them apart and reassembling them elsewhere. The Regional Centre for Historic Monument Preservation even organized a conference, in March 1969, on the possibilities of saving the houses. It entailed not only specialist discussions about various ways of moving the buildings, but was also an occasion at which preservationists as well as architects involved in the construction of the new Most could express their support for the plan to preserve the historic buildings.[517] Eventually, however, this plan was also dropped; it turned out that the preservationists had presented it too late. In any case, the north Bohemian preservationists also came in for criticism in a specialist periodical for their having been ill-prepared and unable to effectively push through the preservation of the historic traces of the town against the interests of the mining company.[518] After the failure of their efforts to achieve a more substantial revision of the demolition plan, the champions of old Most concentrated instead on only one preservation project, which had long enjoyed political support – the saving of the Deanery Church.[519]

In the atmosphere of the Prague Spring and during the year after the Soviet-led intervention in Czechoslovakia, intellectuals, journalists, historians, and preservationists thus formulated an opposition

---

516 NA, f. SÚPPOP (uncatalogued), Letter from the chairman of the Most Municipal National Committee, Miroslav Fleišer, to the director of the State Institute for the Preservation of Historic Monuments and Environmental Protection (SUPPOP). 24 May 1968

517 NA, f. Státní ústav památkové péče a ochrany přírody (nezprac.), Mostměsto – záznam z porady k záchraně měšťanských středověkých domů, 30. 4. 1969, dále SOkA Most, f. 207 (ONV II), inv. č. 1223–1233, ev. j. 444, Záznam z konference k otázkám záchrany měšťanských středověkých domů ve starém Mostě, 20. 3. 1969.

518 Helena Drábková, 'Jak se dělá konference o záchraně', *Památková péče*, 10 April 1969.

519 See the 'Reconciliation' section.

position rejecting the project to demolish old Most, not just how it was to be carried out, but the very principle of swapping this cultural heritage and the home of many people for coal, money, and a contribution to economic growth. Though these remained minority voices at this time too, and they were unable stop the demolition of the historic town which had already begun, they are clear traces of the advent of a new discourse, which had come to the fore throughout Europe and would in the next two decades also influence the public space and the treatment of cultural heritage in socialist Czechoslovakia. It is not clear what to call this way of thinking, because, at least in the socialist *Sinnwelt*, it was not necessarily conservative; but it was critical of industrial modernity, productivism, and a certain kind of technocratic mindset based on the quantification

25. Maintaining and modernizing a town that has been written off: asphalting the road at the corner of Palackého and Tylova ulice.

of all aspects of social life. Perhaps, then, it is fair to talk about the formation of a discourse of reflexive modernity in the conditions of state socialism.

After the crushing of the reform movement in the Party and with the 'consolidation' of the situation in the summer and autumn of 1969, criticism was no longer possible in the forthright form in had taken in the articles of the 1960s. The public space was regulated far more thoroughly than it had been not only during the Prague Spring but even in comparison with the whole post-Stalinist period, at the latest from 1956 onwards. The supervision and regimentation of the public space nevertheless proceeded slowly and unevenly, and so, still at the beginning of the 1970s – two years after the Soviet-led intervention and a year after Husák had been elected General Secretary of the Central Committee of the Czechoslovak Communist Party – critical voices appeared in the press, inspired by the debates of 1968–69. 'We should not eliminate from the final phase of the debate the opinion that historic Most surely has a higher absolute value than a billion Kčs,' declares an anonymous article in *Lidová demokracie*, the daily of the Czechoslovak People's Party, in April 1970, and continues in the same spirit:

> Perhaps in fifty years, that is, in the not too historically distant future, it will be recognized that this had not been worth it, because coal will no longer be mined there and all that will remain of one billion Czechoslovak crowns will be an item in an old record of state-budget revenues – or that there was not as much coal as had previously been thought and the costs of new construction and mining where higher than anticipated.[520]

Stanislav Ráček (1939–2014), who repeatedly wrote newspaper reports and journalistic essays about Most in the late 1960s and first half of the 1970s, formulated in *Mladý svět* what was at the time

---

[520] 'Město za 90 milionů tun', *Lidová demokracie*, 4 April 1970.

quite a bold statement: 'Future generations may call us barbarians who destroyed the landscape and razed a once rich Bohemian historic town, which had ranked amongst the top ten of the thirty royal boroughs.' Ráček also makes the remarkable observation that it was 'only the death sentence', the decision to demolish old Most, that had awakened interest in the past and the historic value of the town, which had not been present in people's thoughts at all until the mid-1960s, let alone a matter of public interest.[521]

But these voices too, cautiously interpreting the demolition of old Most as a project that would 'perhaps' with time be called barbarian or at least an act that had not been 'worth it', gradually fell silent or the criticism lost more of its edge and was transformed into allusions, forcing one to read between the lines. All in all, given the advance of the demolition, the struggle for the preservation of old Most, carried on by a few interested intellectuals, journalists, and preservation specialists still at the end of the 1960s, no longer made sense by the mid-1970s.

Neither the regimentation of the public space in the normalization years, nor the actual end of old Most, however, meant the end of critical reflection on the whole project. Once formulated, fundamental critiques or proposed alternative solutions usually do not vanish from the world so easily. And that was also true regarding the extraction of all the coal from under old Most. Now, melancholic or dark reflections sought new ways of expression, and by far not only in private correspondence. They were balanced between the private and the public in the milieu of culture that lacked state approval, in the form of photographs, paintings, sculptures, installations, poems, and stories.

Old Most almost does not exist. Instead, a gaping black pit has opened up, as romantic as other pits, but this one is where a town used to be

521 Stanislav Ráček, 'Až teprve ortel smrti', *Mladý svět*, 17 March 1970.

[...] The landscape is in motion: what is extracted has been filled back in, so that when a village or town does not have to give way to mining itself and is on the route to the spoil tip, it is buried. The population movement is sizeable, and so it is that we have a landscape in front of us where cultural tradition yields to industry and is quickly replaced by a pseudo-culture and the inhabitants, largely immigrants [Czechs from the interior and from Volhynia, Slovaks, and Roma], do not assimilate to the historic centre in the traditional environment of the town [...] It is common that people leave their home and go somewhere else, but it is not common that they bury their tradition in slag heaps of clay and coal and actively participate in the demolition. [...] I would very much like to [...] capture all of this in art.[522]

These words were written by the independent artist Jiří Sozanský (b.1946) in the early 1980s in a letter to the art historian Jiří Kotalík (1920–1996), the then director of the National Gallery. The rugged landscape of north Bohemia, which says a lot about human beings' power over the world they inhabit, had attracted artists for decades. Amongst those artists in the 1960s were the photographer Josef Sudek (1896–1976), the poet Emil Juliš (1920–2006), and the painter Bohdan Kopecký (1928–2010). It was Kopecký, who, in about 1970, opened up the topic of the north Bohemian landscape for Sozanský, a man one generation younger than himself. But it took ten years before Sozanský and eventually other independent artists chose the depopulated, vanishing, old Most as a place for their art projects. The message of Sozanský's 'environments', as he called his installations, is also clear from his lively correspondence with Juliš and from the *Most 81/82* catalogue.[523] By means of installations, Sozanský sought to confront for the last time the forsaken and lifeless quality of the disappearing town, to raise questions, to

---

522 Jiří Sozanský, letter to Jiří Kotalík, August 1981, in Jiří Sozanský, *Zóna*, Prague, 2014, pp. 7–9.
523 Jiří Sozanský, *Most 81/82*, Prague: Jazzová sekce, 1982.

26. and **27.**
An installation
by Jiří Sozanský
in vacated houses
awaiting demolition.

remind the viewer that this was where people's stories had once unfolded.[524] The atmosphere of the dying town, whose downfall had been brought about by people themselves, attracted other independent artists, including the architect Jiří Borl (b.1950), the sculptor Lubomír Janečka (b.1948), the photographers Jiří Putta (b.1935), Ivan Dolejšek (b.1947), Petr Kovář (b. 1950), Ondřej Šik (1944–1997), and Pavel Jasanský (b.1938), the poet and artist Miroslav Urban (b.1953), the painter Václav Bláha (b.1948), who by means of silhouettes of silent passers-by, people randomly encountering each other, gluttons, and bellowers parodied the alienation and consumerist narrow-mindedness of people in the Ore Mountains, and the film-maker Michal Baumbruck (b.1956), who made a documentary about old Most and these art projects. The distinguished composer Petr Eben (1929–2007) accompanied the exhibition of photographs of the Most installations, which Sozanský (b.1946) organized in the arts and community centre in Dobříš, about 65 km southwest of Prague, with his piano composition inspired by the topic.

The position of these independent critics in 'normalized' Czechoslovakia, though largely typical, is still remarkable. They had an absolutely marginal impact on 'public opinion' and at least until the 1980s it was inconceivable that their views on the demolition of old Most would have been published in, say, *Mladá fronta* (if we remain with the comparison with the second half of the 1960s). Yet Sozanský was at this time regularly being granted permission to make art in an otherwise off-limits zone of a town being demolished, and a book of his was being published by a state-owned publishing house; Eben was teaching at Charles University, generally considered to be a leading ideological institution; and the Most installations were being held under the wing of the director of the National Gallery, Kotalík, who together with Sozanský and his friends, even went to look at the ruins of old Most, and by no means incognito. The photographer

---

524 See the quotation from *Most 81/82*, in Sozanský, *Zóna*, pp. 14–15.

Dolejšek later recalled how Kotalík took him and Sozanský to Most in a government Tatra 613 limousine.[525]

The ostensibly impassable boundary between the opposition, society, and the authorities seemed, and not only on that day, to have vanished into the fog of the Ore Mountains, into an indefinite zone of negotiation and unexpected coalitions.

✕✕✕

In any event, criticism of the demolition of old Most after 1970 was pushed to the margins and changed form. But official discourse also changed. Though the normalization period meant the return of a more authoritarian mode of domination on the model of the late 1950s and early 1960s (including the mass media, now even more strictly controlled), there could be no mechanical return to the *Sinnwelt* of those days. The official discourse of 'real socialism' in the Czechoslovakia of the 1970s thus did not consist in a resuscitation of the enthusiastic building of socialism of the early 1950s, nor could it be the purely technocratic productivism dominating the late 1950s and first half of the 1960s. A number of the emphasized points that had been made by social critics in the 1960s who were now marginalized, were sophisticatedly integrated not only into what was now admissible, but also into what was officially proclaimed. That included not only condemnation of the Stalinist show trials, but also an area that was central to the Most story – namely, respect for the cultural heritage and the preservation of historic monuments. Taking a closer look at the transformations of the ways in which the demolition of old Most was justified and the ways the image of the new Most was constructed enables us to observe the creation of a new paradigm, the synthesis of an engineering and technocratic mentality with a humanist emphasis on consideration for the cultural heritage, which together created the environment of the work and everyday life of modern people.

525 Ivan Dolejšek, *Most*, in Sozanský, *Zóna*, pp. 165–66.

Reconciliation

In 1973, the state-owned Krátký film Praha made a documentary film for a general audience about the demolition of the old Most and the building of the new city, both of which were then under way. The film did not deal with coal mining or energy policy and only in its last minute is the viewer presented with a couple of shots of the modern urban planning and architectural designs of the new Most. During its 25 minutes, the film relates the 'long, glorious past' of Most, from its founding by the north Bohemian House of Hrabischitz and kings of Bohemia in the thirteenth century to alleged combat between the Germans, who 'identified with the Catholics', and the Czechs, for whom, according to the documentary, the town was won back to the Kingdom of Bohemia by the Hussite leader and King of Bohemia George of Poděbrady (*reg.* 1420–71), all the way to the working class's revolutionary struggle for social justice. The title of the film, which was made and broadcast by Československá televize at the impetus of the Party and the Government just when its subject, Most, was being razed, is *Historie nezanikne* (History will not die).[526]

The way the Most story was told now changed, though not dramatically and not in every respect. 'High-quality brown coal' continued to form the unquestionable treasure for which many things had to be sacrificed. And the image of the new Most as the City of Roses, which enabled modern people to lead lives with dignity was not challenged in the official discourse either. The 'feudal and capitalist' past, which, from the perspective of the 1950s, was supposed to be rejected or overcome, gradually began to play another role. The city, which was a graphic example of the ruthless demolition of the cultural legacy, was now to become the showcase of how to preserve

526 *Historie nezanikne*, Krátký film Praha, Československá televize, 1973, 29:03, archiv ČT, IDEC 273 531 15718.

the traces of the glorious past, which the Communist elites sought to use as an instrument for the legitimation of late socialist domination. How the reconciliation of the apparently irreconcilable took place is related in the following section.

THE NEW FACE OF MODERNITY

In the first half of the 1970s, international efforts to make the preservation of the cultural heritage a global political topic came to a peak. In 1972, the World Heritage Convention was created, governed by the World Heritage Committee supported by the World Heritage Centre of UNESCO (United Nations Educational, Scientific and Cultural Organisation). And that same year the United Nations Conference on the Human Environment (also known as the Stockholm Conference) was held. Three years later, European Architectural Heritage Year was declared by the Council of Europe, to 'mobilize the interest and support of all sections of the [European] community'. Though these last two events were rooted in western Europe, they also elicited a response in the state-socialist countries of central and eastern Europe.[527] The World Heritage Convention, whose signatories included the Soviet Union, but not the Czechoslovak Socialist Republic, is evidence of the role that conservation played in the development of the preservation of historic monuments and the cultural heritage: the convention includes both of these components, which were (and continue to be) threatened by the expansionist nature of modern civilization. At the same time, the convention is concerned with the protection of the cultural landscape, a phenomenon that links natural wealth and cultural heritage. Apart from the wide scope of what it covers, the convention is extraordinary in the global reach of the countries it relates to. The UNESCO list of World Heritage Sites, which has been made on the basis of the convention, today contains more than a thousand sites (mostly historic monuments and whole cities), which thanks to it enjoy greater prestige and protection. The list serves as an international instrument that can be used to encourage states to adopt important

---

527 Glendinning, 'Heritage Complexities in the Socialist Bloc, 1945–89', *The Conservation Movement*, pp. 359–89.

measures or at least to prevent the worst violations against the conservation of the historic character of individual protected sites.[528]

Like the countries of western Europe and North America, many of the state-socialist countries in the decades after the Second World War also confronted the threat of industrialization, urbanization, and many-layered modernization at their high point. Although the influence that urban modernization had on widening the gaps between the individual income groups, which in the 1960s drew criticism especially in the United States,[529] could not really manifest itself in the state-socialist countries, the ethos of rational planning for the future was that much stronger here.[530] The absence of a market and a plurality of private owners, moreover, sometimes made it possible in the socialist countries to carry out grandiose projects such as would have required years of negotiation and compromise in the liberal capitalist West.

In the socialist countries, however, criticism of modern urban planning, modern architecture, and lack of consideration for the cultural heritage was articulated more cautiously than in the West and the critics spent more time looking for a suitable vocabulary. One of the reasons was the incontestable fact that the authoritarian regimes, by means of censorship, were able to delay the emergence of critical discourse. Nevertheless, censorship and limitations on the space of public debate, as is evident from the intellectual history of the socialist dictatorships, did not necessarily prevent the gradual formulation of a critical vocabulary and its emergence. It happened in complicated twists and turns, first in opposition circles

---

528 Francesco Francioni (ed.), *The 1972 World Heritage Convention: A Commentary*, Oxford: Oxford University Press, 2008; Dennis Rodwell, 'The Unesco World Heritage Convention, 1972–2012: Reflections and Directions', *The Historic Environment: Policy & Practice* 3 (1), June 2012, pp. 64–85.
For the full text of the convention in English and seven other languages, https://whc.unesco.org /en/conventiontext/ Accessed December 2018.
529 Jacobs, *The Death and Life of Great American Cities*.
530 For more on this, see the 'Utopia' section.

and unpublished reports by expert groups and then, fragmentarily, in critical discourse, making its way into specialist or intellectual periodicals, until eventually, often in coded language, it penetrated the mainstream media.

The authoritarian form of government and its efforts to control the flow of information were not the only reasons for the long absence of criticism of modernity and lack of consideration for historic built-up areas, and they definitely do not offer a satisfying explanation for it. In connection with the criticism of the reconstruction of towns in the modernist spirit, the special circumstances of the attitude towards works of the past played an important role in the state-socialist countries, perhaps even more important than that played by the regimentation of the public space. One of the special circumstances was the breaking with the past, as emphasized by Communist ideology, in consequence of which everything old was linked with inimical categories: religion, feudalism, and the bourgeoisie. This break with the past was adopted by people as a starting point even more in areas where there had been a mass exchange of population – as, for example, in western and northern Poland and the Bohemian borderlands. Another complication in people's attitudes towards the historic built-up areas (which was intensified by Czech admiration for modernist architecture in the late 1950s and early 1960s) was the temporarily autonomous development both of the architectural debate and of building practice in the socialist countries of central and eastern Europe in the 1950s (and in the Soviet Union as early as the 1930s). These were anomalies of socialist realism.

In many Western countries the 1950s were the high point of modernist optimism in the attitude towards the cultural heritage, the urban environment, and the construction of new cities and neighbourhoods, which had only been marginally slowed down by the Revivalist 'preservationist' discourse. From the end of the 1940s onwards, the socialist countries of central and eastern Europe adopted from the Stalinist Soviet Union socialistic realism in architecture based on a marked Revivalism, pathos, and a conservative attitude towards space. For that reason, in connection with criticism of Stalinism in the second half of the 1950s, the gates swiftly opened to moderate, even purist, mass-produced housing, which was not only a reaction to the continuing housing crisis, but was also an ideological rejection of Stalinist Revivalism.[531] The prefab concrete-panel block and the housing estate thus did not penetrate the towns of the socialist countries as something specifically Communist, but as modernist pro-Western criticism of the Stalinist diktat of conservative architecture. In the early 1960s, when Jacobs was writing about the death of American cities, not only architects but also intellectual elites of the socialist countries perceived the triumph of modernism in urban planning and construction as part of post-Stalinist revisionism, and therefore, in a way, as liberation from the dogmatic constrictions of the recent past. This is why it would still be a while before the emergence of a full appreciation of the values of the historic town and criticism (based on the experience of living in an historic town) of the alienation caused by modernity and, for example, by the diktat of the transportation infrastructure. The emphasis on the preservation of historic monuments and renovation, which stems from the late Stalinist revulsion towards modernist architecture, although selective, is surprising at first sight, that is, it was not necessarily in contradiction with the destruction or neglect of Church monuments or monuments of non-dominant ethnic groups. In the Khrushchev years, generally considered to have been less irreconcilable to the feudal and bourgeois past, plans from the early 1950s for historic reconstruction which were never carried out were replaced by projects that even Le Corbusier's studio would not have been ashamed to have come up with.[532]

---

531 For more on this topic in Czechoslovakia, see the 'Utopia' section.
532 See the discussion of the plans for the restoration of the large Plac Grunwaldzki (Grunwaldzki Square), Wrocław, Poland, in Glendinning, *The Conservation Movement*, p. 375.

The struggle against the relics of the Stalinist past and the even earlier past in the towns of the Soviet bloc had a strong legitimacy until the second half of the 1960s, because it linked the socially and revolutionarily associated Marxist-Leninist starting points with criticism of the Stalinist dictatorship. In the Soviet Union and in other countries in its sphere of influence during the 1960s, projects emerged or began to emerge which fundamentally corroded the structure and compactness of historic towns, for example, Kalinin Prospekt (1962–68) in Moscow, the Hotel Rossiya (1967–2006) near the Kremlin, and the demolition of many historic buildings in East Germany which had survived the war, like Schinkel's Bauakademie in Berlin and the Paulinerkirche in Leipzig. Just as the incursion of modernism, critical of Stalinism, had been inspired by rational planning and the Constructivist building in western countries, so the new wave of historical consciousness which arose in the socialist bloc in the late 1960s, together with the related movement for the preservation of the cultural heritage, was also inspired by Western models.[533]

The socialist states of course sought to neutralize the independent activity oriented to the conservation of the cultural heritage. It turned out, however, that as in environmental questions in this respect too censorship was only temporarily effective. In the long term, it was far more effective to incorporate these activities into official structures, like the All-Russian Society for the Preservation of Historical and Cultural Monuments (VOPIiK).

Like the organizations for the protection of the natural environment, it too awakened considerable interest and enjoyed public favour, so that by the mid-1970s it had 22 million members (400,000 in Leningrad alone). Already at the end of the 1960s, the Soviet Union began to offset calls for the preservation of the cultural heritage by

---

533 That is evident in criticism of the demolition of old Most, which was expressed from 1967 to 1970. See the chapter 'For the Old Town' in the 'Criticism' section.

means of specific actions, at first highly selective, for example, when the relevant authorities earmarked a group of exceptionally valuable Russian Orthodox churches to be saved from demolition and then restored. In 1973, the historic centre of Moscow was divided into nine conservation zones, so that henceforth projects like the Hotel Rossiya or the dividing up of the Arbat District were no longer possible.[534]

Developments in the socialist countries of central and eastern Europe were similar. After the demolition of the Paulinerkirche in Leipzig in 1968 led to public protests, East German cultural policy started to change fundamentally, and in the 1970s began to be oriented more to the Prussian tradition than to the International Modern.[535] A similar emphasis on national and historical continuity, entailing increased investment in the repair of historic built-up areas and the avoidance of demolition of historically valuable buildings was characteristic of most of the state-socialist countries in the 1970s and 1980s. Czechoslovakia, which could follow on from a long tradition of historic-monument preservation and from an emphasis on national tradition, personified in the 1950s by Zdeněk Nejedlý, was no exception in this regard.

534 See Glendinning, *The Conservation Movement*, pp. 379–73.
535 East Germany, in reaction to European Architectural Heritage Year, in 1975, passed a new law intended to provided more effective preservation for architectural monuments of the past and to facilitate the renovation of some. The centre of East Berlin was definitely moved from the former Stalinallee to Unter den Linden in the 1970s, a street lined with monumental buildings from the eighteenth and nineteenth centuries, which were being restored at that time. Another significant gesture was the reconstruction of the Nikolaiviertel, in Berlin, in a Revival style in the 1980s.

THE AMALGAM OF NORMALIZATION

> Historic settlements that are the cradles of the history of each of us,
> and of the whole commonwealth of human settlements, regions, and
> states, became the clearest evidence of the continuity of human life and
> the meaningfulness of work and of making things, the truest record of
> the history of society and its efforts to better its lot and the conditions of
> living in ever-greater dimensions, from the courts of monarchs
> to the totality of today's commonwealth.
>
> (Otakar Nový, 1977[536])

We encountered the architect Nový in this book once before, when,
in *Mladá fronta* in June 1968, he roundly criticized what he called
Gründerzeit socialism and the demolition of old Most as one of its
worst manifestations. Less than ten years later, in *Památky a příroda* (Historic monuments and nature), the periodical of the State
Institute for the Preservation of Historic Monuments and Environmental Protection, he defended essentially the same view. Emphasizing considerate progress, which could not come to a halt for fear
of unnecessary slum clearances or new construction in historic settlements, while respecting the strict rules of preventing the 'spread
of technological high-handedness'. As in Richta's work during the
normalization years,[537] here too one perceives an effort to change
former criticism into a constructive, loyal attitude, to which some
'details' of the criticism of course fell victim and its edge was dulled.

Nový's article was in fact a revised version of a paper he had given
at an international symposium entitled 'New Life in Historic Sites'
in early October 1976. The symposium, on the regeneration of historic settlements, was held under the auspices of the Czech and Slovak

---

536 Otakar Nový, 'Funkce historických sídel v podmínkách současného rozvoje společnosti',
Památky a příroda: Časopis Státní památkové péče a ochrany přírody 2 (1), 1977, pp. 7–16.
537 See the chapter 'City, Forest, Smoke: The Birth of Environmental Consciousness in Socialist
Czechoslovakia'.

ministers of culture in collaboration with UNESCO. Attended by 143 participants from 22 countries, it was held from 30 September to 5 October 1976 in Prague and Bratislava.[538] In addition to the presentation of plans for the regeneration of the historic centre of Prague and the Prague Castle precinct, papers were given by architects and preservation specialists from western and central Europe. The topics ranged from the regeneration of the historic core of Edinburgh to reviving historic settlements in Poland and in East and West Germany, to the revalorization of the Belgian architectural heritage and to specific examples from Switzerland and Greece. The symposium was also attended by deputies of the Czech and Slovak ministers of culture and the deputy mayors of Prague and Bratislava. The Czech minister of culture, Milan Klusák (1923–1992), hosted Czech and foreign preservationists and other experts in Waldstein House, Prague, thus making it clear that the preservation of the cultural heritage was a priority of Czechoslovak policy.

It was no coincidence that the former quarterly of the State Institute for the Preservation of Historic Monuments and Environmental Protection began in the second half of the 1970s to be published ten times a year, and, moreover, under the new name *Památky a příroda*, indicating that two related areas required care (*péče*) and protection (*ochrana*). The two terms became standard at that time in the official discourse of normalization Czechoslovakia.[539] That fully

---

538 Concerning the symposium, see *Památky a příroda* 2 (1), 1977, p. 23. See also Aleš Vošahlík (ed.), *Nový život v historických sídlech: Symposium ČSSR* Prague: L'Institut d'Etat de la Protection des Monuments Historiques et de la Sauvegarde de la Nature, [1977].
539 The protection of historic monuments has a long tradition in Czechoslovakia and particularly in Bohemia and Moravia-Silesia, not interrupted even after 1948 (see the chapter 'In Defence of the Old Town' in the 'Criticism' section). The officially sanctioned discourse of the period called normalization thus followed on both from the ideology of national Communism, which was embodied throughout the 1950s by Zdeněk Nejedlý in particular, and from the conservative emphases of the post-Stalinist period, when the Historic Monuments Protection Act 1958 (Zákon o památkové péči) was passed, which was in force until 1987, when a new act was passed. The emphasis on the value of protection of the national heritage (and its role in officially sanctioned discourse), however, increased considerably from the late 1960s and the early 1970s,

comported with the broader European change in the discourse about tradition and cultural heritage, whose protection and further development were now increasingly understood throughout Europe and North America as important aspects of modern civilization. Again comporting with important international documents, including the World Heritage Convention, the periodical also linked the two spheres to which the central values of informed capitalism and 'real socialism' could be applied. Both the specialist debate about monument preservation and the policy of protection and preservation of cultural heritage developed in normalization Czechoslovakia in interaction with the Western world. These were not only one-off events, like the conference in the autumn of 1976. Though it did not ratify the World Heritage Convention until 1990, Czechoslovakia remained a member of UNESCO. An important role in international cooperation in the protection of the cultural heritage was played by the Czechoslovak National Committee of ICOMOS (the International Council for Monuments and Sites, based in Paris, and, since 1972, the main advisory body of UNESCO for questions of cultural heritage).[540] From 1971 until his death, the chairman of the Czechoslovak National Committee was the distinguished architect and urbanist Emanuel Hruška (1906–1989), who in the 1970s and 1980s significantly contributed to the plans for the repair and revival of the urban preservation zones (*městské památkové zóny*). Throughout the 1980s, Hruška was, among other things, an honorary member of the General Assembly of ICOMOS, and gave papers in European capitals from Vienna to Paris, while chairman of the Club for the Preservation of Old Prague (Klub za starou Prahu).

in reaction both to domestic criticism of the destruction of historic monuments and to international attention paid to the topic.

540 The periodical *Památky a příroda* (published ten times a year by the State Institute for the Preservation of Historic Monuments and Environmental Protection (Státní památkové péče a ochrany přírody), regularly ran articles on the topic in collaboration with UNESCO. In 1981, it had a special issue on the fifteen years of the existence of the Czech branch of ICOMOS and its prospects. See *Památky a příroda* 6 (4), 1981, pp. 193–257.

From the perspective of the late-socialist state, monuments of the past were important not only as sources of historical knowledge or as repositories of aesthetic values. They were also assigned 'culturally educational' and 'culturally ideological' importance, and both the socialist State and every one of its citizens were responsible for their preservation. The preserved traces of the past in the form of historic monuments thus, from the perspective of those days, made it possible 'to gain historical knowledge and to build a new culture'. They were an 'indispensable part of man's environment', helping him 'in his education, up-bringing, and development of aesthetic feeling [...] to create his own sense of national pride and awareness.'[541]

The emphasis on the past and the care of heritage was not only a defensive reaction presenting critics and the whole world with the feigned considerateness of the socialist State. At least two aspects attest to this having been more than merely an ideological pretence: the increased efforts of the socialist State to inculcate in its citizens an interest in, and positive attitude towards, historic monuments and real efforts, supported by the political elites, to protect both individual monuments and whole historic entities.

The popularization of important places of Czech and Slovak history, including visits to castles and manor houses, as a generally welcome way of spending leisure time (besides the weekend cottage craze, probably the most widespread way), especially for families with children, also as a way of teaching Czech history and geography in the school curriculum, and in a wide variety of instructional publications and manuals for the preservation of historic monuments all bore fruit. During the 1970s and 1980s, cultural heritage went from being a topic of intellectuals in the humanities, specialists, and oddballs to being a widely experienced aspect of the environment in which Czechs lived. It became something that they sought out,

541 Antonín Sum (ed.), *Památky a mládež: Příručka pro mladé ochránce památek*, Prague: Státní zemědělské nakladatelství, 1983, p. 8.

did not want to miss, and identified with. For example, according to public opinion research from the second half of the 1970s, in reply to the general question how the Prague transport situation should be resolved, only 6 per cent of the respondents replied that they preferred a more economical variant if it entailed violating the historic character of the city, whereas a full 82 per cent of the respondents were clearly in favour of a markedly more expensive solution that was more considerate of historic monuments. Twenty-one per cent of the respondents did not consider monument preservation to be currently sufficient and amongst respondents with post-secondary education more than half felt it was lacking. Forty-four per cent of the respondents at that time often visited heritage sites, and slightly more than fifty per cent had so far visited only occasionally or not at all.[542]

Why did the State invest so much effort and money into encouraging its citizens to love and respect traces of the past which it had sometimes grossly neglected or destroyed? Apart from the discursive shift, thanks to which care for cultural heritage and familiarity with it began in the most developed countries to be generally considered a sign of being highly civilized, several other reasons typical of state-socialist regimes, including normalization Czechoslovakia, naturally suggest themselves. Although already in the 1970s the number of people interested in the cultural heritage, including those who considered its preservation to be of greater value than, for example, economical management of public funds, clearly rose, the feeling that the socialist State was responsibly looking after historic monuments still predominated.[543] Since in the socialist system, where there were no private owners of larger properties or rich patrons, it was almost exclusively the State that looked after monuments, its elites could count on the increasing gratitude of the citizenry for

---

542 Květoslava Křížová, 'Památky a veřejné mínění', *Památky a příroda* 2 (4), 1977, pp. 157–59.
543 For the public opinion polls on this, see ibid.

this care and protection in the future – just as they expected it in the spheres of education, social security, including old-age pensions and health care. From public opinion research in Czechoslovakia, it is also known that the vast majority of the population did not agree with an overly benevolent approach to those who damaged or destroyed cultural monuments and they demanded stricter punishment for them, including the obligation to return damaged monuments to their original condition at their own expense.[544] Demands of this sort were fully in keeping with the normalization discourse about strict measures to be taken against 'elements that refuse to conform', various 'hooligans', and 'losers', to whom the State should make it absolutely clear that they do not belong to the decent society of law-abiding citizens. In the 1970s it was hardly obvious that historic awareness would gradually lead to a more critical view of the State's neglect or destruction of cultural monuments and old built-up areas, and could ultimately turn against the original intentions to foster that awareness, let alone that, like environmental awareness, it could serve to delegitimize state socialism.

That the socialist State took seriously the preservation of monuments of the past as a sign of an advanced culture, that is, the protection and care of cultural heritage, should be evident from the following examples. In the 1970s and 1980s, in addition to smaller protected areas, large urban preservation zones were established and expanded. There were more than thirty of them in Czechoslovakia at the beginning of the 1980s. This was not merely a legislative category to boast about internationally. In subsequent years, many of these historic urban preservation areas (*městské památkové rezervace*) were either completely reconstructed or the national committees, in collaboration with the preservationists, at least took measures to ensure that the most valuable parts of these historic centres, like the city walls, would be saved. Such steps were taken in the

---

544 Ibid., p. 157.

1970s, for example, in the towns of Český Krumlov, České Budějovice, Telč, Slavonice, Olomouc, Tachov, Tábor, Čáslav, Litoměřice, Úštěk, Cheb, Loket, Hradec Králové, Polička, and Pelhřimov.[545] In the Czech Republic in the first half of the 1980s, there were only two regions in which no urban preservation area or zone had been established – one of them was the Most district.[546]

The largest preservation area in Czechoslovakia, indeed one of the largest in the world, is the Městská památková rezervace Praha. It was established in 1971 and its existence has considerably limited highhanded building projects, particularly for skyscrapers, not only in the medieval core of Prague, but also in the New Town, whose built-up areas consist mostly of nineteenth-century buildings. It was this linking of the protection of the medieval core together with the urban fabric from the nineteenth century and first third of the twentieth century which in its day made the Prague preservation area an example of a modern comprehensive approach to heritage preservation.[547] The overall restoration of the Prague preservation area was planned beginning in the mid-1970s and was carried out ten years later. In the meantime, however, still in the 1970s, Prague Castle was restored and, in 1981, so was the National Theatre.[548]

It is in the attitude towards the heritage of the 'glorious past' and particularly in the discourse and practice of monument preservation that one can observe probably the greatest instances of convergence between, on the one hand, criticism of Stalinist and post-Stalinist productivism, as it developed in the second half of the 1960s, and,

545 Aleš Vošahlík, 'Příklady regenerace městských památkových rezervací v ČSR, *Památky a příroda* 2 (2), 1977, pp. 81–87.

546 Aleš Vošahlík and Alena Hanzlová, *Koncepce památkové ochrany historických měst v ČSR*, Prague: Státní ústav památkové péče a ochrany přírody, 1983, p. 169, with a map of the Czech Socialist Republic showing heritage towns.

547 See Aleš Vošahalík, 'Pojetí ochrany historických měst v České socialistické republice', *Památky a příroda* 6 (4), 1981, pp. 225–32.

548 Josef Hobzek, *Vývoj památkové péče v českých zemích*, Prague: Státní ústav památkové péče a ochrany přírody, 1987; Vošahlík and Hanzlová, *Koncepce památkové ochrany.*

on the other, the official normalization discourse, which, in keeping with this criticism, put the emphasis, in the 1970s and 1980s, on the tradition of preservation and heritage. The constellation, peculiar to the normalization period, of suppressing certain forms of criticism while actually accepting them – that is, gradually integrating the starting points of the critical discourse into the ideological structure of 'real socialism' – is a feature of Czechoslovak politics in this period.

The dictatorship of consensus,[549] however, did not allow unresolvable or hard-to-resolve conflicts amongst the individual aims and principles which it professed. Though at a general level it praised the development of heavy industry, the expansion of mining, and increasing energy production as fundamental prerequisites for the happy life of socialist man, while professing a considerate approach to the cultural heritage of the Bohemian Lands and Slovakia, it could avoid such conflicts of values and concrete policies only at the cost of pushing some topics and even whole spheres of life out of the public space – and to a certain extent also out of internal political debate. One result was the creation of parallel realities. And they did not necessarily exist only on the margins, in areas left to the mercy of the interests of mining and production. Part of the Lesser Town of Prague was marked for demolition because of a planned, but never carried out, motorway. In the district of Vinohrady, a local market was meant to be demolished. And, in connection with the building of the Žižkov Television Tower most of the Jewish cemetery there was demolished and paved with concrete. Violence could be surprisingly close to non-violence, destruction to preservation, without the political elites' willingness to really admit these contradictions.

---

549 This term is used especially by the German historian Martin Sabrow for late socialism. See Martin Sabrow, 'Der Konkurs der Konsensdiktatur', in Konrad H. Jarausch and Martin Sabrow (eds), *Der Weg in den Untergang: Der innere Zerfall der DDR*, Göttingen: Vandenhoeck & Ruprecht, 1999, pp. 83–116.

The linguistic construction of the world, mediated by politicians, the mass media, and many specialists, in which the disparate and inconsistent could exist side by side undisturbed – a world that pretended that all of this had created one ever-perfecting whole – could have a temporarily stabilizing effect and thus provide legitimacy to late socialist domination. It was precisely this feature, however, that contained the germ of its future disintegration.[550]

One of the most glaringly different parallel realities was in the Ore Mountains. Whereas representatives of the national committees and local Party organizations consulted with experts on how most sensitively to repair and revise the historic centre of, say, Litoměřice or Úštěk, a few dozen kilometres away bulldozers were tearing up the pavement of the streets of old Most and demolition crews were blowing up historic buildings, farm houses, chapels, churches, convents and monasteries. Just as state-organized or at least state-approved physical violence in normalization Czechoslovakia was pushed into special and, if possible, hidden zones of psychiatric hospitals, prisons, secret-police interrogation rooms, and off-limits border areas,[551] it was as if the destructiveness and ruthlessness of industrial modernity had been banished to a kind of zone where other rules applied and one said little about that. North Bohemia, together with several other places, constituted such a 'war zone', a special place in which one need not feel particularly bound by values that one would otherwise so vehemently profess. It was a zone in the war against the landscape and the past, so noisy that it

550 See Alexej Yurchak, 'Soviet Hegemony of Form: Everything Was Forever, Until It Was No More', *Comparative Studies in Society and History* 45 (3), June 2003. For the Czech milieu, see Michal Pullmann, *Konec experimentu: Přestavba a pád socialismu v Československu*, Prague: Scriptorium, 2012. For more on the sources of the legitimacy and delegitimization of the socialist dictatorship in the period of reflexive modernity, see the conclusory section of the present book.
551 See Michal Pullmann, '"Ruhige Arbeit" und die Einhegung der Gewalt: Ideologie und gesellschaftlicher Konsens in der spätsozialistischen Tschechoslowakei', in Volker Zimmermann and Michal Pullmann (eds), *Ordnung und Sicherheit, Devianz und Kriminalität im Staatssozialismus: Tschechoslowakei und DDR 1948/49–1989*, Göttingen: Vandenhoeck Ruprecht, 2014, pp. 39–56.

seemed to be impossible to hear the voices talking about respect for, and preservation of, the fruits of previous generations as the basis of civilized socialist society.

As I suggested in the introduction to this part of the book, the impression of such a total lack of interconnections is misleading. It is, then, all the more important to try, using the example of Most, the most savage front line of the north Bohemian 'war zone', to understand the persistent efforts to reconcile the parallel realities of destruction and thoughtfulness. The political and economic elites of the Party, the State, and the region of the Ore Mountains needed to persuade not only the Czechoslovak public and, indeed, the international public, but also, and perhaps mainly, themselves, that the reality there is not a zone of wrack and ruin, but, on the contrary, an essential part of peace-loving, considerate, socialist modernity.

THE VELVET DEMOLITION

Unknown men appear in a village graveyard. They pull up the wooden crosses and demolish the gravestones. The people in the picturesque village of Matyora, on an island in the middle of the River Angara, in Siberia, have known for some time that their homes would in a few months be submerged by the water behind the dam being built. Nevertheless, they are overcome with rage. Their ancestors, parents, friends, everyone who thought they would rest there for ever, lie in that graveyard. It is an inviolable site of memory, and strangers, the workers who have been told to clear it out, have now escaped from the enraged locals who have lived here for generations.

Thus begins the novel *Farewell to Matyora* by Valentin Rasputin (1937–2015), one of the first environmentalist works of fiction published in the Soviet Union.[552] The engineers from the government commission coordinating the demolition of old Most may not have had an opportunity to learn something from Rasputin's story (it was not published in the Soviet Union until 1976 and not in Czech translation until four years later), but they acted considerably more cautiously than their Soviet colleagues in distant Siberia.

Already in the 1960s, the representatives of the town were aware that the demolition of the Most cemetery would be harder to justify than the demolition of the rest of the town, which most of the people perceived as consisting of crumbling old houses and a non-functioning infrastructure. And this was true even though many of the descendants of the dead no longer lived in Most or even in Czechoslovakia, for they had been expelled to Germany right after the war. From the beginning, in connection with the cemetery, most of the talk was about moving, not about demolition. Like the living, even the dead were to be moved out of old Most.

---

552 Rasputin, *Proshchaniye s Matyoroy.*

The chairman of the Most Municipal National Committee, Miroslav Fleišer (d.1975) sought to find a way to inform the public about 'moving' the cemetery shortly after it had ceased to be used for burials, in other words, a few years before its final demolition. He did not fail to emphasize that the 'moving of the remains of the dead will be carried out with reverence'. The living could also choose how they wanted their ancestors remains to be dealt with – to have them moved to separate graves in the new Most cemetery or to a common grave there, or to have them cremated in the Most crematorium, where they could go to pick up the urns. In the first instances, to have the 'accessories of the graves', for example, tombstones, plaques, and granite kerbs, also moved to the new cemetery, all at the expense of the SHD mining company. If, however, the second or third option were preferred, next of kin could, within a year of moving their ancestors' remains, pick up the tombstones and the rest of the graves at the old cemetery.[553]

The moving of the cemetery was also discussed in the mass media in a similar spirit, in papers published in cities ranging from Ústí nad Labem in north Bohemia to Bratislava, the capital of Slovakia. The story was most covered by a newspaper intended for the remaining members of the German minority in Czechoslovakia, *Die Volkszeitung*. In a page-long interview, entitled '24,000 Dead People Are Moving', two SHD officials knowledgeably explained how a 'team of twelve stonemasons and five gravediggers, in other words, all experts, are making sure that the work is carried out absolutely right', and, they emphasized, 'everybody is working under strict supervision'.[554] They mentioned the generosity of the SHD, which

---

553 NA, f. ÚPV – běžná spisovna (nezprac.), kart. 204, sign. 371/1/575, Přemístění hlavního hřbitova v Mostě, 30. října 1965.

554 'Bei den Arbeiten wird ein Kollektiv von zwölf Steinmetzen und fünf Totengräbern beschäftigt, also durchwegs Fachkräfte, welche eine sachgemäße Durchführung der Arbeiten garantieren, wobei ich die strenge Aufsicht, unter der sie stehen nicht unerwähnt lassen will.' '24 000 Tote ziehen um: Gespräch mit Direktor Motl vom Braunkohlenrevier Most und seinem Stellvertreter Marek.' *Die Volkszeitung*, 29. 9. 1967.

was covering all the costs, even if some next of kin did not make their application by the announced deadline, 30 April 1968. If they applied late, the responsible officials would try not to proceed in an overly bureaucratic manner. There would be a fee to pay only if urns had to be sent abroad at the request of an expelled descendent of the deceased. The transfer of the dead was planned to take four years and it anticipated moving a total of 2,000 family plots and single graves – the remains of about 24,000 people. Because in the new cemetery everyone buried since 1853 was to have a common monument, at which a memorial ceremony would be held annually on All Souls Day, the SHD suggested that the dead would be recalled here more than anywhere else.[555] Other newspapers also wrote in a similar spirit about the thoughtful moving of the dead and the reviving of their memory.[556]

Unlike in the Rasputin story, the originators of this project anticipated the emotions linked with the demolition of the place where one's ancestors had been laid to rest. They faced them with a certain understanding and were able to neutralize them. The problem was more that a large number of the next of kin showed no interest in their ancestors' remains and particularly not in their gravestones. The District National Committee therefore deduced that any abandoned and forgotten gravestones could be demolished with a clear conscience. The local officials thus discharged their duties towards the next of kin, but forgot that even if there were a lack of interest a cemetery still has a historic value that should be documented, as followed from the general agreement with the preservationists concerning the procedure of the demolition of the town. Employees of the State Institute for the Preservation of Historic Monuments and Environmental Protection complained that the District National Committee, when demolishing part of the cemetery, had failed to

555 Ibid.
556 See 'Práca s mrtvými', *Smena*, 26 July 1966.

arrange for the documentation 'of the abundant sepulchral architecture' and important information, which the cemetery provided, about ethnic relations in the history of north Bohemia (particularly the 'monuments of the former Czech minority pioneers and Czech institutions of old Austria').[557]

Projects for the preservation of the cultural heritage of Most, mainly the moving of the Gothic buildings and their composition into a large-scale memorial of some kind, were not pushed through, despite the increasingly dominant discourse about considerateness[558] – with one fundamental exception, which the next chapter will discuss. All the more, however, did the authorities devote themselves to documentation of the town, the preservation of small monuments and also, especially after 1970, the publicity of this conservationist-documentary dimension of the Most experiment.

Thus, apart from the State Institute for the Preservation of Historic Monuments and Environmental Protection and its regional branch, a team of archaeologists was also working intensively in Most. And, in connection with the years of research, the Archaeological Institute of the Czechoslovak Academy of Sciences even set up a branch here. Apart from these specialized institutions, the commission of the district preservationists attached to the District National Committee was also active; for example, in 1975, the commission proposed that about 200 architectural and decorative elements or small statuary from 96 Most buildings should be preserved. Thus, not only first-rate works of art were saved (documented and preserved mainly thanks to the regional centre), but so too were a wide variety of small statues and reliefs from the houses of burghers, together with ornamentation of windows, gables, and balconies, columns, entrance ways, corbels, bossages, railings, grilles, festoons, doors,

---

557   NA, f. SÚPPOP (nezpracovaný), Hřbitov v Mostě – exhumace starší části. Dokumentace, 5. března 1968.
558   See the chapter 'In Defence of the Old Town' in the 'Criticism' section.

volutes, gables, arches, and parts of vaults.[559] Of the state list of 53 immovable monuments in Most (not counting Hněvín Castle, which stands at a safe distance on a hill above the town), which had been listed already in 1971,[560] only a handful of them could be saved. The commission of the district preservation office also recorded 75 small church items, ranging from altars to statuary, which for various technical reasons could not be moved. All the more feverishly, then, did the local authorities, institutions, and individuals work to save what they could – there was no time to spare. The battle was waged not only with the demolitions in progress, which were freeing the space for mining, but also with the Most 'gold-diggers' – private collectors and petty thieves who understood in time that 'old junk' would one day be valuable.[561] The SHD and the political authorities did not put any obstacles in the way of those preservationist efforts and in some respects even provided all kinds of support. That can be interpreted as looking for excuses, as a sophisticated political strategy, but also as evidence that those behind the demolition of the old town, the people responsible for the whole project, were aware or were gradually becoming aware that something irreplaceable was being lost.

During the demolition of Most, particularly in the course of the 1970s, the preservationists, archaeologists, and institutions they worked for could thus, at least with partial success, demand the fulfilment of the conditions that they had once set for their acceptance of the demolition of the historic town. In addition to meeting the terms of the trilateral agreement between the Ministry of Culture, the SHD, and the North Bohemian Regional National Committee in Ústí nad Labem, concerning the permission to enable detailed

---

559 SOkA Most, f. 207 (ONV II), inv. č. 1234–1243, ev. j. 445, Zápis z komise okresní památkové péče ONV v Mostě ze dne 1. 2. 1975.
560 SOkA Most, f. 207 (ONV II), inv. č. 1223–1233, ev. j. 444, Státní seznam nemovitých památek Severočeského kraje, k 1. 9. 1971.
561 'Gibt es in Most Goldgräber?', *Volkszeitung*, 1 May 1969.

28. Detail of the façade of a house on Mírovo náměstí (Peace Square). To save it or to sacrifice it?

documentation and preservation of all historically valuable movable objects, there were also several dozen concrete documentary works, as well as the dismantling and moving of various objects, in connection with a total of 22 large historic buildings or sets of buildings, another roughly 25 houses of burghers, and several monuments related to the labour movement.[562] Monuments and commemorative plaques were also moved. The situation became somewhat more complicated when individual institutions and government offices (including cultural commissions and departments of the Municipal National Committee and the District National Committee, the

562 SOkA Most, f. 207 (ONV II), inv. č. 1223–1233, ev. j. 444, Documents to ensure the preservation of historic monuments during the demolition of Most, March 1964.

district museum, groups of volunteer preservationists, the Archae-ological Institute of the Academy of Sciences and its Most branch, and the State Institute for the Preservation of Historic Monuments and Environmental Protection and its regional branch) vied with each other in the work and overlapped, lacking a common coordi-nating body.

Today, many years later, the situation seems absurd. Under the pressure of the SHD and under the supervision of the State and the Party, a whole historic town was changed into piles of rubble and dozens of people in its streets were at the last minute measuring, photographing, dusting off objects, taking them out of meaningful spatial relations and moving them into warehouses or showing them in various little exhibitions.

People who in other circumstances would probably be among the irreconcilable critics of the Most experiment were now involved in this feverish activity. With regard to the preservation of at least frag-ments of memory and the cultural heritage, they were giving this beneficial activity their all. This was a project that they thus helped to legitimate.

At the time when the demolition of the old town was coming to a peak, occasional visitors, who by chance found themselves in the Regional Centre for Historic Monument Preservation in Ústí nad Labem, could in the corridor of the building see a small exhibition about the work done to save wall paintings and statues. They could see two cartouches with the coats of arms of the City of Most and a Renaissance relief that had once decorated the old Most town hall, now taken down from the courthouse. According to a document about the carrying out of monument preservation in the Most dis-trict, elaborated by the department of culture at the Most District National Committee, these 'attractive exhibits', together with vari-ous forms of documentation, provided evidence not only of the diffi-culty and seriousness of saving historic items, but also, 'last but not least, of the importance of their presentation to the public'. It is not known how many people actually saw this exhibition in the corridor or what thoughts it evoked in them. Bureaucrats of the department, however, were convinced (or for some other reason considered it important to emphasize in internal documents) that exhibiting the saved cultural items in a new place (eventually, for example, in the public space of the new Most and in government offices there) would 'become lasting evidence of the socialist State's preservation of the cultural heritage'.[563]

The most fundamental manifestation of the remarkable emphasis on history face to face with the destruction of its material traces was the detailed systematic documentation of the Most project beginning in the 1960s. With the support of the local and top-level authorities, two large and costly research projects, one by preservationists, the other by archaeologists, were carried out in parallel in Most beginning in the mid-1960s, resulting in detailed documentation. Apart from this, other research projects were carried out with the participation of a wide variety of institutions, including several at the Academy of Sciences: specialists on ethnology and folklore gathered evidence 'about the lifestyle of the inhabitants of the town', scholars from the Institute for the Theory and History of Art considered the development of the production of art objects as aspects of human labour, and sociologists were supposed to use the example of Most to add to our understanding of the dynamics of contemporary society. The dying town was thus a unique subject in which the humanities and social sciences had an opportunity to test a technique normally used only in biology and medicine – the autopsy.

The preservationists' research on the historic built-up areas of the town was carried out from 1965 to 1969 under the direction of the architectural historian Václav Mencl (1905–1978). With regard to the value of its monuments, old Most was moved, thanks to the

---

563 SOkA Most, f. 207 (ONV II), inv. č. 1234–1243, ev. j. 445, Výkon památkové péče na okrese Most (bez datace, po r. 1975).

research results, many rungs up the hierarchy of historic towns, now among the top twenty most valuable in Czechoslovakia. Though the conclusions were interesting and prompted lively debate, nothing at all was deduced from them which would have changed the approach to the demolition of the town.[564]

The archaeologists' research of the town was conceived even more grandly than the preservationists'. The local branch of the Archaeological Institute had been operating in Most since 1953. The Ore Mountains and the Central Bohemian Uplands had a number of important archaeological sites, especially of the early medieval period. In view of the current mining, it was, moreover, evident that there was little time to research many of them. This problem was of course even more acute right in Most. Archaeological research here was carried out under absolutely extraordinary conditions, in the awareness that before the town was devoured by mining the research, in view of the huge area of the investigated terrain, would succeed in answering only the most important questions. Naturally, the research was accompanied by conflicts between the archaeologists and the SHD. These came to a head in late 1969 and early 1970.[565] Several generations of distinguished Czech archaeologists worked in Most, in particular Antonín Hejna (1920–1986) and Jan Klápště (b.1949), and the then head of the Archaeological Institute Jan Filip (1900–1981) also used to travel here from Prague. The research, which until that time had probably been the most extensive in Czechoslovak medieval archaeology, included detailed documentation, and was thus described as evidence of the high level of culture of socialist Czechoslovakia. The key phase of the research, from 1970 to 1975, was described in a travelling exhibition, which could

---

564 SOkA Most, f. 207 (ONV II), inv. č. 1223–1233, ev. j. 444, Záznam z konference k otázkám záchrany měšťanských středověkých domů ve starém Mostě, 20. 3. 1969.
565 Concerning this, see NA, f. Ministerstva kultury ČSSR (nezprac.), kart. 249, Připomínky ředitele Archeologického ústavu ČSAV k provádění komplexního průzkumu v historickém areálu města Most a jeho okolí, 4. prosince 1969.

be attended not only by people in north Bohemia, but also, in the summer of 1976, by visitors to the Museum of the City of Prague (Muzeum hlavního města Prahy). At the same time, the research was also mentioned in the daily press, popular-science magazines, and documentary films.[566] The documentation of the glorious past of a town yielding to the interests of the present was the most cogent expression of the contemporary emphasis on the all-embracing responsibility of socialism, which had respect for the great national past, aware of the role of collective memory while building a world based on systematic scientific knowledge.

From the contemporary made-for-television documentaries, speeches, and newspaper articles it is clear that the main argument justifying the Most project was extremely simple. It was the fact that the socialist State had at its disposal economic and educational potential which enabled the carrying out of such a spectacular project: to destroy one town and build a modern one, to clear away millions of tonnes of earth and to extract millions of tonnes of coal, to free people from the misery of their old houses and enable them a modern dignified life with central heating and hot and cold running water. The positive attitude to history and the preservation of the remnants of the past face to face with the large-scale (and from the then point of view inevitable) destruction of the cultural landscape, certainly did not form the core of the discourse about the Most project even in the 1970s. But it is remarkable that, despite the reality of north Bohemia and of Most in particular, this emphasis on considerateness towards the traces of the past and consciousness of memory was not hushed up or made taboo, indeed, quite the opposite. Simultaneously with what was probably the most thorough demolition of a historic European town since the end of the Second World War, attempts were made during those two decades in normalized Czechoslovakia

---

566   See 'Výstava o archeologickém výzkumu města Mostu v l. 1970–1975', *Památky a příroda* 2 (1), 1977, pp. 28–29.

to adopt the discourse of reflexive modernity, in which the Most experiment is not seen as an exception but as a spectacular example of taking such a stance towards the world. In order to understand how it was possible that such a construct could be credible and why it gave the socialist project, at least for a while, legitimacy, rather than delegitimizing it, we must now turn to the last, intentionally postponed, part of our story.

A BRIDGE BETWEEN THE PAST AND THE FUTURE

Thus the former Deanery Church will stand here for centuries to come
and its story will become the stuff of legend.
(From the film *Jak se stěhuje kostel* [How to move a church],
Československá televize, 1988)

29. Taking down the spire of the Deanery Church in March 1972; part of the preparations for moving
the church beyond the reach of coal mining.

Most Czechs do not know that Most was once a valuable historic
town of 30,000 inhabitants. One Most story, however, did make history. When Most of the days of state socialism is discussed, people
usually recall the moving of a church. In the autumn of 1975, the
late Gothic Church of the Assumption (built from 1517 to 1550 to
replace the early Gothic church that had burnt down in 1515), the
most valuable monument of Most, was moved east of its original

location in the centre of the old town to a safe place under which there was no longer any coal to be mined. In the course of one week, the 10,000-tonne church was moved on specially built trollies along specially laid rails a distance of 841.1 metres from its original site. The operation, the likes of which had never been carried out before anywhere in the world, was a success.

The technology entailed an exceptionally sophisticated and forward-looking solution to a demanding task, which remains remarkable even today.[567] But what interests us here is rather the genesis of the whole plan and particularly the role that rescuing the late Gothic Catholic church played in the official narrative of the transformation of Most and, more generally, in the normalization discourse about the attitude of the socialist State towards the cultural legacy.

Rescuing the church, one of the scenarios in the event of the demolition of old Most, was first discussed at the end of the 1950s, that is, a few years before the Party and then the Government took the final decision about the fate of the town. The 1960 proposal for the future planning of the Most–Litvínov territory already includes the information that in connection with the planned demolition of old Most it would be necessary to consider the fate of the historic monuments there, even though they were in very bad repair. In particular, it states that 'the most remarkable of them is the Gothic church', noting that 'the solution to the problem of preserving this important monument will have to begin immediately'.[568]

---

567 In the late 1960s, an acrimonious dispute arose between the state-owned Transfera company in the town of Pardubice and the engineer Josef Wünsch over the technical solution. Wünsch eventually had to accept the fact that his solution would not be implemented, and Transfera thus became the main party to write the script and carry out the transfer. For more on this, see Krejčí, *Most*, pp. 141–65. For documentation of the preparation, technical solution, and legal questions (including the agreement with the Church), see NA, f. Ministerstvo kultury a informací 1965–1975 (nezprac.), kart. 248.

568 SOA Litoměřice, f. 668 (SKNV Ústí nad Labem), kart. 137, Zasedání rady 8. 11. 1960, Materiál 'Podrobná organizace území Most – Litvínov', p. 31.

The members of the national committees and other political bodies also knew about the great value of the church and its fate was from the start an open question. Ministers and senior Party officials, at least some of them, did not exclude the possibility of saving the church. The reasons were probably diverse, ranging from the cultural awareness of some of the decision-makers to the general atmosphere of the late 1950s and early 1960s, when, among other things the Historic Monuments Preservation Act (Zákon o památkové péči 1958) was passed and the topic generally became important. It was clear that the institutions in charge of monument preservation would not have the final word about the demolition of the town; nevertheless, they could not be completely ignored, partly because of the current emphasis on obeying 'socialist law'. Political elites in Prague and the SHD officials may have seen the saving of the church as a concession to the preservationists, who, in the interest of pushing through the protection of the most valuable buildings, would not obstruct the plan to demolish the whole of Most. This pragmatic consideration, if it in fact existed, did indeed have this effect: their plan to win over the preservationists was a success. Another partner in the talks about the fate of the church was of course the Roman Catholic Church. The surviving documents about the relationship between the State, the SHD and the Church, however, confirm that that no efforts were made to achieve a compromise with the Church on this matter. Here, in a working-class north Bohemian town, the Church was extraordinarily weak and it agreed, with little resistance, to deconsecrate the Deanery Church. Its efforts to build a replacement in the new town were unsuccessful.[569]

The Czechoslovak Government first decided to save the church soon after passing the resolution on the demolition of old Most, in

---

[569] See NA, f. Ministerstvo kultury a informací 1965–1975 (nezprac.), kart. 248, Dohoda uzavřená mezi Římskokatolickým děkanským kostelem v Mostě zastoupeným kapitulním ordinariátem v Litoměřicích a Ministerstvem kultury ČSR (1969) a kart. 249, Dopis kapitulního vikáře Ministerstvu kultury a informací (sekretariát pro věci církevní), 22. 1. 1968.

other words, in 1964[570] – but, as it turned out, it was not the final decision. The various possible ways that were considered for its rescue[571] – some of which, like leaving the church where it was on a giant pillar in the middle of the mined-out pit, seemed utterly bizarre – were often described in the press, documentary films, and specialist periodicals and books.[572] This is probably the most popular part of the whole story, corresponding fully to the intentions of the people who were in charge of the fate of Most especially in the 1970s.

Among the main proponents of saving the church as a whole (most feasibly by moving it) were Čestmír Císař (1920–2013), who was the minister of education and culture from 1963 to 1965, a reform Communist, and a native of nearby Hostomice nad Bílinou, and Jiří Hájek (1919–1993), his successor; their brief included the preservation of this historic monument.[573] Although for ideological reasons or simply pragmatic ones a number of important and powerful State and the Party representatives had from the beginning sided with saving the church, the project also had its opponents. To many politicians and mining-company managers, it seemed an onerous task whose outcome was far from certain. And mainly it was in

---

570 Usnesení vlády 612/1964.

571 For the original detailed elaboration of these variants, including the cost calculations and plan drawn up by the State Institute for the Reconstruction of Historic Buildings (Státní ústav pro rekonstrukci památkových staveb), see NA, f. ÚPV – běžná spisovna (nezprac.), kart. 163, sign. 356/1/12, Vyhodnocení a závěrečný protokol komise expertů, 29. května 1964. Among the advocates of what from today's point of view appears to be the most remarkable variant – namely, leaving the church on a high pillar in the middle of the mined-out landscape, was the President of Czechoslovakia, Antonín Novotný (1904–1975), who argued that it was one of the cheapest solutions and that the only disadvantage would be to leave 'coal worth 100 million crowns under the church', which, according to him, did not matter because 'coal is not a scarce commodity for us today'. For Novotný's comments on the various proposed solutions, see NA, f. 1261/1/43 (Kancelář 1. tajemníka ÚV KSČ A. Novotného, 1951–1967), Návrh na záchranu gotického kostela v Mostě, 23. srpna 1967 (loose, handwritten notes).

572 For specific articles, documents, and studies, see below in this chapter.

573 See NA, f.ÚPV– běžná spisovna (nezprac.), kart.163, sign. 356/1/12–I (1965–1967), vládní materiály a korespondence k záležitosti děkanského chrámu.

their view a huge expenditure,[574] particularly since saving church-es was not an investment priority of a socialist state. Among the most active fighters against the preservation of the whole church by means of its costly transfer were the officials of the North Bohemian Regional National Committee, who feared it meant siphoning off money from other items in the regional budget which to them were more important.[575] The whole operation understandably meant a huge complication for the SHD. Its interests were defended by, among other people, the minister of fuel and energy (and eventually his deputy) Odvárka, who chaired a key committee for the coordi-nation of the demolition of old Most and the construction of the new town.[576]

It was the chairman of the North Bohemian Regional National Committee, Jan Jelínek (1909–?), who in 1965, together with Jo-sef Odvárka, presented a draft government resolution for rescind-ing the previous resolution on the saving of the church by moving it. Instead of the original plan, both men, thinking economically, proposed selling the church to someone or some institution abroad. It could of course not get there by rail, and thus they foresaw its being dismantled here and reassembled outside Czechoslovakia. The main thing was that it was all meant to be settled by December of that year, so that the construction of the utility corridor would not

---

574 According to estimates from that period, saving the Deanery Church by moving it cost about 58,000,000 Czechoslovak crowns. NA, f. SÚPPOP (nezprac.), Ekonomické vyhodnocení dosud zpracovaných variant záchrany gotického kostela v Mostě (1965). All other historic preservation, including the preservation of small monuments, which was required by mining in Most would, according to the 1964 estimates, amount to 4,620,000 crowns. NA, f. SÚPPOP (nezprac.), Vyjádření Krajského střediska památkové péče a ochrany přírody Ústí nad Labem pro SKNV Ústí nad Labem, 4. září 1964.

575 NA, f. ÚPV – běžná spisovna (nezprac.), kart. 163, sign. 356/1/12–I (1965–1967), vládní materiály a korespondence k záležitosti děkanského chrámu, dopis předsedy SKNV Ústí nad Labem Jana Jelínka ministru školství a kultury Jiřímu Hájkovi, 17. 9. 1966.

576 SOA Litoměřice, f. 668 (SKNV Ústí nad Labem), kart. 558, inv. č. 123, Návrh předsedy SKNV a předsedy koordinační komise na zrušení usnesení vlády o přesunu kostela, bez datace [1964/65].

be held up because of the church.[577] On 21 April 1965, the Government did, indeed, pass the resolution and in the following year they made it more specific that it would, in addition to the transfer, also allow for the dismantling or demolition of the church.[578] The resolution thereby opened up the space for all the scenarios – and thus for a battle amongst the individual interest groups. At that time, apart from the Ministry of Education and Culture, the head of the State Institute for the Preservation of Historic Monuments and Environmental Protection was now vehemently speaking up in favour of moving the church (although where to move it remained an open question).[579] Jelínek, by contrast, in correspondence with the minister of culture, Hájek, urged the Government 'to take into consideration' that in the North Bohemian Region it was necessary to deal with more pressing questions than the preservation of churches.[580] This uncertainty continued until the beginning of the 1970s.

It was by far not only ambitious regional politicians or SHD engineers with little interest in culture who opposed preservation in this period. In the mid-1960s, this operation would probably have been met with the least understanding from ordinary people, that is, a considerable number of the workers and farmers who actively or passively still supported the Communist project. The fact that the 'larger part of the population would set this extraordinarily demanding preservationist operation into its natural opposition to the unsolved and urgent problems of the Most district'[581] is mentioned in official correspondence and other records of the state-wide and

577 SOA Litoměřice, f. 668 (SKNV Ústí nad Labem), kart. 598, inv. č. 123, Návrh vládního usnesení o zrušení usnesení vlády č. 612/1964 o zabezpečení památkového objektu gotického kostela v Mostě při vyhlovací akci podloží pod historickým jádrem města.
578 NA, f. SÚPPOP (nezprac.), Projednání návrhu vládního usnesení o zabezpečení gotického kostela v Mostě, 25. 8. 1966.
579 NA, f. SÚPPOP (nezprac.), Stanovisko SÚPPOP k alternativám záchrany kostela (červen 1966).
580 NA, f. ÚPV – běžná spisovna (nezprac.), kart. 163, sign. 356/1/12–I (1965–1967), vládní materiály a korespondence k záležitosti děkanského chrámu, dopis předsedy KNV Ústí nad Labem Jana Jelínka ministru školství a kultury Jiřímu Hájkovi, 17. 9. 1966.
581 Ibid.

north Bohemian political bodies. The costly preservation of a late Gothic European monument was for the same reason politically risky also from the perspective of the Most District National Committee. At the September 1966 session, its members mentioned the absurdity of the whole situation, that while the Most district was suffering from an acute shortage of services, the State was fighting against religious prejudices, and, at the same time, was about to undertake the costly preservation of a church. Nevertheless, the Most District National Committee, in its statement, eventually came out in support of saving the church despite the anticipated public opinion, arguing that 'in view of our current difficulties, it is impossible, after all, to agree to the preservation of this important architectural monument which has survived for centuries'. The District National Committee at the same time expressed a readiness to explain the point of this unpopular measure to the members of the working class.[582] That probably did not always meet with success, at least not at the state-wide level, as is evident from sporadic, but preserved letters from ordinary Czechoslovak citizens protesting against uneconomical expenditures on unnecessary things.[583]

Saving the church, which ultimately required an investment of almost 100 million Czechoslovak crowns, was thus, in the second half of the 1960s, both a technically and a politically risky step even though it complied with the wishes of preservationist experts and leading intellectuals in the humanities. But it was also a potential threat to the legitimacy of the Communist Party as the avant-garde

---

582   NA, f. ÚPV – běžná spisovna (nezprac.), kart. 163, sign. 356/1/12–I (1965–1967), vládní materiály a korespondence k záležitosti děkanského chrámu, Stanovisko Rady ONV Most pro Ministerstvo školství a kultury, 30. 9. 1966.

583   Some workers and other ordinary citizens perceived the investment of the staggering sums in the preservation of the church, which was from their point of view a relic of an irrelevant past, as truly unnecessary, when, in their opinion, it was necessary to build roads, factories, hospitals, sports grounds, housing estates, and towns. See the 1966 letter sent by workers of the Kladno area, NA, Úřad předsednictva vlády – běžná spisovna, kart. 167, sign. 356/1/12, II (další doklady – ONV II, 445–07. See also a remark in the 1988 film *Zánik a znovuzrození města*.

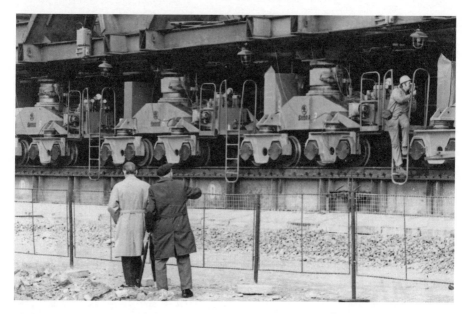

30. Detail of some of the 53 trollies, made for the Transfera company by Škoda Plzeň, used in the extraordinarily successful technical execution of moving the church (Photo from 11 October 1975).

of progress. Preparations for the operation were made quietly, in government secretariats and in communication with the relevant national committees and with the engineers who would eventually prepare the chosen variant for moving the intact church along rails. In the press, apart from the local *Kulturní kalendář*, saving the church was only sporadically written about until 1968 and it was clear that neither the national committees, nor the Government, nor the Party wanted to hold it up for show.

All of that changed radically at the end of the 1960s and mainly in the first half of the 1970s. Regardless of the twists and turns of the political situation and the dramatic swings in the social atmosphere from 1967 to 1975, we can observe a continual increase in the attention paid to this operation. Even the coming of normalization policy did not sideline the topic. On the contrary, the Government of Prime Minister Štrougal first of all nullified each and every one of the numerous resolutions on the Most church from the 1960s[584] and, taking into consideration the 'interest of professionals' and the possibilities of 'promoting the technological level of the CSSR and the socialist State's attitude to cultural monuments,'[585] decided once and for all, in March 1971, to save the church as a whole. The government resolution also stipulated the specific manner in which the church would be moved and the route it would take.[586]

The political elites of the consolidation period understood that the times had changed. It was clear that saving the church was no longer a matter of internal agreement between individual ministries and national committees, but was something observed by a large part of the public. If there were any outrage now, it would not be, as it had been from the steelworkers of Kladno in the mid-1960s, over the costly transfer of the church, but more likely would arise if the Government decided to sell the church or demolish it. Saving the church was not cheap, but the political elites understood that by paying for the transfer of the church they would be paying to buttress the legitimacy of the system they represented.

Already beginning in 1970, therefore, the Government started to develop various forms of publicity about saving the church.[587] This plan gradually acquired considerable breadth and was becoming an increasingly important part of the whole operation. The Government and the relevant national committees thus sought to ensure that the 'saving of the church in Most became an important cultural and political event that provided evidence of the extraordinary care

---

584 Usnesení vlády č. 258 z 25. října 1970.
585 NA, f. ÚPV – běžná spisovna (nezprac.), kart. 210, sign. 356/1/12, Informace pro předsedu vlády ČSSR s. dr. L. Štrougala, 23. listopadu 1970.
586 Vládní usnesení č. 48 ze 4. března 1971, confirmed and specified by Government Resolution No. 103, 12 May 1971.
587 NA, f. ÚPV – běžná spisovna (nezprac.), kart. 210, sign. 356/1/12, Informace pro předsedu vlády ČSSR s. dr. L. Štrougala, 23. listopadu 1970.

that the socialist State takes of its cultural heritage'.[588] The promotion of the operation was meant to take place at many levels, ranging from information in the press to documentary films for the cinema and television, inviting guests from abroad to witness the transfer, temporary and permanent exhibitions about saving the church, and its being made ready for tourists once it had reached its destination.

Dozens of journalists, in keeping with the wishes of Party officials and members of the national committees, grasped the now popular topic with new energy and for several months, even years, they made it the main story, overshadowing the demolition of old Most, the construction of the new Most, and the related development of lignite mining. It is clear that the people who ordered or inspired the writing of these several hundred articles, which, between 1970 and 1975, extolled the saving and moving of the Most church, were aware of the changed *Sinnwelt* of that time.

The transfer of the church thus became emblematic of the whole Most story. The vast majority of articles about Most from the 1970s are about this single aspect of the destruction of the historic town in the interest of mining and industrial development.[589] Yet it was not purely a matter of exchanging a technocratic or, more narrowly, productivist conception of the world for nostalgia and publicity of the preservation of the cultural heritage. Indeed, the two narratives had been intertwining and were complementing each other. The transfer of the church was presented as a 'technological event of

---

588 SOkA Most, f. 207 (ONV II), inv. č. 1234–43, ev. j. 445, Politickohospodářské využití přesunu děkanského kostela v Mostě do nového prostředí, 21. ledna 1970.

589 From the beginning of the debate about the preservation of the church, from the first half of the 1960s to the end of 1967, only ten articles were published in the regional press (*Průboj*) and the Czechoslovak press, and they were lost amongst the dozens of articles about other aspects of the Most project. Slightly more was written about the church in 1968, but at that time, most articles concerning Most were about other topics. In 1969–70, the situation changed and of the roughly eighty articles published in the short period from 1970 to 1975 in dailies and weeklies about the demolition of old Most and the construction of the new town roughly 50 were exclusively about moving the church.

31. The church being moved through the grounds of the former abattoir (October 1975).

global importance,'[590] and to all appearances was also perceived as such. Journalists sang the praises of 'technology, which is a bridge [*most*] between the past and the future'.[591] The transfer was even explicitly called an international advertisement for Czechoslovakia, that is, an 'example of the advanced state of technology in the republic'[592] and it did indeed attract international attention.[593]

To the engineers' euphoria over the unlimited technological possibilities enabling the achievement of the once inconceivable was added the theme of care for lasting values and respect for the work of past generations.[594] Dozens of articles thus extolled the saving of the church as evidence of the socialist State's responsible attitude

590 'Kostel versus uhlí', *Československý horník*, 11 June 1970.
591 'Kostel na kolech', *Svět práce*, 8 October 1975.
592 Ibid.
593 See *L'Humanité Dimanche*, 14 December 1974.
594 The attempt to link the two discourses is clear. Period sources basically already talk about it and it also appears in the secondary literature. See Glassheim, 'Most, the Town that Moved'.

towards cultural values, which many people set in contrast to the ruthlessness of Western capitalist concerns:

> Because [the Deanery Church] is an extremely valuable cultural monument, the socialist State has not hesitated to spend resources on its conservation, even if it is a piece of church architecture.
> In the capitalist world, an enterprise involved in coal mining would definitely not spend resources to save a church. Nor would a bourgeois state have enough resources for such an operation [...] Even though the operation is exceptional by world standards [...], our efforts to conserve cultural monuments is not at all exceptional. These efforts are typical of socialism; they are systematic. By moving a church that stood in the way of the essential development of the economy, we are therefore providing evidence not only of the advanced level of technology, of our scientists, engineers, and workers, but also the advanced level of our culture, which we are able to demonstrate with more than just ideas.[595]

According to other articles as well, the moving of the church was evidence of the 'attention that Czechoslovak society pays to the preservation of cultural values', and also demonstrated the lead that socialism had over the capitalist West, for example, the sinking city of Venice, the eroded sculptures of Cologne, the potential collapse of the Acropolis of Athens or the Colosseum: 'It is a matter of the fundamental attitude towards man and his works, towards the past and towards future generations.'[596]

Neither the construction of this narrative about the church nor the scale and energy with which it was publicly 'told' in many variations was of course a coincidence in the authoritarian system of state socialism; rather it was above all the intention of the people in power. That is demonstrated, for example, by the documentary films about

---

595 'Hmota v pohybu', *Zemědělské noviny*, 2 October 1975.
596 'Kostel na kolech', *Svět práce*, 8 October 1975.

saving the church. Since the 1970s, the State Institute for the Preservation of Historic Monuments and Protection of the Environment had some of the conservation work filmed. This footage was then used in 1974–75, when the Institute, at the impetus of the Czech Ministry of Culture and in collaboration with the Transfera company, had the moving of the church filmed and an eleven-part series made from that, each part of which was twenty minutes long. The first part explains the value of the church as an historic monument. The next parts discuss the economic justification for the specific version of the transfer, the construction work to save the church, and the technical solution for the transfer, and the last two parts depict the moving of the church to its new location in September 1975.[597]

The anticipated cost of filming and producing these documentaries was about 3.5 million Kčs,[598] but the final costs were of course higher, because the last two parts, which required night filming, ran over budget. Some parts were screened in cinemas all over north Bohemia and on television,[599] but the Government made it clear, through the Ministry of Culture, that this rather technical documentation did not meet the main aim, which was to popularize the saving of the church, that is, 'to promote the effective form of care that the socialist State provides to historic monuments, and to emphasize that economic interests in the socialist State are not pursued insensitively or to the detriment of the cultural heritage'.[600] For that reason, a shorter popular film of between 30 and 40 minutes was to be made from the existing footage, suitable especially for television,

---

597 NA, f. SÚPPOP (nezprac.), Filmové zpracování přesunu mosteckého chrámu, scénáře dílů 1–11 (březen 1974–říjen 1975).
598 NA, f. SÚPPOP (nezprac.), Návrh témat jednotlivých krátkých filmů dokumentujících a propagujících přesun gotického kostela v Mostě (září 1973), časový rozvrh a finanční náklady.
599 The film was shown on Czechoslovak television on 17 October 1975. See NA, f. SÚPPOP (nezprac.), Informace o propagaci přesunu mosteckého kostela (exp. MK ČSR).
600 NA, f. SÚPPOP (nezprac.), Most – komplexní program filmové dokumentace a jejího využití, correspondence between the Czech Ministry of Culture and the State Institute for the Preservation of Historic Monuments and Environmental Protection (SUPPOP), 1974.

followed by an even shorter promotional film of between 10 and 15 minutes for a wide variety of purposes, including publicity abroad in various language editions. The final, shortened version was not produced until 1988,[601] because the adaptation of the church (which was also meant to be part of the narrative) and its being opened to the public at its final destination were achieved ten years later than planned. Thanks to the generous support for publicity about saving the church and of course thanks to the attractiveness of the topic for the mass media, two other documentaries were produced and shown on Czechoslovak television. They are focused exclusively on the saving of the Deanery Church. The story formed an important part of many other TV documentaries and newsreels about Most, the Most district, and north Bohemia in general.[602]

The publicity plan was fully met. The people of Czechoslovakia and the international public in 1975 marvelled at the advanced state of technology in the socialist State and subconsciously accepted, together with the message (transported together with the church) about the consideration and care which this State, despite all the negative impacts of industrial modernity, devoted to cultural heritage. This success, however, was not limited only to the period of moving the church or even to the period of Late Socialism; it continues to this day. It is the topic of the church, which again and again attracts attention, not only of the general public, but also of many scholars, including historians, archaeologists, museum professionals, and preservationists. And thus since the mid-1970s more has been written about saving the church than about the destruction of the whole of old Most.[603]

601 Jak se stěhuje kostel, directed by Jindřich Fairaizl, Krátký film Praha, 1988, 13:40.
602 Deset tisíc tun gotiky v pohybu, documentary film, Československá televize, 1976, 13:22, Archiv ČT, IDEC 27553105298; Husarský kousek v gotice, a television programme, Československá televize, 1976, 22:57, Archiv ČT, IDEC 276 531 22637.
603 The Deanery Church of Most, including the problem of relocating it, is discussed by Heide Mannlová-Raková, Kulturní památka Most: Děkanský kostel a jeho stavitelé, Most: Okresní muzeum v Mostě, 1989; Jan Klápště and Otakar Novák, Gotický kostel Nanebevzetí Panny Marie

32. The Deanery Church at its new location shortly after being opened to the public in 1988, thirteen years after it was moved.

The change in the way that the Most project was written about in the first half of the 1960s compared to the 1970s and 1980s is striking. The cultural achievement on which the State under the normalization regime built its legitimacy could no longer be reduced to millions of tonnes of coal mined and kilowatt hours of electric power generated, or even to the replacement of old hovels with a clean

v Mostě, Prague and Ústí nad Labem: Propagační tvorba and Památkový ústav Ústí nad Labem, 1992 (published at the same time as *Gothic Church of the Ascension [sic] of the Virgin Mary in Most*, trans. Anděla Kunstová, also in French and German editions); Zdeňka Štefanová, 'Přesun gotického kostela v Mostě', in Libuše Pokorná and Ivan Jakubec (eds), *Mostecko, Litvínovsko, Lounsko, Žatecko: Sborník učitelských prací z kursů univerzitních extenzí v Mostě*, with a German abstract, Most, [Prague], and [Liberec]: Okresní muzeum v Mostě, Univerzita Karlova, Dialog, 2002, pp. 93–105; Zdeněk Budinka, 'Most – město, jeho osudy i osud přemístěného chrámu', *Dědictví Koruny české* 3, 2006, pp. 10–14; Pavel Koukal, *Přesunutý děkanský kostel Nanebevzetí Panny Marie v Mostě*, Ústí nad Labem: Národní památkový ústav, 2007, and other articles in journals of historic preservation.

modern city providing everyone with comfortable housing. The political elites of the normalization regime, far more than their predecessors, accepted the conservative ethos of preserving cultural heritage. The swapping of the historic town of Most for the coal under its streets could thus be problematic with regard to the legitimacy of Communist domination. The already planned saving of the church could thus help to justify the whole project that was now irreversibly under way.

The cultural contribution of real socialism was thus supposed, at least according to the image it created of itself, to consist in a synthesis of economic productivity and self-sufficiency, utopian visions of a sunny town, and the cultivation of historical consciousness. The power holders and the mass media under their control sought to persuade the Czechoslovak and the international public that the city of Most had been demolished in accordance with the imperative of consideration and respect for the supreme artistic achievements of the past and therefore also with understanding for the essentially human desire that memory overcome physical death.

The narrative about the demolition of the old town opening the gate to 'black gold' was eclipsed by the story of the saving of the late Gothic church. The elites of normalized Czechoslovakia found an outstanding way to link the technocratic discourse with the humanist one, to keep in step with the times. It was almost a successful squaring of the circle. The technocratic discourse, founded on the conviction that human beings can dismantle the world they live in and then, at no loss (indeed, at a net profit), put it together somewhere else, turned out to be remarkably flexible and viable. The saving of the old church, originally (from the perspective of the authorities) a compromise with the preservationists, became the triumph of that way of thinking.

Today, when you visit the saved church, located in something like no-man's land outside the new city, you can see in its crypt the shortest version of a film about how it was saved, made in the late 1980s.

In the course of ten minutes you learn that the church once stood on high-quality brown coal and could therefore definitely not remain there, and that Czech engineers, architects, urban planners, experts in the preservation of historic monuments, and also representatives of the town, the district, the region and the Government ultimately found the best solution for extracting the coal and saving the church, and that it was a great success, admired by the world. And nothing more. As if this were the whole true story.

A Laboratory
of Modernity

WHERE THE PRESENT BEGINS

In the spring of 1961, humankind entered a new age. A hitherto un-known 27-year-old Soviet pilot orbited the earth at an altitude of 327 kilometres, at one point above an unsuspecting America fast sleep. He was the first human being to see Earth from outerspace before eventually parachuting successfully down from the clouds to the fields of Eastern Siberia. The news of his flight travelled around the earth quicker than the cosmonaut himself and generated enthusiasm that seemed to know no bounds. Upon his return, Yuri Gagarin (1934 –1968), the first envoy of humankind in outer space, was welcomed by crowds of people in capital cities of the East and the West. In June, he lunched with the Queen of the United Kingdom and shared his feelings in a special broadcast of the BBC.

The possibilities of humankind once again seemed infinite. The barrier of Earth's gravitation may have briefly been surmounted for one man but it was generally believed to be only the beginning. It was anticipated that space colonization would begin in the foresee-able future. 'Please convey to the moon, and the stars too, what today we all want to say, that we'll be with them soon' sang the big-band leader Gustav Brom (1921–1995) in 'Pozdrav astronautovi' (Greet-ings to the astronaut) also known as 'Dobrý den, majore Gagarine' (Good-day, Major Gagarin), a Dixieland-like hit that topped the charts in Czechoslovakia. Suddenly, no obstacle seemed too big to be surmounted.

And it was in that atmosphere that the engineer Karel Šamberger, the head of the Ležáky Mine, was given authorization to devise the plan for the demolition of Most. Officially, the authorization came from the SHD management in a letter of 13 April 1961, on the day when the news of the first man in space spread around the world. Seen from today, the two events seem to have little in common. The conquest of space still fascinates people, but mining coal less so. And surface mining, for which a unique historic town had to be eliminated, leaves an impression of barbarity.

It was, nevertheless, a manifestation of the same faith in the power of science and technology to change the world to the benefit of humankind. The exploitation of the wealth concealed under the surface of our planet was not understood much differently from space flight. Both of these achievements, the penetration of the heavens or the centre of the earth, together with other achievements like the production of the first high-performance computers or increasingly accessible treatment with antibiotics, confirmed a new way of constructing the identity of modern political systems and societies. It was a new era in which states no longer defined themselves primarily on the basis of their ability to conquer – or physically eliminate from their territory – people whom they did not consider to be part of a healthy or just society, and physical force was an index not of barbarity but of the strength, determination, and viability of the given political and social order. That is true of the countries not only to the west but also to the east of the Iron Curtain. In the east too there was a clear shift towards more civilized, less violent, forms of control, together with emphasis on the standard of living, contingent on technological development. A clear milestone in that process was Khrushchev's (1894–1971) speech at the 20th Congress of the CPSU, in 1956, in which he, as First Secretary of the Communist Party of the Soviet Union and de facto head of the whole Eastern Bloc, distanced himself from some elements of the tyranny of his predecessor, Stalin (1878–1953). The ability to control society and production by physical force and superior power alone was supposed in future not to determine the success and wealth of nations.

From Washington to Moscow, an increasingly more significant part of society perceived the emphasis on science and technology as the guarantee of a more peaceful, better, and just world. Only the future would reveal the risks of technological progress, from the growing scarcity of natural resources to environmental disasters to the global widening of the gap between the developed and the developing countries, the consequences of which for the poorer majority of our planet have often been more devastating than enslavement by means of the European colonizers' guns and chains.

The hopes pinned on science, technology and the possibilities of uninterrupted growth in the standard of living, in the West and the East, ideas about the civilized nature and risks connected with that discursive formation or practice – that is, all the substantial aspects which by the second half of the 1950s at the latest began decisively to determine the nature of Euro-Atlantic (and eventually even global) civilization – are still definitely comprehensible to us today. We still share these hopes, though perhaps with more questions and doubts, and, mainly, we are still fully faced with the risks stemming from the practice of technological civilization. The short period from the late 1950s to the early 1960s, when being civilized began to be measured primarily by means of technological progress and economic performance, was, at least in central Europe, the start of the era that we are still living in today.

THE DIALECTICS OF THE AGE
OF THE TECHNOCRACTS

In hindsight, the demolition of old Most seems to be the story of Communist despotism. An authoritarian state, basing its legitimacy on the development of heavy industry, did not hesitate to destroy one of the most valuable historic towns on its territory in order to be able to extract as simply as possible millions of tonnes of low-quality coal and to change it into electric power for factories and the increasing consumption of households. It robbed thousands of people of their homes and moved them to concrete housing estates.

Although such a story sounds credible, the wider context of the period and the accessible documents contradict it. The post-war history of the town of Most is obviously also a particular manifestation of the productivist approach to the world and the command and control regulation practised by the state-socialist regime. But it is far more a laboratory of industrial modernity in Europe and elsewhere, in other words a mirror of the character of modern society, of various forms of alienation and the self-propulsion of the technology and economic development of human beings and their environment as they change.

The particular aspects of life in a mining region, which helped to determine the thinking of the people in the Most district well before the Second World War and then the expulsion of a large part of the population after the war, turned out to be extraordinarily compatible with the typical discourse at the peak of European modernity in the first three post-war decades – namely, the faith of human beings in their own ability to plan the future technologically. After the experiences of the Great Depression and the Second World War, this conviction offered Europe the hope that it would succeed not only in overcoming the current crisis, but also in preventing future catastrophes. The conviction took a variety of forms, several of which are evident in the Most experiment – ranging from economic reduction of the world we live in, as in productivism (Communist and non-Communist), to a more complex technocratic approach, which manifested itself in urban planning and architecture, to visions of reshaping the landscape. Though these approaches stem from quite different conceptions of the world and are held by different actors, they share a fascination with, and faith in, values that can be precisely calculated and whose trajectories towards the future can be determined in the way physicists work with the laws of gravity and the conservation of mass.

In the Czechoslovak context, this conception of the world draws considerable inspiration from Marxist philosophy, but was fully developed in the 1960s and 1970s, and stands in opposition to the Stalinist conception of social revolution. And observing the decision-making processes, we can see how the Stalinist style of governance, personified by the authoritarian old Communists and local dictators, was partly replaced in the late 1950s and early 1960s by economic and other expert elites. The revolutionary ethos was replaced by technocratic rationality.

If one pole of technocratic thinking is economic reductionism and productivism, measuring the world on the basis of economic indices, the other pole is the utopia of a rationally organized world of the future, guaranteeing a good life with dignity for everyone. One of the plotlines of the Most story, the promise of a new city and its subsequent construction, can usefully be read as the technocratic adaptation of utopian thinking.

The ideological starting points of the expert plans and popular notions accompanying this aspect of the Most experiment – namely, the efforts to create the same living conditions for every citizen – were strikingly egalitarian. Nor did the final form of the city built in the 1960s and 1970s permit of marked differences in housing standards. From this perspective, the planning and building of the new city appears to be a particular manifestation of Communist ideology and of the politics of the Communist Party dictatorship in practice. Not only the obviously French inspiration of Le Corbusier or the First Republic inspiration of Zlín, however, points to the considerably broader modernist contexts of 'real existing utopias'. Faith in a rational solution to all social problems and the disciplining and upbringing of law-abiding citizens by means of the spatial organization of their habitat were part of a long tradition stemming from the Enlightenment. In the twentieth century, the Enlightenment was one of the sources of modern technocratic thinking east and west of the Iron Curtain. The scientific and technological revolution, with its emphasis on expert models of governance and its promise of carrying out the best possible model of the State and society, found extraordinarily literal, but otherwise symptomatic application in the story.

The period of the scientific and technological revolution, however, also shares with the Enlightenment the ambivalence that Adorno and Horkheimer defined in their renowned *Dialektik der Aufklärung* (1944, rev. 1947), that is, an era that aimed at 'liberating human beings from fear and installing them as masters'.[604] The fundamental points of Enlightenment thinking – namely, the rational overcoming of myths and binding hierarchies, together with the liberating power of human rationality (and therefore the freedom to which every society and every individual could aim) – contains regressive elements in its very foundations: false clarity, which has a tendency to become a new myth, the destruction of culture by emphasizing technologies and calculable effects of production, the exclusion of otherness, and identifying the conceptualizable, mathematizable world with truth.

The period that I call 'technocratic', for lack of a better term, was born of the optimism sustained by technology breaking boundaries that may just a few decades ago, during the lives of the actors of the middle and older generations, have seemed to them to be the final

---

604 Adorno and Horkheimer, *Dialectic of Enlightenment*, p. 1.

frontiers. Machines were no longer supposed to merely obey human beings, but were meant to be able to manage them. Poverty and illness were no longer meant to be part of human fate, but a task to be dealt with. Human beings were not meant to be entirely dependent on Earth; instead, the gates to the infinite universe were opened to them. The scientific and technological revolution at the same time promised to rectify the existing narrowmindedness and thoughtlessness of human beings, who, with their blinkered orientation to one factor or another threatened future prosperity and development. As I sought to demonstrate in the chapter on technocracy, the idea of scientific management was perceived as the way to government deriving its steps from the most complex knowledge of reality. The creation of the environment, the linking together of education and labour, the problems of civilization, and taking health and beauty into consideration were meant to be integrated into disciplines even as technological as cybernetics and the system of economic management.

The 'technocratic age' in practice, as reflected in, among other things, the modern history of Most, manifests not complexity but a reduction of the world which is in some respects more dramatic than what one might (even in the first half of the twentieth century) have attributed to the Enlightenment project in general. Whereas the Enlightenment had gradually equated thinking with mathematics,[605] in the era of faith in rational planning of the future thinking was equated with economics, with the simple calculation of investment and profit. Faith in the liberation of creative abilities by means of the standard of living and increasing leisure time gained thanks

605 See Edmund Husserl, *Krize evropských věd a transcendentální fenomenologie*, Prague, 1972, p. 42; 'Die Krisis der europäischen Wissenschaften und die transzendentale Phänomenologie: Eine Einleitung in die phänomenologische Philosophie', *Philosophia* (Belgrade) I, 1936; *The Crisis of European Sciences and Transcendental Phenomenology: An Introduction to Phenomenological Philosophy*, trans. David Carr, Evanston, Ill: Northwestern University Press, 1970.

to efficient management seems remarkably naive, particularly when compared with the uniformity of the housing estates of the new towns of the 1960s and 1970s or with uniform mass entertainment consuming that leisure time. Together with the technocratic meg-aprojects that disregarded soft factors like respect for the past, con-servation of the land, or the sense of home, criticism of them also emerged at the beginning of the 1960s. It turned out that the tech-nocratic way of thinking was to some extent capable of reflection, which – somewhat bizarrely – turned out to be the salvation of the Most church.

In an interview ten years before his death (but, as agreed, pub-lished only posthumously), Martin Heidegger (1889–1976) was asked: 'Can the individual man in any way still influence this web of fateful circumstance? Or, indeed, can philosophy influence it? Or can both together influence it, insofar as philosophy guides the in-dividual, or several individuals, to a determined action?' Heidegger replied: 'If I may answer briefly, and perhaps clumsily, but after long reflection: philosophy will be unable to effect any immediate change in the current state of the world. This is true not only of philosophy but of all purely human reflection and endeavor. Only a god can save us.' And a bit further on, he was asked whether it was 'not a little too pessimistic to say: we are not gaining mastery over this surely much greater tool [that is] modern technicity' Another part of his lengthy reply reads: 'The essence of technicity I see in what I call "pos-ure" (*Ge-Stell*), an often ridiculed and perhaps awkward expression. To say that pos-ure holds sway means that man is posed, enjoined and challenged by a power that becomes manifest in the essence of tech-nicity – a power that man himself does not control.'[606] It seems,

---

606 Martin Heidegger, 'Už jenom nějaký bůh nás může zachránit', *Filosofický časopis* 43 (1), p. 21. This is a Czech translation of an interview with Martin Heidegger conducted by Rudolf Augstein and Georg Wolff for *Der Spiegel* in 1966. In keeping with the terms by which Heidegger agreed to discuss his political past, the interview was published posthumously as 'Nur noch ein Gott kann uns retten' (Only a God Can Save Us), *Der Spiegel*, 31 May 1976, pp. 193–219. An

however, that despite the continuing devastation of the landscape and the human soul, which has been made possible by technology, we may see hope in the ambivalence of the project of modernity and its scientific and technological application, that is, in the element of reflection, which this project, despite everything, is open to. For that matter, even Gagarin, after returning from his short space flight, which became one of the most powerful symbols of the era of boundless technological optimism, declared: 'Orbiting Earth in the spaceship, I saw how beautiful our planet is. People, let us preserve and increase this beauty, not destroy it!'

English translation is published online, http://www.ditext.com/heidegger/interview.html Accessed 28 October 2018. The page number from the German original is 209, appearing in square brackets in the translation.

DESTRUCTION AS THE ACHIEVEMENT OF VICTORY

Marxism was created in reaction to the problems of nineteenth-century urban society. The socialist dictatorships, which in the twentieth century based themselves on its ideological principles, were thus in essence, despite their otherwise very different forms, connected with industrialization and modernity, either with the change from agrarian society (as in countries ranging from the Soviet Union to Bulgaria) into a society more urbanized and industrialized or (as in East Germany or Czechoslovakia) with the elimination of the tensions and social differences resulting from capitalist industrialization. The policies of the Communists, based on Marxism, were able to achieve both these things – vigorously to transform an agrarian society into a society that was urban and industrial, and, with similar vigour, to close the social gaps, that is, to take from the rich (or, more brutally, to eliminate them physically) and give to the poor. The socialist dictatorships thus reacted to the class divisions of society and were able, by administrative means and physical force, to eliminate them. That is what gave them their initial legitimacy, which was reflected in mass support from a considerable part of the population.

With the accomplishment of this mission and at the same time with the successes of Western social democracy, which began in the second half of the 1950s – using considerably more moderate means while maintaining liberal civil liberties – to achieve a comparable equalization of the dramatic differences in property and income in the population, there was a danger of the first big legitimacy crisis in the 'people's democracies'. The question why this crisis was prevented or how the socialist dictatorships were able to overcome it is answered by the key circumstances of the events related in this book.

The global optimism of the post-war period, particularly its technocratic form which triumphed in the late 1950s and early 1960s, and the policies of the state-socialist systems based on the doctrines of Marxism-Leninism, had the same starting point. Apart from the key role of positivism and the technology that was subordinated to it as an instrument of economic growth, this shared starting point consisted mainly in the conviction that progress is indisputably good, needs to be worked for, and brings people increasingly greater freedom and happiness. As long as these two pillars (in addition at least to the generationally based and lasting faith in the necessity of overcoming the effects of class society) – that is, the ideal of positivism and faith in progress – met with reality or with the *Sinnwelt* of a large part of society, then state socialism, despite the blunders and the legacy of the Stalinist terror, was able to defend its legitimacy. In such a constellation, experiments like the one in Most, helped to buttress, rather than weaken, the domination of the state-socialist regime that was able to achieve such great things.

As events began to move along the spiral of the decisions eventually leading to the demolition of the old Most, the Czechoslovak version of state socialism could boast considerable successes. In the preceding five years, from 1955 to 1960, Czechoslovak industrial production had increased by 60 per cent and real wages by 40 per cent. People were doing considerably better because the State was now systematically concerned not only with production but also with their satisfaction as consumers. The Stalinist idol, the Stakhanovite, gradually gave way to the citizen-consumer and the State had to accommodate him or her. This achievement and the transformation of everyday reality were determined by, among other things, a twofold increase in the quantity of mined coal in merely a decade, from 1950 to 1960.[607] Considering the continuation of the welcome trend, the claim that a dirty old town with decrepit houses or that a piece of landscape which engineers would return to its original condition had to be sacrificed to this mining was thus completely comprehensible. At that time, in the early 1960s, actually, as long as one

---

[607] See the chapter 'The Destruction of the City as an Investment Plan' in the 'Numbers' section.

was not an expert in the preservation of historic monuments or an art historian, it was difficult to argue with the alleged benefits of such a project. The determination of the political elites not to shrink from the demanding task, together with their ability to make good use of it as an opportunity to build a model modern city with decent housing for a hundred thousand people (in keeping with the original plans), thus in the atmosphere of the times naturally increased confidence in the powers that be and in the political leadership's legitimacy to execute power.

The story, however, began to get complicated in the second half of the 1960s and in the 1970s, not only because of the Warsaw Pact military intervention and the initially dubious legitimacy of the men installed at the head of the Party and the State by the Kremlin to normalize the situation. The main reason was because throughout the developed world, including the richest and most industrialized socialist countries, primarily Czechoslovakia and East Germany, the era of unbounded faith in the progress of civilization and in the unquestionable results of positivistically understood science was slowly drawing to a close. The reduction of the world to economic indices and technicists' forecasts was in the 1960s already beginning to meet with critical reactions throughout Europe, first in circles of intellectuals in the humanities, but gradually also in wider social strata. Soft factors in the life of society, such as environmental protection, the value of home as a slowly established habitat (rather than a rationally constructed one) or respect for the cultural heritage and efforts to preserve, it became more important.

As we saw in the previous section of the book ('Reconciliation'), the political elites of normalization Czechoslovakia also sought to surmount this second crisis of legitimacy and, already in the 1970s, to integrate some elements of revised modernist paradigms into the ideological structure and political practice of state socialism. National parks were established, periodicals popularizing care for the cultural heritage and for nature were published, urban preservation zones were established, and eventually even the Deanery Church was moved. The normalization censorship and self-censorship may have stifled open dialogue, but it could not reverse the change in people's *Sinnwelt*. The power elites of normalization Czechoslovakia were well aware that the achievement of civilization on which the legitimacy of their restored dictatorship was standing could no longer be based only on the increasing efficiency of mining or production or on fairly distributed housing in dignified conditions. In the 1970s, the great final demolition of old Most was therefore not usually presented as the victory of progressive forces over the past. And when it was thus presented, then it was in a markedly less violent, more sophisticated form than in the sense of how the transformation of the town had been discussed in the late 1950s or the early 1960s.

It could thus seem for a while that the struggle for the new face of socialism in step with the demands of the times would be won. But it turned out, and not only in Czechoslovakia, that the historic change under way was deeper than it had initially seemed. When faced with the fall of the two Enlightenment ideals, connected with questioning the direct proportionality between, on the one hand, economic and technological development and, on the other, the degree of freedom, state-socialist domination was unable to offer any other, comparably strong, credible narrative.

The consensual character of late socialism and its displaying non-violence and considerateness may for a while have prevented the gulf from widening, but they could not permanently bridge it, let alone fill it in. The ability to remedy some destructive manifestations of the technological and economic exploitation of the world in the era of reflexive modernity[608] could not be conceived as the normalization elites had imagined it, that is, as a supplementary

---

608 Ulrich Beck, *Risikogesellschaft: Auf dem Weg in eine andere Moderne*, Frankfurt am Main: Suhrkamp, 1986. For an English translation, see *Risk Society: Towards a New Modernity*, trans. Scott Lash and Brian Wynne, London: Sage, 1992. I discuss this further in the chapter 'Faces of Modernity' in the 'The Story' section.

agenda that could be affixed to an otherwise unchanged ideological structure and political practice. The discourse and political practice of the normalization years, seeking to achieve a synthesis of material and aesthetic interests, economic growth, and consideration for the works of those who had gone before, of progress and memory, only seemingly responded to the challenges of the new face of modernity. In fact, it was mainly a manifestation of an increasingly conservative regime of 'decent' people (that is, disciplined and quietly carrying out their tasks), a regime that had lost the ability to change completely from within, which, in reflexive modernity, necessarily required democratization and an opening up of critical public debate.

In the era of individualization, of the questioning of the central narrative of progress, of the undermining of faith in objective science, but also of the new mulling over of hitherto obviously understood hierarchies and values (like traditional gender roles), the original strategy for the legitimation of state socialism changed into its opposite, symptoms of the intensifying corrosion of a system that was unable to react to changes in thinking and the demands of practice. Unlike the Communist elites (to their detriment), the dynamics of the modern age did not come to a standstill in the era of technocratic planning for the future. The tenacious conducting of the Most experiment right to the bitter end, together with its decreasingly credible justification in the second half of the 1980s, is one of the ubiquitous symptoms of the fundamental crisis of legitimacy. The demolished houses, excavated streets, millions of tonnes of extracted lignite, the concrete housing estates of the new Most, and the moved church – only a few years before the showpiece and symbol of an extraordinary achievement of civilization by socialist Czechoslovakia – now became its disgrace. The same city, the same coal, the same people – and a story with quite a different point.

THE STORY CONTINUES

Autumn had arrived once again and Most, like the rest of north Bohemia, was drowning in fog. The pungent air, buses with little signs warning 'Inversion' placed behind their windscreens, special hours in schools, and suffering from a choking cough were typical of everyday life from Chomutov to Ústí nad Labem in that season. Despite the usual restrictions on going outdoors, especially for small children and senior citizens, this time hundreds of people gathered on Náměstí Zdeňka Nejedlého (Zdeněk Nejedlý Square) in Teplice about 35 kilometres north of Most. Not Charter 77 signatories and their acquaintances, they were just ordinary people, and until that time most of them had been loyal to the prevailing order. But they wanted to breathe clean air. It was Saturday, 11 November 1989, and the Velvet Revolution had just begun.

Throughout the 1980s, from East Germany to Hungary, and from Bulgaria to Estonia, environmental criticism pointed out the inability of the state-socialist states to keep their own promises to improve the quality of the living conditions of all their citizens. This criticism was made at many levels, from the associations tolerated by the State and from the state-funded scientific institutions to independent initiatives and opposition circles. Right after the collapse of the socialist dictatorships, which this criticism had in no small measure helped to bring about, periodicals, specialist and popular, and the other mass media of the countries of the former Soviet bloc were flooded with evidence that had been gathered for many years about the unprecedented devastation of nature and the cultural landscape, the pollution of the air and the rivers, and dying forests. The inability to prevent the large-scale destruction of the landscape and health threats for millions of people were among the most tangible and consequently most influential causes of the delegitimization of Communist domination, which only shortly before had been determining the fate of nearly a quarter of the world.

Czechoslovakia was among the countries where the discrepancies between the promise and the reality of the environment became most glaring. Within three days of being sworn in, Václav Havel (1936–2011), in his first New Year's speech as Czechoslovak President, summarized in two sentences this aspect of the state-socialist legacy: 'We have polluted the soil, rivers and forests bequeathed to us by our ancestors, and we have today the most contaminated environment in Europe. Adults in our country die earlier than in most other European countries.'[609] Three leading critics of the way the late socialist State had treated the natural environment, both from dissident circles and from the ranks of tolerated experts, Ivan Dejmal, Josef Vavroušek, and Bedřich Moldan, were made the first Czechoslovak and Czech ministers of the environment.

Deputies of the Federal Assembly, the Czech and the Slovak legislatures, and the three governments (the federal, the Czech, and the Slovak) soon began to work on practical steps to rectify the situation. First of all, limits were set on the mining of lignite, which were meant to prevent once and for all the further devastation of the cultural landscape. It was not long before the first clearly critical documentary films on the devastation of old Most were made. The story of this town became an example of the destructive nature of Communist productivism, demonstrating the guilt of the Communist rulers who had not hesitated to physically dispose of their own country.

The rude awakening from the dream of victory over the ruthless power of the technicist conception of the world came in 1993, in the form of the demolition of Libkovice, a village about 20 km southwest of Teplice, founded in the twelfth century. This time not even its church would be saved; the owners of the Hlubina

609 'Novoroční projev prezidenta Václava Havla', 1 January 1990, in Václav Havel, *Projevy z let 1990–1992/ Letní přemítání*, vol. 6 of the collected works, Prague: Torst, 1999, pp. 9–19, here p. 9. An English translation is available online: http://old.hrad.cz/president/Havel /speeches/1990/0101_uk.html Accessed 28 October 2018.

Mine had it demolished almost twenty years later, in 2002. But perhaps more important than the bulldozing of people's homes 'in the conditions of freedom' was the discovery that the environmentalists opposing them were again on the defensive. With the advent of the long-lasting government of the Civic Democratic Party (Občanská demokratická strana – ODS) and the ideology of a 'market without modifiers' (*trh bez přívlastků*), the proponents of being considerate towards the soft factors of life were losing one battle after another: from the nuclear power station in Temelín, south Bohemia, to the conversion of a former barracks on four-teenth-century foundations into the Palladium shopping centre in Prague. In the Czech Republic, in the second decade of the twenty-first century, at a time when the importance of renewable resources was growing worldwide, mining limits that had been set more than 25 years before were now, paradoxically, being lifted. Debates were carried on about the demolition of Horní Jiřetín and perhaps also various ways to save its church. 'What was human increasingly yielded to what was economic,' Hníková and Losos once wrote about Communist productivism in north Bohemia, 'and eventually it was neither human nor economic.'[610]

Today, we feel that we are living in a different world from the one in which our parents grew up. All the more reason, then, are we surprised that we are continuously losing battles that should have been won long ago. How can that be?

Despite the growing and deepening critical reflections on the consequences of the productivist approach to the world, movement in the wrong direction continues before our eyes; questioning the possibilities of engineers managing society is paradoxically leading to the accentuation of a strikingly more limited criterion – namely, simple economic advantage. And that is true even though economic

---

610 Hníková and Losos, 'Odepsané město'. 21 June 1968. For the full quotation, see the chapter 'In Defence of the Old Town' in the 'Criticism' section.

profit has long ceased to be linked clearly with progress and has become merely confirmation of efficient operations, that is, actually, confirmation of itself.

The vision of technological progress offering solutions to all the problems of civilization and of the rationally managed society of the future has in recent decades truly lost much of its persuasiveness. The cybernetic utopia of the theorists of the scientific and technological revolution, rather than filling most people with enthusiasm and faith in a brighter future, more likely terrifies them. At the same time, however, exploitation enabled by technology was long ago emancipated from human beings. The eroded faith in this way of relating to the world does not mean, however, that it no longer influences our lives. The wealth connected to the technological control of the world – concentrated in the hands of those who control the technological means – is probably a sturdier structure than the political elites who once believed in progress and relied on teams of experts.

Under the strict supervision of engineers, the pit that was left at the foot of Hněvín after the demolition of the medieval town was made into an artificial lake. Near it stands a city of prefab concrete-panel housing blocks, into which so much hope had been invested. The mining company still has its offices in the 23-storey highrise that dominates the city. The nature of the company has changed: it has gone from being a state-owned enterprise to being a joint-stock company. The monies from the sale of coal and electric power flow elsewhere than before, into private hands. But the message of the board of directors, billowing over the town, remains the same as before: Your fate and your happiness, O town, O district, depend solely on us.

The future, it seems, is open both to subjugation and to emancipation. The former requires only inertia, the latter requires the continuous defence of thinking. But 'some god' will not save us. We have to save ourselves.

MAPS

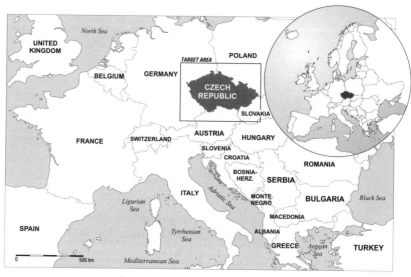

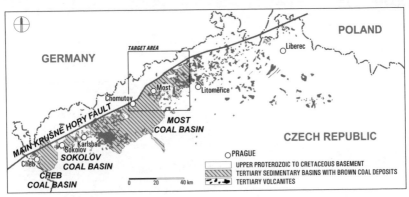

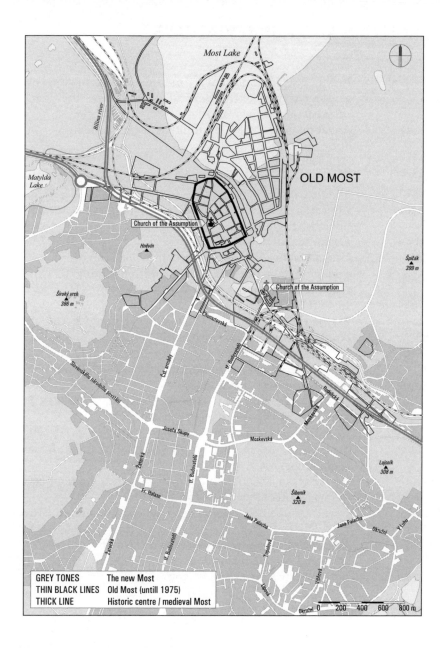

Most Lake

Bílina river

Matylda
Lake

OLD MOST

Church of the Assumption

Hněvín

Špičák
399 m

Široký vrch
386 m

Church of the Assumption

Chomutovská

tř. Budovatelů

Čsl. armády

Slovenského národního povstání

Rudolická

Moskevská

Josefa Skupy

Zámecká

Moskevská

tř. Budovatelů

Lajsník
308 m

Fr. Halase

Šibeník
320 m

Jana Palacha

Jana Palacha

Okružní

V Úžku

Zámecká

tř. Budovatelů

Topolová

Vtelenská

Úšová

Okružní

GREY TONES	The new Most
THIN BLACK LINES	Old Most (untill 1975)
THICK LINE	Historic centre / medieval Most

0   200   400   600   800 m

ACRONYMS AND ABBREVIATIONS

AÚV KSČ	Archiv Ústředního výboru Komunistické strany Československa (Archive of the Central Committee of the Czechoslovak Communist Part)
AV ČR	Akademie věd České republiky (Czech Academy of Sciences)
č.	číslo (number)
ČSAV	Československá akademie věd (Czechoslovak Academy of Sciences)
ČSSR	Československá socialistická republika (Czechoslovak Socialist Republic)
ČSR	Česká socialistická republika (Czech Socialist Republic)
ČST	Československá televize (Czechoslovak Television)
ev. j.	evidenční jednotka (uncatalogued item number)
f.	fond (record group)
inv. č.	inventární číslo (inventory number)
kart.	karton (box)
KNV	Krajský národní výbor (Regional National Committee)
MěNV	Městský národní výbor (Municipal National Committee)
NA	Národní archiv, Praha (National Archive, Prague)
nezprac.	nezpracované (uncatalogued)
ONV	Okresní národní výbor (District National Committee)
s.	strana, strany (page, pages)
sign.	signatura (shelf mark)
SHD	Severočeské hnědouhelné doly (North Bohemian Browncoal Mines)
SHP	Severočeská hnědouhelná pánev (North Bohemian Basin; today, Mostecká pánev, Most Basin)
SHR	Severočeský hnědouhelný revír (North Bohemian Brown Coal District)
SKNV	Severočeský krajský národní výbor (North Bohemian Regional National Committee)
SKV KSČ	Severočeský krajský výbor Komunistické strany Československa (North Bohemian Regional Committee of the Czechoslovak Communist Party)

SNB	Sbor národní bezpečnosti (National Security Corps, i.e. national police)
SOA	Státní oblastní archiv (State Regional Archives)
SOkA	Státní okresní archiv (State District Archives)
SÚPPOP	Státní ústav památkové péče a ochrany přírody (State Institute for the Preservation of Historic Monuments and Environmental Protection, today's Národní památkový ústav, National Heritage Institute)
sv.	svazek (file)
ÚPV	Úřad předsednictva vlády (Office of the Government)
ÚSD	Ústav pro soudobé dějiny (Institute of Contemporary History)
ÚV KSČ	Ústřední výbor Komunistické strany (Central Committee of the Czechoslovak Communist Party)

BIBLIOGRAPHY

Primary Sources (I): Unpublished Materials

Records from the following collections and classes:

Národní archiv (NA, National Archives), Prague
Archiv Ústředního výboru Komunistické strany Československa (AÚV KSČ, Archive of the Central Committee of the Czechoslovak Communist Party), Osidlovací komise (Settlement Commission)
Ministerstvo energetiky a vodního hospodářství (Ministry of Power and Water Resource Management) 1958–1960
Ministerstvo paliv (Ministry of Fuels) 1955–1960
Ministerstvo paliv a energetiky III (Ministry of Fuels and Power) 1960–1965
Ministerstvo paliv (Ministry of Fuels) III 1963–1965
Ústřední správa energetiky (Central Office of Energy Management) 1963–1968
Ústřední správa vodního hospodářství (Central Office of Water Resource Management)
Úřad předsednictva vlády (Office of the Government)
Ministerstvo školství a kultury (Ministry of Education and Culture)
Politické byro Ústředního výboru Komunistické strany Československa (ÚV KSČ, Politburo of the Central Committee of the Czechoslovak Communist Party) 1968–1971
Ideologické oddělení (Ideology Department) 1951–1961
Ideologická komise ÚV KSČ (Ideology Commission of the Central Committee of the Czechoslovak Communist Party) 1958–1968
Ideologická komise ÚV KSČ 1969–1971
Národohospodářská komise ÚV KSČ (Economics Commission of the Central Committee of the Czechoslovak Communist Party)
Oddělení stranických orgánů (Department of Party Bodies) 1960–1967
Předsednictvo ÚV KSČ (Presidium of the Central Committee of the Czechoslovak Communist Party) 1962–1966
Předsednictvo ÚV KSČ 1966–1971
Předsednictvo ÚV KSČ 1971–1976
Předsednictvo ÚV KSČ 1976–1979
Předsednictvo ÚV KSČ 1981–1986

Porady tajemníků ÚV KSČ (Meetings of the Secretaries of the Central Committee of the Czechoslovak Communist Party) 1954–1966

Sekretariát ÚV KSČ (Secretariat of the Central Committee of the Czechoslovak Communist Party) 1954–1962

Sekretariát ÚV KSČ 1962–1966

Sekretariát ÚV KSČ 1966–1971

Sekretariát ÚV KSČ 1971–1976

Sekretariát ÚV KSČ 1981–1986

Komise ÚV KSČ (Commission of the Central Committee of the Czechoslovak Communist Party) 1963–1968

Kancelář 1. tajemníka ÚV KSČ A. Novotného (Office of the First Secretary of the Central Committee of the Czechoslovak Community Party Antonín Novotný) 1951–1967

Politické byro ÚV KSČ (Politburo of the Central Committee of the Czechoslovak Communist Party), 1962

Ministerstvo kultury (Ministry of Culture)

Státní památková správa (State Office of Monument Preservation, until 1964)

Státní ústav památkové péče a ochrany přírody (State Institute for the Preservation of Historic Monuments and Environmental Protection)

Zemský památkový úřad Praha (Office of Historic Monument Preservation in Bohemian and Moravia-Silesia, Prague)

Státní oblastní archiv Litoměřice (SOA Litoměřice, State Regional Archives, Litoměřice)

Severočeský krajský národní výbor (SKNV) Ústí nad Labem (North Bohemian Regional National Committee in Ústí nad Labem)

SKNV – zasedání pléna (plenary sessions)

SKNV – zasedání rady (council sessions)

Severočeský krajský výbor Komunistické strany Československa (SKV KSČ, North Bohemian Regional Committee of the Czechoslovak Communist Party)

Státní oblastní archiv Litoměřice – pobočka Most (State Regional Archive, Litoměřice, Most branch)

Severočeské hnědouhelné doly (SHD), generální ředitelství (North Bohemian Brown-coal Mines, general management)

Státní oblastní archiv Litoměřice – Státní okresní archiv Most (SOkA Most)

Okresní národní výbor (ONV, District National Committee) Most I 1945–1960

ONV Most II 1960–1975

Městský národní výbor (MěNV, Municipal National Committee) Most 1945–1990

KSČ – okresní výbor Most (Czechoslovak Communist Party, district committee, Most)

Kronika města Mostu (Chronicle of the City of Most)

Zpravodaj ONV (Bulletin of the District National Committee)

Zpravodaj MěNV (Bulletin of the Municipal National Committee)

Fotografický fond (Photo Library)

Archiv Československé televize (Archives of Czechoslovak Television)

Primary Sources (II): Published Materials, Periodicals

ABC mladých techniků a přírodovědců
Ahoj na sobotu
Architekúra & Urbanizmus
Aufbau und Frieden
Beseda
Co vás zajímá
Československá hygiena
Československý architekt
Československý horník
Československý svět
Czechoslovak Life
Dialog
Filmový přehled Praha
Für Sie aus der Tschechoslowakei
Hospodářské noviny
Im Herzen Europas
L'Humanité Dimanche
Izvestia (USSR)
Journal magazín
Katolické noviny

Krásy domova
Kulturní kalendář Mostecka
Kvart
Květy
Lidé a země
Lidová demokracie
Literární noviny
Ľud
Magazín aktualit a zajímavostí
Mladá fronta
Mladý svět
Moderní řízení
Naše rodina
La nuova Sardegna Sassari
Obrana lidu
Osvětová práce
Památková péče
Památky a příroda
Práce
Pravda
Pravda (Bratislava)
Právo lidu
Průboj
Přítomnost
Reportér
Rudé právo
Sedmička
Signál
Sloboda
Smena
Svět
Svět motorů
Svět socialismu
Svět sovětů
Svět v obrazech
Svobodné slovo
T70
Technická práca
Technické noviny (Bratislava)

Tribuna
Tschechoslowakisches Leben
Tschechoslowakisches Leben (Romania)
Tvář
Tvorba
Večerní Praha
Věda a technika mládeži
Věda a život
Vesmír
Vlasta
Volkszeitung
Výber
Výtvarná práce
Zápisník
Zář
Zemědělské noviny
Zemědělský a lesní zaměstnanec
Život
Životní prostriedie

Primary Sources (III): Period Publications, Collections of Documents, and Other Published Sources

Campanella, Tommaso, *La città del sole: Edizione complanare del manoscri o della prima redazione italiana (1602) e dell'ultima edizione a stampa (1637)*, trans., notes and appendices by Tonino Tornitore. Milan: UNICOPLI, 1998; An English translation is available online at http://www.gutenberg.org/ebooks/2816 Accessed 28 October 2018.

Cikáni ve starém Mostě, Most: ONV v Mostě a ÚHA, 1975.

Císařovská, Blanka, and Prečan, Vilém (eds), *Charta 77: Dokumenty 1977-1989*, 3 vols, Prague, 2007.

Cori, Johann Nepomuk, *Geschichte der Königlichen Stadt Brüx bis zum Jahre 1788*, Brüx: Verlag d. Stadt Brüx, 1889.

Dickens, Charles, *Hard Times*, London: Bradbury & Evans, 1854.

Engels, Friedrich, *Die Lage der arbeitenden Klasse in England: Nach eigner Anschauung und authentischen Quellen*, Leipzig: O. Wigand, 1848.

Fakta o severočeském hnědouhelném revíru, nositeli řádu Klementa Gott-walda za budování socialistické vlasti, OR SHD, 1972.

Fröhlichová, Zdena, 'Socialistické Mostecko', 3 vols, typescript, 1975, pp. 248–51. Deposited in the Library of the Most District Museum.

Forman, Zdeněk, Jasný, Vojtěch, and Kachyňa, Karel, *Budujeme pohraničí*, Prague, 1950.

Havel, Václav, 'Novoroční projev prezidenta Václava Havla', 1 January 1990, in Václav Havel, *Projevy z let 1990-1992/ Letní přemítání*, vol. 6 of the collected works, Prague: Torst, 1999, pp. 9–19, here p. 9. An English translation is available online: http://old.hrad.cz/president/Havel /speeches/1990/0101_uk.html Accessed 28 October 2018.

Hejdánek, Ladislav, *Filosofie a politika: Patnáct let nepolitické politiky.* A samizdat collection of articles written from 1963 to 1978. Prague, 1978. Quoted in Václav Tollar, 'Emancipáty a problém lidských práv', in Martin Šimsa (ed.), *Nepředmětné výzvy české filosofie: K myšlení Ladislava Hejdánka*, Ústí nad Labem: Univerzita J. E. Purkyně, 2013, pp. 333–57.

——, 'Pojetí pravdy a jeho ontologické předpoklady', PhDr Dissertation, Charles University, Prague, 1952. Online at: https://www.hejdanek.eu /digiarchiv.php?id_detail=265 Accessed 25 October 2018.

Hilpert, Thilo (ed.), *Le Corbusiers 'Charta von Athen': Texte und Dokumente - Kritische Neuausgabe*, Braunschweig: Vieweg, 1984.

Hojdar, Josef, and Vrbová, Marie, *Počítání dluhů minulosti*, Most: INFO-PRINCIP, 1999.

Honzík, Karel, *Tvorba životního slohu: Stati o architektuře a užitkové tvorbě vůbec.* Preface by Jan Mukařovský, Prague: Václav Petr, 1946.

——, Kuchyňka, Zbyněk, and Klivar, Miroslav, *Aktuální problémy socialistického životního slohu*, Prague: Čs. společnost pro šíření politických a vědeckých znalostí, 1963.

Juliš, Emil, *Pod kroky dýmů*, Most: Dialog, 1969.

Jurová, Anna, *Rómska problematika 1945-1967. Dokumenty.* Pt 3, Prague: Ústav pro soudobé dějiny AVČR, 1996.

Le Corbusier, *Vers une Architecture*, Paris: G. Crès, [1923]; published in English as *Towards a New Architecture*, trans. Frederick Etchells, (1931)New York: Dover, 1986, also available online: https://archive.org /details/TowardsANewArchitectureCorbusierLe/page/n1

——, *Za novou architekturu*, trans. Pavel Halík. Prague: Petr Rezek, 2004.

London, Jack, *The People of the Abyss*, London: Isbister, 1903. Online at <http://london.sonoma.edu/Writings/PeopleOfTheAbyss/>

Marx, Karel, and Engels, Bedřich, *Vybrané spisy*, 2 vols., Vol. 2, trans. Ladislav Štoll, ed. Miluše Svatošová, preface and indexes trans. Milena Kirschnerová, Prague: Svoboda, 1950.

Mearns, Andrew, *The Bitter Cry of Outcast London: An Enquiry in to the Condition of the Abject Poor*, London: James Clarke & Co., [1883].

More, Thomas, *Utopia*, Trans. from the Latin by Paul Turner, (1516) New York: Penguin, 1965.

Most: Dostavba nového Mostu a zrušení staré části města, [Most], 1965.

Péče o občany cikánského původu na území města Mostu, MěNV v Mostě, Most 1979.

Prečan, Vilém, *Die sieben Jahre von Prag, 1969-1976: Briefe und Dokumente aus der Zeit der 'Normalisierung'*, trans. from the Czech by Ilse Löffler, Frankfurt am Main: Fischer, 1978.

Rasputin, Valentin, *Loučení*, translated from the Russian by Dagmar Šlampová, Prague, 1980.

——, *Прощание с Матёрой*, 1976, in English as *Farewell to Matyora*, translated by Kathleen Parthé and Antonina W. Bouis, Evanston (IL), 1995.

Richta, Radovan et al., *Civilizace na rozcestí*, Prague, 1969.

——, *Civilization at the Crossroads: Social and Human Implications of the Scientific and Technological Revolution*, trans. Marian Šlingová, Prague: International Arts and Science Press, 1967.

——, *Člověk a technika v revoluci našich dnů*, Prague: Čs. společ. PVZ, 1963.

Šimečka, Milan, *Obnovení pořádku, Příspěvek k typologii reálného socialismu*, samizdat, Prague: Edice Petlice, 1978.

——, *The Restoration of Order: The Normalization of Czechoslovakia*, with an introduction by Zdeněk Mlynář, trans. A. G. Brain [Alice and Gerald Turner], London: Verso [1984].

Štěpánek, Ladislav, 'Horníci na Mostecku', in Jiří Elman (ed.), *Regionální studie VII: Krušnohorský historický sborník*, Most: Dialog, 1968, pp. 127–37

Štýs, Stanislav, *Problémy rekultivace devastovaných pozemků v severočeském hnědouhelném revíru*. Z celostátního semináře pracovníků Státní ochrany přírody, Teplice v Čechách, 18–20 January 1961. Ústí nad Labem: Vydáno péčí Krajského střediska státní památkové péče a ochrany přírody v Ústí nad Labem, 1961.

———, 'Rekultivace a životní prostředí v SHD', *Hnědé uhlí* (special issue) 1980.

———, *Rekultivace území postižených těžbou nerostných surovin*, Preface Ctibor Blattný, Prague, Budapest, Berlin: SNTL, Könyvkiadó, VEB Verlag Technik, 1981.

Sum, Antonín, and Štěpinová, Naďa (eds), *Památky a mládež: Příručka pro mladé ochránce památek*, Prague: Státní zemědělské nakladatelství, 1983. Taut, Bruno, *Die Stadtkrone* with contributions by Paul Scheerbart, Erich Baron, and Adolf Behne, Jena: Eugen Diederichs, 1919.

Technik, Svatopluk, *Budujeme osvobozené kraje v Liberci roku 1946*, Liberec: Česká beseda, 2001.

Teige, Karel, *Nejmenší byt*, Prague: Václav Petr, 1932.

———, *The Minimum Dwelling*, trans. from the Czech by Eric Dluhosch, Cambridge, Mass.: MIT Press, 2002.

With Heritage So Rich: A Report of a Special Commission on Historic Preservation under the Auspices of the United States Conference of Mayors, New York: Random House, 1966; the 1999 re-edition is available online: https://www.slideshare.net/PreservationNation/with-heritage-so-rich -compressed Accessed 18 November 2018.

Vošahlík, Aleš, and Hanzlová, Alena, *Koncepce památkové ochrany historických měst v ČSR*, Prague: Státní ústav památkové péče a ochrany přírody, 1983.

Žák, Ladislav, *Byt a krajina*, ed. and intro. Dita Dvořáková, Prague: Arbor vitae, 2006.

Secondary Literature

Adorno, Theodor W., and Horkheimer, Max, *Dialektik der Aufklärung: Philosophische Fragmente*, Amsterdam, 1944.

———, *Dialectic of Enlightenment*, ed. Gunzelin Schmid Noerr, trans. Edmund Jephcott, Stanford: Stanford University Press, 2002. Available online at https://archive.org/details/pdfy-TJ7HxrAly-MtUP4B Accessed 2 November 2018.

———, *Dialektika osvícenství*, trans. from the German M. Hauser a M. Váňa, Prague: OIKOYMENH, 2009.

Arendt, Hannah, *The Human Condition*, Chicago, 1958,

———, *Vita aktiva oder Vom tätigen Leben*, trans. from the English by Hannah Arendt, Stuttgart: Kohlhammer, 1960.

Amery, Colin, and Cruickshank, Dan, *The Rape of Britain*, foreword by John Betjeman, London: Elek, 1975.

Beck, Ulrich, *Risk Society: Towards a New Modernity*. New Delhi, 1992, translated from the German, *Risikogesellschaft: Auf dem Weg in eine andere Moderne*, Frankfurt am Main: Suhrkamp, 1986.

——, *Riziková společnost: Na cestě k jiné moderně*, Prague: SLON, 2011.

——, Giddens, Anthony, and Lash, Scott, *Reflexive Modernization: Politics, Tradition and Aesthetics in the Modern Social Order*, Stanford, Calif.: Stanford University Press, 1994.

Bell, Daniel, *The Coming of Post-industrial Society: The Venture in Social Forecasting*, New York: Basic Books, 1973.

Benevolo, Leonardo, *Die sozialen Ursprünge des modernen Städtebaus*, Gütersloh, Berlin: Bertelsmann-Fachverlag, 1971, trans. from the Italian, *Le origini dell'urbanistica moderna*, Bari: Laterza, 1963.

Bennett, Michael, and Teague, David W., *The Nature of Cities: Ecocriticism and Urban Environments*, Tucson, AZ: University of Arizona Press, 1999.

Bernal, John Desmond, *Science in History*, 4 vols, London: Watts, 1954.

——, *Věda v dějinách* (2 vols), Prague: Státní nakladatelství politické literatury, 1960.

——, *The Social Function of Science*, London: George Routledge & Sons, 1939.

——, *World without War*, London: Routledge & Kegan Paul, 1958.

Beyme, Klaus von, et al. (eds), *Neue Städte aus Ruinen: Deutscher Städtebau der Nachkriegszeit*, Munich: Prestel,1992.

——, *Der Wiederaufbau: Architektur und Städtebaupolitik in beiden deutschen Staaten*, Munich and Zurich: Piper, 1987.

Bodenschatz, Harald, Post, Christiane, et al. (eds), *Städtebau im Schatten Stalins: Die internationale Suche nach der sozialistischen Stadt in der Sowjetunion 1929–1935*, Berlin: Verlagshaus Braun, 2003.

Bohn, Thomas M. (ed.), *Von der 'europäischen Stat' zur 'sozialistischen Stadt' und zurück? Urbane Transformationen im östlichen Europa des 20. Jahrhunderts*, Munich: Oldenbourg, 2009.

——, *Minsk - Musterstadt des Sozialismus: Stadtplanung und Urbanisierung in der Sowjetunion nach 1945*, Vienna, Cologne, Weimar: Böhlau, 2008.

Brimblecombe, Peter, *The Big Smoke: A History of Air Pollution in London since Medieval Times*, London: Methuen, 1987.

Budinka, Zdeněk, 'Most – město, jeho osudy i osud přemístěného chrámu', *Dědictví Koruny české: Časopis ochránců a přátel našeho kulturního dědictví*, vol. 15, (2006) no. 3, pp. 10–14.

Burkett, Paul, *Marxism and Ecological Economics: Toward a Red and Green Political Economy*, Leiden: Brill, 2006.

Burley, Jon Bryan, *Environmental Design for Reclaiming Surface Mines*, Lewiston, NY: Edwin Mellen Press, 2000.

Carson, Rachel, *Silent Spring*, Boston: Houghton Mifflin, 1962.

Conrads, Ulrich, *Programme und Manifeste zur Architektur des 20. Jahrhunderts*, Braunschweig: Vieweg, 1981.

Cortekar, Jörg, Jasper, Jörg, and Sundmacher, Torsten, *Die Umwelt in der Geschichte des ökonomischen Denkens*, Marburg: Metropolis, 2006.

Crocker, Geoff, *A Managerial Philosophy of Technology: Technology and Humanity in Symbiosis*, Houndmills, Basingstoke and New York: Palgrave Macmillan, 2012.

Čapka, František, Slezák, Lubomír, and Vaculík, Jaroslav, *Nové osídlení pohraničí českých zemí po druhé světové válce*, Brno: Akademické nakladatelství CERM, 2005.

Darmer, Gerhard, *Landschaft und Tagebau: Ökologische Leitbilder für die Rekultivierung*, Hanover: Patzer, 1973.

Das Denkmal als Altlast? Auf dem Weg in die Reparaturgesellschaft, Munich: K. M. Lipp, 1996.

Diefendorf, Jeffry M., *In the Wake of War: The Reconstruction of German Cities after World War II*, New York and Oxford: Oxford University Press, 1993.

Dolejšová, Drahomíra, 'Genius Loci Mostecka', MA thesis, Jan Evangelista Purkyně University, Ústí nad Labem, 2009.

Dominick, Raymond, 'Capitalism, Communism, and Environmental Protection: Lessons from
the German Experience', *Environmental History* 3 (3), July 1998, pp. 311–32.

——, *The Environmental Movement in Germany: Prophets and Pioneers, 1871-1971*, Bloomington and Indianapolis: Indiana University Press, 1992.

Drucker, Peter F., *Landmarks of Tomorrow*, New York: Harper & Brothers, 1957.

——, *The New Society: The Anatomy of Industrial Order*, New York: Harper & Bros., [1949].

Duignan, Peter, and Gann, L. H., *The Rebirth of the West: The Americanization of the Democratic World, 1945–1958*, Cambridge (Mass.): Blackwell, 1992.

Eagleton, Terry, *Ideology: An Introduction*, London and New York: Verso, 2007.

Ekbladh, David, 'Mr. TVA: Grass-Roots Development, David Lilienthal, and the Rise and Fall of the Tennessee Valley Authority as a Symbol for U.S. Overseas Development, 1933–1973, *Diplomatic History* 26 (3), 2002, pp. 335–74.

Erder, Cevat, *Our Architectural Heritage: From Consciousness to Conservation*, Paris: Unesco, 1986.

Fergusson, Adam, *The Sack of Bath*, Salisbury: Compton Russell, 1973.

Fishman, Robert, *Urban Utopias in the Twentieth Century: Ebenezer Howard, Frank Lloyd Wright and Le Corbusier*, New York: Basic Books, 1977.

Flanagan, Maureen A., 'Environmental Justice in the City: A Theme for Urban Environmental History', *Environmental History* 5 (2), April 2000, pp. 159–64.

Foster, John Bellamy, *Marx's Ecology: Materialism and Nature*, New York: Monthly Review Press, 2000.

——, Brett Clark, and York, Richard, *Der ökologische Bruch: Der Krieg des Kapitals gegen den Planeten*, Hamburg: Laika-Verlag, 2011.

Foucault, Michel, *Les mots et les choses: Une archéologie des sciences humaines*, Paris: Gallimard, 1966.

——, *The Order of Things: An Archaeology of the Human Sciences*, New York: Pantheon, 1970.

——, *Slova a věci*, trans. Jan Rubáš, Brno: Computer Press, 2007.

——, *Surveiller et punir: Naissance de la prison*, Paris: Gallimard, 1975

——, *Discipline and Punish: The Birth of the Prison*, London and New York: Alan Lane and Random House, 1977.

——, *Dohlížet a trestat*, trans. Čestmír Pelikán, Prague: Dauphin, 2000.

——, *Naissance de la clinique: Une archéologie du regard médical*, Paris: Presses Universitaires de France, 1963.

——, *The Birth of the Clinic: An Archaeology of Medical Perception.* London: Tavistock, 1973.

——, *Zrození kliniky*, trans. Jan Havlíček and Čestmír Pelikán, Červený Kostelec: Pavel Mervart, 2010.

Franc, Martin, and Knapík, Jiří, *Volný čas v českých zemích 1957-1967*, Prague: Academia, 2013.

Francioni, Francesco (ed.), *The 1972 World Heritage Convention: A Commentary*, Oxford: Oxford University Press, 2008.

Freeden, Michael, 'Ideology and Political Theory', *Journal of Political Ideologies* 11(1), February 2006, pp. 3–22.

Freese, Barbara, *Coal: A Human History*, Cambridge, Mass.: Perseus, 2003.

Friedrichs, Jürgen, *Stadtentwicklungen in West- und Osteuropa*, Berlin and New York: De Gruyter, 1985.

Fröhlichová, Zdena, 'Socialistické Mostecko', 3 vols, typesript, 1975. Deposited in the Library of the Most District Museum.

—— and Heide Mannlová, *Most 1932-1982*, Ústí nad Labem: Severočeské nakladatelství, 1982.

Garnier, Tony, *Die ideale Industriestadt/Une cité industrielle. Eine städtebauliche Studie.* Text by Rene Jullian, Forward by Julius Posener, Tübingen: Ernst Wasmuth Verlag, 1989.

Glassheim, Eagle, 'Ethnic Cleansing, Communism, and Environmental Devastation in Czechoslovakia's Borderlands, 1945–1989', *The Journal of Modern History* 78, March 2006, pp. 65–92.

——, 'Most, the Town That Moved: Coal, Communists and the "Gypsy Question" in PostWar Czechoslovakia', *Environment and History* 13, 2007, pp. 447–76.

Glendinning, Miles, *The Conservation Movement: A History of Architectural Preservation*, London and New York: Routledge, 2013.

Gottlieb, Robert, *Forcing the Spring: The Transformation of the American Environmental Movement*, rev. edn (1993)Washington, DC, and London: Island Press, 2005.

Gutzeit, Ina, *Denkmäler im Braunkohleabbaugebiet Leipzig Süd: Möglichkeiten und Grenzen der Denkmalpflege im Umgang mit sakralen Baudenkmälern und deren Ausstattung*, Hamburg: Diplomica, 2007.

Habermas, Jürgen, *Legitimationsprobleme in Spätkaptalismus*, Frankfurt am Main: Suhrkamp, 1973.

——, *Legitimation Crisis*, trans. Thomas McCarthy, Boston: Beacon Press, 1975.

——, *Problémy legitimity v pozdním kapitalismu*, trans. from the German by Alena Bakešová and Josef Velek, Prague: Filosofia, 2000.

——, *Strukturwandel der Öffentlichkeit: Untersuchungen zu einer Kategorie der bürgerlichen Gesellschaft*, Neuwied Berlin: Luchterhand, 1962.

——, *The Structural Transformation of the Public Sphere: An Inquiry into a category of Bourgeois Society*, trans. Thomas Burger with Frederick Lawrence, Cambridge, Mass.: MIT Press, 1989.

Harris, Chauncy D., *Cities of the Soviet Union: Studies in Their Functions, Size, Density, and Growth*, Chicago: Rand McNally, 1970.

Hardy, Dennis, *Utopian England: Community Experiments, 1900-1945*, London and New York: Routledge, 2000.

Häussermann, Hartmut, and Rainer Neef, *Stadtentwicklung in Ostdeutschland: Soziale und räumliche Tendenzen*, Opladen: Verlag für Sozialwissenschaften, 1996.

Heidegger, Martin, *Vorträge und Aufsätze*, Pfullingen: Neske, 1954.

——, *The Question Concerning Technology and Other Essays*, trans. and with an introduction by William Lovitt, New York and London: Garland, 1977.

Hobzek, Josef, *Vývoj památkové péče v českých zemích*, Prague: Státní ústav památkové péče a ochrany přírody, 1987.

Hoffmann-Axthelm, Dieter, *Wie kommt die Geschichte ins Entwerfen? Aufsätze zur Architektur und Stadt*, Braunschweig: Vieweg, 1987.

Hohensee, Jens, and Salewski, Michael (eds), *Energie, Politik, Geschichte: Nationale und internationale Energiepolitik seit 1945*, Stuttgart: F. Steiner, 1993.

Holubec, Stanislav, *Lidé periferie: Sociální postavení a každodennost pražského dělnictva v meziválečné době*, Pilsen: Západočeská univerzita, 2009.

Horáček, Martin, *Za krásnější svět: Tradicionalismus v architektuře 20. a 21. století*, with an English abstract, Brno: Barrister & Principal and VUTIUM, 2013.

Horňáková, Ladislava (ed.), *The Baťa Phenomenon: Zlín Architecture, 1910-1960*, Zlín: Regional Gallery of Fine Arts, 2009.

Hughes, Donald J., *An Environmental History of the World: Humankind's Changing Role in the Community of Life*, London: Routledge, 2001.

Husserl, Edmund, *Die Krisis der europäischen Wissenschaften und die transzendentale Phänomenologie: Eine Einleitung in die phänomenologische Philosophie*, vol. 6 of the collected works, ed. Walter Biemel, (1936) The Hague: Nijhoff, 1954.

——, *The Crisis of European Sciences and Transcendental Phenomenology: An Introduction to Phenomenological Philosophy*, trans. with an introduction by David Carr, Evanston, Ill.: Northwestern University Press, 1970.

——, *Krize evropských věd a transcendentální fenomenologie*, (1972) trans. from the German by Oldřich Kuba, Prague: Academia, 1996.

Jarausch, Konrad H. (ed.), *Dictatorship as Experience: Towards a Socio-cultural History of the GDR*, New York and Oxford: Berghahn, 1999.

——, and Sabrow, Martin (eds), *Der Weg in den Untergang: Der innere Zerfall der DDR*, Göttingen: Vandenhoeck & Ruprecht, 1999.

Jacobs, Jane, *The Death and Life of Great American Cities*, New York: Random House, 1961.

——, *Smrt a život amerických velkoměst*, afterword and editing by Jiří Hrůza, trans. Jana Solperová, Prague: Odeon, 1975.

Judt, Tony, *Postwar: A History of Europe Since 1945*, New York and London: Penguin, 2005.

Jünger, Ernst, *Der Arbeiter: Herrschaft und Gestalt*, Hamburg: Hanseatische Verlagsanstalt, 1932.

——, *The Worker: Dominion and Form*, ed. Laurence Paul Hemming, trans. from the German by Bogdan Costea and Laurence Paul Hemming, Evanston, Il.: Northwestern University Press, 2017.

Kabisch, Sigrun, 'Revitalisation Chances for Communities in Postmining Landscapes', in *Postmining Landscapes: Reclamation, Ecology, Nature Conservation and Socio-economy in Practice, Peckiana 3*, ed. Willi E. R. Xylander, Görlitz: Senckenberg Museum für Naturkunde, 2004, pp. 87–99.

Kaelble, Hartmut, *Sozialgeschichte Europas 1945 bis zur Gegenwart*, Munich: C. H. Beck, 2007.

Kalia, Ravi, *Chandigarh: The Making of an Indian City*, New Delhi: Oxford University Press India, 1999.

Kaška, Václav, *Neukáznění a neangažovaní: Disciplinace členů Komunistické strany Československa v letech 1948–1952*, Prague: Conditio humana ÚSTR, 2014.

Keyes, Jonathan, 'A Place of Its Own: Urban Environmental History', *Journal of Urban History*, March 2000, pp. 380–90.

Khan-Magomedov, Selim O.: *Pioneers of Soviet Architecture: The Search for New Solutions in the 1920s and 1930s*, trans. from the Russian by

Alexander Lieven, London and New York: Thames and Hudson and Rizzoli, 1987.

Kladnik, Ana, 'The Formation and Development of the Socialist Town in Yugoslavia and Czechoslovakia, 1945–1965', PhD thesis, University of Ljubljana, 2013.

Klápště, Jan, and Novák, Otakar, *Gotický kostel Nanebevzetí Panny Marie v Mostě*, Prague and Ústí nad Labem: Propagační tvorba and Památkový ústav Ústí nad Labem, 1992.

——, *Gothic Church of the Ascension [sic] of the Virgin Mary in Most*, trans. Anděla Kunstová, Prague and Ústí nad Labem: Propagační tvorba and Památkový ústav Ústí nad Labem, 1992 (also in French and German editions).

Komořansko - minulost a současnost, ed. Vlastimil Novák, Komořany: Doly a úpravny Komořany, 1993.

Kopeček, Michal, 'Ve službách dějin, ve jménu národa', *Soudobé dějiny* 8 (1), 2001, pp. 23–43.

Kotkin, Stephen, *Magnetic Mountain: Stalinism as a Civilization*, Berkeley, Calif., and London: University of California Press, 1995.

Koukal, Pavel, *Přesunutý děkanský kostel Nanebevzetí Panny Marie v Mostě*, Ústí nad Labem: Národní památkový ústav, 2007.

Krejčí, Václav, *Most: Zánik historického města, výstavba nového města*, [Ústí nad Labem]: AA 2000, 2000.

Černý, Bohumil, Křen, Jan, Kural, Václav, and Otáhal, Milan (eds), *Češi, Němci, odsun*, Prague: Academia, 1990.

Kuča, Karel, *Města a městečka v Čechách, na Moravě a ve Slezsku*, vol. 4: 'Most', Prague: Libri, 2000, pp. 161–201.

Landsman, Mark, *Dictatorship and Demand: The Politics of Consumerism in East Germany*, Cambridge, Mass.: Harvard University, 2005.

Larkham, Peter J., *Conservation and the City*, London and New York: Routledge, 1996.

LeCain, Timothy J., *Mass Destruction: The Men and Giant Mines That Wired America and Scarred the Planet*, New Brunswick, NJ: Rutgers University Press, [2009].

Lefebvre, Henri, *La production de l'espace*, Paris: Éditions Anthropos [1974].

——, *The Production of Space*, trans. by Donald Nicholson-Smith, Oxford and Cambridge, Mass.: Blackwell, 1991.

Lindenberger, Thomas (ed.), *Herrschaft und Eigen-Sinn in der Diktatur: Studien zur Gesellschaftsgeschichte der DDR*, Cologne, Weimar, and Vienna: Böhlau, 1999.

Lipp, Wilfried, *Natur, Geschichte, Denkmal: Zur Entstehung des Denkmalbewusstseins der bürgerlichen Gesellschaft*, Frankfurt and New York: Campus Verlag, 1987.

Loewenstein, Bedřich, *Problemfelder der Moderne: Elemente politischer Kultur*, Darmstadt: Wissenschaftliche Buchgesellschaft, 1990.

——, *Projekt moderny*, trans. Robert Kalivoda and Dana Kalivodová, Prague: ISE, 1995.

Lüdtke, Alf, *Herrschaft als soziale Praxis: Historische und sozial-anthropologische Studien*, Göttingen: Vandenhoeck & Ruprecht, 1991.

Mannlová Raková, Heide, *Kulturní památka Most: Děkanský kostel a jeho stavitelé*, Most: Okresní muzeum v Mostě, 1989.

Marx, Karl, and Engels, Friedrich, *Die deutsche Ideologie: Kritik der neuesten deutschen Philosophie in ihren Repräsentanten, Feuerbach, B. Bauer und Stirner, und des deutschen Sozialismus in seinen verschiedenen Propheten,* (1845–46) Berlin: Dietz, 1953. Online at <http://www.mlwerke.de/me/meo3/meo3_009.htm>

Massard-Guilbaud, Geneviève, and Stephen Mosley, *Common Ground: Integrating the Social and Environmental in History*, New Castle upon Tyne: Cambridge Scholars: Cambridge Scholars, 2011.

Mattern, Hermann, *Gras darf nicht mehr wachsen: 12 Kapitel über den Verbrauch der Landschaft*, Braunschweig: Ullstein, 1964.

Mazower, Mark, *Dark Continent: Europe's Twentieth Century*, London: Allen Lane The Penguin Press, 1998.

McDonough, Tom (ed.), *The Situationists and the City: A Reader*, London and New York: Verso, 2009.

Meadows, Donella H., Meadows, Dennis L., Randers, Jørgen, and Behrens III, William W., *The Limits to Growth*, Washington, DC: Potomac Associates – Universe Books, 1972. Available online: http://www.donellameadows.org/wp-content/userfiles/Limits-to-Growth-digital-scan-version.pdf Accessed 27 January 2019.

Meier, Hans Rudolf, and Scheuermann, Ingrid (eds), *Denkmalwerte: Beiträge zur Theorie und Aktualität der Denkmalpflege*, Berlin and Munich: Deutscher Kunstverlag, 2010.

Meller, Helen B., *Towns, Plans and Society in Modern Britain*, Cambridge: Cambridge University Press, 1997.

——, *European Cities, 1890-1930s: History, Culture, and the Built Environment*, Chichester: Chichester: John Wiley, 2001.

Mikšíček, Petr et al., *Zmizelé Sudety*, Domažlice: Pro občanské sdružení Antikomplex vydalo Nakladatelství Českého lesa, 2006.

Milyutin, Nikolay Alexandrovich, *Соцгород: Проблемы строительства социалистических городов* (Sotsgorod: Problems of building socialist cities), Moscow and Leningrad: GIZ, 1930.

Miljutin, Nikolaj A., *Socgorod*, trans. from the Russian by Petr Denk, Prague: Knihovna Levé fronty, 1931.

Mitscherlich, Alexander, *Die Unwirtlichkeit unserer Städte: Anstiftung zum Unfrieden*, (1965)Frankfurt am Main: Suhrkamp, 1969.

Míšková, Alena, Franc, Martin, and Kostlán, Antonín (eds), *Bohemia docta: K historickým kořenům vědy v českých zemích*, Prague: Academia, 2010.

Montrie, Chad, 'Expedient Environmentalism: Opposition to Coal Surface Mining in Appalachia and the United Mine Workers of America, 1945-1975', *Environmental History* 5 (1), January 2000, pp. 75–98.

Mörsch, Georg, *Denkmalverständnis: Vorträge und Aufsätze 1990-2002*, Zurich: vdf Hochschulverlag, 2005.

Mosley, Stephen, 'Common Ground: Integrating the Social and Environmental in History', Special Issue on the Future of Social History, *Journal of Social History* 39 (3), 2006, pp. 915–33.

Murphy, Priscilla Coit, *What a Book Can Do: The Publication and Reception of* Silent Spring, Amherst and Boston: University of Massachusetts Press, 2005.

Myllyntaus, Timo, and Saikku, Mikko (eds), *Encountering the Past in Nature: Essays in Environmental History*, 2nd rev. edn, (1999) Athens, OH: Ohio University Press, 2001.

Nairn, Ian, 'Outrage: On the Disfigurement of Town and Countryside', *Architectural Review*, special issue, vol. 117, no. 702 (1955).

——, 'Counter Attack: Counter Attack Against Subtopia' vol. 120, no. 719 (December 1956).

——, *Your England Revisited*, London: Hutchinson, 1964.

Nash, Roderick Frazier, *The Rights of Nature: A History of Environmental Ethics*, Madison, WI: , University of Wisconsin Press, 1989.

Novák, Aleš, *Moc, technika a věda: Martin Heidegger a Ernst Jünger*, Prague: Togga, 2008.

Novák, Vlastimil, *Magický Most*, Most: Hněvín, 2005.

Ševčík, Jiří, Bendová, Ivana, and Benda, Jan, 'Obraz města Mostu', *Architektúra & urbanizmus* 12/3 (1978), nos. 1–4.

Ohlenmacher, Karl, *Sind die Dörfer zum Sterben verurteilt?*, Limburg: Self-published, 1975.

Panerai, Philippe, Castex, Jean, and, Depaule, Jean-Charles, *Formes urbaines de l'îlot à la barre*, Paris: Dunod, [1977].

——, *Vom Block zur Zeile: Wandlungen der Stadtstruktur*, Braunschweig: Vieweg, 1985.

——, *Urban Forms: The Death and Life of the Urban Block*, Boston, Mass., and Oxford: Architectural Press, 2004.

Papageorgiou, Alexander, *Stadtkerne im Konflikt: Die historischen Stadtkerne und ihre Rolle im künftigen räumlichen Gefüge*, Tübingen: Wasmuth, 1970.

Parker, Simon, *Urban Theory and the Urban Experience*, London and New York: Routledge, 2004.

Pavelčíková, Nina, *Romové v českých zemích v letech 1945-1989*, Prague: Úřad dokumentace a vyšetřování zločinů komunismu PČR, 2004.

Petráš, René, *Menšiny v komunistickém Československu: Právní a faktické postavení národnostních menšin v českých zemích v letech 1948-1970*, Prague: VIP Books, 2007.

Pokorná, Libuše, *Most*, photos Jan Reich and Jaroslav Rajzík, Prague: Pressphoto, 1991.

—— (ed.), *Osud Mostecka: Člověk a životní prostředí včera a dnes. Sborník odborných prací*, Most: Okresní muzeum, 1996.

—— (ed.), *Kniha o Mostecku/Das Buch über Mostecko/A Book on the Most region*, Litvínov: Dialog, 2000.

Prakash, Vikramaditya, *Chandigarh's Le Corbusier: The Struggle for Modernity in Postcolonial India*, Seattle: University of Washington Press, 2002.

Průcha, Václav et al., *Hospodářské a sociální dějiny Československa 1918-1992*, vol. II, Brno: Doplněk, 2009.

Pullmann, Michal, *Konec experimentu: Přestavba a pád socialismu v Československu*, Prague: Scriptorium, 2012.

——, 'K sociální dynamice teroru', in Wendy Goldmanová, *Vytváření nepřítele*, Prague: Karolinum, 2015, pp. 267–86. (This is the Afterword to the Czech translation of Wendy Z. Goldman, *Inventing the Enemy*, Cambridge and New York: Cambridge University Press, 2011.)

Reinborn, Dietmar, *Städtebau im 19. und 20. Jahrhundert*, Stuttgart: Kohlhammer, 1996.

Řezníček, Jiří (ed.), *Moderní metody řízení v soudobém kapitalismu*, Prague: Svoboda, 1966.

Rigby, Thomas Henry, and Fehér, Ferenc (eds), *Political Legitimation in Communist States*, New York, London, and Basingstoke: St. Martin's Press and Palgrave Macmillan, 1982.

Rodwell, Dennis, 'The Unesco World Heritage Convention, 1972–2012: Reflections and Directions', *The Historic Environment: Policy & Practice* 3 (1), June 2012, pp. 64–85.

Rodwin, Lloyd, and Hollister, Robert M. (eds), *Cities of the Mind: Images and Themes of the City in the Social Sciences*, New York and London: Plenum Press, 1984.

Sabrow, Martin, 'Sozialismus als Sinnwelt: Diktatorische Herrschaft in kulturhistorischer Perspektive,' *Potsdamer Bulletin für Zeithistorische Studien* 40/41, 2007, pp. 9–23,

——, 'Socialismus jako myšlenkový svět: Komunistická diktatura v kulturněhistorické perspektivě', *Soudobé dějiny* 2, 2012, pp. 196–208.

Sarin, Madhu, *Urban Planning in the Third World: The Chandigarh Experience*, London: Mansell, 1982.

Sayer, Derek, *Prague, Capital of the Twentieth Century: A Surrealist History*, Princeton, NJ, and Oxford: Princeton University Press, 2013.

Schehl, Hellmuth, *Vor uns die Sintflut? Ökologie, Marxismus und die herrschende Zukunftsgläubigkeit*, Berlin, 1977.

Schott, Dieter, Luckin, Bill, and Massard-Guilbaud, Geneviève (eds), *Resources of the City: Contributions to an Environmental History of Modern Europe*, Aldershot: Ashgate, 2005.

Schumpp, Mechthild, *Stadtbau-Utopien und Gesellschaft: Der Bedeutungswandel utopischer Stadtmodelle unter sozialem Aspekt*, Gütersloh: Bertelsmann, 1972.

Schwab, Alexander, *Das Buch vom Bauen*, (1930) Basle: Birkhäuser, 1973.

Šimsa, Martin (ed.), *Nepředmětné výzvy české filosofie: K myšlení Ladislava Hejdánka*, Ústí nad Labem: Filozofická fakulta Univerzity J. E. Purkyně, 2013.

Smoud, T. C., *Exploring Environmental History: Selected Essays*, Edinburgh: Edinburgh University Press, 2009.

Sozanský, Jiří, *Zóna*, Prague: Kant, 2013.

Spurný, Matěj (ed.), *Proměny sudetské krajiny*, Prague: Antikomplex, 2006.

——, *Nejsou jako my: Česká společnost a menšiny v pohraničí 1945-1960*, Prague: Antikomplex, 2011.

Štefanová, Zdeňka, 'Přesun gotického kostela v Mostě', in Libuše Pokorná and Ivan Jakubec (eds), *Mostecko, Litvínovsko, Lounsko, Žatecko v historických studiích: Sborník učitelských prací z kursů univerzitních extenzí v Mostě*, Most, [Prague], and [Liberec]: Okresní muzeum v Mostě, Univerzita Karlova, Dialog, 2002.

Storchová, Lucie et al., *Koncepty a dějiny: Proměny pojmů v současné historické vědě*, Prague: Scriptorium, 2014.

Štýs, Stanislav, *Problémy rekultivace devastovaných pozemku v severočeském hnědouhelném revíru*. Z celostátního semináře pracovníků Statní ochrany přírody, Teplice v Čechách, 18–20 January 1961. Ústí nad Labem: Vydáno péčí Krajského střediska státní památkové péče a ochrany přírody v Ústí nad Labem, 1961.

——, 'Rekultivace a životní prostředí v SHD', in *Hnědé uhlí* (special issue), 1980.

——, and Helešicová, Liběna, *Proměny měsíční krajiny*, Prague: Bílý slon, 1992.

——, and Větvička, Václav, *Most v zeleném*, Most: Hněvín, 2008.

Sutcliffe, Anthony, *Towards the Planned City: Germany, Britain, the United States and France, 1780-1914*, Oxford: Basil Blackwell, 1981.

Sýkorová, Jana, *Zmizelé domovy: Příspěvek k historii zlikvidovaných obcí v okrese Most*, Photo selection and captions by Eva Hladká, Most: Okresní muzeum v Mostě and Státní okresní archiv v Mostě, 2002.

Therborn, Göran, *European Modernity and Beyond: The Trajectory of European Societies, 1945-2000*, London, Thousand Oaks, and New Delhi: Sage, 1995.

Uekötter, Frank, *Von der Rauchplage zur ökologischen Revolution: Eine Geschichte der Luftverschmutzung in Deutschland und in den USA 1880-1970*, Essen: Klartext, 2003.

——, *The Age of Smoke: Environmental Policy in Germany and the United States, 1880-1970*, trans. Thomas Dunlop, Pittsburgh: University of Pittsburgh Press, 2009.

Valášek, Václav, and Chytka, Lubomír, *Velká 'kronika' o hnědém uhlí: Minulost, současnost a budoucnost těžby hnědého uhlí v severozápadních Čechách*, Pilsen: G2 studio, 2009.

Vaněk, Miroslav, *Nedalo se tady dýchat: Ekologie v českých zemích v letech 1968-1989*, Prague: Maxdorf, 1996.

Vidler, Anthony, *Claude-Nicolas Ledoux: Architecture and Utopia in the Era of the French Revolution*, Basle: Birkhäuser Architecture, 2006.

Vietor, Richard, *Environmental Politics and the Coal Coalition*, College Station and London: Texas A & M University Press, 1980.

Vorlík, Petr, *Dějiny architektury dvacátého století*, Prague: České vysoké učení technické, 2010.

Wagner, Peter, *A Sociology of Modernity: Liberty and Discipline*, London and New York: Routledge, 1994.

Watt, Laura A., Raymond, Leigh, and Eschen, Meryl L., 'On Preserving Ecological and Cultural Landscapes', *Environmental History* 9 (4), October 2004, pp. 620–47.

Weber, Max, *Wirtschaft und Gesellschaft*, (1921 and 1922) Cologne: Kiepenheuer & Witsch, 1956.

——, *Metodologie, sociologie a politika*, edited by Miloš Havelka, (1998) Prague: OIKOYMENH, 2009.

Wiener, Norbert, *The Human Use of Human Beings: Cybernetics and Society*, Boston, Mass.: Houghton Mifflin, 1950.

——, *Kybernetika a společnost*, trans. Karel Berka, preface Arnošt Kolman, 'O filosofických a společenských názorech Norberta Wienera', Prague: Československá akademie věd, 1963.

Williams, Raymond, *Problems in Materialism and Culture: Selected Essays*, London: Verso, 1980.

Worster, Donald (ed.), *The Ends of the Earth: Perspectives on Modern Environmental History*, Cambridge and New York: Cambridge University Press, 1988.

Young, John E., *Mining the Earth*, Worldwatch Paper 109, Washington, DC: Worldwatch Institute, 1992.

Yurchak, Alexei, *Everything Was Forever, Until It Was No More*, Princeton, NJ: Princeton University Press, 2006.

Zajoncová, Jana, 'Architektura a urbanismus Mostu, Litvínova a Teplic, 1945–1989', MA thesis, Palacký University, Olomouc, 2011. Online at: <http://theses.cz/id/covm66/Zajoncova_Jana_Architektura_a_urbanismus_Mostu_Litvnova_a.pdf>

Zarecor, Kimberly Elman, *Manufacturing a Socialist Modernity: Housing in Czechoslovakia, 1945–1960*, Pittsburgh, PA: University of Pittsburgh Press, 2011. Online at: https://chisineu.files.wordpress.com/2014/02/manufacturing-a-socialist-modernity.pdf Accessed 28 October 2018.

Zwoch, Felix, and Novy, Klaus, *Nachdenken über Städtebau*, Braunschweig and Wiesbaden: Vieweg, 1991.

Zelinka, Inge, *Der autoritäre Sozialstaat: Machtgewinn durch Mitgefühl in der Genese staatlicher Fürsorge*, Vienna and Münster: LIT, 2005.

Zimmermann, Volker, and Pullmann, Michal (eds), *Ordnung und Sicherheit, Devianz und Kriminalität im Staatssozialismus: Tschechoslowakei und DDR 1948/49-1989*, Göttingen: Vandenhoeck & Ruprecht, 2014.

LIST OF PHOTOGRAPHS

Cover

Most, from the railway station, 1983. SOkA Most, fotografický fond.

The Story

Old Most (after 1945). SOkA Most, fotografický fond.
1. Sterngasse (Hvězdná ulice), Most, 1930s. SOkA Most, fotografický fond.
2. Tuchrahme (Soukenická ulice), Most, 1905. SOkA Most, fotografický fond.
3. Most, 1960s. SOkA Most, fotografický fond.
4. Náměstí Ludvíka Svobody (Ludvík Svoboda Square), dominated by the Deanery Church, old Most. SOkA Most, fotografický fond.
5. The Gasthaus zum weißen Lamm (White Lamb Inn), Švermova ulice, 1965. SOkA Most, fotografický fond.
6. Švermova ulice with the museum building, Most, September 1965. SOkA Most, fotografický fond.
7. Remains of Koněvova ulice (Koněv Street) at Smetanovo náměstí (Smetana Square), waiting for demolition in November 1978. SOkA Most, fotografický fond.
8. Demolition of the Repre arts and community centre. SOkA Most, fotografický fond.

Alienation

Fountain (detail), old Most, hotel Muron in the background. Photo Johana Kratochvílová (signatura.cz).
9. The Opera café, 1970s. From *Most Jiřího Baláše,* Most: Hněvín, 2001, pp. 61, 65. Photos Jiří Baláš.
10. Collecting junk in partly evacuated old Most. From *Most Jiřího Baláše,* Most: Hněvín, 2001, pp. 61, 65. Photos Jiří Baláš.

Numbers

Old Most and the spoil tip. NA Praha, fond ÚPV (Úřad předsednictva vlády, běžná spisovna).

11. Landscape with Ervěnice and Komořany power stations. NA Praha, fond ÚPV (Úřad předsednictva vlády, běžná spisovna).

Utopia

Most, central park, Hněvín dormitory, 1960s. SOkA Most, fotografický fond.

12. Supreme Court building, Chandigarh. Photo Kryštof Kříž (ČTK).

13. Upper Brook Street, Manchester, England, 1965. Photo Shirley Baker (ČTK).

14. Most, view from a temporary tram terminus, 1970s. SOkA Most, fotografický fond.

15. The Podžatecká housing estate still as a suburb of old Most, 1950s. SOkA Most, fotografický fond.

16. The centre of new Most, early 1980s, with the partly erected Municipal National Committee building. SOkA Most, fotografický fond.

17. Final construction work on the hospital grounds, c.1975. SOkA Most, fotografický fond.

18. The theatre, new Most, 1985. SOkA Most, fotografický fond.

Criticism

Oblouková ulice, Old Most (autumn 1974). SOkA Most, fotografický fond

19. Surface mining in the Appalachian Mountains, USA. Photo George Steinmetz (Corbis).

20. Josef Sudek, *The Shores of Soot* (1960). Josef Sudek, *Smutná krajina*, 2nd edn, Prague, Kant, 2004, p. 9.

21. North Bohemian Basin. NA Praha, fond ÚPV (Úřad předsednictva vlády, běžná spisovna).

22. Bezručova ulice (Bezruč St), looking towards Mírové náměstí (Peace Sq.), May 1978. SOkA Most, fotografický fond.

23. Josef Sudek, *The New Most* (1962). Josef Sudek, *Smutná krajina*, 2nd edn, Prague, Kant, 2004, p. 10.
24. Václavské náměstíčko (Wenceslas Sq.), old Most. SOkA Most, fotografický fond.
25. Asphalting the road at the corner of Palackého and Tylova streets. SOkA Most, fotografický fond.
26. and **27.** *Panic*, installation by Jiří Sozanský, with Jiří Novák, September 1982. Photo Jiří Putta. Jiří Sozanský, *Zóna*, Prague: Kant, 2013, pp. 90, 92.

Reconciliation

Moving the Church of the Assumption, Most (9 October 1975). SOkA Most, fotografický fond.
28. Detail of a façade on Mírové náměstí (Peace Sq.). SOkA Most, fotografický fond.
29. Taking down the spire of the Church of the Assumption (Deanery Church) in March 1972. SOkA Most, fotografický fond.
30. Detail of trollies used to move the church. Photo from 11 October 1975. SOkA Most, fotografický fond.
31. The church being moved through the former abattoir grounds. October 1975. SOkA Most, fotografický fond.
32. The Deanery Church at its new location. SOkA Most, fotografický fond.

Laboratory of Modernity

Utility corridor and moved church, Most. Photo Johana Kratochvílová (signatura.cz).

INDEX